THE OXFORD MO

Europe and the Wider World 1830–1930

EDITED BY

STEWART J. BROWN

and

PETER B. NOCKLES

CAMBRIDGE
UNIVERSITY PRESS

University Printing House, Cambridge CB2 8BS, United Kingdom

Published in the United States of America by Cambridge University Press, New York

Cambridge University Press is part of the University of Cambridge.

It furthers the University's mission by disseminating knowledge in the pursuit of education, learning and research at the highest international levels of excellence.

www.cambridge.org
Information on this title: www.cambridge.org/9781107680272

First published 2012
First paperback edition 2013

A catalogue record for this publication is available from the British Library

Library of Congress Cataloguing in Publication data
The Oxford movement : Europe and the wider world 1830–1930 / [edited by] Stewart J. Brown, Peter Nockles.
pages cm
Includes bibliographical references and index.
ISBN 978-1-107-01644-6
1. Oxford movement. 2. Church of England–History–19th century.
I. Brown, Stewart J. (Stewart Jay), 1951– editor of compilation. II. Nockles, Peter Benedict, editor of compilation.
BX5098.094 2012
283′.4209034–dc23
2012011698

ISBN 978-1-107-01644-6 Hardback
ISBN 978-1-107-68027-2 Paperback

THE OXFORD MOVEMENT

The Oxford Movement transformed the nineteenth-century Church of England with a renewed conception of itself as a spiritual body. Initiated in the early 1830s by members of the University of Oxford, it was a response to threats to the established Church posed by British Dissenters, Irish Catholics, Whig and Radical politicians and the predominant evangelical ethos – what Newman called 'the religion of the day'. The Tractarians believed they were not simply addressing difficulties within their national Church, but recovering universal principles of the Christian faith. To what extent were their beliefs and ideals communicated globally? Was missionary activity the product of the movement's distinctive principles? Did their understanding of the Church promote, or inhibit, closer relations among the churches of the global Anglican Communion? This volume addresses these questions and more with a series of case studies involving Europe and the English-speaking world during the first century of the movement.

STEWART J. BROWN is Professor of Ecclesiastical History at the University of Edinburgh. He is the author or editor of ten books, including *Providence and Empire: Religion, Politics and Society in the United Kingdom 1815–1914* (2008), *The Cambridge History of Christianity*, vol. VII, *Enlightenment, Reawakening and Revolution 1660–1815* (co-edited with Timothy Tackett, Cambridge 2006), *The National Churches of England, Ireland and Scotland 1801–46* (2001) and *Thomas Chalmers and the Godly Commonwealth in Scotland* (1982).

PETER B. NOCKLES is Curator and Librarian in the Department of Printed Books, Special Collections, John Rylands University Library, University of Manchester, and Research Fellow in Religions and Theology, University of Manchester. He is the author of *The Oxford Movement in Context* (Cambridge, 1994).

To Nigel Yates
(1944–2009)

An eminent scholar and a generous friend

Contents

Notes on contributors

ANGELA BERLIS is Professor of the History of Old Catholicism and General Church History, and Head of the Department for Old Catholic Theology (*Departement für Christkatholische Theologie*) at the Faculty of Theology, University of Berne (Switzerland). From 2007 to 2011 she was president of the European Society of Women in Theological Research (ESWTR). Her publications include *Frauen im Prozess der Kirchwerdung. Eine historisch-theologische Studie zur Anfangsphase des deutschen Altkatholizismus (1850–1890)* (1998).

JOHN BONEHAM earned his Ph.D. in 2009 from the University of Wales, Bangor, with a thesis on 'Isaac Williams (1802–65), the Oxford Movement and the High Churchmen: A Study of His Theological and Devotional Writings'. His publications include 'Isaac Williams and the Oxford Movement: The Importance of Reserve in His Poetry and Scriptural Commentaries' in the *Welsh Journal of Religious History* (2009) and 'The Poetry of Isaac Williams (1802–65)' in *Studies in Church History* (2012).

STEWART J. BROWN is Professor of Ecclesiastical History and Head of the School of Divinity at the University of Edinburgh. His publications include *The National Churches of England, Ireland and Scotland, 1801–1846* (2001); *The Cambridge History of Christianity*, vol. VII, *Enlightenment, Reawakening and Revolution 1660–1815*, edited with T. Tackett (2006); and *Providence and Empire: Religion, Politics and Society in the United Kingdom, 1815–1914* (2008).

MARK CHAPMAN is Vice-Principal of Ripon College Cuddesdon, Oxford, Reader in Modern Theology at the University of Oxford and Visiting Professor at Oxford Brookes University. His books include *Ernst Troeltsch and Liberal Theology: Religion and Cultural Synthesis in Wilhelmine Germany* (2001); *Bishops, Saints and Politics:*

Anglican Studies (2007); and *Anglicanism: A Very Short Introduction* (2006).

AUSTIN COOPER lectures in Church History and Christian Spirituality at Catholic Theological College in Melbourne, where he has served as Master and Head of the Church History Department. His publications include *A Little by Ourselves: A History of the Oblates of Mary Immaculate in Australia* (Melbourne 1984) and a soon to be published study of the spirituality of John Henry Newman. He was awarded the Order of Australia in 2004 for services to theological education.

JAN DE MAEYER is professor at the Katholieke Universiteit Leuven and director of KADOC (Documentation and Research Centre for Religion, Culture and Society). His publications include *Gothic Revival. Religion, Architecture and Style in Western Europe 1815–1914*, edited with L. Verpoest (2000) and 'Between "défense sociale" and Anticommunism: The Belgian Aristocracy in the Interwar Period' in K. Urbach (ed.), *Noble Fascists? European Aristocracies and the Radical Right* (2007).

ALBRECHT GECK is *Privatdozent* in Ecclesiastical History at the University of Osnabruck in Germany and Director of the Institute of Contemporary Church History of the Recklinghausen church district (*Kirchenkreis Recklinghausen*). His books include *Schleiermacher als Kirchenpolitiker* (1996) and *Autorität und Glaube. Edward Pusey und Friedrich Tholuck im Briefwechsel* (2008).

DAVID HILLIARD was an Associate Professor in History at Flinders University, Adelaide, Australia, and since 2002 he has been an adjunct associate professor. His publications include *Godliness and Good Order: A History of the Anglican Church in South Australia* (1986) and chapters in *A World History of Christianity*, ed. A. Hastings (1999) and *Secularisation in the Christian World*, ed. C. G. Brown and M. Snape (2010).

JEREMY MORRIS is Dean and Fellow in Theology at King's College, Cambridge. His recent publications include *F. D. Maurice and the Crisis of Christian Authority* (2005) and *The Church in the Modern Age* (2007). He is also editor of one of the twentieth-century volumes of a projected History of Anglicanism to be published by Oxford University Press.

PETER B. NOCKLES is Assistant Librarian (Printed Books) and curator of the Methodist Archives and Record Centre, John Rylands University Library, University of Manchester, and was Visiting Fellow of Oriel College, Oxford, 2007–11. His many publications include *The Oxford Movement in Context: Anglican High Churchmanship 1760–1857* (1994) and contributions to a *History of Canterbury Cathedral* (1995), vol. VI of the *History of the University of Oxford* (1997) and *Newman in His Time* (2007).

GEOFFREY ROWELL is the Anglican Bishop of Gibraltar in Europe and a former Chaplain of Keble College, Oxford. His books include *Hell and the Victorians* (1974); *The Vision Glorious: Themes and Personalities of the Catholic Revival in Anglicanism* (1983); and *Love's Redeeming Work: The Anglican Quest for Holiness*, edited with Kenneth Stevenson and Rowan Williams (2001).

KAREL STROBBE is a research assistant at the Centre for Historical Research and Documentation on War and Contemporary Society (Ceges-Soma) in Brussels.

ROWAN STRONG is Associate Professor of Church History at Murdoch University, Perth, Australia. His books include *Alexander Forbes of Brechin: The First Tractarian Bishop* (1996); *Episcopalianism in Nineteenth-Century Scotland* (2002); and *Anglicanism and the British Empire c.1700–1850* (2007). He is the series editor (and a volume editor) of a multi-volume History of Anglicanism to be published by Oxford University Press.

NIGEL YATES (1944–2009) was Professor of Ecclesiastical History at the University of Wales, Lampeter, and provincial archivist to the Church in Wales. His recent books include *The Religious Condition of Ireland 1770–1850* (2006); *Eighteenth Century Britain: Religion and Politics 1714–1815* (2007); *Liturgical Space: Christian Worship and Church Buildings in Western Europe 1500–2000* (2008); and *Preaching, Word and Sacrament: Scottish Church Interiors 1560–1860* (2009).

Abbreviations

AR	*L'Ami de la Religion*
BL	British Library
EHR	*English Historical Review*
IKZ	*Internationale Kirchliche Zeitschrift*
JEH	*Journal of Ecclesiastical History*
JHL	*Journal Historique et Littéraire*
JRH	*Journal of Religious History*
LDN	*Letters and Diaries of John Henry Newman*, ed. I. Ker, T. Gornall, *et al.* (Oxford and London, 1978–), vols. 1–
LPL	Lambeth Palace Library
MCL	Moore College Library, Sydney
OCA	Oriel College Archives
ODNB	*Oxford Dictionary of National Biography*, ed. H. C. G. Matthew and B. Harrison, 60 vols. (Oxford, 2004)
RC	*Revue Catholique*

Introduction

Stewart J. Brown and Peter B. Nockles

I

The Oxford Movement transformed the nineteenth-century established Church of England with a renewed conception of itself as a spiritual body. It reminded adherents of the established Church that theirs was a branch of the holy, catholic and apostolic Church, and not merely a creation of the Tudor state at the Reformation, as many of its critics asserted. In the 'mind of the Oxford Movement', to borrow Owen Chadwick's phrase,[1] the Church of England was an integral part of the Church Catholic that had been instituted by Christ, guided through time by the Holy Spirit, directed by the apostles and then by their episcopal successors, preserved in doctrinal truth, enriched by long centuries of tradition, venerated by generations of the faithful, infused with divine grace through the sacraments and destined to abide until the return of Christ in glory.

The Oxford Movement was initiated in the early 1830s by members of the University of Oxford, notably Oriel College, largely as a response to the threats to the established Church posed by British Dissenters, Irish Catholics and Whig and Radical politicians who seemed poised to subjugate or even abolish the established Church and appropriate its property and income. It was also, as the late Frank Turner has argued, a response to the predominant evangelical ethos – what John Henry Newman called 'the religion of the day' – with its emphases on individual piety, the conversion experience, justification by faith and personal Bible study and its sense that the Ordinances of the Church were relatively unimportant when compared to the religion of the heart.[2] The movement became particularly associated with the ideas expressed in a series of ninety 'Tracts for the Times', conceived by Newman, written by various authors and issued between 1833 and 1841. The Tractarians, as supporters of the movement

[1] O. Chadwick, *The Mind of the Oxford Movement* (London, 1960).
[2] F. M. Turner, *John Henry Newman: The Challenge to Evangelical Religion* (New Haven, 2002).

became known, proclaimed boldly that the Church of England represented the divine authority that society needed in order to meet the challenge of the spread of religious and political liberalism and unbelief, and was a counterpoise to the growing influence of evangelical individualism with its emphasis on private judgement. In contrast to the latter, the movement's leaders promoted an unostentatious but deep spirituality which emphasised awe, obedience, reverence and the principle of reserve when communicating religious knowledge. The Tractarians placed a particular value on fasting, self-denial and asceticism.

By the later 1830s, some Tractarians also began directing attention to the worship, devotion and architecture of the medieval Church. Their thought reflected a more general revival of interest in the Middle Ages as well as the early Church that was also finding expression in Romantic literature, especially the historical novels of Sir Walter Scott or the celebration of chivalry in Kenelm Digby's *The Broad Stone of Honour*. Some Tractarians went beyond a traditional high church insistence on observance of the rubrics and called for more elaborate ceremonial and liturgical dress, and the marking of saints' days and festivals of the Christian year. They were drawn to more ornate church furnishings – including stone altars, sedilia, lighted candles, reredoses, crosses, pointed arches, tapestries, stained glass and wall murals. Some Tractarians, or to be more precise, their Cambridge counterparts associated with the Camden Society, became advocates of church restoration and aimed at recovering the original beauty and symbolism of medieval structures. A few eventually became drawn to devotional practices associated with the medieval Church, including private confession, clerical celibacy, the monastic life and sisterhoods. Continued reflection on the history and nature of the Church, meanwhile, brought a minority of more extreme Tractarians to question whether the established Church of England was indeed a true branch of the universal Church after all. They grew openly critical of Protestantism, and began to look towards the Roman Catholic Church as a model, if not the one true Church. The minority who eventually submitted to the Roman Church did so because they could not feel sure of salvation outside her fold. These 'Romanisers' aroused bitter opposition from those who cherished the Protestant identity of the Church of England. Some viewed the conversion of John Henry Newman in October 1845 as marking the effective end of the Oxford Movement; certainly growing distrust of the 'Romanising' tendencies of the movement had by now seriously weakened its influence in the Church of England, and Newman's conversion, along with a number of his followers, did represent a milestone. Many more Tractarians, notably E. B. Pusey and John Keble, however, remained within the Church of England after 1845, and these Anglo-Catholics, as they became known, continued the work of transforming the established Church through what they termed 'Church principles', or a fuller understanding of the essential marks of the true Church.

There is a rich theological and historical literature on the Oxford Movement within the Church of England. We have a detailed understanding of how the movement contributed, not only to conflict and controversy in England, but also to the revival of the Church and religious belief in nineteenth-century English national life. We have some fine scholarly biographies of Newman and other key figures and an increasing understanding of the role of personal influence and friendship in shaping the movement. We have a growing appreciation of how the Oxford Movement – in practice, though certainly not in its original intent – helped to reshape the Church of England into a more diverse and pluralistic religious body, in which Anglo-Catholics, high churchmen, evangelicals and liberal churchmen alike could find a spiritual home. What is far less well known, however, is the nature of the influence of the Oxford Movement on Churches outside England. To what extent were the beliefs and ideals of the Oxford Movement communicated or exported to other Churches and to other countries? Did the Oxford Movement promote missionary activity and if so, how was this activity the product of its distinctive Church principles? The Tractarians believed that they were recovering and restoring universal principles of the Christian faith, and not simply addressing certain difficulties within their own particular national Church. How far was this view shared by Christians outside England? Did the Tractarian understanding of the Church promote, or inhibit, closer relations among the Churches of the world-wide Anglican Communion? Did the Oxford Movement contribute in significant ways to the emerging ecumenical movement of the nineteenth century? What role did the Oxford Movement play in the nineteenth-century global expansion of Christianity?

The essays of this volume engage with these questions through a series of case studies involving different regions of the English-speaking world and the European continent during the first century of the movement, from approximately 1830 to 1930. In what is the first volume on this theme since the classic *Northern Catholicism: Centenary Studies in the Oxford and Parallel Movements* of 1933,[3] our international team of authors have viewed

[3] N. P. Williams and C. Harris (eds.), *Northern Catholicism: Centenary Studies in the Oxford and Parallel Movements* (London, 1933).

the Oxford Movement as an international movement within a global context. Most of the chapters in this volume began life as contributions to an international conference on the Oxford Movement in its world context organised by Professor Nigel Yates and Dr Peter Nockles and held in September 2008 in Pusey House, University of Oxford. Following the conference, a number of authors were invited to develop their papers into book chapters, and another chapter was commissioned. This volume owes a particular debt to the vision and inspiration of the late Professor Yates, who recognised that the influence of the Oxford Movement extended far beyond its English heartland and that a proper understanding of the movement must involve consideration of its global context. We dedicate the volume to him, in warm gratitude for his many contributions to the history of the modern Church, and especially of the high church movements within the Anglican Communion.

II

Peter Nockles opens our volume with an account of the origins of the Oxford Movement at Oriel College, Oxford. His chapter, 'The Oxford Movement in an Oxford college: Oriel as the cradle of Tractarianism', explores how a small group of gifted and devout young churchmen largely emerging from within the confines of a single college brought to life a movement of religious revival that would profoundly affect the wider Church. While the movement soon flourished on a wider canvas, Oriel College, Nockles demonstrates, 'was truly the cradle, crucible and making of Tractarianism'. The beginnings of the movement reflect its origin in a particular milieu or 'genius loci', and demonstrate the power of religious ideas, and of a small community of thinkers, banded together in order to seek to restore the Church of their day to what they conceived to be its primitive glory.

In the first part of the volume, our authors consider the expanding influence of the Oxford Movement in the English-speaking world, first within the British Isles and then beyond. In chapter 2, 'Isaac Williams and Welsh Tractarian theology', John Boneham explores the impact of the Oxford Movement on the Church in Wales, especially the Welsh-speaking community. As he shows, despite the predominance of evangelical dissent, the Oxford Movement did establish an early presence in Wales, largely through the influence of Isaac Williams and his circle of followers. The Welsh Movement, Boneham demonstrates, was moderate and pastoral in nature, and was implacably opposed to any Romanising positions. In chapter 3, Stewart Brown considers 'Scotland and the Oxford Movement', discussing both the impact of the movement on the small and struggling Scottish Episcopal Church, and also the rather surprising and hitherto largely unchartered influence of the movement on the established Presbyterian Church of Scotland through the Scoto-Catholic movement of the later nineteenth century.

In chapter 4, 'The Oxford Movement and the British Empire: Newman, Manning and the 1841 Jerusalem bishopric', Rowan Strong provides fresh perspectives on Tractarian involvement in the debates over the formation of the Jerusalem bishopric in 1841, giving particular attention to the role of the Tractarian-influenced high churchman Henry Manning in the expansion of the colonial Church, and to the formation of the Colonial Bishoprics Fund in 1841. As Strong demonstrates, in spite of John Henry Newman's opposition to co-operation with the 'heretical' German Lutheran Church, Manning and other Oxford Movement sympathisers initially viewed the Jerusalem bishopric as a promising move towards the expansion of Anglicanism world-wide through missionary bishops. In chapter 5, 'The Australian bishops and the Oxford Movement', Austin Cooper develops the theme of Tractarianism, missionary bishops and the further expansion of Anglicanism overseas. He considers the influence of the Oxford Movement on the six Australian Anglican bishops who met in synod in the autumn of 1850 in Sydney, noting how they gave a practical expression to Oxford Movement principles and conceived of themselves as establishing the 'Church catholic' in Australia, despite 'the tyranny of distance' separating them from the mother Church. David Hilliard then explores the longer-term impact of the Oxford Movement in Australia in chapter 6, 'Anglo-Catholicism in Australia, *c.*1860–1960', noting both the importance of the movement in Australian Anglicanism, and also the way in which the Australian context gave a distinctive shape to the Anglo-Catholicism that grew out of the Oxford Movement. This distinctive Australian Anglo-Catholicism included the work of the bush brotherhoods, which carried on a mission in the more remote regions of the continent. Hilliard's account of Australian Anglo-Catholicism carries him beyond the end date of the volume, to 1960, but the nature of his material required the longer time period. Peter Nockles closes the first section with a chapter on 'The Oxford Movement and the United States', in which he examines Tractarian influence on the Protestant Episcopal Church in the new republic. He notes how Tractarian views contributed both to an existing, if embattled, high church movement in the Episcopal Church and also to the growing cultural divergence between England

and the United States, especially from the mid 1840s, as more and more American Protestants grew hostile to the 'Romanising' elements of the Oxford Movement and left the Episcopal Church vulnerable to its critics as a consequence.

The second section of the book shifts attention from Britain and the wider English-speaking world to the influence of the Oxford Movement on the European continent. In chapter 8, Geoffrey Rowell, bishop of Gibraltar, provides a broad survey of the European context of the Oxford Movement, exploring the engagement of leading Tractarians with the scholarship and Church movements on the Continent. He observes that there were 'important continental parallels to and influences on the Oxford Movement', not least in the shared response to the 'mythological reductionism' of the German biblical scholar David Friedrich Strauss. He concludes by reminding us that his own diocese of Gibraltar was formed in 1842, and that soon afterwards churches were being formed 'which clearly affirmed that the Church of England in Europe had a catholic inheritance and a catholic identity'.

Rowell's opening survey is followed by three chapters that examine the engagement of the Oxford Movement in specific Western European nations. Albrecht Geck gives an account of the movement's engagement with Germany in chapter 9, 'Pusey, Tholuck and the reception of the Oxford Movement in Germany'. He considers the responses of the different theological schools in Germany to the Tractarians, including that of the celebrated 'Tübingen school' to Tractarian views on the history and nature of the Church. The affinities between the English and German cultures helped ensure a close German interest in the Oxford Movement, though it is also clear that Tractarians continued to view German theology of all schools with intense suspicion. In chapter 10, 'The Oxford Movement: reception and perception in Catholic circles in nineteenth-century Belgium', Jan De Maeyer and Karel Strobbe explore the reception and perception of the Oxford Movement in Belgium through a systematic analysis of leading Roman Catholic French-language cultural and Church periodicals, as well as tracts, treatises and books. As they demonstrate, the prevailing Anglophilia in mid-nineteenth-century Belgium helped to ensure considerable initial interest in the Oxford Movement. At the same time, many Belgian Roman Catholic observers also believed the movement would soon bring the Church of England under the authority of Rome, and when it became clear that this was not going to happen, Belgian interest in the movement waned. In chapter 11, '"Separated brethren": French Catholics and the Oxford Movement', Jeremy Morris considers the reactions in France to the Oxford Movement. French responses to the Oxford Movement, he observes, demonstrated 'the tenacity and ubiquity of French suspicion of Britain', with concern over British misgovernment of Irish Catholics becoming a major cause of continuing distrust. There was little confidence in France that the Church of England could be reformed. For most French commentators, the greatest hope was that the Oxford Movement might bring the English nation, the 'separated brethren', into conformity with the Roman Catholic Church. As in Belgium, interest in and enthusiasm for the movement tended to be predicated on its potential for conversions or submission to Rome.

The final three chapters explore the impact of the Oxford Movement on emerging ecumenical visions in nineteenth-century Europe. In chapter 12, 'The Oxford Movement, Jerusalem and the Eastern Question', Mark Chapman discusses how Tractarian responses to the proposal for the Jerusalem bishopric contributed not only to a new interest in, and sensitivity to, the situation of the Eastern Churches, but also to the ecumenical hopes for reunion with the Eastern Churches. Angela Berlis further considers ecumenical concerns in her chapter on 'Ignaz von Döllinger and the Anglicans', giving particular attention to the correspondence of the Roman Catholic historian Döllinger and the Tractarian Edward Bouverie Pusey, conducted over several decades, and to their search for understanding and unity. Finally, in chapter 14, 'Anglicans, Old Catholics and Reformed Catholics in late nineteenth-century Europe', Nigel Yates closes our volume with a survey of Anglo-Catholic ecumenical commitments in the later nineteenth century, giving particular attention to controversial efforts by some Anglo-Catholics to seek unity with Old Catholics and Reformed Catholics in Europe on the basis of the historic episcopate and catholic order.

There has been a tendency for the Oxford Movement to be viewed too much in insular terms and within the confines of a familiar historiography of Anglicanism. To understand how the Oxford Movement transformed the Church of England is certainly important but it is only half the story. Broader continental vistas have been occasionally opened up, notably by the work on Anglo-French interactions over the movement by the late Louis Allen and as exemplified in W. G. Roe's important study of Lammenais (1966), but a certain Anglican insularity in the treatment of the movement has prevailed. Therefore, it is hoped that our collection of essays breaks away from Anglocentricity to new ground and adopts a fresh approach. The case studies in this volume aim to present fresh interpretations of the impact of the Oxford Movement outside England

and the Church of England in a more systematic and sustained way than has hitherto been the norm, and seek to explore the movement in its broader world context. Within the confines of our volume, it has not been possible to present a comprehensive world history of the Oxford Movement, however desirable such a study might be. We are aware that there are notable gaps in our coverage. There is, for example, no chapter on the Oxford Movement in Ireland – although two of our authors, Peter Nockles and Austin Cooper, have published studies on this subject, to which interested readers are directed.[4] We have not explored the impact of the Oxford Movement in Canada, New Zealand and Sweden,[5] where there are interesting stories to be told, nor of the Tractarian influence on the high church Society for the Propagation of the Gospel. All this said, we do believe that our volume provides valuable new perspectives on the impact of the Oxford Movement, not only on world Anglicanism but also on the global expansion of Christianity.

[4] P. Nockles, 'Church or Protestant Sect? The Church of Ireland, High Churchmanship and the Oxford Movement, 1822–1869', *Historical Journal*, 41 (1998), pp. 457–93; A. Cooper, 'Ireland and the Oxford Movement', *JRH*, 19 (1995), pp. 62–74.

[5] See O. Bexell, 'The Oxford Movement as Received in Sweden', in A. Jarlert (ed.), *Kyrkohistorisk årsskrift*, Publications of the Swedish Society of Church History (Uppsala, 2006), pp. 143–52. Peter Nockles has explored the insights into the Oxford Movement of the Swedish Lutheran Church historian Yngve Brilioth, one-time archbishop of Uppsala. See P. Nockles, 'The Oxford Movement and Its Historiographers: Brilioth's "Anglican Revival" and "Three Lectures on Evangelicalism and the Oxford Movement" Revisited', *ibid.*, pp. 133–42.

Prelude

CHAPTER I

The Oxford Movement in an Oxford college: Oriel as the cradle of Tractarianism

Peter B. Nockles

An essay essentially covering the theme of Thomas Mozley's two-volume classic *Oriel College and the Oxford Movement* (1882) may seem out of place in a volume that treats the much wider canvas of 'The Oxford Movement, Europe and the Wider World'. However, that wider international canvas can only be made sense of through an appreciation of the movement's context, origins, cultural and intellectual milieu and physical location. In short, the 'wider world' can be understood only in relation to the core centre of the Oxford Movement. Hence, our volume begins with a revisiting of the Oxford Movement's background, 'birth pangs' and emergence within a unique and particular time and place. Without the unique role and place of Oriel common room, for example, the Oxford Movement may never have acquired the impetus and strength to develop into a religious movement that would influence the wider world in Europe, the British Empire and the United States of America.

For Newman, the academic context of a particular Oxford college lay at the heart of what that movement represented and did much to explain its birth. Every college had its own distinctive character and ethos.

> It will give birth to a living tradition, which in course of time will take the shape of a self-perpetuating tradition, or genius loci as it is sometimes called, which haunts the home where it has been born, and which imbues and forms, more or less, and one by one, every individual who is successively brought under its shadow.[1]

Newman's evocative description of the intellectually and morally formative potential of an academic community, based on personal influence, to kindle, nurture and promote a living religious tradition contained in his *Idea of a University*, sheds light on the forces involved in the genesis

[1] See J. H. Newman, *The Idea of a University*, ed. I. Ker (Oxford, 1976), pp. 129–32.

of the Oxford Movement. For Newman, a college provided the arena in which personal influence could best operate in nurturing and propagating a living religious tradition. As he put it elsewhere: 'It is the shrine of our best affections, the bosom of our fondest recollections, a spell upon our afterlife, a stay for world-weary mind and soul, wherever we are cast, till the end comes.'[2]

The origins and roots of the Oxford Movement can be ascribed to many causes. There were theological, literary and cultural precursors elsewhere, parallel awakenings on the European continent, but at heart, it was the University of Oxford and its colleges, and in particular, though by no means exclusively, one college, Oriel, which provided the *genius loci* for its birth, growth, early struggles and its denouement.

With the notable exceptions of David Newsome's *Parting of Friends* (1966) and the nineteenth-century volume of the recent *History of the University of Oxford* (1997), too often in Oxford Movement literature, the university and its colleges serve as a mere backdrop and *scenae dramatis* rather than the formative influences on ideas and events. It was not for nothing that the sobriquet 'Oxford Movement' eventually gained, though only very slowly, wider currency over other terms of description.[3] By 1882, it seemed natural for Thomas Mozley to throw that term and Oriel College into inseparable conjunction with his *Reminiscences of Oriel College and the Oxford Movement.*

Of course, originating in a particular place or milieu is not in itself sufficient to account for the character and progress of a religious movement. An instructive contrast with the Oxford Movement can be provided by John Wesley's Methodist movement that emerged a century earlier. Like Newman, Wesley was a fellow of an Oxford college, Lincoln. The origins and first phase of the Wesleyan movement, the so-called 'Holy Club', took place within the University of Oxford, but unlike Newman, Wesley sat lightly to his Oxford college connections. The 'Holy Club' may have met in Wesley's Lincoln College but early Methodism was not an academic or intellectual movement and its early areas of growth and fields of influence lay elsewhere. It was otherwise with the Oxford Movement – though the *Tracts for the Times* were widely distributed, Oxford remained the nerve-centre and the movement's spread into the parishes formed a second stage in its history.

[2] J. H. Newman, 'The Rise and Progress of Universities', *Historical Sketches*, 3 vols. (London, 1909), vol. III, p. 215.

[3] O. Chadwick, *The Spirit of the Oxford Movement: Tractarian Essays* (Cambridge, 1992), pp. 135–6.

The ruling orthodoxy at Oxford in the later 1820s, according to William Gladstone's later reminiscences, was a 'high and dry' churchmanship,[4] with most religious zeal emanating from the preaching of the ultra-Calvinist evangelical, Henry Bellenden Bulteel, fellow of Exeter, supported by others of the same stamp such as J. C. Philpot, fellow of Worcester College.[5] However, the seeds of a deeper high church religious revival to which some younger generation evangelicals would prove susceptible, was already taking root. These seeds were not confined to Oriel. One of the striking features of the 1820s and 1830s, the two decades of nineteenth-century Oxford's great intellectual and theological ferment, was the way in which previous barriers between colleges were broken down, aided by such factors as the growth of reading parties often made up of undergraduates from various different colleges.[6] This necessarily meant that ideas nurtured by individuals in one college were transmitted more widely than they otherwise would have been.

Several colleges, alongside Oriel, notably Exeter, Magdalen and Merton, soon gained a reputation for being 'Tractarian' or 'Puseyite' in sympathy or basis. On the other hand, St Edmund Hall and Wadham gained reputations for being avowedly anti-Tractarian. The evangelical party was weak and in a minority within the university. It was only at St Edmund Hall (with its vice-principal, John Hill), 'where', according to William Tuckwell, 'prevailed tea and coffee, pietistic Low Church talk, prayer and hymnody of portentous length',[7] that it gained a significant foothold.

The reasons why so many younger scions of evangelical families were to become especially susceptible to the lure of the Oxford Movement are complex, and the points of spiritual affinity between moderate evangelicalism and nascent Tractarianism, often overlaid by later polemic, need recognition. The correspondence of the Tractarian leaders in the mid 1830s is filled with quiet rejoicing that such and such an evangelical, or '*Peculiar*' in their terminology, was becoming 'Apostolical' in his

4 W. E. Gladstone, *A Chapter of Autobiography* (London, 1868), pp. 52–3; D. C. Lathbury, *Correspondence on Church and Religion of W. E. Gladstone*, 2 vols. (London, 1910), vol. 1, pp. 2–6.

5 P. B. Nockles, '*Floreat Vigornia*: Worcester College and the Oxford Movement', *Worcester College Record* (2007), pp. 63–71.

6 D. Newsome, *The Parting of Friends: A Study of the Wilberforces and Henry Manning* (London, 1966), p. 68.

7 W. Tuckwell, *Reminiscences of Oxford* (London, 1901), p. 96. Thomas Mozley, albeit an unreliable witness, deserves credence when he stated: 'St. Edmund Hall was then the head-quarters of the Evangelical system. It is difficult to convey an idea of the very low position it had in the university.' T. Mozley, *Reminiscences of Oriel College and the Oxford Movement*, 2 vols. (London, 1882), vol. 1, p. 23.

principles. As Newman exulted in May 1837, 'at Exeter right opinions are strong. At Magdalen, Trinity, University and Oriel, nucleuses are forming ... Christ Church alone is immobile.'[8] In fact, Newman was being over-optimistic. A few colleges, notably St Edmund Hall and Wadham, soon gained reputations for being avowedly anti-Tractarian. While the private diaries of John Hill (vice-principal of St Edmund Hall) are surprisingly free from anti-Tractarian animus, there are some unflattering references to the preaching of Newman and actions of other Tractarians. For example, Hill wrote: 'St Peter's day, 29 June 1840: Newman preached a miserable sermon at St Mary's, more calculated to produce Scepticism than any other feeling.'[9]

Many colleges, however, were not committed in either religious direction. Newman seems to have been wrong about University College, as has been suggested by the author of its new college history, Robin Darwall-Smith.[10] University College, like Lincoln and some other colleges, remained relatively untouched, either above or below the fray. Sometimes the attitude of a particular head of house was crucial here. Darwall-Smith suggests that the emollient character and prudent course of its master, Henry Plumptre, was crucial in helping it to avoid serious strife.[11] A similar case can be made out for Worcester College under its mildly evangelical provost, Richard Lynch Cotton.[12] On the other hand, while Balliol gained something of a Tractarian reputation thanks to the prominence of its tutors, W. G. Ward and Frederick Oakeley, the vigorous anti-Tractarianism of its master, Richard Jenkyns (1782–1854), ensured that the Tractarian label did not stick.[13] Similarly, in the case of Brasenose under the mastership of Ashurst Turner Gilbert (1786–1870),[14] Tractarian leanings were kept in check and the college rallied to support an anti-Tractarian member, James Garbett, for the poetry professorship in 1841. In the case of Oriel, it was probably the intransigent and irreconcilable personalities of Newman and its provost, Edward Hawkins, in such contrast to Plumptre's handling of University, which ensured that that college would remain in the cauldron of controversy and become torn apart by theological conflict.

[8] J. H. Newman to H. W. Wilberforce, 14 March 1837, *LDN*, vol. VI, p. 42.
[9] Bodleian Library, Oxford, MS St Edmund Hall 67/12, fol. 12. 'John Hill's Diary', 'Monday June 29, 1840'.
[10] R. Darwall-Smith, *A History of University College Oxford* (Oxford, 2008), p. 360.
[11] *Ibid.*, p. 359.
[12] Nockles, '*Floreat Vigornia*', esp. pp. 63–4.
[13] E. Cannan, M. C. Curthoys, 'Richard Jenkyns', *ODNB*, vol. XXIX, p. 998.
[14] P. B. Nockles, 'Ashurst Turner Gilbert', *ODNB*, vol. XXII, pp. 169–70.

Much has been written on why the movement should have been born in Oxford, and not Cambridge – its curricular emphasis on Aristotelian studies, the close-knit, smaller scale of its colleges, the increasingly close pastoral relationship of tutor to pupil, its historic religious traditions, associations and distinctive ethos.[15] Yet why was Oriel to be its birthplace? In the first instance, the fact that Oriel College was to be the *genius loci* and epicentre of the Oxford Movement owed much to the presence of John Henry Newman, a fellow from April 1822 until his secession to Rome in October 1845. And Newman in turn, and the course of the Oxford Movement that he led, was shaped by the context, atmosphere, setting and ethos of Oriel College.

Newman owed much, spiritually, educationally and pastorally, to Oriel. The very circumstances of his fellowship election were indicative of how the college helped form him. Although Oriel's remarkable academic ascendancy in the early decades of the nineteenth century was achieved partly on the back of Oxford's far-reaching examination and curriculum reforms of the 1800s, Oriel chose its fellows not so much on the basis of honours achieved in the schools (examinations), but by 'a trial, not of how much men knew, but of *how* they knew'. The entrance examination was not so much a test of knowledge but of quality of mind and character. As it was put to Newman, an Oriel fellowship was a 'great point of emolument, in point of character it was immortality'. Newman, who had not distinguished himself in the schools, was an outstanding beneficiary of this far-sighted policy, which was pregnant with profound consequences for the future history of the Oxford Movement.

Newman's intellectual formation at Oriel was at the hands of Richard Whately, John Davison, Edward Hawkins, Joseph Blanco White (an exotic exiled Spanish former priest with whom he shared a love of playing the violin) and Edward Copleston (provost 1814–27). They were part of that firmament of Oriel fellows, also including Thomas Arnold and Renn Dickson Hampden, which was accorded the label Noetic (implying 'free thinkers'). An influential network of theologians engaged in a rational defense of Christianity against the challenge of heterodoxy, the Noetic contribution to political and social reform was also pronounced and gave them an influence beyond Oxford.[16]

[15] P. B. Nockles, 'An Academic Counter-Revolution: Newman and Tractarian Oxford's Idea of a University', *History of Universities*, 10 (1991), pp. 137–97; P. B. Nockles, 'Newman and Oxford', in P. Lefebvre and C. Mason (eds.), *Newman in His Time* (Oxford, 2007), pp. 21–47.

[16] For the Oriel Noetics, see R. Brent, 'The Oriel Noetics', in M. C. Brock and M. Curthoys (eds.), *History of the University of Oxford*, vol. VI, *Nineteenth-Century Oxford, Part I* (Oxford, 1997),

Whately's and Hawkins's personal influence on the young Newman is well known but it extended to other future Tractarians within the college. The Oriel Noetics were never an organised party in the way the Tractarians would become. Whately, for example, had no time for party conflict, and regarded both 'high church and low church as equal bigotries'.[17] While they certainly had their contemporary critics from among the 'high and dry' party then dominant within Oxford,[18] it was only later, and from a Tractarian perspective, that the Noetics came to be portrayed as incipient secularists.

The division in Oriel between Newman and his followers and the Noetic circle first surfaced at the time of the university's formal repudiation of Sir Robert Peel when he sought re-election as its MP in 1829 after his volte-face over Catholic Emancipation. Whately was appalled by Newman's part in this episode and apparent alignment with what he regarded as the bigoted 'two bottle' orthodox high churchmen.[19] After 1831, when Whately was elevated to the archbishopric of Dublin, their paths did not cross and the breach was complete.[20] At the root of this parting of the ways, were other Oriel influences quietly working upon the young Newman and his like-minded friends and would-be disciples within Oriel? It was at Oriel that Newman first met and got to know Pusey and Hurrell Froude. Pusey, then liberal in his churchmanship, left for Germany in 1825, but Newman's friendship with Froude grew steadily from then onwards. Froude was an Oriel pupil of John Keble and, through the agency of Froude, the influence of Keble was also crucial. It was Keble and Froude who helped rescue Newman around this time from the proud liberal intellectualism to which he later felt he was succumbing under Noetic influence.[21]

Froude and Keble inculcated the importance of sound ethos, one's dominant moral habit and proclivity and ruling motive. Newman

pp. 72–6; Brent, *Liberal Anglican Politics: Whiggery, Religion, and Reform* (Oxford, 1987); P. Corsi, *Science and Religion: Baden Powell and the Anglican Debate, 1800–1860* (Cambridge, 1988), pp. 73–83.

[17] Mozley, *Reminiscences*, vol. 1, p. 23.

[18] The comment of a London 'high and dry' churchman and former Oriel man, John Hume Spry, is revealing. He accused Whately of being 'the leader and mouthpiece and indefatigable supporter of a party in the church which promises to do more harm to her doctrine and discipline than all the Calvinism, or dissent, or evangelism of the last century has effected'. J. H. Spry to H. H. Norris, 10 December 1829, Bodleian Library, MS Eng Lett. c. 789, fol. 201.

[19] See P. B. Nockles, '"Lost Causes … and Impossible Loyalties": The Oxford Movement and the University', in Brock and Curthoys (eds.), *History of the University of Oxford*, pp. 195–267, at pp. 201–3.

[20] J. H. Newman, *Apologia pro vita sua* (London, 1864), p. 69.

[21] *Ibid.*, pp. 71–2.

imbibed a deepening sense of the necessity of inculcating a 'catholic' or 'Apostolical' ethos, in accord with the spirit of the primitive Church. As James Pereiro has conclusively shown in his *'Ethos' and the Oxford Movement*, ethos lay at the heart of Tractarianism, its theological principles being shaped and coloured by this conception. Pereiro has focused on one of Newman's star Oriel pupils, Samuel Francis Wood, younger brother of Charles Wood, first Viscount Halifax and scion of a famous Yorkshire Whig family, and a much neglected figure in the Oriel Tractarian firmament.[22] For Wood, as for his mentor Newman, ethos was not a mere matter of taste or feeling but embodied moral characteristics which included self-resignation, self-denial, obedience, reverence, reserve, awe, submissiveness to authority and an openness to the Divine Will. An apostolical ethos was opposed to intellectual pride, self-sufficiency and speculation, the claims of private judgement and mere mental agility and dialectical skill. It was also rooted in a theory of religious knowledge by which orthodox belief was linked to moral conduct. Moral or ethical flaws could be productive of doctrinal error or heresy. As Pereiro shows, the Tractarians imbibed deeply and reapplied certain key precepts of Aristotle's *Nicomachean Ethics* and Bishop Butler's *Analogy of Religion, Natural and Revealed* (1736) – works prominent in the Oxford academic syllabus and lectured upon in Oriel.[23]

The Tractarian understanding of ethos coloured its view of university education and Oriel was to be a focal point for its application. The conviction that religion came first and 'head-knowledge' second permeated Newman's philosophy as a public tutor at Oriel College from January 1826 until June 1832 (the provost having closed his supply of new pupils from June 1830 onwards). It also left its mark on pupils such as Henry Wilberforce and Wood. Academic standards needed to be raised, but alongside religious and moral ones, and this underpinned Newman's determination to reduce the numbers and influence of gentlemen-commoners for whom Oxford sometimes was no more than a 'finishing school' of pleasure and for whom a degree often did not matter. In Newman's view, the role of a college tutor involved more than the imparting of knowledge or preparation for examinations. It possessed an inherent moral, spiritual and pastoral dimension. He regarded his tutorship as part of his ordination vow. Newman could claim countenance from the Laudian Statutes (1636) for his view that a college tutor 'was not a mere

[22] J. Pereiro, *'Ethos' and the Oxford Movement. At the Heart of Tractarianism* (Oxford, 2008), chap. 1.
[23] *Ibid.*, pp. 89–90.

academical Policeman, or Constable, but a moral and religious guardian of the youths committed to him'.[24]

It is possible to determine the extent to which Newman put his educational principles into practice in his time as Oriel tutor and to measure some bench-marks of the religious, pastoral and academic successes of his tutorship. In a recent study of Newman as tutor at Oriel (private and public) from 1821–31, Philippe Lefebvre has demonstrated that there was a decline among the student population in the number of men of family and fortune (the gentlemen-commoners), a decrease in the number of students who did not graduate (with fewer gentlemen-commoners among them), an increase in the number of undergraduates sitting for honours and an increase in the number of future clergy among his pupils.[25] Lefebvre shows (from evidence in Newman's A*utobiographical Memoirs* and his published correspondence) that Newman had a clear conception of what he identified as evils in the existing system, one of which was the over-preponderance of the aristocratic gentlemen-commoners. Such internal reforms helped prepare the ground for a greater receptivity to Tractarian ideals when the time came.

Newman admired Hawkins and had preferred him over Keble at the election of a new provost in 1828. Hurrell Froude had urged Keble's claims, arguing that he 'would bring in with him a new world, that donnishness and humbug would be no more in the College, nor the pride of talent, nor an ignoble secular ambition'. Yet Newman at the time was unmoved, backing Hawkins as 'the more practical man', and famously declaring, 'that if an Angel's place was vacant, he should look towards Keble, but that they were only electing a Provost'.[26] Newman himself conceded that Hawkins initially supported his tutors 'in their measures of enforcement of discipline and the purification of the College'. However, a conflict between the two came to a head in 1830 when Newman, along with two other Oriel tutors, Hurrell Froude and Robert Wilberforce, sought to exercise greater control in the choice of undergraduate students and rearrange classes in order them to give more pastoral attention to favoured pupils. Hawkins obstructed them and all three resigned as tutors. Newman argued that the heads of houses had 'usurped, or at least

[24] J. H. Newman, *Autobiographical Writings. Edited, with an Introduction by Henry Tristram* (London, 1956), p. 91.

[25] P. Lefebvre, 'The Student Population at Oriel College and Newman's Pupils (1821–1933)', Annexe 1.A. 'John Henry Newman: Tradition, rupture, developpement (1826–1831)' (unpublished thesis, Université de Paris III, 2004), pp. 105–15.

[26] Newman, *Autobiographical Writings*, p. 91.

injuriously engrossed power in University matters, and that those who did the work, the resident fellows, not those who had no work to do, should have the power'.[27] Copleston stiffened Hawkins's resolve in countering this view. He insisted that the examination reforms of the 1800s had necessarily changed the academic balance of power in the university by increasing the educational responsibility of the heads, thus making the action of the Oriel tutors the more dangerous.[28]

Newman felt let down by Hawkins, who became an adherent of the academic status quo as well as distant and remote from the fellowship body once he had assumed the provostship.[29] Hawkins was also accused of sacrificing college interests on the altar of Westminster political allegiances and non-Oxonian influences. However, it was the nature as well as extent of Newman's personal influence as college tutor that gave Provost Hawkins misgivings – misgivings shared by the former provost, Copleston, who had first developed the idea that there should be greater and more personal intercourse between tutor and pupil. The development itself owed much to Oriel's system of 'open fellowships' which Provost Eveleigh (d. 1814) had instigated. It is difficult to represent Hawkins and Copleston as part of any secularising trend. The two sides differed not so much over the importance of the religious dimension of the tutorial office as over its application and direction. The dispute and its outcome damaged Oriel. Some indeed have traced the slow decline of Oriel's stunning academic supremacy to the removal of Newman, Froude and Robert Wilberforce as tutors.[30]

The evidence of Lefebvre's recent study shows that academic achievement as well as religious orthodoxy and cultivation of moral habits was a high priority for Newman as tutor. The care that Newman took over his pupils as individuals whom he took into his confidence is shown in the manuscript memorandum books on his pupils which he kept, the originals of which are in the archives of the Birmingham Oratory. However, it is also clear from this evidence that Newman regarded his tutorial office as a way of preparing some of his pupils for a defence of the Church in certain future trials which he evidently foresaw.[31] The names of many of Newman's and Froudes's Oriel pupils and tutorial associates read like a roll-call of Tractarian disciples in the 1830s: Robert Wilberforce, Thomas

27 *Ibid.*, p. 96.
28 D. W. Rannie, *Oriel College* (London, 1903), p. 201.
29 Newman, *Autobiographical Writings*, p. 97.
30 For example, see M. Pattison, *Memoirs* (London, 1885), p. 99.
31 Lefebvre, 'Student Population at Oriel College'.

Mozley, Charles Marriott, Samuel Wood, Frederic Rogers, Sir George Prevost, George Dudley Ryder, Charles Page Eden, Robert Francis Wilson and John Frederic Christie. When the crisis came in 1833, many of his former pupils were indeed at their posts and ready to enter the fray. Newman always had a deep sense of the providential destiny and special work to be accomplished by each individual, in accordance with his powers and particular circumstances.[32]

Newman remained hopeful that Oriel fellows might be appointed from among his former pupils and followers. As early as 1829 the suggestion was put about by Whately and others that the college was becoming packed with Newman's favourites, with the claim that many fellowship candidates were of inferior academic ability and only brought forward 'on the strength of party cabal'.[33] Certainly, the fortunes of Oriel continued to be everything to Newman, even when he was on his Mediterranean journey in 1832–3. His letters home at that time are full of expectant references to Oriel fellowship elections and whether disciples and friends such as Frederic Rogers had been successful.[34] Mark Pattison later maintained that for about ten years from 1830 elections to Oriel fellowships were protracted struggles between Newman endeavouring to fill the college with men likely to carry out his ideas and the provost 'endeavouring, upon no principle, merely to resist Newman's lead'. Pattison felt that this led to some inferior elections, but, for all his anti-Newman animus, laid the blame for the worst decisions on 'the Provost's party', claiming that Newman was the more true to the old Oriel principle of looking for promise rather than performance in candidates.[35]

The provost's writ did not extend to appointments to certain college offices, such as that of dean, treasurer, junior treasurer and librarian. The provost was overruled by a faction of Newman's supporters in college office elections in October 1833, and Newman was dean in 1833–4 and 1834–5. Newman's aspirations for Oriel anyway always extended far beyond what he could achieve under his remit as college tutor. At a time when government-inspired liberal reformers were seeking to modernise

[32] Thomas Mozley had first-hand experience of this aspect of Newman's influence, citing as an example Newman's letter of appeal to him in May 1832: 'You have various gifts and you have good principles, for the sake of the church, and for the sake of your friends, who expect it of you, see that they bring forth fruit.' Mozley, *Reminiscences*, vol. 1, p. 449.

[33] R. Whately to E. Hawkins, 29 April 1836, OCA, Letterbook 3, no. 216.

[34] For example, see J. H. Newman to F. Rogers, 5 June 1833, in A. Mozley (ed.), *Letters and Correspondence of John Henry Newman during His Life in the English Church*, 2 vols. (London, 1891), vol. 1, p. 404.

[35] Pattison, *Memoirs*, p. 99.

Oxford's college statutes, Newman advocated a return to the spirit of Oriel's fourteenth-century founder, Adam de Brome, with the provost and fellows living together in spiritual brotherhood, sharing a common table, all devoted to a life of study in the service of God.[36] Comparing the college statutes with current practice, Newman found 'only two things which are not in substance … observed; the Provost living with the Fellows, and the Fellows residing. This excepts of course the great deviation common to all the Catholic Foundations; the cessation, i.e. of Prayers for the Founders.'[37] Prayers for the dead being one of the practices of the primitive Church that the Tractarians wished to restore, Newman made a special point of praying for Oriel's founders and benefactors. Newman also wished to highlight the criteria of 'good character, good capacity, and poverty' as criteria in elections to fellowships. He wished to encourage fellows to reside, living frugally, and not be lured off to secure livings or get married. His aim was a rekindling of spiritual and scholarly brotherhood among all members of collegiate society, regardless of academic status. His educational vision found at least limited expression in a private initiative which he and Pusey inaugurated in 1836–7 involving his younger followers working with him in collaboration on the 'Library of the Fathers'. In 1837, Newman took a house in St Aldate's for those without fellowships who wished to stay in the university.[38] However, it was at Littlemore after 1840 that Newman and his associates fully embraced a semi-monastic community life.

The controversies in the mid 1830s over proposals to modify undergraduate subscription to the Thirty-Nine Articles so as to allow the admission of Dissenters to the university, and also over the appointment by the Whig ministry of the Oriel latitudinarian Noetic Renn Dickson Hampden to the regius chair of divinity in 1836, fatally divided Oriel and the university as a whole.[39] Oriel Tractarians turned on their former Noetic mentors, now portrayed as assailants of 'the foundation of the faith' in Oxford.[40] Hampden became a bogeyman for the Tractarians as much for the qualified support for the admission of Dissenters that he expressed in his *Observations on Dissent* (1834) as for his apparently 'Socinianizing' but unreadable Bampton lectures of 1832. Newman's critique of Hampden

[36] For wider discussion of the conflicting models of university reform, see Nockles, 'An Academic Counter-Revolution', esp. pp. 156–77.

[37] J. T. Coleridge, *Memoir of the Rev. John Keble* (London, 1869), p. 248.

[38] J. B. Mozley to A. Mozley, 9 November 1837, in *Letters of the Rev. J. B. Mozley. Edited by his Sister* (London, 1885), p. 69; Pattison, *Memoirs*, pp. 180–81.

[39] Nockles, 'The Oxford Movement and the University', esp. pp. 212–31.

[40] [H. W. Wilberforce], *The Foundation of the Faith Assailed in Oxford* (Oxford, 1835).

particularly incensed the latter's Oriel Noetic allies, with Whately later characterising Newman's polemical *Elucidations of Dr Hampden* (1836) as 'a tissue of deliberate and artful misrepresentations'.[41] However, though Oriel names were in the forefront of the anti-Hampden campaign, its main headquarters were at Corpus Christi and Brasenose colleges. Oriel was still more affected by the impact of Newman's Tract 90 in early 1841. In this work, Newman had sought to demonstrate that the Thirty-Nine Articles were 'patient' of a 'catholic' sense but thereby provoked the charge of 'duplicity'.[42] Tract 90 roused a chorus of opposition from older liberals, Protestant high churchmen and evangelicals alike. The 'Board of Heads' (the university's governing body) denounced Tract 90, with only two dissentient voices, Routh of Magdalen and Richards of Exeter. Tract 90 gave the provost of Oriel a unique opportunity to reassert his authority. The provost conducted an inquisition of fellowship candidates on their attitudes to religious parties and opinions, insisting that candidates completely repudiate Tract 90's interpretation of the Articles. It was claimed that Hawkins was the only head of a college to have adopted this policy. Judge Sir John Taylor Coleridge, scion of a famous Devon family, nephew of the famous poet and Keble's lifelong friend from their Corpus Christi college days, advised his younger son, Henry James Coleridge, when preparing to stand for an Oriel fellowship in February 1845, to beware 'of the Provost's one-sided bigotry in religious matters' and to abstain even from reading Tract 90.[43] The young Henry Coleridge took his father's advice, and could in consequence report that during his interview with the provost in March, he 'was not very roughly handled by him'. He had pleaded theological ignorance, and had got off lightly with the remark, 'You have a very great deal to learn.'[44] Existing fellows lacked this option. Richard Church's refusal to disavow Tract 90 or to refrain from lecturing on the Articles prompted Hawkins to remove him from his Oriel tutorship after much agonising.[45] The granting of a testimonial to another Oriel

[41] R. Whately to E. Hawkins, 22 April 1843, OCA, Letterbook 3, no. 252. In the same letter, Whately commented: 'The author … had nothing to learn from "The Slanderer" Himself!'

[42] For fuller discussion of the crisis, see P. B. Nockles, 'Oxford, Tract 90, and the Bishops', in D. Nicholls and F. Kerr (eds.), *John Henry Newman: Reason, Rhetoric and Romanticism* (Bristol, 1991), pp. 28–87.

[43] Sir J. T. Coleridge to H. J. Coleridge, 14 February 1845, BL, Ms Add 85887.

[44] H. J. Coleridge to Sir J. T. Coleridge, 8 March 1845, BL, Ms Add 85931.

[45] R. W. Church to G. Moberly, 26 June 1842, in M. C. Church (ed.), *The Life and Letters of Dean Church* (London, 1895), pp. 36–7. As another Oriel fellow, Frederic Rogers, explained, academic considerations made the provost reluctant to act in this case. See F. Rogers to Miss S. Rogers, 27 June 1841, in G. E. Marindin (ed.), *Letters of Frederic Lord Blachford. Under Secretary of State for the Colonies, 1860–1871* (London, 1896), p. 105.

luminary, Charles Page Eden (Newman's successor as vicar of St Mary's, the university church), was delayed on similar grounds.[46]

Albany Christie, another disciple of Newman among the Oriel fellows, also fell under Hawkins's scrutiny. Christie emanated from the eminent family of auctioneers and had come up to Oriel with special testimonials from the Noetics Blanco White and Whately, before coming under Newman's spell. After taking high honours and gaining a fellowship, he assisted Newman in his edition of select portions of the *Ecclesiastical History* (1743) by the Gallican divine, the Abbé Fleury. Christie found himself the object of the provost's displeasure on account of what the provost regarded disdainfully as 'Romanising' publications, including an edition of St Ambrose's *Holy Virginity* (1843).[47] The former provost's nephew and Oriel fellow, William Copleston, pushed Hawkins to take disciplinary action against Christie in November 1843 after publication of the latter work: 'Really such vagaries are no longer tolerable and as an Oriel man I feel no doubt in common with many others, that something must be done to rescue the College as a body from the imputations sure to be brought upon it by this publication.'[48] In fact, Hawkins had had Christie in his sights for some time. Among his papers, Hawkins left a record of notes made on him covering the years 1841–4. He records his expressions of displeasure to Christie at 'his idea of taking pupils to pass the Long Vacation in France & attend a RC cathedral, his intention not to read the state services for 5th Nov & yet conceal such intention from the Bishop, his turning to the east, & intoning the service'.[49] Hawkins used Christie's frequent absences from Oxford in order to threaten him with deprivation of his fellowship, but Christie defended himself robustly, explaining the necessity of looking after his ailing mother and complaining to the provost: 'nor do I think that you take a view of my position on the side of considerateness ... I believe your conscientiousness is scrupulosity.'[50] In response, the provost hit back: 'I think I ought to tell you that the letter itself was an improper one. You probably did

46 E. Hawkins to C. P. Eden, 20 October 1843, OCA, Letterbook 1, no. 78. Eden bluntly informed the provost: 'I do not find myself at liberty to accept a testimonial which is offered me as "in the confidence that my sentiments" in reference to Tract XC "have not really undergone any change".' C. P. Eden to E. Hawkins, 21 October 1843, OCA, Letterbook 1, no. 83. Eden complained that the provost was seeking to impose 'a new Test'. C. P. Eden to E. Hawkins, 20 September 1843, OCA, Letterbook 1, no. 77.

47 A. J. Christie (ed.), *On Holy Virginity: with a brief account of the Life of St Ambrose: (from which the Tract is derived)* (Oxford, 1843).

48 W. J. Copleston to E. Hawkins, 18 November 1843, OCA, Letterbook 1, no. 8.

49 E. Hawkins, 'Notes 1841–44', 20 April 1844, OCA, Letterbook 1, no. 19.

50 A. J. Christie to E. Hawkins, 22 January 1845, OCA, Letterbook 1, no. 15.

not intend to make it so, but so it was.'[51] In fact, refused testimonials for taking orders in 1844, Christie absented himself to London, where he studied medicine at St Bartholomew's Hospital, while spending long vacations with Newman at Littlemore.[52] Christie and Hawkins remained locked in conflict. The provost could not resist a final condescending lecture when news of Christie's abandonment of his fellowship and conversion to Rome broke in October 1845:

> That you have at last taken refuge from infidelity in credulity (as, of course, I must call it) is very melancholy, considering the great advantages with which you have been blessed – blessed & tried. But ... you will have acuteness enough, by & by, to detect the hollowness of the system of Rome, and you will be in imminent danger of relapsing into infidelity.[53]

In December 1845 Hawkins was also prompt in forcing another fellow, Frederick Neve, to declare his intentions, after hearing that Neve was deliberating on whether to join the Church of Rome. Hawkins himself implied that he was acting more strictly than other college heads, suggesting to Neve that 'if you suppose that I am acting against the law it is open to you to get your name inserted into the books of some other college or Hall within three months from this day, if any Head of house will receive your name, and then your privilege will be preserved'.[54]

There were instances of Hawkins making a candidate's repudiation of Tract 90 a condition of his signing college testimonials for deacon's and priest's orders. In 1848 Hawkins delayed signing testimonials for Henry Coleridge himself owing to the latter's scruples about the Thirty-Nine Articles. Henry's father, Judge Coleridge, shared his anxieties on the matter to his friend, Charles Dyson, in a letter of September 1848, in which he laid the blame 'at the door of the repulsive scrupulosity & pugnaciousness of the Provost'.[55] The provost would regard his misgivings as well founded, given that Henry Coleridge, like Albany Christie, later seceded to Rome, and both became prominent Jesuits. On the other hand, Judge Coleridge had earlier warned that the provost's policy would drive 'the inconsiderate, the unstable, the wrongheaded' into the arms of Rome.[56]

[51] E. Hawkins to A. J. Christie, 10 March 1845, OCA, Letterbook 1, no. 16.

[52] R. G. Clarke, *In Memoriam. A Short Sketch of Father Albany Christie of the Society of Jesus* (London [1893]), pp. 8–9.

[53] E. Hawkins to A. J. Christie, 25 October 1845, OCA, Letterbook 8, no. 710.

[54] E. Hawkins to F. R. Neve, 23 December 1845, OCA, Letterbook 8, no. 714.

[55] Sir J. T. Coleridge to C. Dyson, 11 September 1848, BL, Add Ms 86162.

[56] Sir J. T. Coleridge to E. Hawkins, 13 January 1844, OCA, Letterbook 11, no. 1087.

On the other hand, the provost's obsessive anti-Tractarianism could create difficulties in an opposite theological direction. In 1842, Hawkins approved Arthur Hugh Clough's election as fellow. Although Clough had briefly come under Newman's influence,[57] by 1842 Hawkins 'believed him to be [free] from all Tract views generally and a sound and well principled man';[58] the fact that he had been one of Thomas Arnold's star pupils at Rugby also favoured his cause. Clough's subsequent doubt about the veracity of Christianity itself and eventual resignation from his fellowship in 1848 proved something of an embarrassment and unpleasant surprise for the provost. The provost's old-fashioned 'evidence theology' approach, attempting to hold Clough in the faith by setting him to read Paley's *Natural Theology*, was evidently counterproductive.[59] In short, college business in the 1840s was at the mercy of theological controversy in a way unthinkable twenty years earlier. As Copleston observed to Hawkins: 'In my quiet times, when there was no faction or cabal in college, and confidence was reposed in the Governors of the Society, observance of forms was less necessary and less attended to. No college meeting was held for the matter of ordinary testimonials.'[60]

In a reversal of roles, liberals now appeared as conservative defenders of the Articles, while Newman and the Tractarians, who had defended the Articles up to the hilt in 1836, were now accused by Hampden of regarding them as a 'bondage'.[61] The condemnation of Tract 90 by the Oxford authorities and, subsequently, most of the episcopal bench, was one of the blows that led to Newman's protracted Anglican 'death bed' from 1842 in self-imposed retreat at Littlemore.

Tractarians blamed Hawkins for enforcing submission to a narrow interpretation of the Articles, but private correspondence shows that Copleston was the real driving force behind his policy. In September 1843 Copleston asked Hawkins's views as to 'the disposition of the majority of your Fellows, and whether you think they would support you in decisive measures for the suppression of this heresy within your society'. Copleston clearly sought to strengthen Hawkins's hand against what he

57 [F. T. Palgrave], *Poems by Arthur Hugh Clough* (London, 1862), p. vi.

58 E. Hawkins to R. Whately, 26 November 1845, OCA, Letterbook 8, no. 715.

59 E. Hawkins to A. H. Clough, 25 October 1848, OCA, Letterbook 8, no. 737. Clough later questioned Hawkins as to whether Christianity was 'really so much better than Mahomatanism, Buddhism ... or the old heathen philosophy'. A. H. Clough to E. Hawkins, 28 February 1849, OCA, Letterbook 8, no. 742.

60 E. Copleston to E. Hawkins, 22 November 1844, OCA, Letterbook 1, no. 58.

61 R. D. Hampden, *The Thirty-Nine Articles of the Church of England*, 2nd edn (Oxford, 1842), pp. 40–41.

called 'the fanatical party', urging him that 'It is however high time that open war should be proclaimed against this conspiracy and that the true sons of the church should declare themselves and rally the authorities of the University.'[62] Copleston rejoiced that the provost was making Tract 90 the 'touchstone' of 'eligibility to office in college'. He was anxious that Oriel should 'regain its credit for sound opinions in religion'.[63] He wanted Hawkins to go further by refusing testimonials to any fellowship or ordination candidate whom he even suspected of 'an inclination towards the new heresy'.[64] Oriel's Tractarian fellows recognised that their former provost was their most implacable enemy. It prompted opposition to an attempt in December 1841 to hang Copleston's portrait in Oriel Hall, moves matched by Newman and Keble's resistance to the presentation to the college of a bust of Whately. Copleston smarted under the display of antagonism aroused, lamenting to Hawkins:

> Thirteen years of my absence (just the period of my Provostship) ought to have prepared me for the change of disposition in so changeable a body. Yet I am surprised at it more perhaps than I ought to have been – for I had imagined that there were other grounds for placing a memorial of me than mere personal regard.[65]

Although no other Oxford college became quite so internally divided as Oriel, Oxford continued to be plagued by theological controversy, often stirred up by Newman's tormentor, Charles Portales Golightly, a former Oriel undergraduate and one-time candidate to be Newman's curate at Littlemore.[66] There was the Oxford poetry professorship contest in late 1841, the suspension of Pusey from preaching from the university pulpit in 1843 after a controversial sermon on the Eucharist and its condemnation by a committee of six 'Doctors of Divinity' (presided over by Hawkins) and the Tractarian challenge to the evangelical warden of Wadham, Benjamin Symons, who was candidate for vice-chancellor in 1844.[67] However, Newman's direct involvement in university affairs waned, even though battles continued to be fought by his disciples in his name.

After 1835 Newman held no college office and was rarely seen in hall, though he gave receptions every Tuesday evening in the common room. As Mozley recalled, he 'could no longer do at Oxford the work he had

[62] E. Copleston to E. Hawkins, 26 September 1843, OCA, Letterbook 5, no. 404.

[63] E. Copleston to E. Hawkins, 10 April 1843, OCA, Letterbook 5, no. 405.

[64] E. Copleston to E. Hawkins, 26 November 1845, OCA, Letterbook 1, no. 40.

[65] E. Copleston to E. Hawkins, 8 December 1841, OCA, Letterbook 9, no. 864.

[66] A. Atherstone, *Oxford's Protestant Spy: The Controversial Career of Charles Golightly* (Milton Keynes, 2007), pp. 9–14, 28–31.

[67] For fuller discussion of these episodes, see Nockles, 'The Oxford Movement and the University', p. 246–58.

to do', and 'was cribbed and crabbed in rooms no better than might be assigned to an undergraduate'.[68] By the early 1840s there was a growing note of bitterness in Newman's correspondence as he felt himself growing apart from Oxford. In February 1842, he wrote from Littlemore: 'For some years, as is natural, I have felt I am out of place at Oxford, as customs are. Everyone about is my junior … I have long given up all intention, if it were in my opinion, of being Provost myself.'[69] The despondent tone had deepened by August 1844: 'I do fancy I am getting changed. I go into Oxford, and find myself out of place. Everything seems to say to me, "This is not your home". The college seems strange to me, and even the college servants seem to look as if I were getting strange to them.'[70]

Newman even feared that Hawkins would use new disciplinary powers to threaten his position in Oriel. As Newman confided to Elizabeth Bowden in November 1844:

> I verily believe that the Provost will not let me rest in peace long, even if I do not retire from the fellowship myself. I am disposed to think he would not let me vote an Election. One of his tests the other day to one of our fellows who proposed to take orders was 'Whether he thought me an ill-used man'.[71]

He also observed a lack of support in Oriel among those whom he had helped. Newman observed of Charles Page Eden, his successor at St Mary's: 'Eden who has come near enough to know me, has shown no tenderness, no real respect, no gratitude.'[72] Newman felt sore about Eden because he had sacrificed his own marked preference for his former pupil, friend and disciple, Samuel Wood, for an Oriel fellowship in 1832 to the claims of Eden, because the latter's needs then seemed materially greater than those of Wood, who had independent means.[73] Other fellows resident in 1842 included Edward Arthur Litton, an evangelical, and James Fraser, a 'high and dry churchman', neither of whom were close to Newman or Tractarian ideals. Of course, there were exceptions among younger fellows such as Rogers, Church, Marriott, and Charles Dayman, but Newman was struck by the embarrassing incongruity that Blanco White, who had finally apostatised from Christianity, should almost alone among his earliest Oriel friends speak of him with affection.[74]

[68] Mozley, *Reminiscences*, vol. II, p. 210.
[69] J. H. Newman to Mrs J. Mozley, 15 February 1842, *LDN*, vol. VI, p. 463.
[70] J. H. Newman to Mrs J. Mozley, 13 August 1844, *LDN*, vol. X, p. 312.
[71] J. H. Newman to E. Bowden, 16 November 1844, *ibid.*, p. 412.
[72] J. H. Newman to H. W. Wilberforce, 27 April 1845, *ibid.*, pp. 641–2.
[73] Pereiro, *'Ethos' and the Oxford Movement*, p. 8.
[74] J. H. Newman to H. W. Wilberforce, 27 April 1845, *LDN*, vol. X, p. 641.

Nonetheless, in spite of its unsympathetic elements, C. S. Emden has demonstrated by examination of the Buttery Books that Newman's withdrawal from Oriel was more gradual than has been supposed. Newman's regular visits to Oriel suggest they were not merely to do duty at St Mary's, since they continued after his resignation as vicar in autumn 1843. His visits were to close friends among the Oriel fellows such as Richard Church and Charles Marriott, and he hoped to vote for Marriott as a candidate for provost if Hawkins (like Copleston) were given a bishopric;[75] hence his concern that Hawkins might prevent him from taking part in future elections. J. W. Burgon (fellow 1847–76) suggested on good authority that Hawkins was not raised to the episcopal bench during these critical years because of the expectation that Newman would then have been elected provost.[76]

Thus, Newman's withdrawal to Littlemore did not mark a complete severance from Oriel. On the contrary, Newman's Oriel ties were the very last to be broken and may even have delayed his final departure from the Church of England. He only finally resigned his fellowship six days before joining the Church of Rome on 9 October 1845. His friends among the Oriel fellows appealed to his college loyalty, and this may have delayed his departure. In November 1844, Newman had told his friend and follower John Frederic Christie, fellow of Oriel, that he had become 'useless as a child of Adam de Brome', since he was no longer filling college offices and was a stranger to his juniors. In response, Christie both reassured and pleaded with him:

> [I]s really a life of study and devotion now unsuitable to a child of Adam de Brome[?] Can you ever affirm that there is any one fellow who fulfils more nearly what Adam de Brome's own notion of a fellow would be than yourself, except indeed in this one point that you have latterly shut yourself up much at Littlemore[?]

Christie declared that he owed everything to Newman as teacher and mentor, but wished that 'you would not treat us as aliens to you'.[77]

The last act in the drama of Newman's troubled Oxford career played out in his absence in Convocation in the Sheldonian Theatre on 13 February 1845. This memorable meeting considered three proposals. The first two proposals, a condemnation of certain objectionable passages

[75] C. S. Emden, *Oriel Papers* (Oxford, 1948), p. 173.

[76] J. W. Burgon, 'Edward Hawkins. The Great Provost', in *Lives of Twelve Good Men*, 4th edn, 2 vols. (London, 1889), vol. I, p. 424.

[77] J. F. Christie to J. H. Newman, 17 November 1844, *LDN*, vol. x, pp. 419–20.

in W. G. Ward's *Ideal of a Christian Church* (1844) and the deprivation of Ward's degrees, were passed, but the third, a proposal to condemn Newman's Tract 90, was defeated by the intervention of the two proctors, the senior being Oriel's Richard Church. The Oxford heads had won a pyrrhic victory. In fact, Convocation's rejection of what was regarded as a 'new Test' represented a personal defeat for Provost Hawkins. Many of the members of Convocation who addressed their thanks to the proctors for their action were from Oriel.

Dean Church's use of the title 'catastrophe' to describe the events of 1845 in his history of the movement really was applicable to Oriel. After Newman's departure, there were a few to put on the Tractarian mantle, most notably Charles Marriott, but for many of his disciples in college a light had gone out. As Marriott observed to Judge Coleridge on the day after Newman's secession, 10 October 1845: 'It is strange and painful to feel going on without Newman, but we are going on at a rate that that at once encourages and alarms me.'[78] The sombre atmosphere in Oriel emerges from an entry in Judge Coleridge's diary for 19 October 1845, when he refers to his son Henry's recent return to Oriel as a new fellow: 'Henry left us on Friday morning ... very much out of spirits, even to tears, at the prospect before him there.'[79]

In conclusion, the early phase of the Oxford Movement was to a remarkable extent bound up with the history of Oriel College. The role of the Oriel common room was crucial. As an acute observer noted in 1852:

> It is our object, to appeal to anyone who was acquainted with the inner life of the Oxford religious world twenty and five-and-twenty years ago, whether two very opposite, and now very prominent, parties in the English Church, are not the development of private discussions and every-day conversations within the walls of Oriel common-room.[80]

It is remarkable that the source of a world-wide religious movement can be ascribed not only to one university, not only to one college, not only to one common room within that college but to one table within that common room!

Newman himself admitted that Keble and Froude were primary authors of the Oxford Movement, long prior to the catalyst provided by political events in 1833. James Pereiro also indicates that Newman was as deeply influenced, notably in formulating his theory of development of doctrine,

78 C. Marriott to Sir J. T. Coleridge, 10 October 1845, OCA, Letterbook 11, no. 1072.

79 Sir J. T. Coleridge, 'Ms. Diary (1845)', entry for 19 October 1845, BL, Ms. Add 86047.

80 'Memoir of Bishop Copleston', *Christian Remembrancer*, 23 (1852), p. 18.

by his one-time Oriel pupil Wood as Wood was by Newman. Some of Newman's former Oriel pupils and disciples ran far in advance of himself in the direction of Rome, while some other one-time acolytes, notably the Oriel fellow Arthur Hugh Clough, in reaction against Newman, drifted into rationalism or outright unbelief. Other contemporary Oriel men, later holding high office in the Church, such as Samuel Wilberforce and George Anthony Denison, however, were impervious to his personal influence partly because they had no wish to become any man's disciple. As archdeacon of Taunton and protagonist of the Eucharistic controversy of the 1850s, Denison gained a reputation as an extreme high churchman. He would spend decades fighting for the cause of what became known as 'the Catholic Revival' in the Church of England. Yet in his autobiography, he makes very little of his time at Oriel or of Tractarian influences on him there.[81] In fact, his description of the atmosphere and style of Oriel common room is distinctly unflattering, though his main complaint was that it was socially 'dull' and constrained – in stark contrast to Newman's experience. As for Samuel Wilberforce, after becoming bishop of Oxford in 1845 he seemed to go out of his way to court provost Hawkins, informing him, for example, after a visit to Littlemore in October 1845, that he had 'been much struck by the inferior character of all of Newman's comrades'.[82] Newman's formerly close Tractarian friend Isaac Williams drew back as Newman advanced towards Rome and is thus a not unbiased witness. He did not go as far as Samuel Wilberforce in belittling Newman's second-generation followers, but in his *Autobiography* (published in 1892 but largely composed in 1859), he made a telling point:

> [T]here does not appear to have been any who associated with Newman on terms of equality, either from age, or position, or daily habitual intercourse, or the like, in unrestrained knowledge, who have followed his example in seceding to the Roman Church, such, I mean, as Fellows of Oriel, who lived with him.[83]

Newman could not control his followers, even had he wished. If anything, he understated in his *Apologia* the part that Oriel had played in shaping the movement but he acknowledged there the debt which he owed others in Oriel:

> I had lived for ten years among my personal friends; the greater part of the time, I had been influenced, not influencing; and at no time have I acted upon others,

[81] G. A. Denison, *Notes of My Life. 1805–1878* (Oxford, 1878), pp. 49–50, 67–8.

[82] S. Wilberforce to E. Hawkins, 25 October 1845, OCA, Letterbook 11, no. 1097.

[83] *The Autobiography of Isaac Williams* (London, 1892), pp. 121–2.

without their acting upon me … it was through friends, younger, for the most part, than myself, that my principles were spreading.[84]

The Oriel Tractarian debt to their Noetic mentors is clear. As Wood observed, Whately's 'Lectures on Logic and Rhetoric' 'were a remarkable preparation for what was to follow'.[85] Logical precision was a vital intellectual tool, and Froude's as well as Newman's logical powers gave coherence to Tractarian principles, but for the Tractarians, the ultimate truth of religious doctrines did not rest on logical demonstration. On the other hand, the Oriel influence on Pusey was not paramount. Pusey was a fellow only from 1823 until 1828, part of which time he was anyway in Germany. Moreover, he departed for Christ Church to take up the regius chair of Hebrew in 1828, some years prior to the dawn of the movement.

Newman suggested in his *Apologia* that he was 'driven' from Oxford by the old liberal party, once dominant in Oriel.[86] Given their later history of antagonism, it was ironic that he should have supported the candidature of Hawkins rather than Keble, whom Froude had wanted, for the provostship in 1828. Yet Hawkins at that time seemed to Newman to be the stronger candidate for what the office ought to entail.[87] Hawkins's promotion also enabled Newman to become vicar of St Mary's and thereafter to wield his well-known influence from that pulpit and also to have the time and independence to commence the *Tracts for the Times* and lead the movement. For all this, he owed Hawkins and Oriel a profound debt of gratitude for unforeseen consequences, a debt which he acknowledged.[88]

Personal presence was a key element in Oxford's and Oriel's tutorial system and became a conduit for the dissemination of Tractarian principles. Newman was a charismatic influence as tutor, preacher and propagandist, marking for ever the lives of many of his Oriel pupils, thereby ensuring that the movement took deep root in that college. From Oriel, he orchestrated a religious movement that captivated an idealistic and serious-minded younger generation of 'juniors' in the university in reaction against a combination of academic conservatism and relative religious laxity among the 'seniors'.

84 Newman, *Apologia*, p. 133.
85 Newman later recalled that Whately 'was the first person who opened my mind, that is who gave it ideas and principles to cogitate upon'. J. H. Newman to W. Monsell, 10 October 1852, *LDN*, vol. xv, p. 176.
86 Newman, *Apologia*, p. 329.
87 Newman, *Autobiographical Writings*, p. 91.
88 J. H. Newman to Mrs William Froude, 4 April 1844, in G. H. Harper (ed.), *Cardinal Newman and William Froude, F.R.S: A Correspondence* (Baltimore, 1933), p. 42.

Oriel was truly the cradle, crucible and making of Tractarianism, as it had been of Noeticism. It was also within Oriel that it encountered some of its most effective formal opposition spearheaded by its provost. Copleston took pride in Provost Hawkins's attempts to crush Tractarianism in the college and contrasted this policy with that of what he called 'the disreputable set' of men 'in possession of Exeter College'.[89] Oriel was a house divided, and it was in the internecine strife within its walls that so much of the Oxford Movement's early history was moulded and shaped.

Oriel, however, had no monopoly over the Tractarian brand name, as became clearer in the wake of Newman's departure for Rome in October 1845. Not only is there evidence for the decline of Oriel's intellectual pre-eminence within the university by the early 1840s, but also by the mid 1840s for that of even its Tractarian theological pre-eminence. Thus, when the ultra-evangelical newspaper *The Record* listed individual Oxford colleges in terms of a sliding scale of whether its tutors were 'anti-Romanist', 'neutral' or 'Tractarian', Balliol came out top in the Tractarian stakes with four tutors thus labelled, followed by Exeter and Brasenose with three each. However, Oriel is well down the list, with only one tutor labelled 'Tractarian'.[90] Of course, allowance must be made for the anomalies of *The Record*'s classifications and the fact that only tutors were classified. Further evidence for the waning of Oriel's Tractarian credentials is provided by a letter dated 2 January 1846 from the prominent Balliol fellow and broad churchman Arthur Stanley, to Sir Edward Parry. Stanley discussed in detail both the intellectual and 'Puseyite' character of various Oxford colleges in relation to where Parry's son must go: Oriel does not even get a mention.[91] Moreover, there were staunch anti-Tractarians among the Oriel fellows such as the evangelical Edward Arthur Litton, who became prominent after Newman's defection. Litton was to emerge, after Golightly, as one of the Oxford diocese's foremost enemies of Tractarianism and ritualism in the 1850s and 1860s.[92]

[89] E. Copleston to E. Hawkins, 26 November 1845, OCA, Letterbook 1, no. 38. Copleston told Hawkins: 'I have read with infinite disgust Rawlinson's defence of himself.'

[90] Cited from *The Record* (27 February 1845) in J. Bateman, *Tractarianism as described in Prophecy* (London, 1845), p. 42.

[91] A. P. Stanley to Sir E. [Parry], 2 January 1846, BL, Add Ms 58372, fols. 1–3.

[92] For example, *Address to the Bishop of Oxford of the Rev. E. A. Litton and other clergymen of the diocese, together with his Lordship's reply* (Oxford [1859]). For Litton's repudiation of Tractarian theology, see E. A. Litton, *The Church of Christ in its idea, attributes, and ministry: with a particular reference to the controversy on the subject between Romanists and Protestants* (London, 1851), esp. p. vi.

This chapter has been the story primarily of the Oxford Movement in one college, but it was a movement that stirred many, if not all, Oxford (and some Cambridge) colleges, before it began to make its remarkable influence and impact on the wider world. It is that impact on the wider world which the following essays will explore. These essays will demonstrate, in different ways, that the Oriel Tractarians were by no means insular or Anglocentric. What was happening in Oriel and Oxford soon attracted wider attention, as the number of visitors from the Continent and North America to Oriel and Littlemore testifies. Oriel spoke to Europe and the wider world.

PART I

Beyond England: The Oxford Movement in Britain, the Empire and the United States

CHAPTER 2

Isaac Williams and Welsh Tractarian theology

John Boneham

An important and often neglected aspect of Oxford Movement's effect on the world beyond Oxford can be seen in the extent of its influence in Wales. Although historians have tended to dismiss the significance of Welsh Tractarianism, claiming that it was merely an English movement which had little effect on the Welsh populace,[1] studies by Eifion Evans, A. Tudno Williams, D. P. Freeman and B. M. Lodwick have demonstrated that the Oxford Movement did have a notable effect on a number of Welsh parishes, clergy and lay people.[2] There were a number of Welshmen who came under the influence of the movement while they were students at Jesus College, Oxford, during the 1830–40s; they were to propagate its principles when they returned to Wales through their teaching in their parishes and the publication of devotional and polemical works in both English and Welsh.[3] A prominent individual who formed a connection between Wales and the Oxford Movement was Isaac Williams, a close friend of John Henry Newman, John Keble and Hurrell Froude, who was born at Llangorwen, outside Aberystwyth, and became a prolific writer of Tractarian poetry, as well as sermons, biblical commentaries and three of the *Tracts for the Times*.[4]

While various studies since the 1950s have dealt both with Isaac Williams's contribution to the Oxford Movement and the contribution of many of the Welsh-speaking Tractarians, little attempt has been made

[1] D. B. Rees, *Pregethwr y Bobl. Bywyd a Gwaith Owen Thomas* (Denbigh, 1979), p. 250.

[2] D. E. Evans, 'Mudiad Rhycychen yng Ngogledd Sir Aberteifi', *Journal of the Historical Society of the Church in Wales*, 4 (1954), pp. 45–6; D. E. Evans, "Dylanwad Mudiad Rhydychen yng Ngymru II", *Journal of the Historical Society of the Church in Wales*, 6 (1956), pp. 92–104; D. P. Freeman, 'The Influence of the Oxford Movement on Welsh Anglicanism and Welsh Nonconformity in the 1840s and 1850s' (unpublished Ph.D. thesis, University of Wales, Swansea, 1999); A. Tudno Williams, *Dylanwad Mudiad Rhydychen yng Nghymru* (Denbigh, 1983); B. M. Lodwick, 'The Oxford Movement and the Diocese of Llandaff during the Nineteenth Century' (unpublished M.Phil. thesis, University of Leeds, 1976).

[3] Freeman, 'The Influence of the Oxford Movement', pp. 8, 260.

[4] S. A. Skinner, 'Williams, Isaac (1802–1865)', *ODNB*, vol. LIX, pp. 213–16.

to examine the extent of Williams's influence over the clergy who came to promote the movement in the parishes of rural Wales. This chapter will argue that while Isaac Williams's direct and practical involvement with the Oxford Movement in Wales was somewhat limited, his distinctively conservative approach to the movement's principles was echoed in the writings of many of the Welsh-speaking Tractarians. This suggests that Williams's writings and example may well have had an important influence over the movement's leaders in Wales.

ISAAC WILLIAMS AND THE WELSH-SPEAKING TRACTARIANS

Although Isaac Williams was brought up in London and spent most of his life in Oxford and Gloucestershire, he maintained a deep affection for Wales. He frequently returned to his family's estate at Llangorwen for holidays and the landscape of rural Cardiganshire inspired a number of his poems.[5] His poetic volumes *The Baptistery* and *Thoughts in Past Years*, for example, include descriptions of Clarach Bay near Aberystwyth and the picturesque waterfall at Devil's Bridge in north Cardiganshire.[6] A poem from *The Baptistery* highlights Williams's affection for the country of his birth:

> Yea, if to thee my fancy yearns,
> If early love within me burns,
> At thy dear name, my native land –
> If thrills a pulse in heart or hand
> For home, or shrine or Church below,
> This is the dearest wish I know.[7]

Williams's correspondence with his niece Catherine Williams also suggests that he was deeply interested in Welsh culture and wished to discover more about traditional Welsh legends.[8]

In 1841 Isaac Williams made an important contribution to the Welsh Tractarian cause by becoming involved with his brother Matthew Davies Williams in the plan to build a new church at Llangorwen.

[5] *Ibid.*; C. Taylor, 'Isaac Williams of Cardiganshire – The Christian Poet – An Introduction to His Nature Poetry', *Transactions of the Honourable Society of Cymmrodorion* (1986), pp. 115–26; B. Dennis, 'Isaac Williams, Priest and Poet', *Welsh Review*, 65 (1979), pp. 81, 86–9.

[6] I. Williams, *Thoughts in Past Years* (Oxford, 1838), p. 126; I. Williams, *The Baptistery* (Oxford, 1844 edn), p. 77.

[7] Williams, *The Baptistery*, pp. 234–44.

[8] C. Williams to I. Williams [no date], LPL, MS 4476, fols. 60–66, with permission of the Trustees of Lambeth Palace Library.

This church, which would take the dedication of 'All Saints', was the first Tractarian church to be built in Wales according to ecclesiological principles.[9] The building was praised by *The Ecclesiologist*, the periodical of the Cambridge Camden Society, as a perfect example of church architecture. It contained the first stone altar built in Wales since the Reformation, raised on three steps,[10] which reflected the Tractarian emphasis on the importance of the altar and the belief that the celebration of the Eucharist was the central act of Christian worship.[11] The sermon that Isaac Williams was invited to preach on the morning of the church's consecration emphasised a number of key Tractarian themes, including the doctrines of baptismal regeneration and the real presence, the sacramentality of the created world and the importance of awe and reverence when worshipping in the new church.[12]

Letters to Isaac Williams from his family dated around 1845 make it clear that they wished him to return to Wales, believing that this would greatly aid the Tractarian cause in his native land. In a letter dated 1846, his brother reminded him that he had once expressed a desire to do something that would help the Welsh Church, and he suggested that Isaac's influence would now make a significant contribution to it since there was 'a great necessity for someone to whom the well disposed may look up for advice and example'.[13] Williams's cousin Lewis Evans also claimed that he would be a suitable person to run the college that Evans hoped to establish to train young men for the ministry in Wales.[14]

Despite Isaac Williams's love for Wales and his family's belief that he had the potential to make an important contribution to the Oxford Movement there, it is important not to over-emphasise his contribution to Welsh Tractarianism. For whatever reason, he decided not to return to Wales, and his direct contribution to the Welsh Tractarian cause was therefore restricted to his involvement with the parish of Llangorwen. Moreover, although it is likely that he had a basic working knowledge of Welsh, he did not write in that language and his contribution to the movement was fundamentally English in both language and tone.

9 N. Yates, 'Church Building and Restoration', in G. Williams (ed.), *The Welsh Church from Reformation to Disestablishment, 1603–1920* (Cardiff, 2007), pp. 280–81.

10 *The Ecclesiologist*, 3 (1842), p. 47.

11 Cf. A. Härdelin, *The Tractarian Understanding of the Eucharist* (Uppsala, 1965), pp. 268–80.

12 I. Williams, *A Sermon Preached at the Consecration of the Church of Llangorwen in the Diocese of St. David's* (Aberystwyth, 1841), pp. 14–15, 17–18, 22–4.

13 M. D. Williams to I. Williams, 2 April 1846, LPL, MS 4476, fol. 163.

14 L. Evans to I. Williams, 8 October 1845, LPL, MS 4474, fols. 79–84.

A more direct contribution to the Oxford Movement in Wales was made by the Welsh-speaking Tractarians. These included Isaac Williams's cousins Lewis Evans and Lewis Gilbertson. Evans had been an undergraduate alongside Newman, John Keble and Hurrell Froude at Oriel College and served in the parishes of Llanfihangel-y-Creuddyn and Ysbyty Ystwyth with Ystrad Meurig in Cardiganshire. As the head of a clergy training school in this latter parish, Evans's influence brought many of his students to sympathise with the Oxford Movement and to teach its principles in their future parishes.[15] Lewis Gilbertson became the first vicar of Llangorwen, where he introduced Tractarian practices, including the daily service in Welsh, a weekly celebration of the Eucharist and the singing of Gregorian chant. Later he was appointed vice-principal of Jesus College, Oxford, and he also supported attempts to translate devotional literature, including Thomas à Kempis's *The Imitation of Christ*, into Welsh.[16]

The Oxford Movement's influence was to spread beyond north Cardiganshire through the efforts of a number of Welsh Tractarian clergy who were active in the dioceses of Bangor and St Asaph. These included Morris Williams (*Nicander*), the vicar of Llanllecid and later Amlwch in the diocese of Bangor; Evan Lewis, who succeeded Williams at Llanllechid and later became dean of Bangor in 1884; Phillip Constable Ellis, who was successively incumbent of Penmon and Llanfairfechan, in the diocese of Bangor; John Williams (*Ab Ithel*), the rector of Llan-ym-Mawddwy and later of Llanenddwyn and Llanddwywe; and Richard Williams Morgan (*Môr Meirion*), who served as perpetual curate of Tregynon in the diocese of St Asaph from 1842 until 1853.[17] As fluent Welsh-speakers, these men were able to teach Tractarian principles to their people in their mother tongue, and they published works in both English and Welsh.[18] So effective was their ability to propagate the movement's teaching that their parishioners

[15] D. E. Evans, 'Traethwad: Dylanwad Mudiad Rhydychen yng Nghymru', National Library of Wales MS 21439 D; essay written for the Eisteddfodd Genedlaethol Frenhinol Cymru, Aberystwyth, 1952, pp. 39, 247, 328.

[16] D. E. Evans, 'Mudiad Rhydychen yng Ngogledd Sir Aberteifi', *Journal of the Historical Society of the Church in Wales*, 4 (1954), pp. 48–51.

[17] J. E. Lloyd, rev. D. Ben Rees, 'Williams, Morris (1809–1874)', *ODNB*, vol. LIX, p. 262; D. L. Thomas and D. T. W. Price, 'Lewis, Evan (1818–1901)', *ODNB*, vol. XXXIII, pp. 606–7; J. E. Lloyd, rev. B. Jones, 'Williams, John (1811–1862)', *ODNB*, vol. LIX, pp. 248–9; R. L. Brown, *Ten Clerical Lives: Essays Relating to the Victorian Church in Wales* (Welshpool, 2005), pp. 163–86; D. P. Freeman, 'The Revd Richard Williams Morgan of Tregynog and His Writings', *Montgomeryshire Collections*, 88 (2000), pp. 87–93.

[18] A. T. Williams, *Mudiad Rhydychen a Chymru* (Denbigh, 1983), pp. 54ff.; Freeman, 'The Revd Richard Williams Morgan', pp. 87–93.

became well grounded in its principles and were able to enter into public theological debates with opponents of Tractarianism, as well as to write articles for the Welsh-language Tractarian periodical, *Baner y Groes*.[19]

While the Welsh Tractarians' ability to convey Tractarian teaching in Welsh was invaluable in helping the movement gain a foothold in rural Wales, there is perhaps some truth in the argument that the Oxford Movement remained very much an English import. This was obviously true on one level, since the majority of the Welsh-speaking Tractarians seem to have developed their sympathy for the movement while they were undergraduates at Oxford (though R. W. Morgan learnt his High Church principles from the Episcopal Church of Scotland while he was a student at Edinburgh).[20] However, it is important to remember that there had been a High Church tradition in Wales which pre-dated the beginning of the Oxford Movement and which provided a fertile soil from which Welsh Tractarianism could grow and develop. The origins of this tradition can be seen in the early Stuart Church and James I's appointments of High Church Welsh bishops to the dioceses of Bangor and St Asaph, appointments that owed much to the influence of William Laud.[21] The restoration of the established Church and the monarchy in 1660 was warmly welcomed in Wales, especially by the gentry of north Wales, many of whom had become High Churchmen while they were students at Jesus College, Oxford, before the Civil War, under the influence of the college principal, Francis Mansell.[22] The post-Restoration Welsh bishops were deeply opposed to Protestant dissent,[23] a characteristic trait of High Churchmanship. It is also significant that advocates of the Jacobite cause were active in Wales well into the eighteenth century,[24] while the fact that bishops William Beveridge of St Asaph, George Bull of St David's and Christopher Bethell of Bangor were sympathetic to High Churchmanship must have allowed it some freedom to develop in Wales. Isaac Williams's biographer, Owain Jones, claimed that Williams

[19] R. Roberts, *A Wandering Scholar: The Life and Opinions of Robert Roberts* (Cardiff, 1991 edn), pp. 278–80; D. P. Freeman, '*Baner y Groes*, A Welsh-Language Tractarian Periodical of the 1850s', *National Library of Wales Journal*, 32 (2002), pp. 305–16.

[20] R. L. Brown, *Parochial Lives* (Llanrwst, 2002), pp. 133, 136–7.

[21] G. Williams, 'The Early Stuart Church', in Williams (ed.), *The Welsh Church from Reformation to Disestablishment*, pp. 10–11.

[22] W. Jacob, 'The Restoration Church', in Williams (ed.), *The Welsh Church from Reformation to Disestablishment*, p. 65.

[23] *Ibid.*, pp. 67–8.

[24] R. H. Owen, 'Jacobitism and the Church in Wales', *Journal of the Historical Society of the Church in Wales*, 3 (1953), pp. 111–19.

did not learn his High Church principles from John Keble but that they were already part of his family tradition.[25] It is also interesting to note that, according to Eifion Evans, the High Church tradition which existed in the parish of Llanychaiarn in north Cardiganshire pre-dated the beginning of the Oxford Movement in Wales.[26]

If the Welsh Tractarians first came under the influence of the movement at Oxford, they also gave the Oxford Movement in Wales its own distinctive stamp by producing devotional and polemic literature in the Welsh language. Morris Williams's *Y Flwyddyn Eglwysig*, for example, mirrored John Keble's *The Christian Year* by providing a poem on theological themes for each of the Sundays and feasts of the liturgical year.[27] The leaders of the movement in Wales also tended to be highly nationalistic, as was reflected by R. W. Morgan's and John Williams's interest in Celtic mythology and in the eisteddfod movement.[28] Their nationalism can be seen in their opposition to the government's plan to amalgamate the sees of Bangor and St Asaph in order to fund the new diocese of Manchester, a proposal which was seen as a stark example of English imperialism.[29] R. W. Morgan was a strong advocate of the use of the Welsh language in the established Church in Wales. One of his pamphlets, entitled *Amddiffiniad yr Iaith Gymraeg* (A Defence of the Welsh Language), attacked the use of English in the Welsh Church and was particularly critical of the tendency to appoint non-Welsh-speaking bishops to Welsh sees. In his view it was this scant regard for Welsh national identity that had led so many Welsh people to abandon the established Church for nonconformity.[30] P. C. Ellis also opposed the preferment of senior clergy who were unfamiliar with the Welsh national identity and language.[31]

Bearing in mind Isaac Williams's prominent role in the Oxford Movement and the fact that he was a prolific writer of Tractarian literature, the question of the extent of his influence over the Welsh-speaking Tractarians is an important one. Unfortunately there is no evidence from extant correspondence between them and Williams, though it is interesting to note that, according to his biographer, John Williams spent a year as curate of All Saint's, Llangorwen, and during this time became

[25] O. W. Jones, *Isaac Williams and His Circle* (London, 1971), pp. 94–6.
[26] Evans, 'Mudiad Rhydychen yng Ngogledd Sir Aberteifi', p. 54.
[27] M. Williams, *Y Flwyddyn Eglwysig* (Bangor, 1883).
[28] Brown, *Parochial Lives*, pp. 140–41; Freeman, 'The Influence of the Oxford Movement', p. 310.
[29] Lloyd and Jones, 'Williams, John (1811–1862)', p. 248; Brown, *Parochial Lives*, p. 138.
[30] Brown, *Parochial Lives*, pp. 144–6.
[31] Brown, *Ten Clerical Lives*, pp. 180–81.

acquainted with Isaac Williams and his brother.[32] It is also interesting that R. W. Morgan's writings seem to have been influenced by Isaac Williams's tracts. For example, his claim in *A Vindication of the Church of England* that God would punish those who sought to 'presumptuously attempt to exalt individual reason' by prying into mysteries of the faith is strikingly reminiscent of Williams's Tract 80 on reserve.[33] Another interesting comparison can be seen in an anonymous article printed in the *Baner y Groes* in 1855, which claimed that the linen cloth placed over the consecrated elements after the service of Holy Communion represented the shroud in which Jesus was buried,[34] and Isaac Williams's poetic volume *The Altar*, 1847. Williams's work had linked a description of Jesus' burial to an image of a priest placing the unconsumed consecrated elements under a linen cloth,[35] so it is likely that the author of the article was familiar with it.

It is also significant that the theological perspective of the Welsh-speaking Tractarians seems to have had much more in common with the conservative approach of Isaac Williams and the ' Bisley school' than with that of Newman and the Romanising Tractarians. The Bisley school was a group within the movement which included Isaac Williams, his brother-in-law George Prevost and Thomas Keble (the brother of John Keble), from whose parish of Bisley the coterie received its name. The members of the Bisley school were clergy in rural parishes in Gloucestershire. Although they were supportive of the Oxford Movement in its early stages, they came to view its pro-Roman developments and Newman's leadership of it with increasing suspicion.[36] The Bisley Tractarians were much more restrained in their theological views than their Oxford counterparts, and, while the movement in Oxford became more sympathetic towards Roman Catholicism, they continued to emphasise the importance of loyalty to the Church of England and its Prayer Book.[37] As Newman's

[32] J. Kenward, *Ab Ithel: An Account of the Life and Writings of John Williams Ab Ithel* (Tenby, 1871), pp. 61–2.

[33] Freeman, 'The Revd Richard Williams Morgan of Tregynon', p. 90, quoting R. W. Morgan, *A Vindication of the Church of England* (London, 1849), p. 210; cf. I. Williams, *On Reserve in Communicating Religious Knowledge*, no. 80 in *Tracts for the Times* (London, 1838), pp. 45–50.

[34] Freeman, 'The Influence of the Oxford Movement', p. 348.

[35] I. Williams, *The Altar, or Meditations in Verse on the Great Christian Sacrifice* (London, 1847), image 29 [no pagination], 113–16.

[36] R. H. Greenfield, 'The Attitude of the Tractarians to the Roman Catholic Church' (unpublished D.Phil. thesis, University of Oxford, 1956), pp. 253–4; G. Prevost to T. Keble, 25 November 1838, Gloucestershire Record Office D2962/26; Isaac Williams to Thomas Keble [*c.*1838], Keble Deposit held at LPL, 9/56.

[37] Jones, *Isaac Williams*, pp. 13–20. Other members of the Bisley school were Hubert Cornish, Charles Cornish, Robert Gregory, H. A. Jeffreys, Raymond Barker, Errol Hill and Richard Champerowne.

curate at St Mary's, Oxford, between 1831 and 1842, Williams formed an important link between the Bisley school and the Oxford Tractarians, though his letters to Thomas Keble reflect his concern that both groups were clearly moving in different directions.[38] That Isaac Williams's conservative approach to the movement's principles also tended to be typical of the Welsh-speaking Tractarians is reflected in their emphasis on the doctrine of the apostolic succession, in their attitude towards Roman Catholicism and in their approach to the doctrine of the real presence in the Eucharist.[39]

THE APOSTOLIC SUCCESSION

The doctrine of the apostolic succession, which was central to Tractarian theology and formed the subject of the first of the *Tracts for the Times* (John Henry Newman's *Thoughts on the Ministerial Commission*),[40] is frequently emphasised in the writings of Isaac Williams. In a poem entitled 'The Rule of Faith' published in the *Lyra Apostolica*, for example, he claimed that God's truth had been committed to the Church, which was

> Founded on Jesus Christ the corner-stone,
> With Prophets and Apostles and the Line
> Of ordered Ministers ...[41]

In his *Devotional Commentary on the Gospel Narrative*, Williams claimed that Jesus' commissioning of his apostles conferred upon them the power to bless and to absolve sins,[42] while in one of his sermons he taught that the maintenance of the threefold office of bishop, priest and deacon was an essential mark of the true Church which remained faithful to the form of ministry instituted by Christ.[43]

Isaac Williams's poetic volume *The Cathedral*, which uses specific parts of a cathedral's architecture to evoke reflection on theological themes, presents the chapter house of the cathedral building as a

[38] I. Williams to T. Keble (no date), Keble Deposit held at LPL, 9/34; I. Williams to T. Keble [no date], LPL, Microfilm Box 779, 'Letters from Rev. Isaac Williams to Thomas Keble and His Family' [material not foliated].

[39] Freeman, 'The Influence of the Oxford Movement', pp. 1–3.

[40] J. H. Newman, *Thoughts on the Ministerial Commission*, no. 1 in *Tracts for the Times* (London, 1834).

[41] I. Williams, 'The Rule of Faith (XCVII)' in J. H. Newman (ed.), *Lyra Apostolica* (Derby, 1836), p. 118.

[42] I. Williams, *Devotional Commentary on the Gospel Narrative: The Lord's Resurrection*, vol. VIII (London, 1881), p. 232.

[43] I. Williams, *Plain Sermons on the Catechism*, vol. I (London, 1882), pp. 223–4.

metaphor for the doctrine of the apostolic succession. The chapter house lent itself particularly well to this subject, since it was the place where new bishops were traditionally elected by the cathedral chapter. In Williams's poem, the chapter house was portrayed as having eight walls, which correspond to the eight stanzas of the poem. The image of this octagonal room, supported by one pillar, alluded to the role of the bishop as a source of unity within his diocese. Williams's reference to the seats for the priests placed around the walls of the chapter house also emphasised the relationship between the bishop and his clergy,[44] which the Church Father Ignatius of Antioch, in a passage from his Epistle to the Ephesians quoted by Williams, compared to the strings of a harp:

> The Presbytery, being worthy of God, is united to the Bishop, as the strings are to an harp, thus bound together in union of heart and voice, and in that love of which Jesus Christ is the Leader and Guardian.[45]

Williams began his poem on the chapter house by taking up Ignatius' image and referring to the threefold ministry as the 'Mysterious harp of heaven-born harmony' which was essential to ensure the maintenance of 'order' and 'obedience' in the Church.[46] He also emphasised the belief that the order of bishops was founded personally by Christ through his commissioning of the apostles. It was 'Christ Himself, and His appointed few', Williams claimed, who 'moulded the frame' of the apostolic harp and 'in the silvery bound / Set all the glowing wires',[47] as he passed his own ministry on to the apostles, and they, in turn, handed it on to their successors by the laying-on of hands.

Williams's poem makes it clear that he saw the role of bishops as being more than just a convenient way of ruling and ordering the earthly Church but rather as the means by which God's grace continued to touch the temporal sphere through the sacramental life of the Church. Whereas earthly monarchs represented the kingly rule of God by wearing the 'shadow of God's Kingship', those ordained in the apostolic succession actually made Christ present in the Church:

> But in Thy Priesthood Thou Thyself art here,
> And virtue goeth forth from Thee.[48]

[44] I. Williams, *The Cathedral, or the Church Catholic and Apostolic in England* (Oxford, 1848), pp. 307–8; W. Benham, 'Introductory Analysis of "The Cathedral"', in I. Williams, *The Cathedral, or the Church Catholic and Apostolic in England* (London, 1889), pp. 7–8.

[45] Williams, *The Cathedral*, p. 43, quoting Ignatius' *Epistle to the Ephesians*, c. iv.

[46] *Ibid.*, p. 43. [47] *Ibid.*, p. 44. [48] *Ibid.*, p. 45.

As a result of the apostolic succession, bishops in the contemporary Church continued to fulfil the apostolic ministry by teaching the faith and celebrating the sacraments:

> ... With awe-stricken eyes
> We sit with loved disciples round Thy feet;
> Or, as the growing bread Thy love supplies,
> From Apostolic hands we take and eat.[49]

This suggests that Williams believed that the validity of the sacraments depended upon the apostolic succession, and that it was therefore essential to the very nature of the Church. The sixth stanza of the poem highlights this by alluding to *The Cathedral*'s emphasis on the imagery of church architecture, as the successors of the apostles are described as 'Key-stones' in 'God's sure house', that is, the Church founded on Christ and the apostles.[50] Williams went on to speak of bishops in even more exalted terms as 'visible angels lightening lower skies', who are appointed to represent Christ on earth.[51]

Such an emphasis on the importance of the apostolic succession was also reflected in Morris Williams's *Ecclesia Defensa*, a collection of short essays on Tractarian subjects written in Welsh. Here he claimed that:

> Church history proves that the bishops of the contemporary Church of England receive [their] vicarious authority from Christ himself... This authority was transferred from generation to generation from the apostolic age, and will be transferred until the end of time. From hand to hand the authority will be transferred.[52]

For Morris Williams, the apostolic succession was the only means by which one could receive true authority to absolve sins, administer the sacraments and, in the case of bishops, ordain others.[53] This belief was reflected in his *Y Flwyddyn Eglwysig*:

> As the Father sent Christ,
> Christ sent his servants,
> To convey rightly the Word of the Cross,
> From one age to another.
>
> Christ was anointed with the Holy Spirit,
> To be the Head of his Holy Church;
> He in turn imparts Him to the members thereof,
> Through the hands of his authorised servants.

[49] *Ibid.* [50] *Ibid.*, p. 47. [51] *Ibid.*

[52] M. Williams, *Ecclesia Defensa* (Holywell, 1951), p. 44. I am grateful to the late Canon D. W. Thomas for his assistance with some of these English translations.

[53] Evans, 'Traethwad: Dylanwad Mudiad Rhydychen yng Nghymru', p. 80

The Father-in-God transmits the gift,
By his hand to faithful men;
They consequently become Fathers themselves,
A generation of Ministers.[54]

In his *Letters to a Dissenting Minister*, which sought to defend Tractarian claims against the arguments of the Nonconformists, Philip Constable Ellis emphasised the belief that ordination in the apostolic succession bestowed a real gift of God upon the recipient. Those who were ordained fulfilled their ministry not because of any virtue or authority of their own, but as channels of divine grace, since ordination was 'the gift of God the Holy Ghost, conveyed through the Bishop as a medium'.[55] Richard Williams Morgan's *Notes on Distinctive Verities of the Christian Church* also taught that it was because of the apostolic succession that the true faith, once committed to the apostles by Christ himself, would continue to be 'transmitted, according to [Christ's] promise, uninterruptedly from age to age'.[56]

Closely connected to this emphasis on the importance of the apostolic succession was a strong criticism of Protestant Dissent, which had rejected episcopacy and the threefold ministry. In a poem on the Welsh Church from *The Cathedral* Isaac Williams lamented the fact that the 'Primeval saintly Church' of St David's, one of the most ancient of the Welsh dioceses, had become a stronghold of Protestant Dissent so that, from the south to the north of the diocese,

... from Towy's flood
To Conway springs an ever-teeming brood
Of novelty, to claim thy true domains ...[57]

His use of the word 'novelty' suggests that Williams believed that Nonconformity, in rejecting the ancient apostolic faith, had become merely another form of religious liberalism. Elsewhere he described Nonconformist worship as being a 'conventicle' and was particularly critical of the hymns composed and popularised by Dissenters which, in his view, contained 'egoistical expressions' which were the antithesis of the liturgies of the early Church.[58]

It has been claimed that Tractarian opposition to Nonconformity was much more prominent in Wales, where Dissenters posed more of a threat

[54] M. Williams, *Y Flwyddyn Eglwysig* (Bangor, 1883), pp. 29–30.
[55] P. C. Ellis, *Letters to a Dissenting Minister* (Rhyl, 1879), 43.
[56] R. W. Morgan, *Notes on Various Distinctive Verities of the Christian Church* (London, 1851), p. 169.
[57] Williams, *The Cathedral*, 23.
[58] I. Williams, 'The Psalter, or Psalms of David; in English Verse', *British Critic*, 27 (1840), p. 3.

to the authority of the established Church than was the case in England.[59] This is borne out by the attitudes of the Welsh-speaking Tractarians. Morris Williams, for example, claimed that, since the Church of England was the one true catholic Church in Wales, Dissenters who had removed themselves from its communion were guilty of damaging the Body of Christ. His *Y Flwyddyn Eglwysig* contained the following rebuke of Dissenters:

> You left the Lord's House and Church,
> His sweet Orchard and Fold.
> Will the God of Heaven consider this good
> When He will judge you?
>
> There is but one Spirit, one Father,
> One Faith, one Baptism and one Jesus;
> It is a heavy and a sad thing
> To divide and split up Christ.[60]

The Tractarian belief that, in rejecting the Church and its sacraments, Nonconformists had rejected Christ and cut themselves off from the means of salvation was also expressed in an article printed in *Baner y Groes* in 1857. This claimed that:

> God, in his pity towards man, has arranged the means for him to be saved. He has set up his church in the world, and that church is the Ark in which alone God has promised to save man, and to restore him to his favour for ever.[61]

Like Morris Williams, Richard Williams Morgan claimed that Nonconformist schism from the established Church constituted a 'grievous practical sin' which could never be justified.[62] Dissenting ministers possessed no real authority, since they had not been episcopally ordained.[63] Both Morgan and P. C. Ellis claimed that, since Dissenters had abandoned the apostolic succession, their ministers were judged not according to their spiritual authority but according to their ability as preachers. Ellis claimed that this was ironic since, despite Nonconformity's emphasis on salvation by faith alone, they were guilty of undermining the importance of grace and making 'God's gifts to others conditional on the merit of a fallible man'.[64]

[59] Freeman, 'The Influence of the Oxford Movement', pp. 402–3.
[60] I. Williams, *Y Flwyddyn Eglwysig*, p. 121 [translation by Canon D. W. Thomas].
[61] 'Y Weinidogaeth', *Baner y Groes*, 3 (1857), p. 33.
[62] Morgan, *Notes on Various Distinctive Verities*, p. 24. [63] *Ibid.*, p. 163.
[64] Ellis, *Letters to a Dissenting Minister*, p. 23.

ATTITUDES TO ROMAN CATHOLICISM

Isaac Williams and the Welsh-speaking Tractarians' emphasis on the apostolic succession went hand in hand with a deep antipathy for the Church of Rome. According to a letter from Henry James Coleridge to his father, so great was Isaac Williams's dislike for Roman Catholicism that when W. G. Ward informed him of his decision to convert, Williams's response was to 'burst into a flood of tears'.[65] Robert Gregory, another member of the Bisley school, claimed that Williams never ceased to see the Roman Church as the 'the Scarlet Woman of the Apocalypse', though he never actually wrote this in any of his books.[66] Williams's negative view of Rome is also reflected in an unpublished sermon on Daniel 12:10, in which he claimed that:

> [T]he things spoken against the Church of Rome are in a great measure true and so evident that the Almighty God seems thereby to caution and warn us. Her footsteps have been in every country marked with blood, the deceits and frauds practised by her members and ministers, and that too on a great scale, seems as bad as any that has been in the world.[67]

Central to the Welsh-speaking Tractarians' view of Roman Catholicism, and closely connected to their deep sense of nationalism, was their claim that the Anglican Church in Wales possessed an authority independent of the see of Rome. This was founded on their belief that the apostolic succession had been brought to Wales by St Paul himself centuries before St Augustine had arrived at Canterbury.[68] An article printed in *Baner Y Groes* argued that the re-establishment of the Roman Catholic hierarchy in England and Wales in 1850 was illegitimate, since the true successors of the apostles in England and Wales were the bishops of the Church of England.[69]

The strongest attack by the Welsh-speaking Tractarians upon Roman Catholicism is to be found in Richard Williams Morgan's *A Vindication of the Church of England*, written in response to Viscount Fielding's conversion to Rome in 1850. In this work Morgan challenged the papal claim of absolute supremacy over the Church, arguing that it had no basis in Scripture and was a 'usurpation over the Church

[65] H. J. Coleridge to J. T. Coleridge, 10 November, 1843, from the Coleridge Family Papers held at the BL.
[66] W. Holden (ed.), *Robert Gregory, 1819–1911: An Autobiography* (London, 1912), p. 37.
[67] I. Williams, unpublished and undated sermon on Daniel 12:10, LPL, MS 4479, fol. 199.
[68] Freeman, 'The Influence of the Oxford Movement', p. 264
[69] Freeman, '*Baner y Groes*', p. 312, citing *Baner y Groes*, 1 (1855), pp. 25–7.

of Christ forbidden by Christ Himself'.[70] For Morgan, the Roman Church was a 'corrupt' and 'schismatic' body, whose orders could not be considered valid in England.[71] In his view the corruptions which had grown up in the Roman Church over the centuries included the papal claims to absolute supremacy, the invocation of saints, worship of relics and images, clerical celibacy and the doctrines of purgatory and transubstantiation.[72]

Such a view of Roman Catholicism meant that Isaac Williams and the Welsh-speaking Tractarians tended to hold a more positive view of the Protestant Reformation than did Newman and Hurrell Froude,[73] despite their clear antipathy for Protestant Nonconformity in their own day. In a letter to Newman written in 1838, for example, Williams expressed concern that 'those who agree with us will not feel heartily in such a cause knowing that we are anxious rather to turn away people's minds from the Reformation to earlier principles'.[74] Even in 1851, by which time most Tractarians would have been content to describe themselves as being 'Catholic',[75] Williams, in a letter to Pusey, described himself as a 'Protestant'.[76]

In opposition to Roman Catholic claims, Morris Williams pointed out that the Church of England had not been created at the Reformation and had existed before Henry VIII had separated the English Church from the authority of Rome. Christ had used the political antagonism between the crown and the papacy in the sixteenth century to reform the English Church of its Romish corruptions and to restore its primitive, catholic status:

> [T]he same body continued to exist which had existed before: as no one who washes his face changes the constitution of his body, so the Protestant Reformation did not change the constitution of the church, but rather cleansed it of the filth of the Papacy.[77]

His belief that the Reformation had not broken the connection between the sixteenth-century Church of England and the early Church was

[70] R. W. Morgan, *A Vindication of the Church of England* (London, 1851), p. 26.

[71] *Ibid.*, p. 1. [72] *Ibid.*, pp. 93–4.

[73] P. Avis, *Anglicanism and the Christian Church* (Edinburgh, 1989), pp. 189–94.

[74] I. Williams to J. H. Newman, 1838, Pusey House Library MS, Liddon Bound Volume, no. 1, by permission of the Principal and Chapter of Pusey House.

[75] Cf. P. B. Nockles, *The Oxford Movement in Context* (Cambridge, 1994), pp. 178–80.

[76] I. Williams to E. B. Pusey, 19 December 1851, Pusey House Library MS, Liddon Bound Volume, no. 27.

[77] Evans, 'Traethwad: Dylanwad Mudiad Rhydychen yng Nghymru', pp. 75–6, quoting *Yr Haul* (December, 1841), p. 377.

reflected in one of his poems which presents Cranmer and Ridley as being in the same class as St Stephen, the first Christian martyr, and St Cyprian, the Church Father:

> Stephen is a lamp which will never be extinguished,
> And Cyprian glitters,
> I see Cranmer as a star,
> Second to the sun, and venerable Ridley,
> Beautiful is their appearance; O how fair![78]

This positive view of the Reformation stands in stark contrast to the refusal of Newman, Keble and Pusey to subscribe to the 'Martyrs' Memorial' which was erected in Oxford in memory of Cranmer, Latimer and Ridley.

THE REAL PRESENCE

Central to the theological outlook of Isaac Williams and the Welsh-speaking Tractarians was their emphasis on the real presence of Christ in the Eucharist. While teaching that Christ was truly present in the consecrated bread and wine of the sacrament, they were reticent in defining exactly how this came about and were quick to distinguish their belief from the doctrine of transubstantiation, which they believed taught that Christ was corporeally or physically present in the elements.

In one of his sermons Isaac Williams taught that the Eucharist brought the Christian 'intimately and closely into God's awful presence'.[79] The presence of Christ in the sacrament was described as being 'real' and 'substantial',[80] as opposed to merely figurative or metaphorical. It required serious preparation on the part of the communicant since it was an 'awful and serious matter … to come unto Christ's nearer presence without repentance'.[81] At the same time Williams firmly rejected the doctrine of transubstantiation, claiming that this teaching was an attempt to define rationally what ought to be accepted humbly as a mystery of faith. In his view, the doctrine was a 'low and carnal deceit' that attempted 'to bring out the doctrine of the Eucharist from the holy

78 Freeman, 'The Influence of the Oxford Movement', p. 410, quoting M. Williams, 'Yr Agdyfodiad', *Y Traethodydd* (1851), p. 159.
79 I. Williams, unpublished sermon on John 16:8, 9, 10, 11, LPL, MS 4479, fol. 171.
80 Williams, *Plain Sermons on the Catechism*, vol. II, p. 350.
81 *Ibid.*, p. 372.

silence which adoring reverence suggests'.[82] One of his *Hymns on the Catechism* also expressed this view:

Mysterious words! like priests of old
We eat the sacrifice;
But half the meaning is not told,
Untold the countless price;
We hear and do Thy last command,
Our hearts adore Thy words, but cannot understand.[83]

Whereas, according to the doctrine of transubstantiation, the consecrated elements were in substance completely transformed into Christ's body and blood,[84] Williams believed that they remained bread and wine in their natural substances but contained the real presence of Christ in a spiritual and sacramental sense.[85] This emphasis on the 'spiritual' and 'sacramental' presence of Christ in the sacrament, however, was not meant to imply a merely figurative or metaphorical presence. As Alf Härdelin has pointed out, for the Tractarians, influenced as they were by Bishop Butler's *Analogy*, the invisible, spiritual world was more real than the world which could be perceived by the senses. Their definition of the Eucharistic presence as being 'spiritual' and 'sacramental', in their view, pointed to higher and more 'real' objective presence than the 'physical' and 'carnal' presence which was upheld by the doctrine of transubstantiation, as they understood it.[86]

The importance of the real presence was also reflected in an article in Welsh in *Baner y Groes* which claimed that the sanctuary of the church building was more sacred than the nave since it was here that Christ became present in the Eucharist.[87] In an unpublished sermon on John 6, John Williams taught that 'the mystical body of our Lord which we read of is a reality and not a mere phrase'.[88] The fact that he wrote a Welsh translation of the Latin Eucharistic hymn 'Pange Lingua Gloriosi Corporis Mysterium'[89] by Thomas Aquinas also clearly suggests that he held a high view of the Eucharistic presence. Morris Williams's hymn

[82] Williams, *On Reserve in Communicating Religious Knowledge*, Tract 80, p. 101.

[83] I. Williams, *Hymns on the Catechism* (London, 1843), pp. 118–19.

[84] P. Haffner, *The Sacramental Mystery* (Leominster, 1999), pp. 88–9.

[85] Williams, *Devotional Commentary on the Gospel Narrative*, vol. VI, pp. 456–7; Williams, *Plain Sermons on the Catechism*, vol. II, p. 351.

[86] Härdelin, *The Tractarian Understanding of the Eucharist*, p. 157.

[87] Freeman, '*Baner y Groes*, A Welsh-Language Tractarian Periodical', p. 308, quoting *Baner y Groes*, 4 (1858), p. 23.

[88] J. Williams, unpublished sermon on John 6:56, National Library of Wales, MS 17184, p. 76.

[89] J. Griffiths (ed.), *Emynau'r Llan* (Bangor, 1997), pp. 338–9.

'Gyda'r Saint Anturiais Nesu' (With the Saints I draw near) also provides a vivid portrayal of the weary soul being refreshed and strengthened through the gift of Christ's body and blood in the Eucharist:

> With the saints I draw near,
> Under my heavy load, to God's altar,
> It is a table to feed the poor, hungry one,
> A table to strengthen the weak:
> There I received, as if touching it,
> The broken body of holy Jesus.
> In that place my heart melted
> Like wax before the fire.[90]

It is interesting to note that the words '*as if* touching it' ('*megis gyffwrdd*' in the Welsh original) suggest that the Eucharistic presence was not to be understood in a corporeal or physical sense, since they imply that to touch the consecrated elements was not directly to touch Christ. This emphasis may have been an attempt by Morris Williams to distinguish his understanding of the real presence from the Roman Catholic interpretation of it. Like Isaac Williams, he rejected the doctrine of transubstantiation, claiming that 'Transubstantiation is Papist and a dangerous error, but the Real Presence is a scriptural truth.'[91]

Morris Williams's belief, like that of Isaac Williams, that the nature of the Eucharistic presence was a mystery which had to be accepted in faith, was reflected in part of a poem from *Y Flwyddyn Eglwysig* on John 6:52. Here he asks for the gift of humility to accept Christ's Eucharistic presence in faith, without prying into the nature of the mystery:

> Christ make me very humble
> So that I can believe your words fully,
> Without listening at all to human reasoning,
> When it opposes the words of your lips.[92]

A similar view was also taken by Richard Williams Morgan, who claimed that, while the Church of England taught that Christ was present in the sacrament of Holy Communion, 'wherein the verity and reality of [Christ's] body and blood consists, is a mystery; but no greater mystery

90 *Ibid.*, pp. 336–7. The original verse of this well-known hymn reads: 'Gyda'r saint anturiais nesu, / Dan fy maich at allor Duw, / Bwrdd i borthi'r tlawd newynog, / Bwrdd i nerthu'r egwan yw; / Cefais yno megis gyffwrdd / Corff drylliedig Iesu glân, / Yn y fan fe doddai 'nghalon / Fel y cwyr o flaen y tân.' English translation by J. Gainer.

91 Evans, 'Traethwad: Dylanwad Mudiad Rhydychen yng Nghymru', p. 83, quoting *Cronicl Cymru* (10 December 1869), p. 4.

92 Williams, *Y Flwyddyn Eglwysig*, p. 59.

than every operation of the Infinite, Almighty, and Incomprehensible God'.[93] Like Isaac Williams, Morgan claimed that the consecrated bread and wine became Christ's body and blood sacramentally, while the natural substances of bread and wine remained.[94] In his view, it was impossible to reconcile the doctrine of transubstantiation with the Church of England's definition of a sacrament as a 'visible and outward sign of an invisible and spiritual grace'. Rather, transubstantiation implied that the outward sign in fact became the inward and spiritual grace which it was meant to signify.[95]

CONCLUSION

Although the teaching of the Welsh Tractarians attracted vehement opposition from Nonconformists who accused them of being crypto-papists,[96] their theological views, including those of Isaac Williams and the Bisley school to which he belonged, were actually much more restrained than those held by some of the more advanced Romanising Tractarians in Oxford. Welsh Tractarians were more antagonistic towards Protestant Dissent than their English counterparts; however, they also held a much more negative view of Roman Catholicism and were more sympathetic towards the Reformation. While upholding the doctrine of the 'real presence' in the Eucharist, they rejected any definition of this doctrine in terms of transubstantiation as the Church of Rome understood it. The approach of the Welsh-speaking Tractarians was not just a narrow expression of High Church conservatism; rather, like the churchmanship of the Bisley school, it was a manifestation of the original aims of the Tractarian movement having a very real influence on rural parishes outside Oxford. It is likely that the more pro-Roman tendencies of the Oxford Movement in England would have attracted great opposition and would have stood little chance of gaining ground in the parishes of rural Wales. The more restrained approach reflected in the writings of the Welsh Tractarians was a means of presenting the movement's principles in a way that parishioners could accept. Although it is not possible to assess the precise extent of Isaac Williams's influence over the Welsh-speaking Tractarians, it is surely significant that, as a member of the Bisley school and the only Welshman among the leading Tractarians, he formed a link between two groups.

[93] Morgan, *Notes on Various Distinctive Verities*, pp. 210–11.

[94] Morgan, *Vindication of the Church of England*, p. 64. [95] *Ibid.*, p. 65.

[96] Freeman, 'The Influence of the Oxford Movement', p. 130.

It is likely that Isaac Williams's example and writings were an important influence on the Oxford Movement in Wales, just as they were in America and Scotland.[97] However, it was the Welsh-speaking Tractarians who were ultimately responsible for applying the movement's teaching in the Welsh setting through their parish work.

97 Letters to Isaac Williams from Tractarians in North America and Scotland suggest that his published writings were being read there and were assisting the cause of the Oxford Movement in those countries: H. Potter to I. Williams, 13 June 1846, LPL, MS 4475, fol. 146; J. Stuart to I. Williams, 13 June 1846, LPL, MS 4476, fol. 20.

CHAPTER 3

Scotland and the Oxford Movement

Stewart J. Brown

INTRODUCTION

There was, in the image of the suffering, nonjuring eighteenth-century Scottish Episcopal Church, something that touched the Romantic sensitivities of the Oxford Movement. Here was an Episcopal Church that had, against all odds, preserved its spiritual independence and Church principles; it had been severely tested by adversity and persecution, had known prolonged poverty and humiliation, had been reduced to a remnant, but it had endured. It was, in the words of Sir Walter Scott, 'the ancient but poor and suffering Episcopal Church'.

Many Tractarians looked with deep sympathy upon the Scottish Episcopal Church and its history. They felt a particular call to assist the Scottish Episcopalians – portrayed by John Henry Newman in *Lyra Apostolica* as 'our brethren of the North ... cast forth to the chill mountain air'[1] – and help them preserve their identity and recover their social influence. And according to what was for long the only significant scholarly study of the subject, William Perry's small book on *The Oxford Movement in Scotland*, published in 1933, the Tractarians did just that.[2] They brought the small, suffering Scottish Episcopal Church out of the wilderness and into the mainstream of British religious life. For Perry, the spirit of the Oxford Movement permeated the Scottish Episcopal Church, inspiring a revival of that Church as a spiritual and social force in Scottish national life. Perry's portrayal of the Oxford Movement in Scotland was a story of endurance rewarded, of spreading influence and steady growth.

The story of Scottish Episcopalianism and the Oxford Movement in Scotland was, however, more nuanced than Perry's straightforward and teleological account. The work of Peter Nockles, Nigel Yates, Gavin

[1] Quoted in P. Nockles, '"Our Brethren of the North": The Scottish Episcopal Church and the Oxford Movement', *JEH*, 47 (1996), pp. 655–82, at p. 656.

[2] W. Perry, *The Oxford Movement in Scotland* (Cambridge, 1933).

White and especially Rowan Strong has shown that Tractarian interest in Scotland was by no means welcomed by all Scottish Episcopalians, that English Tractarians could be insensitive to Scottish Episcopalian traditions and foment divisions within the Scottish Church, and that their Scottish supporters could be a difficult and overbearing minority. Tractarianism, moreover, did not bring a large-scale revival of the Scottish Episcopal Church, which remains a small denomination to this day.

This chapter will revisit the impact of the Oxford Movement on Scotland. It will direct attention to the larger religious context in Scotland at the time and consider the Tractarian influence within the Scottish Episcopal Church and also among the Scottish Presbyterian Churches. And it will show that the Oxford Movement did have a profound impact on Scotland, but in an unexpected quarter.

THE SCOTTISH RELIGIOUS SETTING

Two salient features characterised Scottish religious life in the 1830s. First, the Scottish people were overwhelmingly Presbyterian. Probably between 85 and 90 per cent of the Scottish church-going population worshipped in Presbyterian churches, with about two-thirds worshipping in the established Church of Scotland, and about a third worshipping in Presbyterian secession denominations that had broken away from the established Church during the eighteenth century. The different Presbyterian Churches all embraced a Reformed, or Calvinist, theology, as defined by the seventeenth-century Westminster Confession of Faith (adopted by the Scottish Church in 1647), with its emphasis on the awesome power and majesty of God, on salvation by grace alone and on the absolute authority of the Scriptural word. Presbyterian worship in the different denominations was shaped by the Westminster Directory of Public Worship. Services focused upon the word of God, with Bible readings, long sermons and the congregational singing of metrical psalms. There was no instrumental music in public worship, and no readings from a prayer book; ministers instead gave out long, extempore prayers. Church interiors generally had white-washed or bare stone walls, and were dominated by the high pulpit. There were no stained-glass windows, no crosses on the wall and no altars, as such things were viewed as reminiscent of the Romanism that had been rejected at the Reformation. Presbyterian churches normally celebrated communion once or twice a year, in sacramental events that took place over three or four days. Baptisms at this time normally took place in private homes. Most Scottish Presbyterians were adherents of the Church of Scotland, which was the established Church in Scotland, and was governed by a hierarchy of Church courts – kirk-sessions, presbyteries, synods and general assembly – made up of ministers and lay elders. However, as noted above, a large and growing number of Scottish Presbyterians were members of secession denominations – that is, Presbyterian denominations which had broken away from the established Church, mainly over disputes concerning lay patronage in the appointment of established Church ministers.

The second salient feature of Scottish religious life in the 1830s was intense religious conflict. Following the parliamentary reform act of 1832, Scottish Presbyterian seceders, with support from a small number of Scottish Congregationalists and Baptists, had launched a national campaign to disestablish the Church of Scotland and end the connection of Church and state. The campaign included public meetings, marches with drums and banners, petitions to parliament, tracts and pamphlets, refusals to pay the local church rates in Edinburgh and imprisonments for non-payment. The Church of Scotland grew embattled and defensive; and some despaired of its future as an established Church. Then in 1834, the Evangelical party gained a majority in the general assembly of the established Church and, under the leadership of Thomas Chalmers, the Evangelicals embraced a programme of reforms which aimed to make the Church more popular, efficient and dynamic. The general assembly reformed the Church's patronage system to give congregations a greater voice in the selection of parish ministers, and it launched a church extension campaign to increase the number of parish churches and schools and to conduct a vigorous home mission movement among the un-churched labouring classes in Scotland's industrialising society. It petitioned parliament for a grant to support Scottish church extension, similar to the church extension grants parliament had given to the Church of England in 1818 and 1824. But the Scottish Dissenters responded by agitating vigorously against any state grant, and their political influence proved decisive with the reformed parliament. In 1838, Viscount Melbourne's Whig government announced that it would not support a Scottish church extension grant. The Church of Scotland was deeply aggrieved, not only by the government's refusal to support the established Church's efforts to expand its ministry to Scotland's growing population, but also by what seemed unequal treatment for the Church of Scotland in comparison to the Church of England. Worse was to follow. In 1838, the Scottish civil courts declared the Church's reform of patronage to be illegal, and insisted on the enforcement of unrestricted patronage rights in the appointment of parish ministers. The Church resisted what it viewed as the 'intrusion' of unpopular patrons' candidates into parish churches against the wishes of congregations. The result was an escalating conflict between Church and state, including violent confrontations in some parishes, which by the early 1840s threatened the break-up, or disruption, of the Church of Scotland.

The Scottish Episcopal Church had not participated in this ecclesiastical competition and strife. The Scottish Episcopal Church was just emerging from the shadows of persecution and lacked the resources for a large-scale home mission to the people of Scotland. It was only in 1792 that had it been relieved of most of the eighteenth-century penal legislation that had reduced it to a remnant. There were in 1800 six bishops, about seventy clergy and perhaps fifteen thousand adult worshippers. These numbers had increased by the 1830s, but not significantly. Decades of persecution had taken their toll, and the Episcopal Church was far from united. The small denomination was torn by significant and heartfelt internal divisions over liturgy. In the north, and especially the north-east, Episcopalians were deeply attached to the Scottish Communion Office, a liturgy based on a modified version of the Scottish Prayer Book of 1637 and formally agreed by the Scottish Church in 1764.[3] It was venerated for its historical associations and for conveying a clear sense of the real presence of Christ in the sacrament. In the south, on the other hand, Episcopalian congregations tended to use the Book of Common Prayer of the Church of England, and to view the Scottish Communion Office as theologically suspect. In particular, some felt its expressions of the real presence ran too close to the Roman Catholic doctrine of transubstantiation. Moreover, some Episcopalian congregations, known as 'English Episcopalians', refused to accept the authority of the Scottish bishops, claiming that the Relief Act of 1792 had not given state recognition to the Scottish bishops and that those bishops therefore had no legal status.[4]

Scottish Episcopalians, whether they followed the Scottish Communion Office or the Book of Common Prayer, were predominantly High Church in their piety, with a sense of themselves as representing the true Church in Scotland, spiritually independent, defined by their sacramental liturgy against the dominant Presbyterianism,

[3] Nockles, '"Our Brethren of the North"', pp. 662–3; R. Strong, *Episcopalianism in Nineteenth-Century Scotland* (Oxford, 2002), pp. 25–6.

[4] W. Blatch, *A Memoir of the Right Rev. David Low* (London, 1855), pp. 259–61; D. C. Lathbury (ed.), *Correspondence on Church and Religion of William Ewart Gladstone*, 2 vols. (London, 1910), vol. II, p. 201.

preserved by providence and tested and purified through over a century of persecution and suffering. As Peter Nockles has observed, 'the continued witness of the Scottish Episcopal Church in the eighteenth century demonstrated that the Church did not need the buttress of the State to uphold primitive truth'.[5] Alongside this dominant High Church tradition, there was also a small but growing evangelical movement within Scottish Episcopalianism, associated largely with English and Irish Anglican migrants into Lowland towns and cities; the evangelicals were less attached to the sacramental traditions of the past and more interested in carrying a simple gospel message to all who would hear them. Tensions between evangelicals and high church Episcopalians could be acute, and were connected with the conflicts over the Scottish Communion Office, over the authority of the Scottish bishops, and over Scottish, English and Irish ethnicity. In 1842, these tensions contributed to a schism, when the evangelical Revd D. T. K. Drummond of Edinburgh, along with most of his congregation, left the Scottish Episcopal communion.[6] There was real fear that the secession would spread. 'The Drummond party', observed E. B. Ramsay, dean of Edinburgh, to William Ewart Gladstone on 1 May 1845, 'must increase if things go on as they do at present. The chapels of this description will in some places supersede the S. Epl. [Scottish Episcopal] Chapels.'[7]

During the 1830s and early 1840s, Episcopalians were ambivalent about the difficulties of the Church of Scotland. Many families and communities harboured memories, still very raw, of persecution at the hands of the Presbyterian establishment and they could be tempted to view the Presbyterian troubles as the result of erroneous doctrine or divine displeasure. However, Episcopalians also recognised that the Presbyterian Church was the established Church in Scotland and that it helped maintain social order through its hundreds of parish churches and by representing the union of Church and state. And with rapid industrialisation and urbanisation, growing crime, prostitution, drunkenness and class conflict, Scotland was in manifest need of agencies of social order.

It was into this volatile Scotland and divided Episcopal Church that Tractarianism found its way and made its impact.

[5] Nockles, '"Our Brethren of the North"', p. 657.

[6] For a recent account of the Drummond secession, see P. Meldrum, *Conscience and Compromise: Forgotten Evangelicals of Nineteenth-Century Scotland* (Carlisle, 2006), pp. 259–79.

[7] E. B. Ramsay to W. E. Gladstone. 1 May 1845, BL, Gladstone Papers, Add Mss 44283, fols. 99–104.

THE OXFORD MOVEMENT AND THE SCOTTISH EPISCOPAL CHURCH

The Oxford Movement was becoming known in Scotland from the later 1830s, as diverse individuals, mainly from among the wealthy landed or professional classes (and who had been educated in England or had family connections in England), came to embrace Tractarian teachings on the authority of the visible Church, the mystical chain of the apostolic succession, the real presence of Christ in the Eucharist and the beauty of ancient liturgies. Some, to be sure, doubted that the Scottish Episcopal Church had much to learn from the Tractarian movement. This movement, some believed, had emerged in the very different context of an established Church of England that had come under Erastian and rationalist influences through its state connection. 'We Scottish Episcopalians', insisted Michael Russell, bishop of Glasgow, in his *Charge* of May 1842, 'have no immediate concern [with the Oxford Movement], because we, as a body, were free from the deteriorating causes which operated so unfavourably in the case of the Anglican communion.' 'Being cast off by the State', he explained, 'we escaped the malign influences'; indeed, for the persecuted Scottish Episcopalians, 'belief in the holy catholic church' had never waned.[8] Yet Russell was broadly favourable towards the Tractarian principles in his *Charge*, as was the high church bishop of Edinburgh, Charles Terrot, in his *Charge* of that same year.[9] Tractarian teachings, for these Scottish sympathisers, would help to bring the Church of England closer to the Scottish Episcopal Church.

Others in Scotland, meanwhile, went beyond mere sympathy; they found the Tractarian teachings strongly compelling and indeed saw in them the potential for the renewal of the Scottish Church. Prominent among these early supporters in Scotland were some aristocratic lay persons of English birth or education, or with English connections. In the early 1840s, the recently widowed Marchioness of Lothian was drawn to Tractarian writings, in part through the influence of her brother-in-law, the Revd Lord Henry Kerr, high church rector of Dittisham, Devon, and a supporter of the ecclesiological movement in the Church of England. Lady Lothian ceased her late husband's practice of attending the parish church of the established Church of Scotland, and paid

[8] M. Russell, *Charge Delivered to the Episcopal Clergy of the City and District of Glasgow, May 4, 1842* (Edinburgh, 1842), pp. 17–18.

[9] Meldrum, *Conscience and Compromise*, p. 253.

for the building of a sumptuous gothic Episcopal church, St John the Evangelist, in Jedburgh, in the Scottish borders. The church, which seated 180 people, was designed by John Haywood, a member of the Cambridge Camden Society (founded in 1839 to promote the revival of ecclesiological traditions). The church's structure and interior furnishings, including an altar and three sedilia of Caen stone, lectern, aisleless nave, screened-off chancel, alignment with its chancel to the east and steeply pitched roof, reflected Tractarian liturgical practices. The dowager Queen Adelaide, widow of William IV and a patron of the ecclesiology movement, gifted the pulpit, while tiles with sacred images, designed by A. W. N. Pugin, were placed above the altar.[10] The church was, according to Rowan Strong, the 'first Episcopal church to be built to Camden Society principles'.[11] The consecration of the church in August 1844 became a major event for the Scottish Episcopal Church, attended by four Scottish bishops and thirty-two clergy. The clergy included the leading English Tractarians, John Keble, Robert Wilberforce and William Dodsworth.[12] The six sermons preached on the occasion were published in a commemorative volume.[13] W. F. Hook, High Church vicar of Leeds and a close friend and spiritual adviser of Lady Lothian, played a key role in the commemoration, preaching two of the six sermons marking the event.[14] The consecration, Keble informed his friend, John Taylor Coleridge, on 30 August 1844, 'was especially interesting as being the settling of the Church in a place from which it had vanished since the Revolution [of 1688–9]'.[15] Soon afterwards, another Episcopal church, St Mary the Virgin, was built in Dalkeith by the fifth Duke of Buccleuch and his high church wife (and Lady Lothian's close friend), Charlotte Anne Montagu-Douglas-Scott; the Duchess was, in turn, influenced by her brother, the Revd Lord John Thynne, high church canon of Westminster Abbey. The Dalkeith church had a distinctive double hammer-beam roof and fan-vaulting in the chancel. The

[10] Tristam Clarke, 'A Display of Tractarian Energy: St John's Episcopal Church, Jedburgh', *Records of the Scottish Church History Society*, 27 (1997), pp. 196–207; W. H. Teale (ed.), *Six Sermons Preached at the Consecration of the Church of St John the Evangelist, Jedburgh* (Edinburgh, 1845), pp. xx–xxxix.

[11] R. Strong, 'Coronets and Altars: Aristocratic Women's and Men's Support for the Oxford Movement in Scotland during the 1840s', in R. N. Swanson (ed.), *Gender and Christian Religion*, Studies in Church History 34 (Woodbridge, 1998), pp. 392–9; C. Kerr, *Cecil Marchioness of Lothian: A Memoir* (London, [1922]), pp. 43–61.

[12] Clarke, 'Display of Tractarian Energy', pp. 207–9.

[13] Teale (ed.), *Six Sermons.*

[14] Clarke, 'Display of Tractarian Energy', p. 208.

[15] J. Keble to J. T. Coleridge, 30 August 1844, Bodleian Library, Oxford, Ms. Eng. Lett. D. 135, fols. 125–8.

first incumbent was a Tractarian priest, who introduced choral services in the church and who became the private confessor to Lady Lothian from 1847 until her conversion to Roman Catholicism in 1851.[16] Lord and Lady Aberlour built and endowed another church on Tractarian principles, St Mary's, Dalmahoy, a few miles outside Edinburgh; this church was consecrated in 1850. In January 1848, through the initiative of a number of wealthy laymen, a new church in Edinburgh, St Columba's by the Castle, was consecrated. The church combined the Scottish Communion Office with elements of advanced ritualism, including a decorated stone altar, lavish stained glass and a carved oak rood screen with a large cross.[17] Both churches were designed by the architect John Henderson. They were part of a movement that would see eighty-eight new Episcopal churches built between 1840 and 1860, all of them influenced by ecclesiological principles.[18]

In the summer of 1840, two young lay Episcopalians, the Tory MP of Scottish parentage William Ewart Gladstone, and the lawyer James Hope, conceived the project of erecting a college in Scotland for the training of Episcopal priests and lay leaders. Both men had come under Tractarian influence while students at Oxford, and they saw the college project as part of a larger movement for reclaiming Scotland to the true catholic and apostolic Church.[19] For them, the non-intrusionist conflict and threatened break-up of the Presbyterian establishment represented an opportunity for a revival of the social and political influence of the Scottish Episcopal Church. 'Perhaps it is perverseness', Gladstone wrote to Hope in August 1840, but for him the crisis in the Church of Scotland indicated 'that now is the time' to press forward vigorously with the college project – to which Hope responded that 'the sooner our tree is planted the better'.[20] Gladstone insisted that the college should educate not only priests, but also future lay leaders, who would assist the clergy in the spread of 'Church principles'.[21] They enlisted the support of leading Episcopalian aristocrats, among them the Duke of Buccleuch

[16] Kerr, *Cecil Marchioness of Lothian*, pp. 66–71.

[17] Strong, *Episcopalianism in Nineteenth-Century Scotland*, pp. 236–47.

[18] A. Mclean, 'The Scottish Episcopal Church and the Ecclesiological Movement, 1840–60', *Architectural Heritage*, 8 (1997), pp. 47–59, at pp. 47–8.

[19] R. Ornsby, *Memoir of James Robert Hope-Scott of Abbotsford*, 2 vols. (London, 1882), vol. I, pp. 206–12, 242–5.

[20] W. E. Gladstone to James Hope, 16 October 1840; J. Hope to W. E. Gladstone, 27 August 1840, National Library of Scotland, Hope-Scott Papers, Ms 3672, fols. 77–8, Ms 3674, fols. 125–7.

[21] W. E. Gladstone to J. R. Hope, 8 September 1840, in Lathbury (ed.), *Correspondence on Church*, vol. II, pp. 242–3.

and Lord Lothian (who would die in 1841), and substantial funds were raised in Scotland and England. John Henderson's gothic buildings were erected at Glenalmond, near the city of Perth, with the foundation stone laid by Gladstone's father, Sir John Gladstone of Fasque, in September 1846. The College of the Holy and Undivided Trinity was opened several months later in May 1847. By now, James Hope had been removed from the governing council because of distrust over his extreme Tractarianism (he would convert to Roman Catholicism in 1851), and the college sought to distance itself from the Romanising wing of the Tractarian movement. But the first warden, Charles Wordsworth, the High Church nephew of the poet, had come under Tractarian influence while at Oxford.[22] Under his leadership, chapel worship was conducted on Tractarian principles and staff and students wore surplices at worship. Although Wordsworth, who was consecrated bishop of St Andrews in 1853, would later become a fierce opponent of Anglo-Catholics and ritualists, Glenalmond retained many of the Tractarian liturgical practices that Wordsworth had introduced.

The influence of the Oxford Movement was still more evident in the building of St Ninian's Cathedral in Perth.[23] The initiative here came from two young aristocratic laymen who had come under Tractarian influence while students at Oxford. Lord Forbes and George Frederick Boyle (later Earl of Glasgow) were attracted to the notion of restoring the Scottish cathedrals, both to enhance the influence and authority of the bishops and to serve as bases for mission priests who would reclaim the people of Scotland to the true catholic and apostolic Church. The building of St Ninian's was to be the beginning of a movement of cathedral restoration. The venerable Patrick Torry, High Church bishop of St Andrews, Dunkeld and Dunblane, who sympathised with the Oxford Movement, gave the 'noble scheme' his warm support in July 1847.[24] Money was raised in Scotland and England for the new cathedral, the first to be built in Britain since the rebuilding of St Paul's in London. There was, to be sure, considerable Scottish opposition to what was viewed as an English Tractarian project, including opposition from older High Church Scottish Episcopalians. None the less, the grandiose neo-gothic building, designed by the English architect William Butterfield, with pointed arches, high ceiling and frescoes, was consecrated in December 1850. The

[22] C. Wordsworth, *Annals of my Early Life, 1806–1846*, ed. W. Earl Hodgson (London, 1891), pp. 322–6; J. Wordsworth, *The Episcopate of Charles Wordsworth, Bishop of St Andrews, Dunkeld, and Dunblane 1853–1892* (London, 1899), p. 3.

[23] G. T. S. Farquhar, *The Episcopal History of Perth 1689–1894* (Perth, 1894), pp. 292–306.

[24] J. M. Neale, *The Life and Times of Patrick Torry* (London, 1856), pp. 307–15.

leading English Tractarian and ecclesiologist John Mason Neale was invited to be the first dean of the cathedral.[25] Although Neale declined the invitation, he gave the consecration sermon, calling on the Scottish Episcopal Church to embrace its calling as the one true apostolic Church in Scotland, cease trying 'to live and let live in peace' in Presbyterian Scotland and take its mission boldly to the whole Scottish people.[26] The first dean and canons were all zealous Tractarians. Boyle, meanwhile, had in 1849 endowed another Tractarian establishment, the College of the Holy Spirit on the Western Isle of Cumbrae, with a neo-gothic collegiate church (which would later become the Cathedral of the Isles), also designed by William Butterfield and built in strict conformity to the principles of the English Ecclesiological Society. The first provost was the Tractarian G. Cosby White.[27] With its collegiate church and college, Cumbrae would, its promoters hoped, become another Iona, training and sending forth celibate missionary priests for the conversion of Scotland. However, despite an estimated investment by Boyle of over £30,000, the Cumbrae foundation proved too remote to have much impact.[28]

Following the decision of the Judicial Committee of the Privy Council over the Gorham case in 1850, some English Tractarians, among them Neale, contemplated leaving the Church of England for the Scottish Episcopal Church; Neale envisaged finding a sanctuary on Cumbrae.[29] The bishop of Argyll and the Isles, Alexander Ewing, suspected in 1847 that English Tractarians would 'appeal to our Scottish bishops for the consecration of a bishop for themselves, in order to form a second non-juring church'.[30] According to Bishop Charles Wordsworth, 'the more the [Tractarian] leaders were discountenanced in England, the more they looked to our Scottish Church as the field in which they were to carry on their operations, as the soil in which they might still hope to see the growth of their opinions and the success of their cause'.[31]

In 1847, Alexander Penrose Forbes, a Scottish Tractarian priest and Oxford-educated protégé of Pusey, was elected bishop of Brechin – in part through the prominence of the Forbes family in the Scottish

[25] *Letters of John Mason Neale, Selected and Edited by His Daughter* (London, 1910), pp. 149–51.

[26] J. M. Neale, 'The Mission of the Scotch Church', in *Lectures on Church Difficulties* (London, 1852), pp. 71–82, at p. 80.

[27] P. F. Anson, *The Call of the Cloister: Religious Communities and Kindred Bodies in the Anglican Communion* (London, 1955), p. 47.

[28] Strong, *Episcopalianism in Nineteenth-Century Scotland*, 257–8.

[29] *Letters of John Mason Neale*, pp. 142–5; Nockles, '"Our Brethren of the North"', pp. 672–3.

[30] Cited in Nockles, '"Our Brethren of the North"', p. 673.

[31] C. Wordsworth, *Annals of my Life, 1847–1856* (London, 1893), p. 62.

Episcopal Church and in part through the influence of Gladstone. Forbes became the first Tractarian to be appointed to a bishopric in the United Kingdom. He earned a broad respect in Scotland for his committed ministry in the socially deprived districts of Dundee and his zealous support for the Scottish Communion Office, which he embraced as a powerful expression of the real presence in the Eucharist.[32] Forbes was cautious about the introduction of high ritual, which could have the effect of alienating many Episcopalians, especially Irish migrants. He did, however, give his support to the building of a large neo-gothic church in Dundee, St Paul's, which was completed in 1855. Designed by the celebrated English architect Sir George Gilbert Scott, the church's towering spire was visible throughout the city and served as a symbol of the growing confidence of the Scottish Episcopal Church. Forbes was supported in his efforts to preserve the Scottish Communion Office by his brother and fellow Oxford-educated Tractarian priest, the liturgical scholar George Hay Forbes, who in 1848 had become a mission priest in Burntisland, Fife.[33] In 1862, the first Anglican sisters, members of the Society of St Margaret (founded by Neale), began work in Scotland, establishing a house in Aberdeen in 1864.[34]

The years between 1839 and 1854, Gavin White has observed, were a time of unprecedented growth for the Scottish Episcopal Church. Its seventy-six congregations doubled in number, as did the number of its clergy.[35] With the Scottish Presbyterian establishment gravely weakened by the great Disruption of 1843 and the Scottish Episcopal Church experiencing rapid growth, it seemed that something extraordinary was unfolding north of the Tweed. English Tractarians looked to Scottish Episcopalianism as fertile ground for the revival of Church principles. It was free of any state connection and untrammelled by the laws that restricted Tractarian teachings and practices in the established Church of England. The Scottish Episcopal Church, Tractarians also believed, had been tested by decades of persecution and suffering, and 'the iron which entered into the soul of the poor Episcopalian' during the long years of the penal laws had prepared the Church to win Scotland back to the Faith.[36]

[32] R. Strong, *Alexander Forbes of Brechin: The First Tractarian Bishop* (Oxford, 1995); W. Perry, *Alexander Penrose Forbes, Bishop of Brechin: The Scottish Pusey* (London, 1939).

[33] W. Perry, *George Hay Forbes: A Romance in Scholarship* (London, 1927).

[34] Anson, *The Call of the Cloister*, pp. 350–51.

[35] G. White, 'New Names for Old Things: Scottish Reaction to Early Tractarianism', in D. Baker (ed.), *Renaissance and Renewal in Christian History*, Studies in Church History 14 (Oxford, 1977), pp. 329–37, at p. 329.

[36] Quotation in Russell, *Charge delivered … May 4, 1842*, p. 23.

The Tractarian influence, while significant, was not the predominant factor in the growth of the Scottish Episcopal Church from the 1840s. Much of that growth resulted from large-scale migration of Irish Protestants – members of the Church of Ireland – mainly from Ulster, to the industrialising West of Scotland. The number of Episcopalians in Glasgow and the West rose from about 400 in 1800 to perhaps 20,000 by the mid 1860s.[37] These Ulster migrants were largely Evangelical and strongly anti-Catholic, and they had no desire for Oxford ritual, as high church missioners in the Glasgow area discovered.[38] There were also large numbers of English economic migrants, and many of these were also Evangelical. Some Tractarian supporters in Scotland, moreover, could antagonise fellow Episcopalians by their insensitivity to Scottish traditions and insistence that Oxford beliefs and practices must be embraced. 'I grieve to say', Dean Ramsay wrote to Gladstone on 7 August 1845, 'that a small body of young men are actively employed under the mantle of Catholicity to introduce amongst us party-strife, division & sectarian animosity.'[39] None the less, the Oxford Movement had become a force in Scottish Episcopal life and an important contributor to the recovery of the Scottish Episcopal Church.

THE OXFORD MOVEMENT AND THE DISRUPTION OF THE CHURCH OF SCOTLAND

While the Oxford Movement was not the predominant factor in the revival of the Scottish Episcopal Church, many Scottish Presbyterians came to believe that it was. There may have been some Presbyterian sympathy for early Tractarianism. According to Dean Ramsay, writing to Gladstone in December 1838, 'Mr Hannah [William Hanna], a Presbyterian Minister and son in law to Dr Chalmers told me that he venerated the Oxford Divines personally and added that he thought theirs "the extreme to [which] a highly devotional mind was most likely to fall into".'[40] Hanna's father-in-law, the Evangelical Presbyterian leader Thomas Chalmers, was

37 I. Meredith, 'Irish Protestant Migrants in the Scottish Episcopal Diocese of Glasgow and Galloway, 1817–1929' (unpublished Ph.D. thesis, University of Durham, 2007), pp. 101–11.

38 Strong, *Episcopalianism in Nineteenth-Century Scotland*, pp. 165–87; R. Strong, '"A Church for the Poor": High-Church Slum Ministry in Anderston, Glasgow, 1845–51', *JEH*, 50 (1999), pp. 279–302.

39 E. B. Ramsay to W. E. Gladstone, 7 August 1845, BL, Gladstone Papers, Add Mss 44283, fols. 113–18.

40 E. B. Ramsay to W. E. Gladstone, 20 December 1838, BL, Gladstone Papers, Add Mss 44283, fols. 22–3.

very close to Hanna (who would later write his biography) and may have shared this early sympathy. Certainly in early 1833 Chalmers and Pusey had corresponded in warm terms and offered mutual support in defence of 'national Churches'.[41] However, Chalmers and his fellow Presbyterians soon came to view Tractarianism as a serious threat to the established Church of Scotland, and as even part of an Anglican conspiracy aimed at the overthrow of the Presbyterian establishment and its replacement with an Episcopal one.

In truth, most Scottish Presbyterians showed little awareness of the Oxford Movement until January 1837, when the influential *Presbyterian Review* began a series of highly critical articles, which continued over the next five years, on Tractarianism.[42] These articles introduced Scottish Presbyterian readers to the main teachings of the Oxford divines, including apostolic succession, catholicity, the authority of the Church Fathers, the Church of England as the *via media*, the growing emphasis on tradition and ritual, especially the ritual of the Middle Ages, and the criticisms by some of the Reformation. The *Presbyterian Review* was profoundly hostile to the *Tracts*, finding them deeply flawed and condescending. For example, it observed that Tract 7 ('The Episcopal Church Apostolical') explicitly denied that the Scottish Presbyterian establishment was a Christian Church, because it lacked an episcopate.[43] Such Tractarian writings struck a sensitive nerve in a Church of Scotland that saw itself engaged in a life-and-death struggle with the civil state, and the *Presbyterian Review* responded stridently to the Tractarian claims.[44] It insisted that Scripture, which it defined as the sole authority in the Christian Faith, sanctioned neither the episcopal form of church government nor the doctrine of apostolic succession. It denied that the writings of the Church Fathers were authoritative for the Church, and claimed there was 'an immeasurable distance, an impassable gulf' between the inspired writings of Scripture and the merely human testimony of the Fathers and of later Church tradition. It denounced the Tractarians for 'glorying over us' and it extolled the seventeenth-century Presbyterian Covenanter 'martyrs' for their struggle against episcopacy.

[41] S. J. Brown, *The National Churches of England, Ireland and Scotland 1801–46* (Oxford, 2001), p. 187.

[42] 'Oxford Popery, No. 1', *Presbyterian Review*, 9 (January, 1837), pp. 185–210; 'Oxford Popery, No. 2', *Presbyterian Review*, 9 (May 1837), pp. 289–328; 'Hear the Church', *Presbyterian Review*, 11 (January 1839), pp. 559–69; 'Tracts for the Times', *Presbyterian Review*, 14 (January 1842), pp. 615–52.

[43] [J. H. Newman], *Renaissance and Renewal in Christian History: The Episcopal Church Apostolical*, no. 7 in *Tracts for the Times* (London, 1833), p. 2.

[44] 'Scottish Prelacy', *Presbyterian Review*, 15 (April 1842), pp. 1–31.

Other Scottish Presbyterian publications denounced the Tractarians' ambivalence towards the Reformation and their efforts to revive the rituals, church architecture and devotional practices of the Middle Ages, which for Presbyterians were a time of ecclesiastical corruption, priestcraft, ignorance and superstition. According to the evangelical Presbyterian *Edinburgh Christian Instructor* of early 1839, the Tractarian writings revealed the Church of England to be still only a 'half-reformed Church', and the Oxford divines were now reviving those elements of 'Popery' which the English Reformation had failed to eliminate from Anglicanism.[45] There was a sense among Scottish Presbyterians that the Oxford divines not only were seeking to Romanise the Church of England, but also hoped for the destruction of the Church of Scotland, as the major bulwark of Protestantism within the United Kingdom. There was, many believed, a conspiracy, directed from Oxford, behind the non-intrusion controversy, and this conspiracy accounted for the hostility among the Scottish landed classes towards the Presbyterian establishment, and the indifference of parliament to the impending break-up of the Church of Scotland.

For the evangelical Church of Scotland minister in Perth, Andrew Gray, this conspiracy included leaders of the Scottish Episcopal Church. Gray was minister of the West church in Perth from 1836, and a zealous non-intrusionist. He witnessed with consternation the growing confidence of the Scottish Episcopal Church in the city, including the plans for the Episcopal college in Glenalmond. In March 1842, with the non-intrusionist crisis intensifying and the Church of Scotland facing disruption, Gray introduced an overture before the Presbytery of Perth, calling on the Scottish establishment to respond vigorously to the growing threat from its Tractarian adversaries. He quickly published a greatly expanded version of the speech as a pamphlet, which the *Presbyterian Review* lauded as 'altogether unanswerable'.[46] Gray's central argument was that the overwhelming majority of bishops and clergy within Scottish Episcopal Church held Tractarian views on the sacraments and the Church, and openly denied that the Presbyterian Church was a true Christian Church. He published the statements of a number of leading Oxford divines, including Newman, Dodsworth and Palmer, who maintained that the

45 'The Church of England a Half-Reformed Church', *Edinburgh Christian Instructor*, new series, 2 (February 1839), pp. 54–66.

46 A. Gray, *Oxford Tractarianism, the Scottish Episcopal College, and the Scottish Episcopal Church. Substance of a Speech delivered before the Presbytery of Perth, on the 30th of March, 1842* (London, 1842); 'Principles of the Perth Puseyite College', *Presbyterian Review*, 15 (July 1842), pp. 223–35.

Church of Scotland was a schismatic body, and that its clergy lacked any divine authority to administer the sacraments or preach the word. He insisted that the promoters of the Glenalmond college plan held a similar view of the Presbyterian establishment. This included William Gladstone, whose recently published *State in Its Relations with the Church* had argued that the Church of Scotland could not be a Church because it had wilfully rejected the apostolic succession. Indeed, Gray insisted, Gladstone proclaimed 'the duty of "endeavouring to restore the apostolic system" to the ascendancy among us'.[47] Strengthened by Tractarian principles and by influential supporters, Gray concluded, the Scottish Episcopal Church now 'unchurch our denominations, they degrade our clergy, they unchristianise our people'.[48] They were taking advantage of the non-intrusionist crisis in the Church of Scotland in order to overthrow the Presbyterian establishment.[49]

Such perceptions became widespread among evangelical non-intrusionists. 'There is in this part of the country', wrote Dean Ramsay of Edinburgh to Gladstone on 1 May 1845, 'a very deep rooted impression that the Church of England contains a powerful and numerous party whose object is to introduce Romanist opinions and practices, and further ... that the Episcopal Church of Scotland is desirous of hoisting the colours of that party.'[50] In her novel of 1847 depicting the events of the Disruption, Lydia Miller, wife of the leading non-intrusionist Presbyterian journalist, Hugh Miller, portrayed Tractarianism as a Jesuit conspiracy, committed to undermining the established Protestant Churches of both Scotland and England.[51]

In May 1843, the Church of Scotland was broken up by the Great Disruption. Over a third of its ministers and perhaps half its lay membership left the established Church to form the Free Church of Scotland. The national influence of the remnant Presbyterian establishment was severely diminished. But if Scottish Episcopalians had indeed hoped to benefit from the Disruption, and secure converts from among disillusioned Presbyterians, those hopes were not fulfilled. There was, as we have seen, some growth in the Episcopal Church during the 1840s

[47] Gray, *Oxford Tractarianism*, pp. 71–2.

[48] *Ibid.*, p. 79.

[49] 'The Scottish Prelatic Communion Office', *Presbyterian Review*, 16 (October 1843), pp. 325–7.

[50] E. B. Ramsay to W. E. Gladstone. 1 May 1845, BL, Gladstone Papers, Add Mss 44283, fols. 99–104.

[51] [L. Miller], *Passages in the Life of an English Heiress or Recollections of Disruption Times in Scotland* (London, 1847); A. Calder, 'The Disruption in Fiction', in S. J. Brown and M. Fry (eds.), *Scotland in the Age of the Disruption* (Edinburgh, 1993), pp. 116–25.

and 1850s, but there was no mass movement of Presbyterians into the Episcopal fold. Some Scottish Episcopalians would later blame the failure on the divisions within their Church – over the Scottish Communion Office or between evangelicals and high churchmen. 'At the time of the great Presbyterian Disruption', Alexander Ewing, bishop of Argyll and the Isles, later observed,

> had we held forth the spectacle of a church engaged in the weightier verities of religion, and at peace among ourselves, we should have absorbed within our pale the bulk of the sober-minded and educated of Scotland. But it was not so.[52]

By the 1870s, Scottish Episcopal numbers had stabilised and would remain roughly 3 per cent of the Scottish population.

SCOTO-CATHOLIC MOVEMENT IN SCOTTISH PRESBYTERIANISM

In the aftermath of the Disruption, the newly formed Free Church was stridently anti-Catholic and anti-Tractarian. In 1846, Thomas Chalmers, the acknowledged leader of the Free Church, promoted Free Church leadership of the Protestant Evangelical Alliance against what he described as the combined menace of 'Puseyism' and Roman Catholicism.[53] Amid the mass migration of Irish Catholics into Scotland during and after the great Irish famine of 1845–50, and the 'Papal Aggression' excitement of 1851, many Free Church members felt increasingly threatened by a perceived conspiracy of high Anglicanism and Roman Catholicism. Free Church scholars such as William Cunningham, principal of the Free Church's New College in Edinburgh from 1846 to 1861, devoted themselves to the study of the early Church, in part to combat Tractarian and Roman Catholic teachings concerning the apostolic succession and the divine authority of Church tradition. The Free Church held firmly to what it believed was pure Reformation worship and doctrine.

But within the established Church of Scotland, something unexpected occurred. The 1850s witnessed the emergence of a liturgical reform movement that owed much to the ritualism and devotional practices of the Oxford Movement. This movement was initiated by Robert Lee, minister of the historic Greyfriars church in Edinburgh. Lee was a broad churchman, who was concerned with restoring the social influence of the

[52] Quoted in Nockles, '"Our Brethren of the North"', p. 680.
[53] T. Chalmers, *On the Evangelical Alliance* (Edinburgh, 1846), pp. 28–9.

Presbyterian establishment in the aftermath of the Disruption. He was also impressed by what he viewed as the decorum, solemnity and beauty of worship in the Church of England and the Scottish Episcopal Church, including the liturgical and ecclesiological practices that had come in part through the influence of the Oxford Movement. He came to believe that the more decorous services and church interiors of the Episcopal Church were drawing away the educated middle and upper classes of Edinburgh from the Church of Scotland, and contributing to the growth of Episcopal numbers and influence. It had become fashionable to be a high church Episcopalian. This draining away of the educated elite, he believed, would have to stop if the post-Disruption Church of Scotland were ever to recover its former influence. He contrasted the beauty of Episcopal worship with what he viewed as wearisome Presbyterian services, with their long, often tedious sermons, their droning of psalms and their extempore prayers that could ramble on for twenty to forty minutes, and were often ill-digested repetitions of tired phrases, biblical quotations, theological jargon and pious instructions, which had little meaning as addresses to God and which were largely ignored by the dozing congregations.[54]

With the reopening of a rebuilt Greyfriars church in 1857 (the church had been gutted by a devastating fire in 1845), Lee was determined to bring elements of high Anglican liturgy and church decoration into his Presbyterian services. He prepared a printed order of service, with set prayers and congregational responses, opened each service with a solemn call to worship and closed it with a benediction. He worked to improve music, by organising a trained choir to lead congregational singing of hymns, and then, in 1864, by introducing an organ into the church (the first organ in a Presbyterian church since 1807, when one had been introduced by a congregation and then quickly removed on order of the Church courts). He introduced stained-glass windows into the church. The innovations were welcomed by most of his mainly upper-middle-class congregation. However, they aroused a storm of controversy within the Church of Scotland as a whole, with conservative Presbyterians railing in the Church courts against Lee's 'popish' innovations. Lee would have been censured, and very possibly deposed from the ministry by the general assembly of the Church of Scotland, had he not first suffered a stroke which left him unable to stand trial and then brought his early death in 1868.

[54] R. Lee, *The Reform of the Church of Scotland in Worship, Government, and Doctrine, Part I – Worship*, 2nd edn (Edinburgh, 1866), pp. 11–73; R. H. Story, *Life and Remains of Robert Lee*, 2 vols. (London, 1870), vol. II, pp. 54–107.

But by now other Church of Scotland ministers, mainly young broad church Presbyterians, had taken up his cause. They shared Lee's concern to revive the influence and authority of the national Church in the aftermath of the Disruption, and they were also concerned to emphasise their Church's catholicity. In 1865, they formed the Church Service Society, to promote 'the study of liturgies - ancient and modern - of the Christian Church, with a view to the preparation and publication of forms of Prayer for Public Worship'. They sought to draw liturgies from world Christianity, including the Latin and Greek Orthodox traditions. In 1867, the Society published a liturgical collection, the *Euchologion*, containing various forms of service for baptism, communion, marriage and funerals. This proved highly influential, going through seven expanded editions over the next thirty years. The Church Service Society steadily gained support, and by 1900 about a third of the clergy of the Church of Scotland were members.[55] This became known as the 'Scoto-Catholic movement' and it reflected the belief that the Church of Scotland was a true branch of the ancient catholic Church.

As well as members of the clergy, many congregations also responded positively to the use of printed liturgies. Conservatives in the Church had sought to halt the Scoto-Catholic innovations by the so-called 'Pirie Act'. Introduced by the Revd Dr W. R. Pirie and adopted by the general assembly of 1865, the 'Pirie Act' gave local presbyteries the power to suppress innovations they deemed to be un-presbyterian. Conservatives believed that presbyteries would be zealous in sniffing out and putting down any innovations. But in the event presbyteries proved unwilling to interfere in parishes where individual ministers and congregations jointly supported the innovations. As this was increasingly the case, the liturgical innovations spread. There was also a new interest in church music, including the spread of an 'organ movement' from the 1870s and the development of trained choirs. By 1900, a large majority – over 80 per cent – of Church of Scotland parish churches had both an organ and a choir.[56]

Most of those Presbyterian ministers and lay people who embraced Scoto-Catholic ritual, appreciated stained-glass windows, organs and trained choirs, joined the Church Service Society, and took a growing interest in Church history and tradition, would not have viewed themselves as followers of the Oxford Movement. They wished to introduce

55 D. Murray, 'Disruption to Union', in D. Forrester and D. Murray (eds.), *Studies in the History of Worship in Scotland*, 2nd edn (Edinburgh, 1996), pp. 87–105, at p. 97.

56 A. K. Robertson, 'The Revival of Church Worship in the Church of Scotland' (unpublished Ph.D. thesis, University of Edinburgh, 1956), pp. 212–14.

more decorous, dignified and beautiful forms of worship into their churches, and they were influenced by Continental patterns of worship, as well as by Oxford-influenced Anglican worship. Many were concerned to revive the influence of the established Church of Scotland, especially among the educated landed and professional classes. However, their efforts to study historic liturgies and recover a sense of the Church of Scotland as part of the universal catholic and apostolic Church did reflect similar concerns and interests to those of the Oxford Movement.

Some Church of Scotland ministers, moreover, were drawn to very high sacerdotal forms of worship. They included John MacLeod, who was ordained in 1862 and became minister of Govan old church in Glasgow in 1875. Respected for his luminous spirituality, MacLeod revived the celebration of the Christian holy days, and introduced monthly communions, with an altar cloth over the communion table.[57] His book on the holy communion, published in 1889, was immensely influential with its view of communion as a living celebration of Christ's continuing priesthood, 'which He is now fulfilling in the Upper Sanctuary in the heavenly world'.[58] Another Presbyterian who pushed the boundaries was J. Cameron Lees, one of the founders of the Church Service Society. As minister in Paisley, Cameron Lees took a leading role in the restoration of the historic Paisley Abbey. In 1877, he became minister of St Giles in Edinburgh. Here, he promoted, with the support of Edinburgh's lord provost, William Chambers, major restorations which explicitly aimed at recovering the church's medieval grandeur and splendour. The restoration of St Giles' Cathedral was completed by 1883. Cameron Lees also prepared a printed prayer book for worship, which drew from Latin, Greek, Anglican and Continental Reformed traditions. To the north, Dunblane Cathedral was restored between 1889 and 1893, with a new roof built over the nave and public worship restored in the nave.

There was also a new intellectual respect within the Church of Scotland for the ideas of the Oxford Movement. In his influential St Giles lectures of 1884, published under the title *Movements of Religious Thought in Britain during the Nineteenth Century'*, John Tulloch, principal of St Mary's Divinity Hall at St Andrews University, presented a favourable account of the Oxford Movement. He applauded its 'great idea of the Church in its visibility and authority – in its notes of [apostolic] succession, dogma and

[57] D. Murray, 'John MacLeod of Govan: A Distinctive High Churchman', *Liturgical Review*, 8 (1978), pp. 27–32; A. Wallace Williamson, *Dr John MacLeod: His Work and Teaching* (Edinburgh, 1901); T. Marshall, *Dr John Macleod and Church Reform* (Edinburgh, 1906).

[58] J. Macleod, *The Gospel in the Institution of the Lord's Supper* (Glasgow, 1907), p. 102.

sacrament', and he taught a generation of his Presbyterian students to do the same.[59]

By the 1880s, the high Scoto-Catholic movement was beginning to transform the established Church of Scotland. The liturgical reform movement had brought a number of Presbyterians to seek to recover not only ancient liturgies but also the identity of the Church of Scotland as a true branch of the holy, catholic and apostolic Church. Scoto-Catholics insisted on reviving not only ancient liturgical practices but also Church principles, including apostolic succession (through presbyteries rather than bishops), veneration of tradition and sacramental grace. In part, they were responding to a new assault on the established Church, the disestablishment campaign of the 1870s, by reviving the teachings of the Oxford divines about the nature of the Church. 'We must learn to feel more deeply than we yet do', proclaimed the Scoto-Catholic William Milligan, professor of biblical criticism at Aberdeen University, in his closing address as moderator of the General Assembly of 1882, 'that *we* are an integral part of Christ's body, and in vital connection with the whole body . . . We are a portion of what is called in the creed the "holy Catholic Church", planted in Scotland by the Divine Head of the Church Himself.'[60]

One of the most influential of the Scoto-Catholic ministers was James Cooper. Raised in the northeast of Scotland, the heartland of Episcopalianism, Cooper had from an early age embraced a deep respect for the Scottish Episcopal Church. An admirer of Pusey and the Oxford Movement, Cooper introduced a number of ritualist innovations into his Church of Scotland ministries in Broughty Ferry and Aberdeen during the later 1870s and 1880s – including Christmas services, Holy Week services, private communion to the sick and daily services, at which he knelt at a desk, facing eastwards. In 1870, during a visit to St Peter's in Rome, Cooper had a vision of Catholic reunion, a vision that would long inspire him.[61] Beginning in 1886, he worked for a union of the Church of Scotland and the Scottish Episcopal Church on what he termed 'ancient lines', by which he meant the practices of the Church during the first four centuries.[62] It would be a United Church of the British Empire and serve

[59] M. Oliphant, *A Memoir of the Life of John Tulloch*, 3rd edn (Edinburgh, 1889), pp. 437–9; J. Tulloch, *Movements of Religious Thought in Britain during the Nineteenth Century* (London, 1885), pp. 86–124, at p. 123.

[60] Quoted in H. L. Yancey, 'The Development of the Theology of William Milligan' (unpublished Ph.D. thesis, University of Edinburgh, 1970), p. 337.

[61] J. F. Leishman, *Linton Leaves, including a Biography of Dr Thomas Leishman and some Sidelights on Catholic Reunion* (Edinburgh, 1937), p. 144.

[62] H. J. Wotherspoon, *James Cooper: A Memoir* (London, 1926), pp. 146–7.

to unite and elevate the empire through church principles. 'It is', he proclaimed in a sermon in 1902, 'to a united Church – united with a unity which the world shall see – that our Saviour promises the conversion of the world.'[63] In 1898, Cooper's growing influence was recognised with his appointment as professor of ecclesiastical history at the University of Glasgow, a position which he used to spread his high church, sacramental principles.

In 1892, Cooper, Milligan, Macleod and other members of the high church group founded a new association, the Scottish Church Society. Its stated purpose was 'to defend and advance Catholic doctrine as set forth in the ancient Creeds and embodied in the Standards of the Church of Scotland'.[64] 'We have to recognise', insisted Milligan, its first president, in 1893, 'that we are one with all the faithful during the centuries which proceeded the Reformation, as well as during those which followed it.'[65] The Scottish Church Society organised retreats and conferences, and issued publications, including scholarly editions of historical liturgies. 'By some', observed one historian, 'the Scottish Church Society was hailed as Scotland's Tractarian Movement.'[66] There was, to be sure, considerable Presbyterian opposition to the new Society. 'Accusations of treachery, Popery, Sacerdotalism, gibes about man millinery and aping of Anglicanism', according to an observer, 'filled the air and even crept into the church magazines.'[67] None the less, the Society persevered.

Combined with the work of the Scottish Church Society was a renewed interest in church architecture and decoration, including the preservation and restoration of older churches. In 1886, the Aberdeen Ecclesiological Society was founded, largely through the efforts of James Cooper, to promote the study of worship and church architecture. A similar Glasgow Ecclesiological Society was formed in 1893, and in 1903 these two societies joined to form the Scottish Ecclesiological Society. Under the influence of these societies, work was undertaken to restore cathedrals and churches, and to provide more tasteful arrangements in seating and furnishing. But the aims were not simply antiquarian or aesthetic. 'We think', observed Cooper, in his presidential address to the Scottish Ecclesiological Society for the session 1913–14, 'that CHURCHES, whether old or new, are primarily *Houses of God*.' When they were allowed to fall into ruin, he

[63] J. Cooper, *A United Church for the British Empire: A Sermon* (Forres, 1902), p. 8.
[64] Wotherspoon, *James Cooper*, p. 164.
[65] W. Milligan, *The Scottish Church Society* (Edinburgh, 1893), p. 12.
[66] Robertson, 'Revival of Church Worship', p. 271; Perry, *Oxford Movement in Scotland*, pp. 122–3.
[67] Leishman, *Linton Leaves*, p. 137.

added, it was 'the desecration of what is holy'.[68] Through the influence of these societies, one historian has noted, established Presbyterian 'churches were beginning to resemble places of worship, rather than mere auditoria. Chancels, stained glass, Holy Tables, robed choirs, even prayer desks appeared.'[69]

Some Scoto-Catholics followed Cooper in calling for union with the Church of England on the basis of a restored episcopacy within the Church of Scotland. Some influential Anglicans also shared this ideal. For the Scottish-born archbishop of York, Cosmo Gordon Lang, speaking in Aberdeen in 1894, the Scottish Church Society represented an Oxford Movement within the Church of Scotland; this movement was destined to revive catholic and apostolic principles among 'the mass of the laity' and prepare the way for 'Catholic union'.[70]

The hopes for Catholic union would not be fulfilled (though twice in the twentieth century it seemed that there might be such a union). None the less, the Scoto-Catholic movement of the later nineteenth and early twentieth centuries did transform and enhance Presbyterian worship. In most Scottish Presbyterian churches, worship became more ordered and elaborate, with set orders of service, calls to worship, benedictions, read prayers, regular Bible readings, shorter sermons, hymns, choirs and organs. Church buildings increasingly included stained glass, more attractive furnishings and more colour and light. Perhaps more important, the Scoto-Catholic movement, as expressed by such figures as MacLeod, Milligan, Sprott, the Wotherspoon brothers, Wallace Williamson and Cooper, helped congregations in the Church of Scotland to recover a sense of their continuity with the ancient catholic and apostolic Church, to see themselves as part of a long chain of believers stretching back through the centuries and to realise that they were heirs, not simply of a Scottish Reformation heritage, but of the Church universal. In Scotland, the Oxford Movement had its greatest impact upon the Scottish Episcopal Church. However, through the liturgical reform movements and Scoto-Catholic movements, it also had a considerable influence on the Church of Scotland, and it was here that its influence arguably touched the largest proportion of the Scottish people.

[68] J. Cooper, 'The Restoration, Repair and Re-use of Ancient Churches in Scotland', *Transactions of the Scottish Ecclesiological Society*, 4 (1913–14), pp. 116–26, at p. 117.

[69] Robertson, 'Revival of Church Worship', p. 258.

[70] Cosmo Gordon Lang, *The Future of the Church in Scotland* (Edinburgh, 1895), pp. 10–11.

CHAPTER 4

The Oxford Movement and the British Empire: Newman, Manning and the 1841 Jerusalem bishopric

Rowan Strong

In 1841 a scheme was concocted to institute a Protestant bishop in Jerusalem. The idea was initially that of the king of Prussia, and propounded in England by the Prussian diplomat Chevalier Bunsen, a close confidant of Prince Albert. The new bishop would be alternately appointed by England and Prussia, and an Act of Parliament to this effect was passed on 5 October 1841.[1] From the Prussian point of view, the scheme furthered Frederick William IV's hopes of an episcopate in his Lutheran state Church, and also gave him an entrée into the Near East as a protector of Protestants. In England, there were powerful religious proponents of the initiative. These included the evangelicals, for whom the bishopric could be the centre of a Protestant mission to convert the Jews and so hasten one of the conditions for the Second Coming of Christ. High churchmen such as Walter Hook and William Palmer of Worcester College saw it as an extension of the episcopal order. Accordingly, an Orthodox Jewish convert to Christianity, Michael Solomon Alexander, professor of Hebrew at King's College, London, was consecrated bishop in October 1841. John Henry Newman, in November, issued a personal protest which he sent to the bishop of Oxford and the archbishop of Canterbury, but the new bishop was nevertheless conveyed to his new see in the naval warship, HMS *Devastation*. However, in 1886 the joint scheme collapsed under the weight of growing divisions between the German and English local adherents to the Jerusalem bishopric. This disagreement reached a climax in that year when the Anglicans insisted that the bishop be always ordained according to Anglican rites and should assent to the Thirty-Nine Articles.

[1] R. W. Greaves, 'The Jerusalem Bishopric 1841', *EHR*, 64 (1949), pp. 328–52.

This chapter does not seek to revise the narrative of the Jerusalem bishopric project, but rather to put the scheme in a wider context than the histories of the Oxford Movement and biographies of Newman have hitherto set it. In doing so the chapter focuses on the response of another major figure who moved from the Church of England into Roman Catholicism, namely Henry Edward Manning. Manning was influenced by the Oxford Movement's catholicising agenda, but was not entirely captured by it. He had left Oxford and was a married curate by the traditional date of the movement's launch in the summer of 1833. In his important intellectual biography of Manning, James Perieiro makes it clear that Manning was advancing as a high churchman during the 1830s, but he was also attracted by the fervent devotion of the Evangelicals.[2] According to Pereiro, Manning's sympathy with the Tractarians was a question more of coincidence than active discipleship.[3] By 1843, when he at last realised Newman's powerful attraction to Rome, Manning claimed he had supported the Tractarians because he believed 'none were so true and steadfast to the English Church; none so safe as guides'.[4]

Manning's response to the Jerusalem bishopric has been less studied than that of Newman. At the time Manning was a more confident and comfortable Anglican than was Newman, who within two years would resign his living of St Mary's, Oxford, effectively ceasing his Anglican priesthood. Manning's response to the Jerusalem bishopric provides a window through which the Oxford Movement can be understood in a wider, imperial context – rather than the narrow English, Oxford and Newman-centred focus with which it is most often examined. It is a window that opens on to the body of younger high church supporters of the Oxford Movement, such as Manning – the group that provided many of the movement's initial sympathisers, notwithstanding the critical treatment of some high churchmen by Newman and Froude.

Manning was initially, unlike Newman, markedly positive towards the Jerusalem bishopric. This chapter will argue that the difference between the two famous Oxford Movement converts on this matter can be explained by Manning's much greater awareness of the Church of England in the context of the British Empire, an imperial Anglicanism about which Newman was almost entirely unconcerned. When that wider context is addressed, the Oxford Movement can be better assessed as a radical movement which,

2 James Pereiro, *Cardinal Manning: An Intellectual Biography* (Oxford, 1998), pp. 12–13.

3 *Ibid.*, p. 17.

4 Manning to Pusey, 22nd Sunday after Trinity 1843, *ibid.*, p. 55.

despite its catholic concern for Rome, had a wider geographical influence precisely because of the efforts of sympathisers such as Manning.

Newman's understanding of the Jerusalem bishopric remains virtually the sole interpretative framework of the episcopal project as it related to the Oxford Movement. His immediate strong repudiation of it, and the reasons for that rejection, are well known. Newman wrote in his *Apologia* – that seductive reconstruction of his life which he published in 1864 – that the Jerusalem bishopric was what brought him to the beginning of the end of his life as an Anglican. As he had hitherto proposed that Anglicanism was a *via media* between Roman Catholicism and Protestantism, the Jerusalem bishopric 'brought me', he wrote, 'on to the beginning of the end'.[5] It was, he asserted, the alliance of the Church of England with a Protestant state Church, and thus 'the ultimate condemnation' of his theory that the Church of England was a Catholic middle way between Rome and Protestantism; it was an 'abomination', and, along with the opposition to Tract 90, the scheme revived his anxiety about the catholicity of the Church of England and led directly to his conversion to Rome in 1845.[6]

Recent biographers of Newman have largely been content to reiterate his perception of the project. Both Ian Ker and Sheridan Gilley replicate Newman's claim that the Jerusalem bishopric was the third of the 'blows' that caused Newman's Anglican demise. Ker points to Newman's 'disgust' over the bishopric, and to his comments that it was a 'fearful' and a 'hideous' business because it was a 'coalescing with heretics'.[7] Gilley likewise points out that, for Newman, the scheme was appalling because its advocates assumed that the Church of England was a Protestant Church like the Prussian state Church. More devastating for Newman, for whom the episcopate had assumed the *esse* of catholicism in his Church, was the approval of the scheme by the bishops, led by the archbishop of Canterbury.[8] While Ker and Gilley are sympathetic to Newman's stance, Frank Turner's more critical biography portrays Newman's reaction as 'disproportional, extreme, and vehement' and resulting largely from fear over the potential loss of his closest Romanising associates, who he suspected would be driven out of the Church of England by their hopelessness at any prospect of rapprochement with Rome.[9]

There have been two substantial treatments of the Jerusalem bishopric affair. R. W. Greaves, in his 1949 article, points to the religious motivations

[5] J. H. Newman, *Apologia pro vita sua: Being a History of His Religious Opinions* (Oxford, 1967), p. 136.
[6] *Ibid.*, pp. 139, 141, 200.
[7] Ian Ker, *John Henry Newman: A Biography* (Oxford, 1988), pp. 234–5.
[8] Sheridan Gilley, *Newman and His Age* (London, 1990), p. 207.
[9] Frank Turner, *John Henry Newman: The Challenge to Evangelical Religion* (New Haven, 2002), p. 397.

behind many of the progenitors of the scheme, in contrast to Newman, who saw it largely as an Erastian concept. Greaves did not examine the nuanced response of followers of the Oxford Movement, but he did point to the support of high churchmen such as William Howley, archbishop of Canterbury, and John Kaye, bishop of Lincoln, as being induced by the need to put a stop to Tractarian excesses in the immediate post-Tract 90 period. Greaves, however, only examined the very top episcopal level of high churchmen and, once again, allowed Newman's attitude to stand as representative of all Oxford Movement adherents.[10] P. J. Welch in 1957 argued that, initially, very few churchmen, apart from some Tractarians, opposed the scheme, but he observed that disquiet was beginning to set in among high churchmen such as Gladstone by October 1841.[11]

Historians of the Oxford Movement have generally repeated the view that the Jerusalem bishopric was a disaster for the movement because of what it augured for Newman. This interpretation began with Richard Church's classic work, *The Oxford Movement 1833–1845* (1891). Church portrayed the bishopric as a hasty and incautious idea which undermined Newman's hard struggle for the catholicity of the English Church by entering it into communion with German Lutherans and Calvinists. For Church, the bishopric created division, never received broad favour within the Church of England and drove Newman out of it.[12] Marvin O'Connell has also viewed the Jerusalem bishopric entirely from Newman's perspective – that is, in an entirely negative light. O'Connell dismisses Pusey's initial support as the conviction of a 'simple-hearted' man. 'The Jerusalem bishopric was', O'Connell argues, 'Erastian, Protestant, undoctrinal, anti-sacramental, liberal and a wholesale surrender of the apostolicity of the bishops.'[13] Virtually the only significance of the Jerusalem bishopric in most histories of the Oxford Movement was that it contributed directly to the conversion of Newman. But this is a reductionist interpretation that reflects an out-dated view of the Oxford Movement as rising and falling with the Anglican fortunes of its major progenitor.

Newman's extreme antipathy to the Jerusalem bishopric was shared mainly by the ultra-Romanist militants within the Oxford Movement; however, as Simon Skinner has recently reminded us, they were a minority among the movement's adherents. Among the majority of the movement's

10 Greaves, 'The Jerusalem Bishopric 1841'.

11 P. J. Welch, 'Anglican Churchmen and the Establishment of the Jerusalem Bishopric', *JEH*, 8 (1957), pp. 193–204.

12 R. W. Church, *The Oxford Movement: Twelve years 1833–1845* (London, 1891), pp. 275–6.

13 Marvin O'Connell, *The Oxford Conspirators: A History of the Oxford Movement 1833–1845* (Lanham, MD, 1969), p. 351.

followers who did not take the path to Rome, many did accept that the Jerusalem bishopric was a blow – though not as fatal a one as Newman believed – to the Catholic confessional ideal for Anglicanism that the movement upheld.[14] Skinner's reminder about the larger mass of followers of the Oxford Movement who remained Anglicans is a useful corrective to the traditional focus on the movement's university leadership and its relatively small group of ultra-Romanist followers. In 1841, Manning was very much part of this larger fold of more confident Anglican sympathisers of the movement, and his view on the bishopric represented a more mainstream approach than did Newman's.

A focus on the confidently Anglican Manning is at odds with current Manning scholarship. Far too many studies of Manning have been teleological in approach, viewing his Anglican life as simply a preamble to his later Roman Catholic career. Perhaps this is because most of the authors who have written on Manning have been Roman Catholic (with the notable exception of David Newsome), and for them Manning's Roman Catholic life forms the principal interest and significance of their subject. This outlook rather treats Manning's life in a reductionist fashion, diminishing the fact that Manning was an Anglican for nearly half his life, and was an Anglican priest who was confident in his own Church for most of the two decades before he converted to Roman Catholicism in 1851. This period of Manning's Anglican life, from 1808 to 1851, still waits to be fully addressed in its own right.

Manning's unfolding attitude to the Jerusalem bishopric can be traced in his letters during 1841 and 1842 to his close friend Archdeacon Julius Hare. His friendship with Hare was an indication of Manning's personal breadth of outlook, given the diverse theological positions of the two men. Hare was devoted to German literature and scholarship, including higher criticism of the Bible, and was a forerunner of the broad church school with its adaptation to modern scholarship and promotion of religious toleration. Hare was strongly anti-Tractarian, being repelled by what he thought was the narrowness of their outlook.[15] He was also a friend of Chevalier Bunsen and a fervent proponent of the Jerusalem bishopric.

The Jerusalem bishopric first entered Manning's correspondence with Hare in October 1841, when Manning confessed that he had received the news of the prospective bishop with delight, and he wondered how Newman could be in two minds about it.

[14] S. A. Skinner, *Tractarians and the 'Condition of England': The Social and Political Thought of the Oxford Movement* (Oxford, 2004), p. 134.

[15] N. Merrill Distad, 'Julius Charles Hare', *ODNB*, vol. xxv, pp. 256–8.

> You will know with what joy I received the tiding of the intended mission of a Bishop to reside at Jerusalem. In this I don't know how Newman can have two minds, much less two hearts. I have not however sufficient information as to the mode of carrying this into effect to say that I am without fears of dangerous miscarriage. This remark extends to the whole matter & Valetta question. It seems that God is calling us to great works & that we are found unprepared, & to seek for first principles. I do not think we may lawfully consecrate a Bishop as Bishop of Jerusalem or of Palestine, & by any fiction treat as void, or under our jurisdiction, sees which if they belong to any certainly do not belong to us: nor are they in a condition in which we can without most palpable, & infamous delusion add another to the number of contending candidates.[16]

Manning admitted that he did not as yet have complete information about how the bishopric was to be put into effect, and he was not entirely without fears that its execution could involve 'dangerous miscarriage'. He did not think the new bishop, while resident in Jerusalem, should be entitled bishop of Jerusalem or Palestine, as that would be too great a claim, and would suggest that the more ancient jurisdictions of the Eastern Church were invalid. He was anxious that any suggestion of Anglican intrusion would threaten good relations with the Eastern Churches. But he thought that on all this he and Hare were of 'one heart'.[17] James Pereiro believes that this letter already expresses Manning's opposition to the bishopric as undermining the first principles of the Church of England, because it was an illegitimate intrusion into already established ancient sees.[18] But this view overlooks Manning's earlier letter, expressing cautious welcome for the proposal. Manning was certainly anxious that the bishopric should not become an act of intrusion, but otherwise at this point he supported it.

The bishopric scheme first became public in Whitsun 1841 as a direct outcome of the public inauguration in London that April of a Colonial Bishoprics Fund. In the bishops' public declaration at Pentecost regarding possible outcomes from the fund, the bishop in Jerusalem was explicitly mentioned along with a bishopric for Europe.[19] Manning had been a major speaker at the April launch of the fund and the next day had reported to Hare on its success as an experience of 'great earnestness & brotherly unity'. Manning was no doubt referring to the fact that the

16 H. Manning to J. Hare, 28 October 1841, Manning Papers, Bodleian Library, MS Eng. Lett., c. 653/1, fols. 176–9.

17 H. Manning to J. Hare, 28 October 1841, Manning Papers, Bodleian Library, MS Eng. lett., c. 653/1, fols. 176–9.

18 Pereiro, *Cardinal Manning*, pp. 59–60, n. 16.

19 'Declaration of a meeting of Archbishops and Bishops, held at Lambeth, on Tuesday on Whitsun Week 1841', in R. P. Flindall, *The Church of England 1815–1948: A Documentary History* (London, 1972), p. 95.

meeting included prominent evangelicals such as Bishop J. B. Sumner, as well as its moderate high church instigator, Charles Blomfield, bishop of London, and more emphatic high church supporters such as himself and William Ewart Gladstone. As £27,000 had by this point been promised to the fund, Manning was very satisfied with the immediate outcome. 'I think the work of yesterday elicited and set forward right principles of action more than any single act of the Church in my recollection.'[20]

The Colonial Bishoprics Fund in 1841 was a major paradigm shift for the Church of England with respect to its development within the British Empire. Disappointed and disillusioned by the increasing failure of the state to act on its formal partnership with the established Church, Blomfield had proposed in 1840 in a public letter to the William Howley, archbishop of Canterbury, that a capital fund be established to endow colonial bishoprics. It was the beginning of a new form of engagement with global extension on the part of the Church of England. From now on the Church would act autonomously, separate from the state, to extend itself overseas by raising funds to found colonial and overseas bishoprics, notwithstanding continuing uncertainties about the royal supremacy.[21]

Manning had been eloquent in its support at the public launch of the fund. He had a coherent theological view about such imperial extension. God, he maintained, had entrusted Britain with 'guardianship' over much of the earth, and Britain was thus responsible for the evangelisation of those parts of the globe it had direct authority over, namely its colonies. At the present time, he urged, Britain was in 'moral arrears' to God over its spiritual neglect of these overseas populations; however, if this neglect were reversed, it would enhance imperial unity around a global Anglicanism. Such a religiously based imperial unity, in turn, would be the best pledge of the endurance of the empire, as it would then share in the perpetuity Christ had promised to his Church. Manning called for a global Church of England; it would ensure the 'pure restoration of the one Catholic faith' because his Church was, he proclaimed, 'the brightest light in Christendom'.[22]

Hare, for his part, strongly opposed Newman's protest over the Jerusalem bishopric, calling it a 'an awful act' full of party spirit, and the 'hateful fruit of episcopaltry' (probably referring here to Newman's excessively exalted view of the episcopate as virtually the sole guarantee of the

[20] H. Manning to J. Hare, 28 April 1841, Bodleian Library, MS. Eng. Lett. C. 653, fols. 106–7.
[21] Rowan Strong, 'A New Anglican Imperial Paradigm: The Colonial Bishoprics Fund, 1840–1', in *Anglicanism and the British Empire c.1700–1850* (Oxford, 2007), pp. 198–221.
[22] *Ibid.*, pp. 206–7.

Church of England's catholicity). Newman's protest, Hare insisted, was the act of a solitary individual with no ecclesiastical authority against action by the Church's legitimate rulers. Nor would Hare countenance Newman referring to Lutheran and Calvinistic heresies. Those Churches might be schismatic, but they could not be heretical, as the Church of England's own greatest theologians had called the Lutheran and Calvinist theologies 'the best expositions of the truth'.[23] Manning, in a hasty reply, said that he looked forward to talking together about these things. He disagreed with a view Hare had expressed about the evangelicals being sound ecclesiologically (though he said that he honoured the zealous and saintly among them) and he made no further comment about the bishopric other than to give thanks that the two of them were mostly one in belief and heart. This suggests Manning did not strongly disagree with Hare about the actual bishopric at this stage, or he would surely have raised his concerns as he did about their differences over the evangelicals.[24]

The two friends subsequently had their conversation on these matters; according to Hare their meeting was three weeks earlier than his next letter, so that it must have taken place sometime in the first week of December 1841. Manning had reproved Hare for over-strong language, presumably about Newman. But Hare could not overcome his vehement antipathy to Newman, whom he regarded as having a 'portion of the Antichrist' in him.[25] Manning's reply glossed over their differences, and probably because of that he deferred any comment on Newman's protest on the basis that he had not seen it. But Manning did commend to Hare James Hope's pamphlet on the bishopric as expressing views that Hare and he could respect.[26] Hope's pamphlet had largely opposed the bishopric, based on the dubious position that Bishop Solomon occupied according to canon law, and this probably appealed to the orderly side of Manning's character.[27]

Ten days later, at the beginning of January 1842, Manning wrote again, more fully. He expressed dislike for Hare's strong language

[23] J. Hare to H. Manning, 23 November 1841, Manning Papers, Bodleian Library, MS Eng. lett., c. 653/1, fols. 202–4.

[24] H. Manning to J. Hare, 27 November 1841, Manning Papers, Bodleian Library, MS Eng. lett., c. 653/1, fols. 205–7.

[25] J. Hare to H. Manning, 30 December 1841, Manning Papers, Bodleian Library, MS Eng. lett., c. 653/1, fols. 209–11.

[26] H. Manning to J. Hare, 2 January 1842, Manning Papers, Bodleian Library, MS Eng. lett., c. 653/1, fols. 214–17.

[27] Welch, 'Anglican Churchmen and the Jerusalem Bishopric', p. 203.

against the Tractarians, particularly Newman, who were dear to him. While Manning here made no specific reference to the bishopric, he did refer to 'the unhappy distractions of the Church'. Manning clearly did not have the same outraged view of such distractions, which must have included the bishopric, as Newman had expressed in his protest. Manning did not see the bishopric as threatening the catholic claims of the Church of England, as Newman did, but expressed the hope that those who disagreed about it could nevertheless work together.

I see no hope, below God, but this only. Let all work together without eliciting the consciousness of differences, so long as our spiritual Rulers neither separate us from the Holy Communion, nor suspend us from our Common Ministry. Let us not take the judicial acts which they forebear. I know of no principle but this, which will not issue in schism. At least it shall not, by His help, be my act to proceed in any other towards yourself.[28]

In March 1842, in his last word on the bishopric in his correspondence with Hare, Manning mentioned 'three pamphlets'. These pamphlets would seem to be James Hope, *The Bishopric of the United Church of England and Ireland at Jerusalem* (1841); William Palmer of Magdalen College, Oxford, *Aids to reflection on the seemingly double character of the Established Church, with reference to the foundation of a 'Protestant bishopric' at Jerusalem* (1841); and either E. B. Pusey, *A letter to his Grace the Archbishop of Canterbury on some circumstances connected with the present crisis in the English Church* (1842); or F. D. Maurice, *Three letters to the Rev. W. Palmer* (1842). Manning acknowledged that he and Hare would 'differ widely' as to the degree of truth in each of the pamphlets, but he felt that no good would be served by going through those differences in detail. Although Manning believed that Palmer's argument was not without faults, he did not sympathise with Hare's basic objections of the work.[29]

As Palmer's was the only one of the three possible pamphlets to which Manning made any reference, his basic agreement with Palmer's pamphlet indicates the direction Manning's thinking was taking some four months after his initial positive welcome of the Jerusalem bishopric. Among other arguments, including the one that Lutherans were heretical because they lacked bishops, Palmer propounded a view that the

[28] H. Manning to J. Hare, 2 January 1842, Manning Papers, Bodleian Library, MS Eng. lett., c. 653/1, fols. 218–25.

[29] H. Manning to J. Hare, 7 March 1842, Manning Papers, Bodleian Library, MS Eng. lett., c. 653/1, fols. 246–7.

Catholic Church consisted of the 'Anglican, Greek, and Latin branches, which excluded any one of the branches having bishops where an episcopate of either of the other two existed'.[30] Palmer, with his long-standing concern over relations with the Eastern Orthodox Churches, was worried that these Churches would see the Anglican bishop as an intruder and, consequently, be even less willing than they already were to recognise the Church of England.[31] This view would have reinforced the concern that Manning expressed in his correspondence with Hare that there should be no Anglican intrusion into the ancient sees.

But if Manning was clearly against the bishopric by March 1842, and probably even earlier (in January 1842, when he had expressed agreement with James Hope's anti-bishopric pamphlet), how do we account for his initial welcome of it? David Newsome believes it resulted from Manning's deep and close friendship with Hare, and his reluctance to allow the bishopric to be a source of division between them.[32] Certainly a reluctance to face up to their differences is evident in the correspondence between the two archdeacons on the issue. However, that does not explain Manning's own initial delight at the proposal, as expressed in his October 1841 letter to Hare. His expression of 'joy' at the bishopric project is rather stronger than called for if Manning were simply seeking to be agreeable to Hare. Manning would have known about the Jerusalem bishopric for some time prior to this because of its explicit mention in the Whitsun meeting of the bishops, so his October 'joy' over it, months later, cannot have been unconsidered.

Manning was at first well disposed toward the Jerusalem bishopric because he saw it as a small part of that global extension of Anglicanism which was the purpose of the Colonial Bishoprics Fund. This disposition was also influenced by Manning's long-standing interest in the British Empire and the place of the Church of England within it. This is an area of Manning's intellectual and theological life that has escaped the recent rehabilitations of Manning's reputation by David Newsome, V. A. McLelland and James Pereiro, but it is one that dates back to Henry Manning's early adult life.

The earliest evidence for Manning's imperial consciousness appears in one of his notebooks dated 24 January 1831. This is a written transcript of the whole or part of an undisclosed work on the mutual economic

[30] Peter Nockles, *The Oxford Movement in Context: Anglican High Churchmanship 1760–1857* (Cambridge, 1994), p. 161.
[31] Welch, 'Anglican Churchmen and the Jerusalem Bishopric', p. 202.
[32] David Newsome, *The Convert Cardinals: Newman and Manning* (London, 1993), p. 155.

benefits of colonial possessions to both the imperial power and its colonies. None of the published works on Manning makes any reference to the work, but it is an early indication of what became a sustained imperial concern. It comes from the period immediately following his father's financial collapse, the winter of 1830–31, when Manning secluded himself and read widely. There is no mention of any religious dimension in Manning's transcript. It may have been a work he read in connection with the meagre prospect of attaining a clerkship in the Colonial Office, which was the best prospect his connections held out for him at the time.[33] But whatever the initial reason for Manning's reading on the economics of imperialism, the notebook was sufficiently important for him to keep it among his papers for a long time; indeed, it contains the bookplate of the Oblate community at Bayswater, which Manning founded as a Roman Catholic in 1857.[34]

Manning continued to take a strong interest in the British Empire, and particularly in the extension of Anglicanism overseas, throughout the twenty years he spent as an Anglican priest. This is evident not only in his ardent support for the Colonial Bishoprics Fund, but also in his early canvassing for a bishop for New Zealand from 1837.[35] Newman also liked the idea of missionary bishops as the 'right way of missionary-izing', but unlike Manning he did little about it, and neither was the interest sustained, as Manning's was, over many years.[36] Two other sources among Manning's papers also point to his concern for the colonial Church of England almost up to his conversion to Roman Catholicism in 1851. The first is a small commonplace book in which he made notes for a projected essay or sermon on overseas mission. The second source consists of two letters to him from George Augustus Selwyn, bishop of New Zealand.

The main thrust of Manning's projected essay or sermon in his commonplace book, dated by the Bodleian Library catalogue to around 1845, was to support the Society for the Propagation of the Gospel in Foreign Parts. The notes definitely represented Manning the confident Anglican, for he observed that one of the reasons for supporting the work of the SPG was that members of the Church of England were 'members of the finest branch of the Cath[olic]: & Ap[ostolic] Ch[urch]'. After this his

[33] *Ibid.*, p. 46.

[34] Notebook containing an essay on colonial possession 1831, Manning Papers, Bodleian Library, MS Eng. Misc. d. 1279.

[35] David Newsome, *The Parting Of Friends: The Wilberforces and Henry Manning* (Grand Rapids, MI, 1993), p. 218n.

[36] *Ibid.*, p. 217.

first major point was 'the greatness of the Charge committed to us as a people[.] Spain ceased to be a colonial empire when she began to wa[te]r down Cath[oli]c Teaching.' 'England began to be so when she embraces it.'[37] However, with Britain's empire encompassing one eighth of the habitable earth there was a 'great & manifold guilt resting on us for the sins of the Civil Power from James 1st to this day'. There were four such sins, which Manning defined as (1) 'extermination of aborigines'; (2) 'neglect' presumably of the spiritual welfare of either the aborigines, colonists or the extension of the Church, or all three; (3) 'Thwarting of the good', that is, 'hindrances to SPG'; and (4) 'Direct countenance' by Britain of 'schism and 'idolatry', which may refer to the maintenance of Hindu shrines by the East India Company, a commonplace accusation by evangelicals and others since the 1790s.

Manning's next major point is illegible, but what followed is his contention that 'What the state will not do the Church must', and a number of sub-points which clearly refer to the overseas extension of the Church of England, as they include 'Cranmers Mission to China' and the planting of bishoprics so that the 'Ch[urch is] awake and among the 7 sleepers no longer'.[38] Manning then proceeded to a number of points about the SPG. He urged his prospective audience that they were bound to support the Society, first by reason of their baptism, but also by virtue of their citizenship. 'We have a two fold calling Eng[lan]d: a *Ch*[urch]: & an *Empire* And such an Empire as the world never yet saw.' But this was 'a Stewardship for God'. The British must then answer to God for '1. For the Heathenism of India[.] 2. For the destitution of Canada[.] 3. For the degradation of the W.I. Slaves – 1. Inquisition[;] 2. Slave trade[.] – 4. For the Tophet we have made in Australia.'[39] In answer to the objection that there has been 'so little effect' from missions, Manning proposed that this was because 'God is training us in a slow solitary way' – rather like Abraham, who began as a solitary alien and became the father of a nation. The requirement was to persist in the toil from a 'chain 300 years long'.

So an effort was necessary in part for 'The making the Ch[urch]: co-extensive with the empire' for 'the great work is the Empire'. While the empire had one seventh [it was one eighth above] of all the earth and one seventh of all the people 'yet we have only 10 Bps'.[40] He went on to refer to his argument used before at the launch of the Colonial Bishoprics Fund in 1841 that there were 'moral arrears'. Neglect of the Church in the

[37] Commonplace book, Manning Papers, Bodleian Library, MS Eng. fol. 4.
[38] *Ibid.*, fols. 6–8. [39] *Ibid.*, fols. 10–17. [40] *Ibid.*, fols. 19–24.

United States had resulted in the loss of those former British colonies as 'a band of Spoilers grew up & overthrew all'. Other pointers to British moral indebtedness in its empire were 'Idolatry in India', British 'Emigrants' (presumably because they lacked churches) and 'above all Australia', where there was 'A moral antagonism of souls without God in the world'. 'One delay', he urged, 'may be squandering golden opportunities. And I cannot understand many who fail as Citizens & Xtns can doubt or hang back.' Manning further emphasised the colonial ecclesiastical extension required of members of the Church of England as Christians and as citizens on the ground that it was the 'Particular duty of the Ch[urch]'; but also because 'The Divine procedure' was a sort of providential relay race passing the imperial baton to 'Greece, Rome, Spain, Eng[lan]d'. There was also the great extent of Britain's empire. The divine requirement of church extension had been met, to an extent Manning did not spell out in his notes, by the 'founding of Bps [which were] not a mere perfection of mission but the radical principle[.] 1. They potentially contain the Church[.] 2. They always, in effect, draw after them all the rest[.]'[41]

Manning was outlining in these notes an episcopal principle of Anglican world mission. This ecclesiastical basis for mission contrasted with the usual evangelical concern for the missionary preaching of the gospel, not of the Church. For Manning, though the missionary expansion of the Church presumably implied that the Church would preach the gospel, mission fundamentally had to proceed on an ecclesiological basis, which fundamentally meant the Anglican episcopate. As his notes went on, it was through bishoprics that Christendom had been formed and England had been converted, and he therefore looked to bishops, as an office potentially containing the whole Church, to further its imperial mission. 'We are involved in the unity & the responsibility of the B[ritish]. Empire[.] A providential order. A line of Empires. We are on our probation[.] We have a choice to make. To be Evangelists of Xt or to be the body of the AntiXt.'[42]

There are also amongst Manning's papers in the Bodleian Library two letters to him from Bishop Selwyn in New Zealand. The first is from 1847 and the second, much shorter, from 1850. The first is addressed 'My dear Archdeacon', and the second 'My dear friend'. In Selwyn's longer letter of 1847, he belatedly acknowledged the regular receipt of Manning's archiediaconal charges, his 'work on the unity of the Church',[43] his university

[41] *Ibid.*, fols. 25–34. [42] *Ibid.*, fol. 40. The last six pages of the notebook are illegible.

[43] Pereiro, *Cardinal Manning*, pp. 40–41.

sermons, 'and for many other favours, which I cannot now recollect'. Selwyn then explained that he regarded his becoming bishop of New Zealand as owing to the impression Manning had made on him in his speech at the Colonial Bishopric Fund launch. The bulk of the letter, which was about Selwyn's anxiety over education and the fortunes of the National Society, need not detain us here.[44] Selwyn's letter of 1850, written under the shadow of the Gorham judgement, gave Manning '1000 marks for your volume of sermons' and prays that God will strengthen him in his 'present trouble', which was clearly a reference to the Gorham judgement. Selwyn briefly conveyed sentiments of solidarity from his little Church in New Zealand, and on the independence of that Church, which he must have known Manning would endorse. Clearly anxious about Manning, Selwyn urged

> all to stand firm in their own cause; and to cast upon our Holy & injured Mother the blame of the chains which she is compelled to wear. Let us work with you, as we will to the fullest extent of our power, to assent to the freedom of the Church, whether established by law or not. But keep the Church whole, or we shall all be lost. I am so used to beating against a contrary wind in my little vessel, that I care little for it, if the vessel itself be seaworthy.[45]

So Manning had, from the early 1830s to the end of his Anglican days in 1851, a sustained and abiding interest in the British Empire, and in the extension of the Church of England overseas, both as the best and purest Church, and as the divinely appointed vehicle for redressing the moral arrears of an empire that was falling short in its religious responsibilities for the spiritual welfare of its inhabitants, both indigenous and English migrants. It is this concern, I believe, that led Manning at first to welcome the Jerusalem bishopric as part of Anglican global extension until he began to see it in a different light through the influence of his Tractarian friends.

Similarly, the Oxford Movement soon promoted among its sympathisers in various parts of the empire an interest in missionary and colonial episcopacy. We can see this in Manning's concern for the episcopal extension of missionary Anglicanism, rather than some other dimension such as priestly or lay missionaries. It is also evident in Selwyn, who was already reading Tractarian literature before he left for New Zealand in

[44] G. A. Selwyn to H. Manning, St John's College [Auckland], 1 June 1847, Manning Papers, Bodleian Library, MS Eng. Lett. c. 653/3, fols. 724–6.

[45] G. A. Selwyn to H. Manning, 20 December 1850, Manning Papers, Bodleian Library, MS Eng. Lett. c. 653, fol. 804.

1841, and who would centre development of the New Zealand Church around the bishop as 'the source of all diocesan action', albeit acting always in consultation with his clergy.[46] William Broughton, bishop of Australia, also found Tractarian ecclesiology, and particularly by the 1840s its emphasis on the apostolic succession of the Anglican episcopate, to be a growing influence in his self-understanding of his episcopal office and authority.[47] These colonial bishops found the Tractarian views on the independence of the Church from the state, the divine foundation of the Church and the apostolic succession of the Anglican episcopate to be useful theological conceptions when navigating the tricky waters of colonial politics in a period when the state was quickly and obviously withdrawing from its traditional Anglican partnership. The same push towards a Tractarian emphasis on episcopacy in mission can be seen in William Gladstone. The young ultra-Tory Gladstone, whose 1838 book, *The State in Its Relations with the Church*, was a last gasp of advocacy for a confessional Anglican state, at the 1841 launch of the Colonial Bishoprics Fund publicly endorsed the principle of missionary bishops separate from and independent of the state. While Gladstone in 1841 was still a high churchman, the alteration in his theology had begun to occur, as David Bebbington makes clear, and he became a Tractarian during the 1840s.[48] Tractarian influence on imperial Anglicanism continued in the second half of the nineteenth century, when specially consecrated missionary bishops such as John Mackenzie, first bishop of Central Africa, and his successors were able to pursue the mission beyond the bounds of empire with substantial support from a like-minded constituency at home.[49] In addition, the development of religious communities within Anglo-Catholicism gave Anglicanism for the first time an equivalent, albeit on a very much smaller scale, to the communities of men and women so prominent in Roman Catholic missionary history.[50]

Manning seems to have shared these views that the export of Anglicanism by missionary bishops was indispensable to the Church of England's claim to be a catholic Church. This may, in large part, have

[46] G. A. Selwyn, *A charge delivered to the clergy of the Diocese of New Zealand … on Thursday, September 23, 1847* (London, 1849), pp. 90–91.

[47] Strong, *Anglicanism and the British Empire*, pp. 236–7, 249–50.

[48] David Bebbington, *The Mind of Gladstone: Religion, Homer, and Politics* (Oxford, 2004), pp. 55–6.

[49] Andrew Porter, *Religion versus Empire: British Protestant Missionaries and Overseas Expansion 1700–1914* (Manchester, 2004), pp. 225–34.

[50] *Ibid.*, pp. 234–7; for a particular instance of such a missionary community see Alan Wilkinson, *The Community of the Resurrection: A Centenary History* (London, 1992).

to do with his developing theology of the Church and the episcopate which came to fruition in his book, *The Unity of the Church*, published in 1842. In that book Manning upheld the unity of the Church as something more fundamental than the imposed bonds of either political nations or of empires, because the Church's unity was given it by God for the purpose of confining humankind's fallen tendencies.

> The whole history of the world presents a series of empires rising and falling, sometimes crushed by the weight of a mightier kingdom, and sometimes broken up from within by the force of inward collisions. The whole history of each several empire – the Assyrian, the Persian, the Greek, and the Roman – is little more than a baffled endeavour to impose a constraining bond of unity on the repugnancies of the moral world. Even the last iron despotism, which was stronger than all before it, failed in the task ... But the full display of unity and permanence was reserved for the Church Catholic ... As unity is an attribute of eternity, so it is the cause of imperishableness. Mankind stood in need of some common basis, which should be one and the same in all, to hold in check the tendency of imperfect natures to dissolution. And this is the function of the Church.[51]

Manning does not explicitly mention the British Empire in his book. But the implicit reference was there for a contemporary reader to draw, and was applied explicitly, I believe, by Manning himself, in his powerful speech at the launch of the Colonial Bishoprics Fund the previous year.

> Surely as citizens, the only hope we can have for the perpetuity of this great Christian empire, is that ... its unity of organization shall be identified with the unity and organization of the church of Christ, and so be made partaker of her perpetuity. If we look back, as every Christian man will look back, to the history of past empires, – not regarding the history of the world as a turbulent rolling sea, in which empires rise and fall by chance, driven about by some blind destiny, but recognising some moral law, guided by an unerring Governor, determining the rise and fall of empires, of men ... when we behold these things, and see that it has pleased the providence of the same Supreme Governor to raise us up now to stand where they stood, and to commit to us the same deposit – to make us carriers of the light, we surely have a choice to make, whether we shall be the mere beast of burthen for all nations, or the evangelizer of the world. Whether it may please the same Ruler who has raised us up to continue as we are, or to make us an empire which shall last with the perpetuity of his Church.[52]

In this 1841 speech, Manning argued that the endurance of the British Empire would only be secure if it fostered the ecclesiastical organisation

[51] H. E. Manning. *The Unity of the Church* (London, 1842), pp. 221–2, see also 233–4.

[52] *Proceedings of a meeting of the clergy and laity ... held at Willis's Rooms, 27th April 1841, for the purpose of raising a fund towards the endowment of additional colonial bishoprics* (London, 1841), p. 25.

and unity of the Church of England. In his book of 1842, he proposed that the unity of the Church was expressed in both its objective unity in the apostolic succession of the episcopate and the subjective unity of the members of a diocese to their local bishop and the charitable relationship of those local churches around the world. Such local churches were equal. While there could be a primacy of honour, such as had belonged to Rome, there could not be a jurisdictional supremacy, because each local church under its bishop was a direct and equal descendant of the apostles, directly authorised by the divine Head of the Church. There were indeed doctrinal matters of faith and discipline that appertained to the whole Church, in which case the whole Church had to be consulted. But while the local church had areas that were its own concern, it could not impose these on the other local churches as if it could exercise a universal jurisdiction. Both forms of unity were desirable, but only the first, the episcopate, was essential, and hence his support for Anglican colonial and foreign bishoprics.[53] Though no direct influence can be traced, it is interesting to note that this ecclesiology of Manning's is remarkably similar to that which underpinned the Lambeth Conference, inaugurated in 1867, of an Anglican Communion composed of the union of independent dioceses, with no single see, not even Canterbury, exercising an overall judicial primacy.

Manning's imperial concerns indicate the diversity among sympathisers and adherents of the Oxford Movement. The Tractarian antagonism to aspects of the establishment of the Church of England and its exposure to possible Erastianism is well known.[54] Newman certainly viewed the Jerusalem bishopric in this context. At the same time that Manning was expressing to Julius Hare his delight in the project, Newman in October 1841 wrote to Samuel Wood that the bishopric was about using the Church to extend British influence in the Middle East, to counterbalance Russian and French influence there. 'There is not a single Anglican at Jerusalem, we are to place a Bishop (of the *circumcision, expressly*) there, to collect a communion out of Protestants, Jews, Druses and Monophysites, conforming under the influence of our war-steamers, to counterbalance the Russian influence through Greeks, and the French through Latins.'[55]

[53] Manning, *Unity of the Church*, pp. 151, 280; Pereiro, *Cardinal Manning*, pp. 41–4.

[54] For example, J. H. L. Rowlands, *Church, State and Society: The Attitudes of John Keble, Richard Hurrell Froude and John Henry Newman 1827–1845* (Worthing, 1989), where he sees Newman's antagonism to the state connection as particularly catalysed by his friendship with Hurrell Froude.

[55] J. H. Newman to S. F. Wood, 10 October 1841, *LDN*, vol. XXVIII, p. 292.

Two days later he told John Bowden that the reason for the whole iniquitous development was 'because Russia being represented by the Greeks, and France by the Latins, it is very desirable that England should have a Church there as a means of political influence, a *resident power* in that country'.[56] In Newman's protest of November 1841 this ground of Erastianism was not mentioned, but only the alliance with a heretical Lutheran and Calvinistic Church.[57]

Manning did not see the traditional alliance of the Church of England with the state in quite such starkly antagonistic terms. Indeed, at the launch of the Colonial Bishoprics Fund just six months before Newman made these comments, Manning publicly set forth his vision of a Christian British Empire whose religion provided its unity and its principle of longevity because at its heart was the catholic Church of England against which, as the best of all possible Churches, Christ promised that the gates of hell should not prevail. It was true the state had not been living up to its obligations in the partnership, and therefore the Church was forced to act alone by the nature of her divine commission to proclaim the gospel to all the world, and her obligation to extend the apostolic principle of episcopacy. But the implication was that if the state should reverse its recent unilateral withdrawal of support for the Church of England, the traditional partnership was still valid. In the early 1840s Manning saw the Church–state partnership not as inherently Erastian, but as valid though defective on the state's part. It was defective because it had not adequately supported the divine requirement as a Christian imperial power to spread the true faith through the catholic and apostolic Church of England.

Manning, in his initial view of the Jerusalem bishopric, and in his understanding of the Church–state alliance and the British Empire, was also in tune with the views of a number of the younger members of the high church party. Walter Farquhar Hook thought the bishopric was a unique opportunity to spread abroad, even beyond the boundaries of the empire, the apostolic Church of England though the extension of its episcopate. The more Tractarian Arthur Perceval also saw it as an avenue for the reintroduction of episcopacy in the apostolic succession into Lutheranism.[58] Their, and Manning's, advocacy for the colonial Church of England reminds us that some Oxford Movement supporters had their minds on other things than England, Rome and the University of Oxford.

56 J. H. Newman to J. W. Bowden, 12 October 1841, *ibid.*, p. 295.

57 'Protest against the Jerusalem Bishopric', *ibid.*, p. 328.

58 Nockles. *Oxford Movement in Context*, pp. 160, 163.

The Anglican Manning, with his keen and long-standing interest in the British Empire, could very well have been a key figure in the Church of England's global expansion, and not just through his leadership in the Colonial Bishoprics Fund. The books he sent to Selwyn are indicative of his consciousness of the Church of England in the empire and beyond. The first volume of his *Sermons*, published in 1842, is dedicated to the bishop of New Jersey, evoking the Catholic unity of an international Anglican Church:

> To the Right Reverend Father in God, George, Lord Bishop of New Jersey, in remembrance of the day spent with the clergy assembled in visitation at Storrington, July 13th 1841; when, in his own words, he bade God speed, 'as a Catholic bishop, to the Catholic Church in England;' and cheered us with the consciousness that unity and perpetuity still abide in the inheritance of our spiritual mother.[59]

The Anglican Manning had an ecclesiology that consciously and explicitly embraced imperial and global Anglican expansion. The fourth volume of his published sermons was dedicated to Selwyn himself.[60]

The bishop of New Zealand also gave evidence of the how important Manning's theology was to him, in his letter to Manning of 1847 that has already been mentioned.

> I know you too well by character to think that you would like me to tell you all that one feels on the subject of the works which you have sent me; one of which 'The Unity of the Church' was my travelling companion, when I had no other books besides but my Bible & Prayerbook; and no friend with me, but my ever-faithful Maoris. In a canoe voyage of 200 miles along the Wairoa & Kaipara Rivers to Auckland I read it all through with the greatest benefit to myself, and would gladly have imparted the same good to my poor natives, who are distracted between the Church, John Wesley & the Pope. The world here is slow to believe in Christ, because we are not all one. One principal Chief at Taupo, Te Heuheu, who once described to me his state, as that of a man sitting at a three cross road, not knowing which turning to take, has lately been swallowed up in a torrent of mud which burst from the side of the hill under which he lived. He would no doubt have died a Christian, if the Gospel had been presented to him under one form.[61]

In this long journey Selwyn would have had time (as the Maori were doing all the paddling and cooking) to absorb the argument of Manning's book of the central importance of ecclesiastical unity, in Selwyn's missionary context.

[59] H. E. Manning, *Sermons* (London, 1842), p. i. [60] *Ibid.*, p. iv.

[61] G. A. Selwyn to H. Manning, 1 June 1847, Manning Papers, Bodleian Library, MS Eng. Lett. c. 653/3, fols. 724–5.

Unlike Newman, Manning's embrace of the Tractarian emphasis on the apostolic succession of the Anglican episcopate (in the period in which he remained a confident Anglican) included a long-standing support for missionary and colonial bishops. This concern continued beyond the time of the launch of the Bishoprics Fund launch in 1841 and his initial welcome for the Jerusalem bishopric. In 1845 he included episcopal missions among the outcomes of the Oxford Movement in a letter that David Newsome regards as accurately expressing Manning's Tractarian sympathies to that date.

> Certainly there has never been in my memory, any movement when the Church of England has put forth such tokens of life and power. It is almost incredible that a body which 15 years ago was elated at being an Establishment should now be conscious of being a Church. The work that has been done in and by a Church at home and through its Episcopate and Missions abroad seem to me overwhelming signs of Christ's love and power. What may not be hoped from a body which has even conceived such works of Faith? It is not the nature of severed or barren branches to blossom after 300 years, except 'an Aaron's rod that budded'.[62]

In his imperial awareness Manning was motivated by his theological concern to spread abroad the Church of England as the best possible Church and the principal agent of the gospel of Christ. This concern was not fastened to the ideology of imperial state power, nor was it unmindful of the less powerful in the imperial–colonial–indigenous interface. The Anglican Manning would have liked a British state more attuned to what he saw was its Christian duty to support mission and Church extension. However, the lack of such an imperial partner did not deter him from his hopes for his Church's imperial engagement with the colonial world. In this lack of concern for traditional Anglican establishmentarianism, it seems likely that Manning's increasing engagement with the Oxford Movement, with its distrust of Erastianism and its proclamation of the divine foundation and spiritual independence of the Church of England, was a major influence. It is not without significance that one of Manning's most continuous colonial interests was Bishop Selwyn in New Zealand, who helped to shape a missionary Church that moved very quickly to establish structures of ecclesiastical independence from the state under Selwyn's Tractarian-influenced guidance, and also a Church whose focus in Manning's Anglican days was on the indigenous Maori rather than the white settlers. Manning's imperial theology also gave him the resources

[62] Newsome, *Parting of Friends*, p. 316.

to critique Britain's imperial project for its disregard of the conversion of indigenous populations, and for the immorality of its unique penal colony in Australia.

Consequently, it is not surprising that Manning, like a number of slightly younger high churchmen, was initially a supporter of the Jerusalem bishopric, because they viewed the initiative within the context of Anglican mission in contrast to the anti-Protestant-heresy construction of Newman. For Manning and these slightly younger Anglicans, the Jerusalem bishopric was not the unmitigated disaster that it was for Newman. The hope, though an increasingly guarded one, of such high churchmen in the bishopric was also derived from their assertive Anglicanism in 1841. Manning's early support for the bishopric was not only a further indication of the vitality of high churchmanship among the younger generation in the 1840s; it was also demonstrative, even after Newman's self-induced catastrophe of Tract 90, that high churchmen and Tractarians could agree on some major theological agendas. In this case, they agreed on the necessity of the episcopate in the export of a global Anglicanism; even if, for Tractarian-influenced high churchmen such as Manning and Gladstone, the Jerusalem bishopric was by 1842 an increasingly dubious aspect of such extension. While Manning's position indicates the vitality of younger high churchmen in the 1840s it would not do to push this too far. It was, after all, Tractarian influence which enabled Manning to develop a more critical position on the Jerusalem bishopric by 1842. Tractarian doctrinal edginess in theological debate, coupled with the warm spirituality Manning also found attractive among evangelicals, points to the Oxford Movement's power and influence in pushing high churchmen further than they perhaps initially wanted to go. It was, therefore, very much as a Tractarian-influenced high churchman that Henry Manning ultimately criticised the Jerusalem bishopric. For Manning the Jerusalem bishopric was not a blow; that it was initially seen by him and other strong Oxford Movement sympathisers to be a welcome part of a revived and globally extended Anglicanism is a further indication that the Oxford Movement needs to re-examined beyond its domestic influence on the Church of England, and beyond the viewpoint of John Henry Newman and the minority of his ultra-Roman supporters.

CHAPTER 5

The Australian bishops and the Oxford Movement

Austin Cooper

A recent article in the *Ecclesiastical Law Journal* has argued that the traditional Church of England understanding of the episcopate, and the understanding enshrined in the law of the Episcopal Church of the USA, might substantially differ. The author concluded that 'The Church of England still essentially enjoys the hierarchical structure that it has inherited from the western Church ... and its ecclesiology flows from that structure [while] the Episcopal Church still essentially has the democratic and egalitarian structure conceived in the wake of the American Revolution.'[1]

This chapter will argue that the Australian bishops, while subject to similar socio-political trends as their American confrères, maintained the traditional Church of England understanding and indeed strengthened it. While allowing a clear role for lay participation, the Australian bishop is not merely a church officer empowered to ordain, confirm and oversee a particular church; the bishop has a unique authority to witnesses to the faith of the whole Church. Moreover, in this development of the Australian bishopric, the Church in the Colonies was strengthened and encouraged by the Tractarians.

For the purposes of this chapter, the 'Australian bishops' are the six who met in Conference in Sydney from 1 October to 1 November 1850. William Grant Broughton, bishop of Sydney, the senior of the group, was consecrated in 1836; Francis Russell Nixon of Tasmania and George Augustus Selwyn of New Zealand were both consecrated in 1841, and the remaining three, Augustus Short of Adelaide, Charles Perry of Melbourne and William Tyrrell of Newcastle, were consecrated in 1847.

When Broughton first came to Australia as an archdeacon in 1829, the generous provisions of the Church and School Corporation were still in

[1] Colin Podmore, 'A Tale of Two Churches: The Ecclesiologies of the Episcopal Church and the Church of England Compared', *Ecclesiastical Law Journal*, 10 (2008), pp. 34–70, at p. 70.

place: the Church of England enjoyed a unique role and magnanimous financial support.[2] This support, however, was formally and finally revoked by Order-in-Council shortly after Broughton's arrival. In response, he undertook the long, arduous journey home in 1834–6 to seek government redress. His quest failed. But while he was in England, on 14 February 1836, Broughton was consecrated bishop along with George Mountain of Montreal. It is difficult to discern any connection between this relatively quiet event in Lambeth Palace chapel and Tractarian stirrings in Oxford. Rather, Broughton's consecration was political pragmatism at its best: the Colonial Secretary, Lord Glenelg, saw Broughton's appointment as a solution to 'the inconvenience arising from the necessity of appeal in certain cases to the Bishop of Calcutta … [and] for the maintenance of [clerical] discipline and good order'.[3] Broughton, an old-fashioned high churchman, came under the influence of Tractarian thought through a fortuitous meeting with Edward Coleridge at Eton. This marked the beginning of a life-long friendship in which the younger man gently guided the older; indeed, to this Coleridge connection, more than any other, we owe the importation of Tractarian ideals to Australia. This was 'networking' at its best: family connections, familiarity with and close proximity to the leading Tractarians. Coleridge, a man of boundless energy and enthusiasm, proved an invaluable conduit in transferring ideas. Three years after their first meeting, Broughton, who had relied so much on government support, told Coleridge that:

> My augury is that before [long] we shall be called to defend Christian truth not in alliance, incorporation, union or connection with the State, but in positive opposition to it. I think it is better not to shut our eyes against these conclusions because they are disagreeable ones; but to make our preparations betimes 'that we may be able to withstand the evil day, and having done all, to stand.' My reliance, I assure you, begins to rest very little on external aid, but rather on that internal strength of the Church herself.[4]

Broughton was increasingly clear that such 'internal strength' rested in large part on 'the nature and effect of the Holy Sacraments, the office of the ministry, the constitution and authority of the Church'.[5] In the

[2] The Church and School Corporation, established by Letters Patent in 1826 granting the Church of England one seventh of the surveyed land in the colony. Stephen Judd and Kenneth Cable, *Sydney Anglicans* (Sydney, 2000), p. 8.

[3] Lord Glenelg to Bourke, 12 December 1835, Mitchell Library, Sydney, A 1272, fol. 797.

[4] W. G. Broughton to E. Coleridge, 14 October 1839, MCL.

[5] W. G. Broughton, *Speech in the Legislative Council on Education* (27 August 1839) (Sydney, 1839), p. 8.

midst of a political and religious 'Babel',[6] in which each religious tradition sought its place in the sun, the Tractarians provided a discernable Anglican identity. Broughton unashamedly relied on them:

> [Y]our introduction of [Newman's] name reminds me to say that if I might make choice of my fellow labourers, they should come from *his* school. *They* take, I think, the most just and comprehensive view of the true constitution of our Church, and of its actual duties in the present state of the world ... [in them] I should expect to find that temperate professional ardour which appears to me the first requisite for a man's doing his duty well, and finding his *chief* support and reward in the consciousness of doing it.[7]

Broughton told Gladstone that one of his chief aims was to create an impressive visible presence of the Church in Sydney. This was not merely a question of a 'degree of architectural pretension'.[8] An impressive visible presence needed substance, and Broughton found this substance in the Tractarian teachings. To three of the four churches in his diocese, Broughton appointed young Tractarians, the best talent available: Robert Allwood at St James, King Street, William Walsh at Christ Church, St Lawrence (both still Anglican oases in the inner city), and Robert Sconce at St Andrew's (the cathedral, now with its altar removed). The fourth church went to William Cowper, an older evangelical who was already firmly ensconced at St Philip's. Broughton confided that Cowper was

> of the Calvinistic school; but very much of this has worn off (to which I am not without a persuasion that his intercourse with me may have contributed), but yet he is not without a holy horror still, of the Tracts, or rather what he has heard reported of them.[9]

In his Tractarian sympathies, Broughton's concern was always for what might be useful for the Australian scene. For instance, the fracas over the publication in 1838 of Froude's *Remains* left him unmoved, despite the horrified reports from so influential a correspondent as the old high churchman H. H. Norris of Hackney.[10] Broughton's interest centred on the wealth of theology contained in *The Tracts for the Times*, the various volumes of sermons and *The Library of the Fathers*. Not least of the services Coleridge rendered Broughton was the amount of patristic literature he collected from Newman, Pusey, Keble and others; this collection

6 W. G. Broughton to E. Coleridge, 3 April 1840, MCL.
7 W. G. Broughton to E. Coleridge, 19 October 1837, MCL.
8 W. G. Broughton to W. E. Gladstone, 26 July 1836, BL, Gladstone Papers, Add Mss 44,355, fols. 100–103.
9 W. G. Broughton to E. Coleridge, 14 February 1842, MCL.
10 H. H. Norris to W. G. Broughton, 21 March1838, Mitchell Library Sydney, Mss. 913.

now forms the nucleus of the Moore Theological College Library, Sydney. Broughton described himself as being in the midst of numerous occupations, planning for the future 'for my successors to give [the] finishing stroke' to the 'Churches, parsonages, Schools – a Cathedral, a College (added) and a Library'. And Broughton was clear that all of this rested on a firm theological foundation. Here is the *via media* in practice:

> With regard to the Library I am every day more and more convinced that familiarity with ancient literature generally diffused among the clergy, will alone render them able defenders of the evidences of revealed religion against Deists, and of its doctrines against Unitarians; and more over that we must carefully study those monuments of ecclesiastical antiquity with which you have supplied us, if we wish to find and keep the true path of the Church of England; which directs us to preserve our distance from Geneva without running, as some seem half inclined, back to Rome![11]

Broughton found that this stress on patristics offered a practical foundation for his mission, whereas Gladstone's book, *The State in Its Relations with the Church* (1838), while it placed Anglicans 'under the most weighty obligations' of gratitude to the author, was 'too artificially made up to bear the wear and tear of active service'.[12] Given his dependence on Tractarian theology, it is little wonder that Broughton was slow to qualify his respect for the movement. When Tract 90 was published, nearly two years elapsed before he could obtain a copy. Meanwhile he publicly stated: 'I know nothing and I suspect nothing to have been written by any whose kindred with us we acknowledge, which is in any degree contrary to the holy principles which our Reformers taught, and in the defence of which they died.'[13]

When he eventually read Tract 90, he tactfully distinguished between the position articulated by William Palmer in his *Narrative of Events* and the extreme views which he labelled 'Oxford Principles'.[14] One of the great constants in Broughton's mental armoury was an unswerving hostility to anything that smacked of Romanism.

On the wider ecclesial scene, Broughton gave warm support to the proposed St Augustine's College, Canterbury. Broughton thought that the college '*must* be under the control of one versed in Colonial affairs'. While he suggested the name of William Hart Coleridge, bishop of Barbados and the Leeward Islands, who became the first principal, one suspects

[11] W. G. Broughton to E. Coleridge, 25 February 1839, MCL.
[12] W. G. Broughton to E. Coleridge, 14 October 1839, MCL.
[13] W. G. Broughton *Charge Delivered to the Clergy of New South Wales, 6 October 1841* (Sydney, 1841), p. 33.
[14] W. G. Broughton to E. Coleridge, 4 May 1844, MCL.

that Broughton would have been very happy to be invited – though he dutifully added, 'I look for nothing and seek nothing.'[15]

The Colonial Bishoprics Fund was another venture which drew enthusiastic Tractarian support, and one in which Broughton played a hitherto unrecognised part. He wrote to Dr Pusey urging the need to increase the colonial episcopate.[16] Pusey, for his part, then exerted influence on Bishop Blomfield of London, who was a major force behind the plan.[17] The proposal took definite shape with the meeting at Willis's Rooms on 27 April 1841.[18] The meeting was addressed by such Tractarian stalwarts as William Gladstone, J. D. Coleridge (later Baron Coleridge) and Henry Edward Manning. George Augustus Selwyn, one of the first appointments made possible by the new Fund, later observed that Manning's speech 'never faded from my mind' and was largely responsible for his decision to be a missionary.[19]

Shortly before leaving for New Zealand in 1841, Selwyn visited Oxford and met with Newman and others. The meeting was arranged by the Scottish Tractarian lawyer James Robert Hope (later Hope-Scott), who told Newman that Selwyn wanted to see 'all the Oxford men'. Hope thought it would be preferable that 'as many good men and true as will come' should be invited to one meal and 'moderates, or whatever they are to be called' to another.[20] Newman duly invited John Keble to come to Oxford for the meeting.[21] It is clear that Selwyn made no effort to dissemble his Tractarian sympathies in the months following the publication of Tract 90.

The other Australasian appointment resulting from the Colonial Bishoprics Fund initiative was that of Francis Nixon of Tasmania. A committee was formed to raise funds for the diocese of Tasmania in May 1842 and it was a decidedly pro-Tractarian group: Joshua Watson, Edward Coleridge, Lord Courtney, T. D. Acland, T. Allies and W. J. E. Bennett.[22] The Colonial Bishoprics Fund was indeed part of a wider and fast-growing

[15] W. G. Broughton to E. Coleridge, 11 July 1847, MCL.

[16] W. G. Broughton to E. Coleridge, 3 April 1840, MCL. Unfortunately, Broughton's letter to Pusey has not been located.

[17] The role of Pusey was noted for the first time in Ruth Teale, 'Dr Pusey and the Church Overseas' in Perry Butler (ed.), *Pusey Rediscovered* (London, 1983), pp. 185–209.

[18] *Proceedings of a Meeting of the Clergy and Laity Specially called by His Grace The Lord Archbishop of Canterbury and Held at Willis's Rooms, 27th April 1841, for the Purpose of Raising a Fund towards the Endowment of Additional Colonial Bishoprics* (London, 1841).

[19] G. A. Selwyn to H. Manning, 24 December 1867, quoted in Edmund Sheridan Purcell, *The Life of Cardinal Manning, Archbishop of Westminster*, 2 vols. (London, 1895), vol. I, p. 201.

[20] J. R. Hope to J. H. Newman, *LDN*, vol. VIII, pp. 304–5, n. 3.

[21] J. H. Newman to J. Keble, 24 October 1841, *ibid.*, p. 305.

[22] 'Additional Colonial Bishoprics', *Christian Remembrancer*, 3 (1842), pp. 717–18.

enthusiasm for missions.[23] The appointment of Nixon to Tasmania was clearly the suggestion of a committee of bishops. The new government was prepared to accept the nomination to the new sees of Tasmania and New Zealand.[24] There is no indication that Broughton was in any way consulted: for his part he thought Coleridge would be appointed and advised him not to accept but wait for a 'higher and more conspicuous dignity' (by which he obviously meant Sydney).[25]

The appointment of Nixon was hardly surprising. Although he had been at Oxford before the Oxford Movement began, his published works prior to his consecration as bishop indicate his Tractarian sympathies. He had achieved some prominence as one of the Six Preachers at Canterbury Cathedral. He was certainly no uncritical admirer of the Reformation, believing that one of its effects was 'to destroy, in great part the authoritative teaching of the Church'. Nixon never disguised his support for Tractarian views. In his published Canterbury sermon he lauded Pusey and rejoiced that the *Tracts for the Times* were having a marked influence.[26] By the time he published his *Lectures on the Catechism*, prior to his departure for Tasmania, he was even more decidedly Tractarian. Among other things, he argued for a daily celebration of the Eucharist.[27] Nixon never lost his great respect for the 'extraordinary energy that has latterly marked the efforts of the Church at home', although he did distance himself from the extremists 'who have exhibited a lamentable tendency to touch, with undue tenderness, on the glaring defects and corruptions of Rome'.[28] Hostile elements in the colonial press found in Nixon's published work a large store of material to criticise. For instance, after quoting Nixon's claim that in the Eucharist 'a great and mysterious change takes place in the consecration of the bread and wine, a change of character but not of substance', the *Colonial Times* concluded that this was 'just as bad as the Roman Catholic doctrine of transubstantiation, but not half so honestly stated'.[29] This particular journal was typical in asserting that

[23] Anthony Grant, *The Past and Prospective Extension of the Gospel by Missions to the Heathen* (London, 1844); [H. Manning], 'The Missions of the Church', *English Review*, 2 (1844), pp. 137–78. Manning's review of Grant's Bampton lectures was later reprinted in Australia.

[24] Lord Stanley to Sir R. Peel, 17 April 1842, BL, Peel Papers, Add. Ms. 40467.

[25] W. G. Broughton to E. Coleridge 14 January 1843, MCL.

[26] F. Nixon, *A Sermon Preached in the Cathedral of Christ, Canterbury, before His Grace the Archbishop at the Triennial Visitation of the Deaneries of Bridge and Elham* (London, 1840), pp. 10–11.

[27] F. R. Nixon, *Lectures Historical, Doctrinal and Practical, on the Catechism of the Church of England* (London, 1843), p. 625.

[28] F. R. Nixon, *A Charge delivered to the Clergy of the Diocese of Tasmania at the Primary Visitation in the Cathedral Church of St David, Hobart Town* (Hobart Town, 1846), pp. 12, 27.

[29] *Colonial Times* (Hobart), 24 July 1846 and 10 April 1846.

episcopacy was 'more calculated to alienate, than foster and encourage, true religion'.[30] It maintained an unrelenting hostility to bishops, whom it portrayed as those 'greedy, idle, proud, overbearing, and often dissolute men who profanely claim to be the successors of Our Lord's Apostles'.[31] The editor of the *Colonial Times*, although not particularly perceptive in matters theological, confidently pronounced Nixon a 'Puseyist'.[32] In each colony these charges were repeated *ad nauseam*. Charles Perry, bishop of Melbourne, was spared these relentless attacks, and William Tyrrell, bishop of Newcastle, was apparently never subjected to them. But the other Tractarian bishops faced a hostile press.

Nixon was to endure many difficulties in Tasmania. It was one thing to come armed with a high theology of episcopacy buttressed by an authoritarian temperament. It was quite another to assert that authority over a largely recalcitrant clergy. He also faced serious legal difficulties. It appeared that his Letters Patent did not, in fact, ensure that he was competent to establish a consistorial court through which he could discipline clergy. A visit to the United Kingdom in 1846 did not result in any support from the government, whose only suggestion was that he should have recourse to the Colonial Legislative Council; the very idea horrified Nixon. The only alternative was for the bishops and clerical representatives in the various colonies to 'frame a body of canons which would be applicable to the exigencies of our missionary church'.[33]

In the event, the Oxford Movement provided a way forward. Nixon's younger clergy were of a marked contrast in character to the older. Foremost among them was Fitzherbert Marriott (1811–90), a cousin of Charles Marriott and an Oriel man who is often mentioned in the Newman's letters and diaries as being present at breakfast or dinner with Newman; he was, indeed, another instance of successful Tractarian networking. When he returned to the colony in 1846 Marriott brought with him six young clergymen, well educated, hard working and all Tractarians. They gave unstinting loyalty to Nixon, and their collective careers were one of the success stories of the catholic revival within Anglicanism.

The next three dioceses to be established in the 1840s were Adelaide, Melbourne and Newcastle. In none of these was the Church so well developed as in the older centres of Sydney and Hobart. Broughton's fertile mind had even toyed with the idea of extending the episcopate on his own authority, and he did venture to New Zealand before Selwyn's

[30] *Ibid.*, 16 October 1846. [31] *Ibid.*, 5 December 1843. [32] *Ibid.*, 27 July 1843.
[33] F. R. Nixon, MS dated 25 October 1847, Christ College, Hobart [no addressee].

appointment, though his Letters Patent did not authorise him to do so. Another problem exercised Broughton: the Roman Catholics had appointed a bishop in Adelaide before the Anglicans.[34] This 'holy rivalry' to be first past the episcopal post was a feature of colonial life, having little to do with pastoral needs.

Determined not to be caught again, Broughton acted on his own initiative and suggested that one of his clergymen, Robert Allwood, be appointed bishop of Newcastle. Allwood was, as already mentioned, Rector of St James in King Street, Sydney. Broughton had earlier described him as 'a staunch Tractarian but sound and cautious'.[35] This 'soundness', coupled with Broughton's offer to surrender half his £2,000 salary to endow the diocese, was appreciated by the government. It helped enormously to have Gladstone at the Colonial Office from December 1845 to July 1846. All was effortlessly decided. Then Allwood, for his part (appropriately), expressed himself unworthy for so high an office. Broughton completely misinterpreted these pious sentiments and had the already prepared Letters Patent rescinded.[36] Broughton would not recommend any other colonial cleric. However, Allwood's nomination proved a very successful non-event: a reception was given for him 'on the occasion of his *not* being appointed to the bishopric of Newcastle'.[37]

Gladstone's departure from the Colonial Office in 1846 meant that a window of opportunity had closed. While the government was prepared to accept Broughton's cut in salary, and welcomed funds raised by the Colonial Bishoprics Fund, it was adamant that the Crown would make appointments. Moreover, James Stephen at the Colonial Office had little time for an episcopacy based on 'such elements of mysticism and sacerdotal supremacy as are to be extorted from the Anglican liturgy'.[38] In his view the episcopal office was one created by the state.[39] This did not augur well for any further colonial appointments. On the other hand, it did not mean that William Howley, the archbishop of Canterbury, was a mere cipher. Although it is clear that Archbishop Howley did not have the final word, he frequently made clear his preference for the appointment of one who had 'the same principles [as] the Bishop [Broughton]'.[40]

34 W. G. Broughton to E. Coleridge, 15 October 1844, MCL.

35 W. G. Broughton to E. Coleridge, 14 February 1842, MCL.

36 Allwood confided in Charles Kemp (1813–64), part-owner of the *Sydney Herald*. 'Diary of Charles Kemp', Mitchell Library, Sydney, A 2064, p. 7.

37 *Sydney Morning Herald*, 8 October 1847.

38 J. Stephen to J. Venn, 15 November 1842, Church Missionary Society, London, Venn Mss., C.29.

39 J. Stephen to J. Venn, 3 June 1842, Church Missionary Society, London, Venn Mss., C.29.

40 W. Howley to Lord Grey, 21 December 1846, Grey Papers, University of Durham Library, GRE/B80/5/8–10.

As various names were canvassed, it was Stephen who suggested Charles Perry as 'a man of fortune and of most remarkable munificence in the use of it'.[41] He was to assume the poorest of the three new dioceses with but three churches and three clergymen.[42] However, rumours of the horrors of Puseyism had reached distant Melbourne. An anxious layman wrote to Broughton: 'There is much said about it and against it by people here [and it is said] that Puseyism is next door to Popery ... I will never go to Church if [our new clergyman] is a Puseyite.'[43] Local fears, however, were soon assuaged by Perry's warm endorsement of the Bible Society.[44] Unlike Broughton, who had laboured long to articulate a separate Anglican identity, Perry 'rejoice[d] in the opportunity ... of cooperating with Evangelical Protestant Dissenters'.[45] His impeccable credentials were confirmed shortly after his arrival by his public rebuff of greetings from the local Roman Catholic priest, Patrick Geoghegan. Perry was clearly 'an uncompromising anti-Puseyite'.[46] His theological position was clear: '[W]hilst retaining, as I have always done, the right, and deeply impressed with the duty, of private judgement in religious matters, I became practically identified with [the evangelical school] in all their undertakings.'[47] In practice, as a bishop, Perry could be as authoritarian as any. But this was certainly not due to any exalted notion of the episcopal office. Moreover, from a Tractarian perspective his sacramental theology was questionable: any admission of a doctrine of the real presence, he claimed, had only led to 'unscriptural assumption of dignity and power by the clergy'.[48]

Tractarians for their part lamented Perry's appointment.

Of the four ... consecrated Bishops, one is an avowed maintainer of ... doctrinal errors ... We ask, then, in the name of all that is consistent, what possible right can Churchmen have to give an unqualified 'God speed!' to such a Consecration? ... We earnestly deprecate any supineness on the part of our Church at large in conniving at the future admission of these errors into the colonial Episcopate.[49]

Broughton, too, had reservations. Perry's sentiments 'find no echo in *my* mind or principles'. But he relied on his powers of persuasion and wide

[41] J. Stephen to Lord Grey, 18 December 1846, Grey Papers, University of Durham Library, GRE/B126/11–132.

[42] *Colonial Church Chronicle*, 1 (1847), p. 14.

[43] Charles Sladen to W. G. Broughton, 9 July 1843, Society for the Propagation of the Gospel, London, Australian Papers, Box 14.

[44] *Argus* (Melbourne), 12 October 1847. [45] *Ibid.*, 12 October 1847.

[46] *Port Phillip Patriot*, 10 February 1848.

[47] Charles Perry, 'Notes on My Life' in G. Goodman, *The Church in Victoria during the Episcopate of the Right Reverend Charles Perry* (London, 1982), p. 58.

[48] Charles Perry, *A Catechism on the Sacrament of the Lord's Supper* (Melbourne, 1871), p. 15.

[49] *Christian Remembrancer*, 14 (1847), pp. 426, 428, 431–2.

experience: 'I hope he *will* come by Sydney that he may have the opportunity at least of benefiting by warnings which my experience will justify me in communicating.'[50]

If Perry was something of the 'odd man out', the other two 1847 appointments did not disappoint Broughton. Augustus Short's promotion to Adelaide came after protracted efforts to secure an endowment for the bishopric. Plans for both a diocese in Adelaide and a diocese of Tasmania had been mooted in the early 1840s. After lengthy correspondence, the irrepressible Edward Coleridge induced Baroness Angela Burdett Coutts to donate £35,000 to endow the sees of Adelaide and Cape Town. Coleridge schooled the Baroness in suitably Tractarian sentiments. He wrote to her to

> disapprove and dissuade you from supporting the *Church* Missionary Society, as it is called, but which really does not deserve that name, seeing it has [numerous] supporters who hate Episcopacy, deny Apostolical Succession and do not hold some of the most sacred and essential doctrines of Christianity.[51]

With the Burdett Coutts bequest in place, arrangements for the new Australian diocese were completed in record time. It is not clear who nominated Short. It might have been Benjamin Harrison. In any event, Lord Grey (the Colonial Secretary) accepted this nomination without demur: Short having been Bampton lecturer the previous year and being related to the bishop of St Asaph seemed qualifications enough.[52] Archbishop Howley ranked him 'considerably above the level of those who can in general be considered to make the sacrifice required' to assume a colonial bishopric.[53]

Short was a not-uncritical follower of the Tractarians. He consistently distanced himself from any criticism of the Reformation[54] and voted to condemn Ward's *Ideal of the Christian Church*, though he did not agree with disciplinary action taken against Ward.[55] On the other hand, he took part in what the historian of the movement, Yngve Brilioth, regarded as the most important Tractarian project – *The Library of the Fathers*.[56]

50 W. G. Broughton to E. Coleridge, 26 October 1847, MCL.

51 E. Coleridge to Lady A. Burdett-Coutts, 21 March 1846, Burdett-Coutts Papers, LPL, Ms 1384, fols. 4–9.

52 W. Howley to Lord Grey, 6 March 1847; Lord Grey to W. Howley, 9 March 1847, Grey Papers, University of Durham Library, GRE/B80/5/39 and GRE/B80/5/41.

53 W. Howley to Lord Grey, 6 March 1847, Grey Papers, University of Durham Library, GRE/B80/5/39.

54 A. Short to E. B. Pusey, 23 November 1841, quoted in F. T. Whitington, *Augustus Short: First Bishop of Adelaide: A Chapter of Colonial Church History* (Adelaide, 1887), pp. 22–3.

55 A. Short to E. B. Pusey, 29 November 1841, quoted *ibid.*, p. 26.

56 Yngve Brilioth, *The Anglican Revival: Studies in the Oxford Movement* (London, 1933), p. 141.

Short began a translation of St Hilary's *On the Trinity*. Regrettably this was never completed, though he did complete a considerable amount of work. Perhaps Short was discouraged by Newman's meticulous demands as editor.[57]

Rather more controversial was Short's written defence of Tract 90. This was never published, but the manuscript was used extensively by F. T. Whitington, Short's first biographer.[58] It has not, however, been located among any of Short's extant papers. In this defence of Tract 90 Short made clear his belief in a Church that taught with authority:

> How is it objectionable to say that the Article teaches that the Church derives 'the faith' *wholly* from Scripture, and yet not *solely* from Scripture? Do not Article viii, the Homilies, in every page, and the Injunctions of 1571, show plainly that the Church *does* use the medium of Catholic consent to ascertain the *right interpretation* of Scripture. Have *we* not derived our *connected* view of the Articles of our systematic faith from the Apostles' Creed? If so, we cannot say that Scripture is the *sole*, though it is the *supreme* Rule of Faith. That rule is indeed *wholly* Scriptural and yet not *solely* obtained by us from Scripture.[59]

Two friends dissuaded Short from showing his defence to A. C. Tait (one of the four tutors who made the first move against Tract 90).[60] Had the defence been more widely known, it is doubtful that Short would have been considered suitable, even for a colonial diocese.

In 1846, as noted previously, Short was Bampton lecturer at Oxford and in that turbulent time sought to take an eirenical approach in his lectures, which were published under the title *The Witness of the Spirit with Our Spirit*. None the less, Short's basic Tractarian approach was evident, and reflected in part in his firm belief in baptismal regeneration and in part in his views, similar to those of Newman and Isaac Williams, that our knowledge of things divine depends largely on our obedience to the will of God and that for this we need the Church, ministry and sacraments.[61]

The last of those who were to meet in Sydney in 1850 was William Tyrrell of Newcastle. At the time of his appointment the vast diocese of Newcastle had more clergy churches and people than Melbourne. It is not clear how Tyrrell came to be appointed. He had declined an invitation to accompany his close friend Selwyn to New Zealand, but was willing to accept the diocese of Newcastle, once Robert Allwood's nomination had been

[57] J. H. Newman to A. Short, 28 August 1840, quoted *LDN*, vol. VII, pp. 381–3.

[58] Whitington, *Augustus Short*, pp. 31–41. [59] *Ibid.*, p. 32. [60] *Ibid.*, pp. 27–8.

[61] A. Short, *The Witness of the Spirit with Our Spirit* (Oxford, 1846), pp. 4, 9–11, 55–8.

withdrawn. His bishop, Charles Sumner of Winchester, thought highly of him.[62] Once in Australia he enjoyed easy relations with Broughton, who judged him an 'active minded man: full of vigour and indefatigable in his exertions. We agree most cordially.'[63] Tyrrell, for his part, thought much of 'the noble Bishop of Sydney', and was willing to accept him as 'a guide and director on all occasions of doubt or difficulty'.[64] Everything known about Tyrrell confirms Broughton's judgement: he was a man of single purpose and dedication to the task. The wife of Broughton's successor, Mrs Jane Sophia Barker, confided to her diary of Tyrrell: 'he is *all* business … with a downright look that seemed to say "I will work and no man shall hinder me."'[65] His theology was clearly that of the Tractarians and his spirituality was to match. He wrote in his diary on the feast of St Peter in 1853:

> Rise at 5 or as soon after as I wake and give the first two best hours of the day to devotional reading of God's word and to meditation on the duties of my office and to the employment of the present day.[66]

This was no idle boast. His diary gives vivid testimony of his daily dedication to *lectio divina* in the best Benedictine tradition and to the offices of the Church. This celibate was deeply dedicated to his work as a missionary bishop and always refused any other post. If his library reveals him as one deeply steeped in the writings of the Tractarians,[67] his life marks him as one who could well be considered the ideal bishop.

These are the six bishops who met in October/November 1850 in Sydney. If the movement in England was initially transferred from the University of Oxford to the parishes, in Australia, Tractarianism at this stage was still very much an episcopal phenomenon.

It was becoming increasingly clear that the major challenge to the movement was not the conversion of Newman to Rome or the writings of the younger 'extremists' but rather the debate over whether sacramental grace was a reality or not, and whether the bishops could give a clear lead

62 C. Sumner to W. Howley, 8 March 1847, Grey Papers, University of Durham Library, GRE/B80/5/40.

63 W. G. Broughton to E. Coleridge, 4 July 1848, MCL.

64 W. Tyrrell to Hawkins, 10 July 1849, quoted in R. G. Boodle, *Life and Labours of the Rt. Rev. William Tyrrell, DD First Bishop of Newcastle N.S.W.* (London, 1889), p. 60.

65 Mrs Jane Sophia Barker, Diary, 7 July 1855, quoted in K. J. Cable, 'Mrs Barker and Her Diary', *Journal of the Royal Australian Historical Society*, 54 (1968), pp. 67–105, at p. 85.

66 W. Tyrrell, Diary, University of Newcastle Library, NSW, B 6556, fol. 190.

67 The library is in the Archives of the University of Newcastle, NSW. The library contains seventeen works by John Henry Newman, more numerous than those of any other single author; thirty-eight volumes of *The Library of the Fathers*, six volumes of *The Tracts for the Times* as well as works by other Tractarians.

in asserting the essentials of the Catholic faith. That, at any rate, was the way the *Christian Remembrancer* saw it: 'It is, and has long been acknowledged, that the great battle of the Church of England will be fought upon the cardinal doctrine of Regeneration in Baptism.'[68] The Gorham decision of 1850 offered just such an opportunity for battle. In the aftermath of the judgement Gladstone was foremost among those who wanted an authoritative episcopal statement.

While the right of English bishops to meet in synod was problematic at this time, there was no reason why colonial bishops could not do so. Broughton often mentioned to Coleridge his desire to consult with fellow bishops with the aim of 'coming to a decided understanding with one another as to the Church principles upon which we would act together'.[69] This desire assumed greater urgency in the months after the Gorham decision. Gladstone suggested to Selwyn that the colonial bishops might make a statement on baptism. Once Broughton learnt of this he reacted promptly. He now hoped to hold a synod:

> When I trust by God's grace, prompting and directing our determination, we may be enabled to fulfil, not unworthily, the duty which at this crisis we owe to the Church Universal; and more especially to that division of it in which we are ministers.[70]

Broughton informed Gladstone that although he did not know exactly what his fellow bishops thought of the controversy, they 'are perfectly qualified mentally to deal with a question so momentous as this [and would give] what they may hold to be the just interpretation of the formularies of the Church'.[71] Broughton apparently had great confidence in the episcopate and relished the controversy. He wondered why people in England had not protested more vigorously at what he considered the lack of judicial competence of the Privy Council in such ecclesiastical matters. He was confident that the Australasian bishops could act independently. 'We shall be quite free as an assembly of bishops to consult immediately.'[72] Sadly, Broughton's hopes of episcopal unanimity were shattered when he read the *Melbourne Church of England Messenger*.[73] For it was revealed there that Perry had different ideas concerning baptism.

[68] *Christian Remembrancer*, 14 (1847), p. 406.
[69] W. G. Broughton to E. Coleridge, 22 December 1843, MCL.
[70] W. G. Broughton to E. Coleridge, 10 July 1850, MCL.
[71] W. G. Broughton to W. E. Gladstone, 13 August 1850, BL, Add Mss 44,369, fols. 330–32.
[72] W. G. Broughton to E. Coleridge, 15 August 1850, MCL.
[73] W. G. Broughton to W. Tyrrell, 10 September 1850, Mitchell Library, Sydney, Ms. 913.

Not all the difficulties were theological. There was still some lingering uncertainty as to whether the colonial bishops could legally meet. However, the Attorney General made it clear that in his view the praemunire statutes did not apply to the colonies.[74] Broughton none the less thought it better not to call the proposed Sydney meeting a 'Synod' though in fact he referred to it as such in private correspondence.[75]

I have treated the Conference and its aftermath in another place.[76] The interesting fact is that the Australasian bishops did meet and did make a pronouncement on a doctrinal issue. In so readily agreeing to pronounce on the reality of baptismal grace, the bishops clearly understood their task as to witness to the faith once given to the apostles. They undertook this task despite unrelenting criticism verging on abuse mounted by the popular press; and while they were sensitive to (and later accommodating of) the role of the laity in the Church, they still calmly and deliberately exercised their unique authority. Writing to Gladstone, Broughton observed that:

> We have endeavoured to do our duty by declaring such a declaration of our sentiments on the doctrine of Baptismal Regeneration as will evince, we hope, our … adherence to the true faith of the Church and our resolution to support it by our authority … [document damaged] Melbourne … judged it right to make a declaration of his own views separate from his brethren. That he should have done so is a cause of infinite regret to me.[77]

Despite the lack of unanimity, Broughton felt a justifiable pride in having gathered his colleagues and played some part in the Tractarian story. One can argue that these early Australian Anglicans were not a mere addendum to the Tractarian story, but an integral part in it. They displayed something of the extent to which the Oxford reawakening was stirring throughout the Anglican world. However, it is also evident that as one combs through the writings of these several Australian bishops, one finds nothing of originality added to the deposit of Tractarian theology. What they did contribute was more in the area of praxis. They duly addressed a matter of 'doctrine' and did so on the basis of their 'authority'. In a period enthralled by the zest of democratic constitution-making, they took a position which appeared unpopular and which caused them no little trouble. Indeed, Broughton lamented, 'we are consigned over to

[74] *Hansard's Parliamentary Debates* (House of Commons), vol. cx (6 May 1850), cols. 1195–230.

[75] W. G. Broughton to W. Tyrrell, 10 September 1850, Mitchell Library, Sydney, Ms. 913.

[76] Austin Cooper, 'The Bishops and Baptism: Colonial Reverberations of a Tractarian Controversy', *Pacifica Australasian Theological Studies*, 18 (2005), pp. 67–84.

[77] W. G. Broughton to W. E. Gladstone, 19 November 1850, BL, Add Mss 44369, fols. 421–9.

democracy unmitigated, without any hope of escape'.[78] Yet they calmly and deliberately exercised their corporate authority.[79]

Moreover, twenty-two years before the cable link with the Australian colonies was established, and seventeen years prior to the first Lambeth Conference, these six bishops overcame 'the tyranny of distance' and thought of themselves, and acted together, as part of the one Church Catholic. Gladstone certainly thought these Australian bishops proved themselves to be a 'true Anglican episcopate'.[80]

A proper appreciation of people and events at Oxford is not sufficient for an understanding of the whole story of the Oxford Movement. A recent historian of the movement, Fr James Pereiro, has rightly observed that the 'attention focused on the main actors – particularly Newman – seems to have relegated [the supporting cast of secondary figures] even further into the shadow'.[81] The same could be said of the Tractarians beyond the United Kingdom. It is surely time to bring them out of the shadow. Their part was not merely derivative from the great drama being enacted at Oxford. Rather, they are an integral part of it and their achievements are added proof of the vitality and success of what has become known as the Oxford Movement.

[78] W. G. Broughton to E. Coleridge, 15 August 1850, MCL.

[79] This can be seen also in their confidence in adapting the Canons of 1603–4 and the establishment of the Australian Board of Missions to inaugurate missions, both 'domestic' and 'foreign'. In this latter move, they did not seem their episcopal authority limited by their various Letters Patent. 'Minutes of the Australasian Synod, Nos II and x. See 'Project Canterbury', http://anglicanhistory.org/aus/australasian_synod1850.html (accessed 11 October 2008).

[80] W. E. Gladstone to H. Manning, 25 June 1850, BL, Gladstone Papers, Add Ms 44248, fol. 71.

[81] James Pereiro, '*Ethos*' *and the Oxford Movement. At the Heart of Tractarianism* (Oxford, 2008), p. 3.

CHAPTER 6

Anglo-Catholicism in Australia, c.*1860–1960*

David Hilliard

We begin our account at the Anglican church of St James the Great at Jamestown, a small country town in a wheat- and sheep-farming area some 130 miles north of Adelaide, in the diocese of Willochra in the state of South Australia. The rectangular stone church is typical of rural South Australia, without architectural distinction, but the interior is remarkable for it is dominated by a gothic marble altar, installed in 1938 as a memorial at a cost of £700.[1] Today the altar with its six candles and tabernacle is used only on special occasions, having been supplanted by a free-standing table to allow the celebrant to face the congregation. The present priest of the ministry district that embraces Jamestown is a woman who each Sunday conducts services in churches spread over several hundred square miles. As in many other Australian country towns, the ornaments and interior furnishings of this church indicate the past influence of Anglo-Catholicism. Why is this? What does this evidence tell us about the shape and distinctive features of the Anglo-Catholicism that was planted in Australia between the 1860s and the early 1960s, when the influence of the movement reached its peak?

Anglo-Catholicism in Australia was shaped by three main influences.[2] The first was its dependence on the Church of England. Until

[1] *The Church of St James the Great, Jamestown, 1873–1975* (Jamestown, South Australia, 1975), pp. 24, 27, 39.

[2] Historical studies of Anglo-Catholicism in Australia include: Brian Porter (ed.), *Colonial Tractarians: The Oxford Movement in Australia* (Melbourne, 1989); David Hilliard, 'The Anglo-Catholic Tradition in Australian Anglicanism', in M. Hutchinson and E. Campion (eds.), *Re-Visioning Australian Colonial Christianity: New Essays in the Australian Christian Experience, 1788–1900* (Sydney, 1994), pp. 195–215; Colin Holden (ed.), *Anglo-Catholicism in Melbourne: Papers to Mark the 150th Anniversary of St Peter's Eastern Hill, 1846–1996* (Melbourne, 1997); Colin Holden, *From Tories at Prayer to Socialists at Mass: St Peter's, Eastern Hill, Melbourne, 1846–1990* (Melbourne 1996); Colin Holden, 'Rural Ritualism and Frederick Goldsmith: Anglo-Catholicism in Western Australia Before the First World War', *JRH*, 18 (1994), pp. 75–95, and *Ritualist on a Tricycle: Frederick Goldsmith: Church, Nationalism and Society in Western Australia, 1880–1920* (Nedlands, 1997); John A. Moses (ed.), *From Oxford to the Bush: Catholic Anglicanism in Australia. The Centenary Essays from the Church Chronicle, 1932–33* (Canberra, 1997). For

1981 the Anglican Church was officially called the Church of England in Australia, and the movement to create a constitution for a self-governing national church within the Anglican Communion was long and tortuous, only reaching fulfilment in 1962. The great majority of Anglicans in Australia were of British birth or descent, and the Church was numerically strongest in those regions that had been settled by immigrants from southern England. During the nineteenth century the Australian Church drew most of its clergy from England. Some rural dioceses were dependent upon a supply of British clergy until the 1950s. Australian Anglicans celebrated their historical and cultural ties with the mother Church in many ways, such as the custom of placing stones from medieval English cathedrals and ruined monasteries in the walls of cathedrals and parish churches, symbols of continuity with the pre-Reformation English Church.[3] The dominant figures in the planting of Anglo-Catholicism in Australia came to Australia directly from Britain, often inspired by a vision of planting the Catholic faith and practice in the antipodes. Their locally born successors drew their own inspiration from the English Church. A few of them were able to visit Britain themselves and were impressed by its famous ritualist churches. They eagerly read the *Church Times* and the biographies of heroes of the Catholic Revival.

Secondly, there was the vast size of the Australian continent, the rivalry between colonies (illustrated by their different railway gauges), the spread of white settlement over vast areas and a powerful sense of regional identity. This led to a system of Church government in which the diocese was powerful and the national structure was weak. From the 1840s the diocese of Australia (founded in 1836) was subdivided to create new dioceses embracing each colony and region. By 1915 there were twenty-three of them, grouped into four provinces with three extra-provincial dioceses.[4] Anglican bishops in Australia had more power than bishops in England, for they were responsible not only for diocesan administration and spiritual leadership but also for the recruitment and appointment of clergy, pastoral strategy, the raising of funds,

the history of the Australian Church, see B. Kaye, T. Frame, C. Holden and G. Treloar (eds.), *Anglicanism in Australia: A History* (Melbourne, 2002).

[3] David Hilliard, 'The Ties that Used to Bind: A Fresh Look at the History of Australian Anglicanism', *Pacifica: Journal of the Melbourne College of Divinity*, 11 (1998), pp. 265–80, at pp. 272–3.

[4] The four ecclesiastical provinces were New South Wales, Victoria, Queensland and Western Australia. The three extra-provincial dioceses were Adelaide and Willochra in South Australia, and Tasmania.

the encouragement of charitable work and the energising of their flock through regular visitations of every district. Much depended upon a bishop's personality and theological outlook. A bishop who ruled for two or three decades – as many did – placed on the diocese a strong personal imprint, for during that time he had ordained, appointed and promoted most of the clergy. When the see became vacant its clergy and lay people usually elected someone who would continue familiar policies. Over time, therefore, each diocese developed its own ethos, traditions and theological tone, which differed in subtle ways from those of its neighbours. Smaller dioceses, in which the bishop was more dominant, tended to become homogeneous in theological outlook and rarely changed direction. It was the existence of this strong sense of diocesan identity, and the theological differences between dioceses, reinforced by diocesan and provincial theological colleges, that gave the Australian Church its distinctive character. Moreover, there emerged a correlation between geography and churchmanship. Anglo-Catholicism eventually became strongest in the tropical north, the inland regions beyond the coast and the outback. In the 1950s it was said that the hotter the average temperature of the dioceses as they approached the equator, the higher the churchmanship.

Thirdly, there was the religious composition of Australia, where four major religious bodies with their origins in the British Isles – Anglican, Roman Catholic, Presbyterian and Methodist – existed alongside each other and until the mid twentieth century claimed the nominal allegiance of over 80 per cent of the population. After the mid 1830s the Church of England had no special privileges or favours from the government, so Anglicans had to adjust to being the largest of several denominations, all of them with equal status in their relationship with the state. In this religiously mixed society what did the Church stand for? The teaching of the Tractarians seemed to provide a satisfying answer. The Church of England was the ancient Catholic Church of the English people, a branch of the Catholic Church with its own inherent authority, reformed but maintaining the apostolic succession through bishops, without the unscriptural additions of the Church of Rome. In this ecclesiology, the apostolic succession became a central and defining doctrine. Anglicans had it, but other Protestants did not. At the same time, Anglo-Catholics generally had little time for the Roman Catholic Church, which in Australia, until the 1950s, was predominantly Irish in its leadership and ethos, closely linked to the Australian Labor Party. Anglo-Catholics tended to be intensely anti-papalist, quick to spell out their disagreement with the doctrines and practices of modern Roman Catholicism.[5] Unlike the experience of the Church of England, very few Australian Anglo-Catholic clergy in our period converted to Rome, and none of them were well-known or influential figures.

Anglicanism in Australia had evangelical beginnings. In New South Wales and South Australia the early clergy were firmly evangelical; in Van Diemen's Land (Tasmania) and Western Australia the pioneer clergy included a handful of pre-Tractarian high churchmen. Worship from the Book of Common Prayer was conducted exactly as it was in the homeland, churches were unadorned auditoriums dominated by the pulpit, and Holy Communion was celebrated on Sacrament Sunday once a month. During the 1840s the first clergy influenced by the Oxford Movement – moderate Tractarians – arrived in Sydney and Hobart and made modest innovations in the pattern and conduct of worship. Christ Church St Laurence in Sydney, opened in 1845, was the first complete gothic revival church in Australia, with a robed choir of men and boys, and the incumbent wore a surplice in the pulpit rather than the traditional black preaching gown.[6] Among its early parishioners were three brothers of the English 'martyr' of ritualism, Father Arthur Tooth. In Sydney Robert Tooth was a successful merchant, pastoralist and brewer, an owner of what later became one of Sydney's largest breweries, only a few blocks from Christ Church St Laurence. In the isolated Australian colonies no one knew much about 'Puseyism' except that it was Romanism by stealth and a part of a plot to 'de-Protestantize' the English Church. Almost anything that seemed to signify Tractarian influence aroused opposition, but the battle was essentially over theological ideas, not liturgical practice. In those few churches with clergy sympathetic to the Tractarians the worship was dignified but definitely not ritualist.

The second wave of ritualism reached Australia from the mid 1860s. Innovations were introduced a decade or so later than in Britain and on a much smaller scale: moderate ritualism without extremes. The spread of ritualism can be mapped in each region and in particular churches through the reordering of church interiors and the introduction of new ways of conducting worship. These included a weekly 'early celebration'

[5] Hilliard, 'The Ties that Used to Bind', pp. 273–4; Farnham E. Maynard, *The Continuity of the Church of England: A Story of the Kings and Popes of the Sixteenth Century* (Melbourne, 1939); T. M. Robinson, *Why Not Be a Roman Catholic?* (Sydney, 1942); W. H. Johnson, *Roman Catholic Assertions: A Reply* (Ballarat, Victoria, 1952).

[6] John Spooner, *The Archbishops of Railway Square: A History of Christ Church, St Laurence, Sydney* (Sydney, 2002).

of Holy Communion so that the devout could receive communion while fasting, a choral communion at 11 a.m. one Sunday a month (and later each Sunday) instead of morning prayer, the observance of the major saints' days and festivals and the season of Lent, the replacement of the small holy table by a wooden or stone altar decorated with embroidered frontals in the liturgical colours and surmounted by a brass cross, vases of flowers and two lighted candles, and the celebrant at Holy Communion wearing a coloured stole and taking the eastward position. Initially, as in Britain, these innovations were accompanied by the teaching of Tractarian doctrine, but by the 1900s they were becoming accepted as normal Anglican usages, adopted by many churches that did not identify themselves as 'high'.[7]

From the 1880s we see the introduction of more distinctively Anglo-Catholic practices such as the wearing of Eucharistic vestments and the ceremonial use of incense. Vestments were first worn regularly from 1884 at Christ Church St Laurence in Sydney and from 1887 at St Martin's, Hawksburn, in suburban Melbourne. By the beginning of the twentieth century, when the six colonies came together in a federation, vestments were worn in some twenty churches out of more than a thousand: this was a much smaller percentage of the total than in Britain. The first recorded use of incense was at St Oswald's, Parkside, in suburban Adelaide in 1891. Much later it was introduced at four churches that during the twentieth century were seen as flagships of Anglo-Catholicism: St George's, Goodwood, Adelaide 1905; St Peter's, Eastern Hill, Melbourne 1906; Christ Church St Laurence 1921; and All Saints, Wickham Terrace, Brisbane, 1923. Initially no bishop was willing to allow reservation of the sacrament, but a few clergy went ahead without permission. St George's, Goodwood, was the first church in Australia, from 1908, to have permanent reservation, and the first, in 1917, to hold Benediction and to encourage use of the rosary. The rector, Father Percy Wise, delighted in being 'extreme' and shocking Adelaide's staid diocesan establishment.[8]

As in Britain, in Australia Anglican bishops took widely different positions on ritual innovations, ranging from vigorous disapproval to quiet endorsement. Most were willing to tolerate moderate ritual if parishioners did not object. Only the strongly evangelical diocese of Sydney

[7] For the trend in one diocese, see David Hilliard, 'The Transformation of South Australian Anglicanism, *c.*1880–1930', *JRH*, 14 (1986), pp. 38–56.

[8] H. J. Harrison and J. M. Truran, *St George's, Goodwood, 1880–1980* (Adelaide, 1980), chaps. 4–6. Wise was one of the few from Australia who attended the first Anglo-Catholic Priests' Convention held in Oxford in July 1921.

took action to stall the spread of Anglo-Catholic practices, symbolised by the chasuble. From 1910 Archbishop J. C. Wright, newly arrived from Manchester, required that all clergymen licensed in the diocese should sign a declaration that they would not wear Eucharistic vestments.[9] That policy remains in force. The few Anglo-Catholic churches in Sydney took to wearing copes instead.

By 1900 we can see the beginnings of an Anglo-Catholic party, led by clergy who were overseas members of one or more of the English Anglo-Catholic societies. In relation to the total number of churches and clergy in Australia, the Anglo-Catholic party was small in size and unevenly distributed. The number of Anglo-Catholic clergy in Australia appears to have been less than in Canada and South Africa, but there were many more than in low church New Zealand. It is instructive to examine the overseas membership of two societies that attracted the most committed: the English Church Union (ECU) and the Confraternity of the Blessed Sacrament (CBS). The annual directory of the ECU for 1900, for example, recorded only one branch in Australia, based in New South Wales, though with individual members resident elsewhere.[10] Total membership in the antipodes was 112, including 48 in New South Wales, 45 in the other Australian colonies and 19 in New Zealand. Clergy comprised 42 per cent of the total. The highest clerical concentration was in Adelaide, which is consistent with a claim expressed in 1891 that Adelaide was 'one of the most Catholic dioceses in Australia'.[11] In the same year (1900) the CBS had twenty-three 'priests-associate abroad' working in Australia (compared with forty-seven in Canada, sixty-three in South Africa). Of these, thirteen were in the diocese of Adelaide.[12]

Beyond this fervent core there was a much larger body of clergy and a growing number of lay people who did not see themselves as Anglo-Catholics, for this implied a party or sect within the Church, but as English Catholics or Prayer Book Catholics whose worship and piety was based upon a Catholic interpretation of the Book of Common Prayer. They preferred the 'English Use', as expounded in Percy Dearmer's *The Parson's Handbook* (1899), and they disapproved of extravagant ceremonial and Romanising 'extremists'. Significantly, societies on the exotic wing of Anglo-Catholicism such as the Society of Mary and the Catholic League

9 Stephen Judd and Kenneth Cable, *Sydney Anglicans: A History of the Diocese* (Sydney, 1987), pp. 161–5; Spooner, *The Archbishops of Railway Square*, pp. 92–111.

10 *The Annual Directory of the English Church Union for the Year 1900* (London, 1900), pp. 541–4.

11 *The Banner and Anglo-Catholic Review* (Sydney), February 1891.

12 Confraternity of the Blessed Sacrament, *Annual Report*, 1900 (London), pp. 81–2.

have gained only a tiny following in Australia. Very few Australian churches regularly used the English Missal.

In Australia Anglo-Catholic ritualism took root in two very different social environments. In most colonies the first churches to adopt the new styles of worship were in the capital cities. A few – most famously Christ Church St Laurence in Sydney – were in inner-city and working-class districts, but (as was also the case in Britain) many more were in the developing middle-class suburbs. In Sydney, Melbourne and Adelaide the oldest churches with established congregations tended to remain evangelical or low church strongholds, largely resistant to liturgical change, whereas those churches that acquired a reputation for being 'high' (though they did not regard themselves as Anglo-Catholic) were usually located in the new and comfortable residential suburbs. Among them were St Mark's, Darling Point, and All Saints, Hunters Hill, in Sydney; Christ Church, South Yarra, and All Saints, East St Kilda, in Melbourne; and St Andrew's, Walkerville, and St Peter's, Glenelg, in Adelaide. Prosperous urban dwellers, men and women of culture and taste, liked things done 'properly'. They appreciated ornament and symbolism and could afford to beautify their churches with stained-glass windows and imported furnishings, often as family memorials. The trend towards more dignified worship and richer interior decoration to create a more 'religious' atmosphere was not confined to Anglicans. In these same suburbs (as in comparable cities in Britain and North America), it can also be observed in the wealthier Presbyterian, Methodist and Congregational churches.

More distinctive of Australia was the spread of Anglo-Catholic ritualism in the sparsely settled rural areas and the outback. This occurred because bishops of country dioceses found it hard to entice clergy from the old-established dioceses based on the capital cities and had to rely largely on clergy recruited from Britain. These British-born clergy were the instigators of change, for they included a high proportion of young men who were products of high church or Anglo-Catholic theological colleges. From the 1890s onwards, therefore, we see a wave of ritual innovations in churches in small country towns and mining centres. In Western Australia, for instance, the first churches to use vestments were not in Perth, the capital, but in remote towns such as Carnarvon and Coolgardie.

During the first thirty years of the twentieth century Anglo-Catholicism spread rapidly in rural dioceses, initially in Queensland and later in New South Wales and the other states. Under its fourth bishop, J. O. Feetham (1913–47), the diocese of North Queensland gained a reputation as the most Anglo-Catholic diocese in Australia, where by the 1940s almost every parish church had six candles on the altar, Sung Mass on Sundays, reservation of the sacrament and clergy who expected to be called 'Father'.[13] In the metropolitan diocese of Brisbane the dominant tradition was a moderate and restrained Anglo-Catholicism based upon the Book of Common Prayer. Queensland Anglicans were the first in Australia to become accustomed to seeing their bishops regularly wearing a cope and mitre.

Anglicans, if they liked the clergyman, usually adjusted to moderate changes in worship, which eventually became cherished traditions. But in dusty country towns where church life was dominated by conservative businessmen and small farmers, and where offended churchgoers had no alternative church to attend, these innovations, coupled with the new vocabulary of Anglo-Catholicism, sometimes caused explosions that echoed for years. In the isolated mining town of Broken Hill in the far west of New South Wales there were complaints from parishioners about the teaching of Father A. E. Frost and his confirmation manual that advocated confession before communion and prayer to the Virgin Mary and the saints. In 1915 the evangelical bishop of Riverina called him before a diocesan tribunal to answer charges of false teaching and breach of ritual. Frost resigned and left Australia.[14] Later, after his return to England, he became chaplain of the Community of St Margaret at East Grinstead and, under the name of Bede Frost, became a highly regarded spiritual writer. At the coastal town of Port Lincoln in the South Australian diocese of Willochra, the militant Anglo-Catholicism (and socialism) of its Welsh rector, Morgan Davies, produced a permanent split in the parish.[15] Arriving in 1927, Davies pushed and pulled the congregation of St Thomas' from old-fashioned plain worship to extreme Anglo-Catholicism (English Missal, daily Mass, High Mass, shrines, rosary and Benediction). He converted a large section of parishioners to his views but also aroused substantial opposition. In 1932 the low church dissidents formed a new congregation, recognised by the diocese, which held services in a church hall, supported its own clergyman and survived as a separate entity until the 1950s. Davies returned to England and in later years, until his death in 1951, he served as chaplain of Holloway prison in London.

[13] James Norman, *John Oliver North Queensland* (Melbourne, [1953]).

[14] Laurel Clyde, *In a Strange Land: A History of the Anglican Diocese of Riverina* (Melbourne, 1979), pp. 206–9.

[15] David Hilliard, 'The Anglican Schism at Port Lincoln, 1928–1955', *Journal of the Historical Society of South Australia*, 23 (1995), pp. 51–69.

At the local level, the principal Anglo-Catholic influences in these rural dioceses were the bush brotherhoods.[16] As a way of providing a regular ministry in sparsely settled districts – 'the bush' – they were unique to the Australian Church. The brotherhood movement emerged from a mix of ideals in the late Victorian Church: an enthusiasm for university settlements and brotherhoods as a way of meeting pastoral challenges that slipped through the existing parochial system; muscular or 'aggressive' Christianity with its appeal to a young priest's sense of adventure; and imperial loyalty – the call to do a spell of service overseas and build up the English Church in the far corners of the British Empire. In Britain, church work in the Australian outback seemed romantic; few young Australians saw it that way. Each brotherhood comprised a community of unmarried priests who took temporary vows, usually for five years, and received a small stipend and their keep. They itinerated around a vast district by horse or buggy or in a battered motor car from a central community house which maintained the liturgical life of a religious community. The first was the Brotherhood of St Andrew, founded at Longreach in western Queensland in 1897, and four more had been created by 1914. During the interwar years almost every rural diocese attempted to form a brotherhood but none survived for long. The last of the twenty brotherhoods came to an end in 1980. During their first two decades, 90 per cent of the brothers came directly from Britain and two-thirds of these were university graduates, mostly from Oxford or Cambridge. Later the proportion of Australians rose while the number of university-educated Britons declined.

During the first half of the twentieth century, the bush brotherhoods left a strong imprint on the Australian Church. Almost all the brothers were Anglo-Catholics of various hues and they planted a tradition of Anglo-Catholic worship, church decoration and piety among several generations of Anglicans who lived in the regions where they ministered. Nineteen bush brothers, mostly from upper-middle-class English backgrounds, became bishops in Australia. In 1947, the golden jubilee of the brotherhood movement, nine of the twenty-four diocesan bishops were former bush brothers and the dioceses they led were predominantly Anglo-Catholic. Through the influence of the bush brotherhoods, it was

[16] R. M. Frappell, 'The Australian Bush Brotherhoods and Their English Origins', *JEH*, 47 (1996), pp. 82–97; R. A. F. Webb, *Brothers in the Sun: A History of the Bush Brotherhood Movement in the Outback of Australia* (Adelaide, 1978); Peter F. Anson, *The Call of the Cloister: Religious Communities and Kindred Bodies in the Anglican Communion*, rev. edn (London, 1958), pp. 581–4.

the bush rather than the inner-city working-class parish that became the heartland of Australian Anglo-Catholicism. The diocese of Willochra, which includes the church at Jamestown described at the beginning of this chapter, was one of these. Its bishop in 1938 was Richard Thomas, a Welsh Anglo-Catholic who had come to Australia in 1914 to join the Community of St Barnabas in North Queensland, while the rector of Jamestown in the 1950s had once been a member of the Brotherhood of St Stephen, which had worked in the outback of South Australia.

ANGLO-CATHOLIC ORGANISATIONS

In the twentieth century Anglo-Catholics influenced the Australian Church in several fields. The first national organisation was the Australian Church Union (ACU), founded in Adelaide in 1919 and affiliated with the ECU. It soon had branches in each state, though their fortunes fluctuated. However, any hopes that the ACU would became an effective national body fell apart as a result of the diocesan loyalties of the Australian Church. Its chief contribution was to found a journal called *The Defender*, which was later reborn as the *Australian Church Quarterly* (1936–73), one of the Church's few theological journals. In 1921 the Confraternity of the Blessed Sacrament founded an Australian province which twenty-four years later had ten wards and a hundred priests-associate.

The Anglo-Catholic congresses in London in the early 1920s were the model for an Australian Anglo-Catholic convention held in Melbourne over two days in 1925 and a much more ambitious inter-diocesan gathering held in the New South Wales provincial city of Wagga Wagga in 1933 to celebrate the centenary of the Oxford Movement.[17] This was a time when a conservative and combative evangelicalism was gaining ascendancy in Sydney. A polemical pamphlet on the Oxford Movement by a prominent Sydney clergyman claimed that the Tractarian and Anglo-Catholic movements had 'struck a dagger into the heart of the Reformation'.[18]

The effect of the Wagga Wagga celebrations was to produce among Anglo-Catholics a new confidence that they had all the answers and were the way of the future. This militancy in turn helped to stoke the theological animosities that peaked in the Australian Church in the 'red book'

[17] T. R. Frame, 'Recapturing the Vision Splendid: The 1933 Anglican Inter-diocesan Oxford Movement Centenary Celebrations held in Wagga Wagga', in Moses (ed.), *From Oxford to the Bush*, pp. 146–71.

[18] S. H. Denman, *The Oxford Movement and Its Issues* (Sydney, 1932), p. 7.

case of 1944–8.[19] This began when a group of laymen in the New South Wales rural diocese of Bathurst, supported by Sydney evangelical lawyers and theologians, took action in the New South Wales Equity Court against Bishop Arnold Wylde initially for heresy and then for breach of trust, for authorising a red-covered service book that taught doctrine and ritual practices inconsistent with the doctrine of the Church of England. The 'red book' case ended up in the High Court of Australia and Wylde lost, but it did not resolve the legal issues and it poisoned relations between Sydney and the New South Wales country dioceses for years.

THE NATIONAL CHURCH

The federal union of the six colonies in 1900 to form the Commonwealth of Australia encouraged some Anglicans to think about the possibility of a strong national Church within the Anglican Communion, free to adjust its worship to local circumstances and free from the jurisdiction of English courts.[20] This vision was a long way from the Australian Church under its 1872 constitution, which was essentially a loose federation of independent dioceses and legally an integral part of the Church of England. One of the first to expound the ideal of an Australian national Church was Frederick Goldsmith, dean of Perth, who was the most visible Anglo-Catholic in Western Australia; in 1904 he was elected first bishop of Bunbury. At the 1900 general synod Goldsmith moved to change the Church's title from the Church of England in Australia and Tasmania to one that would identify the Church more closely with national life and 'show what they really were'.[21] However, infant nationalism ran up against a rising wave of imperial sentiment. The majority of the general synod, preferring the competing vision of a universal and imperial Anglicanism, opposed any change in the Church's name.

During the first decades of the twentieth century almost all the leaders of the autonomy movement stood in the Anglo-Catholic or the Prayer Book Catholic traditions. They included St Clair Donaldson, archbishop of Brisbane, 1904–21 (who returned to England in 1921 to become bishop of Salisbury); G. M. Long (bishop of Bathurst, 1911–27, Newcastle, 1928–30); J. S. Hart (bishop of Wangaratta, 1927–42); and Francis de Witt

[19] Ruth Teale, 'The "Red Book" Case', *JRH*, 12 (1982), pp. 74–89; David Galbraith, 'Just Enough Religion to Make Us Hate: An Historico-Legal Study of the Red Book Case' (unpublished Ph.D. thesis, University of New South Wales, 1998).

[20] John Davis, *Australian Anglicans and Their Constitution* (Canberra, 1993).

[21] Holden, *Ritualist on a Tricycle*, p. 166.

Batty (bishop of Newcastle, 1931–58). They were opposed by a large body of clergy and prominent lay people who valued the imperial connection and by conservative evangelicals, based in Sydney, who suspected that the call for an autonomous Church was part of a move by Anglo-Catholics to subvert the Church's doctrinal basis in the Reformation Settlement.

The path towards a constitution was long and often acrimonious, stalled at different stages by persistent distrust between dioceses and the difficulty of reconciling deeply held viewpoints. 'In seeking to gain the support of one side', Bishop Batty recalled, 'we were in constant danger of losing the support of the other.'[22] Sydney evangelicals wanted the proposed appellate tribunal (high court), which would decide on disputed matters of doctrine and practice, to have a majority of lay judges, whereas Anglo-Catholics believed that the bishops, as guardians of the faith, should comprise the majority. Another contentious issue was the status of the Prayer Book and the Thirty-Nine Articles. Were these, as the Sydney diocese insisted, 'foundation truths' to which any new formulations should conform, or could they be modified by a majority of the general synod? A few Anglo-Catholics were wary of successive drafts of the proposed constitution for very different reasons: that the structure would be too rigid and that the Church courts would be controlled by lay lawyers. Finally, with some compromise on each side, during the 1950s an agreed constitution was adopted and came into operation in 1962. Anglo-Catholics were relieved that the goal of autonomy had been achieved, but it was not the strong and unified national Church that they had envisaged in the 1920s.

RELIGIOUS COMMUNITIES

From the 1890s the religious communities of the Australian Church were involved in educational, social welfare and pastoral work. They comprised a mixture of British communities that founded branch houses in Australia along with numerous local foundations, initiated by individuals who formed communities to meet particular needs. Without effective guidance, many of these limped along and died. Altogether twenty-two communities have existed in the Australian Church. Their total membership peaked at about 160 at the end of the 1950s.[23]

[22] Joan Murray (ed.), *Francis de Witt Batty: The Bishop, the Leader, the Man. Memoirs and Extracts from His Writings* (Newcastle, NSW, 1996), p. 74.

[23] For a brief account of each community and bush brotherhood, T. W. Campbell, *Religious Communities of the Anglican Communion: Australia, New Zealand and the South Pacific*

Communities of women outnumbered those of men (14:8). Their founders and superiors were the first women to achieve prominence in the Anglo-Catholic movement in Australia. The Community of the Sisters of the Church, at the invitation of the bishops of Adelaide and Tasmania, sent its first party of sisters to Australia in 1892. They founded schools for girls, first in Hobart and then in Adelaide, Sydney, Melbourne, Perth and Canberra. On their arrival in Sydney they encountered fierce opposition from militant evangelicals, but they went ahead without episcopal approval though with the support of high church and Anglo-Catholic clergy.[24] Through their schools in the capital cities the Sisters of the Church inculcated Anglo-Catholic teaching and devotional habits into several generations of young women. The Order of St Elizabeth of Hungary worked in the diocese of Bunbury in Western Australia for almost thirty years from 1928.[25] The Society of the Sacred Advent in Brisbane was the first women's community founded in Australia, in 1892, by Sister Caroline, a former member of the Community of St John the Baptist, Clewer. Her successor, Emma Crawford (Mother Emma), was superior of the society from 1905 to 1939. During these years its work expanded to embrace the management of six boarding schools for girls in different parts of Queensland and a hospital in Brisbane. Another expression of the Australian Church was the Community of the Holy Name, based in Melbourne, which had originated as a community of deaconesses and was formally recognised as a religious sisterhood in 1912.[26] It became the largest of the religious communities in the Australian Church.

The first community of men in Australia (apart from the bush brotherhoods) was the Community of the Ascension at Goulburn, New South Wales, founded in 1921. It lasted only twenty-two years. It was succeeded by the Society of the Sacred Mission (SSM), based at Kelham in England. At the invitation of all but three of the Australian bishops, it set up an Australian province in 1946 and the following year founded a theological

(Canberra, 2007). See also Florence Stacy, *The Religious Communities of the Church of England in Australia and New Zealand* (Sydney, 1929); E. C. Rowland, 'The History of the Religious Life in Australia', *Australian Church Quarterly*, (September 1970), pp. 15–28; Anson, *Call of the Cloister*, pp. 584–7; Gail Anne Ball, 'The Best Kept Secret in the Church: The Religious Life for Women in Australian Anglicanism, 1892–1995' (unpublished Ph.D. thesis, University of Sydney, 2000).

24 T. W. Campbell, 'The Sisters of the Church and the Anglican Diocese of Sydney, 1892–1893: A Controversy', *JRH*, 25 (2001), pp. 188–206.

25 Merle Bignell, *Little Grey Sparrows of the Anglican Diocese of Bunbury, Western Australia* (Perth, 1992).

26 Lynne Strahan, *Out of the Silence: A Study of a Religious Community for Women. The Community of the Holy Name* (Melbourne, 1988).

college at Crafers in the hills overlooking Adelaide.[27] St Michael's House set out to be a Kelham in Australia. At its peak in the 1950s and 1960s the college drew students from across the country. They lived in a community under rule, almost indistinguishable from novices, and undertook a theological course over five years. The Society of the Sacred Mission, through its English members and international contacts, injected new ideas into the inward-looking diocese of Adelaide. By 1960 over a dozen Australians had made their full profession in the SSM. However, the Society was seriously affected by the theological and cultural upheavals of the late 1960s and 1970s and its numbers plummeted. The Society of St Francis (SSF) founded its first Australian house in Brisbane in 1965 as part of an extension of its work to the South Pacific and New Zealand, and for the next few decades it attracted a stream of novices and founded new houses. Until the 1960s religious communities, although numerically small compared with those of the Roman Catholic Church, had a significant role in Australian Anglo-Catholicism.

THEOLOGY

The Anglo-Catholic movement in Australia during this period included some scholarly clergy, but few had opportunities to develop their scholarship in theology or other fields. One of the reasons for this failure was the deliberate exclusion of theology from Australian universities and the small size and isolation of the Australian Church's theological colleges: there were nine in 1960.[28] This meant that the principal and one or two members of staff (often part-time) spent all their energy teaching six or more subjects to students whose educational background varied from graduates to school-leavers. They had neither the time nor intellectual stimulation for sustained thinking and writing. The most creative minds were usually found in city churches. Anglo-Catholic clerics such as Philip Micklem of St James' in Sydney, F. E. Maynard at St Peter's in Melbourne and Peter Bennie at All Saints in Brisbane read new books in theology and other fields and tried to stimulate the Church's intellectual life.

The most significant Anglo-Catholic theologian to work in Australia was Father Gabriel Hebert SSM, who came from England with an

[27] Alistair Mason, *History of the Society of the Sacred Mission* (Norwich, 1993), chap. 11.

[28] David Hilliard, 'Anglicanism', in S. L. Goldberg and F. B. Smith (eds.), *Australian Cultural History* (Cambridge, 1988), pp. 15–32, at pp. 26–8; Bill Stegemann, *Striving Together for the Faith of the Gospel: A History of St Francis' Theological College, 1897–1997* (Brisbane, 1997). St Francis' College in Brisbane was regarded as the most Anglo-Catholic of the Australian theological colleges.

established reputation as a New Testament scholar and a liturgist, and then taught theology at St Michael's House in Adelaide from 1953 to 1961. While in Australia Hebert wrote his important (and eirenic) book, *Fundamentalism and the Church of God* (1957). In the preface he acknowledged the help of two Anglican conservative evangelical friends: one of them was Donald Robinson, then vice-principal of Moore Theological College, later archbishop of Sydney. Hebert's book inspired a conservative evangelical counter-attack by J. I. Packer called *'Fundamentalism' and the Word of God* (1958) which eventually became better known than the work that provoked it. Another mid-twentieth-century Anglo-Catholic intellectual was Barry Marshall, a former bush brother, who became chaplain of Trinity College within the University of Melbourne. Widely read in modern French theology and liturgical scholarship, he influenced many, but left virtually nothing in print. Appointed principal of Pusey House, Oxford, in 1970, he died soon after his arrival in a domestic accident.

ECUMENISM

In the pluralist religious culture of Australia, where in most places Anglicans were outnumbered by other Christians, Anglo-Catholics were compelled to define their attitudes towards other denominations. For those who adhered strictly to the three-branch theory of the Church it was simple enough. Protestant bodies, lacking the apostolic succession, were in schism and properly instructed Anglicans should never attend their services or assist their religious work. Interdenominational organisations such as the Student Christian Movement were dismissed as representing 'pan-Protestantism'. In the 1930s the dean of Adelaide, only half-jokingly, used to divide the Christian world into three parts: there were Anglicans, Roman Catholics and Other Funny Religions.

At the same time, some Catholic-minded Anglicans rejected this exclusivism and played a significant part in the early ecumenical movement as bridge-builders. Among the first of these was Gilbert White, bishop of Carpentaria, 1900–15, and of Willochra, 1915–25. In 1919 he initiated a series of reunion conferences in Adelaide and Sydney, involving representatives of the Anglican and the main Protestant Churches, and he attended the world Christian conference on Life and Work at Stockholm in 1925. A second pivotal figure was Father Hebert (discussed above), who in 1955 became one of a small group of ecumenists who initiated the Australian observance of the Week of Prayer for Christian Unity. In Brisbane there was Archbishop Reginald Halse (archbishop, 1943–62), a former bush brother, who had a warm relationship with the local Roman Catholic archbishop – unusual at the time – and who also encouraged links with the Protestant Churches. He was president of the Australian Council of Churches, 1959–60, and fostered ecumenical involvement among younger clergy in Brisbane. As elsewhere, the ecumenical movement produced a line of division between liberal and conservative Anglo-Catholics.

SOCIAL ACTION

In its attitudes to social and political issues and to the Church's engagement with the wider society, Anglo-Catholicism in Australia reflected two tendencies. The first was the incarnationalist strand, which believed that every area of human life was the concern of God and that the sacramental system provided the basis for a more equitable human society. The second was the redemptionist strand, which stressed the primacy of personal religion and the relationship of the individual soul to God.[29]

Several prominent Anglo-Catholic clergy – most of them in urban parishes – were definite socialists. An early figure was Charles Marson, who served in Adelaide from 1889 to 1892, founded the first Australian branch of the Fabian Society and then returned to England, where he spent his latter years in Somerset collecting folk-songs. John Hope, rector of Christ Church St Laurence from 1926 to 1964 and a disciple of Conrad Noel, was another; he stood in the tradition of the rebellious Anglo-Catholic 'slum priest'.[30] Christian Socialism had its strongest following among Anglo-Catholics in Melbourne. F. E. Maynard, vicar of St Peter's, Eastern Hill, Melbourne, from 1926 to 1964, was an intellectual who knew something about Marxist theory and economics, was active in various left-wing organisations, published many pamphlets and articles and in 1952 visited China and Russia.[31] There was also the Brotherhood of St Laurence, which was founded for urban work by Father Kennedy Tucker in Newcastle and which moved to Melbourne in 1933. It developed into a prominent welfare agency that campaigned publicly on issues of social justice. Although its Church connections later diminished it would still draw inspiration from the Tucker legacy.[32]

[29] Gabriel Hebert SSM, 'Strands in Anglo-Catholicism', *Australian Church Quarterly* (October 1956), pp. 25–32, at pp. 30–32.

[30] L. C. Rodd, *John Hope of Christ Church St Laurence: A Sydney Church Era* (Sydney, 1972).

[31] Holden, *From Tories at Prayer to Socialists at Mass*, chaps. 15–16.

[32] Colin Holden and Richard Trembath, *Divine Discontent: The Brotherhood of St Laurence. A History* (Melbourne, 2008).

In Anglo-Catholic country dioceses, by contrast, the redemptionist tendency was stronger. The political temperature there was very different. Christian Socialists were rare (and kept quiet) and the clergy were more likely to be supporters of the conservative parties, whose politicians were sometimes pillars of the local church. During the Great Depression, in 1931, Bishop Richard Thomas advocated the suspension of parliamentary government for five years – the 'crafty, scheming politician must go' – with the country to be placed under federal and state commissioners under the direct rule of a plenipotentiary sent from England. He thought that Lord Irwin, recently Viceroy of India (and an Anglo-Catholic), would be a wise and experienced leader.[33] Only a small number of Anglicans were interested in social questions and they were rarely influential; the great majority of parish clergy saw social issues as secondary to their primary pastoral role.

In 1955–6 an English Franciscan friar conducted a preaching and teaching tour of Australia during which he visited seventeen of its twenty-four dioceses and conducted retreats for some 40 per cent of the nation's clergy.[34] This tour provided a rough indicator of the outer extent of Anglo-Catholic influence at that time. The diocese of Sydney, the largest in the country, remained an evangelical fortress, with its small Anglo-Catholic minority relegated to the edge of diocesan life. Anglo-Catholics elsewhere, in looking to the future, expected their influence to grow. No one could foresee the contentious issues and the religious and social trends of the next fifty years that would fracture the Anglo-Catholic movement and lead to its disintegration in the Australian Church.

These upheavals were not unique to Australia. Intellectual movements and liturgical changes challenged many Anglo-Catholic certainties. Urban dioceses that had been dominated by the moderate Catholic tradition became more pluralist and open to liberal theology. Anglo-Catholic institutions and organisations faded away. As we have seen, the last of the bush brotherhoods disbanded in 1980. In many areas of Church life the lack of Catholic vitality contrasted with evangelical energy and self-confidence.[35] In response to these trends, there was from the 1970s a reassertion of a more sharply defined Anglo-Catholicism among the

[33] *The Willochran* (diocese of Willochra, South Australia) (April 1931), pp. 616–17; (July 1931), p. 632.

[34] Charles Preston SSF, 'Friar's Australian Adventure', *Church Times* (London), (3, 10 May 1957).

[35] Peter Corney, 'The Future of Anglicanism in Australia in the Light of the Decline of the Anglo-Catholic Movement', *ACL News* (Sydney) (July–August 2003), pp. 5–12 – a sharp critique from an evangelical standpoint.

clergy of some dioceses. They looked towards the Roman Catholic Church and resisted the movement to ordain women as priests. The Catholic Renewal movement of the 1980s fell apart over the issue of the ordination of women (eventually authorised by general synod in 1992), which produced an acrimonious split between liberal Catholics and traditionalists.[36] Some of the latter joined traditionalist organisations with an oppositional stance or they seceded to the Anglican Catholic Church in Australia, formed as a diocese in 1988, which is a member church of the Traditional Anglican Communion. At the beginning of the twenty-first century, a diffuse and mildly liberal Anglo-Catholicism is still an influential force in many parts of the Australian Church and scholars in the Catholic tradition have left their mark on modern liturgies, but only a handful of dioceses, and some twenty parishes elsewhere, maintain a distinctly Anglo-Catholic identity.

CONCLUSION

Although derived from Britain, and introduced and promoted by British clergy, the Oxford and Anglo-Catholic movements in Australia were moulded by their new environment and eventually assumed a distinctive shape. In the expanding settler society of Australia, the emphasis was on imparting Catholic teaching and the provision of a pastoral ministry: elaborate ceremonial and theological scholarship was peripheral. The principal agents of Anglo-Catholic influence were bishops of Anglo-Catholic sympathies and the clergy they recruited, high church theological colleges which prepared locally born candidates for ordination and religious communities, including the bush brotherhoods that were founded from the 1890s to minister in sparsely settled areas. However, the influence of bishops was decisive. For all these reasons, the spread of Anglo-Catholicism was uneven. At its height of influence in the mid twentieth century, it was strongest in rural and outback Australia, notably in Queensland, but was a minor presence in the two largest dioceses of Sydney and Melbourne.

In Australia Anglo-Catholicism was never a tightly organised or unified movement. It contained diverse strands: social and political radicals, conservatives, ecumenists, British Catholic nationalists and those, mostly clergy, who were seen as 'extreme'. The core of committed followers who

[36] Colin Reilly (ed.), *Renewing the Drifting Church: Australian Anglican Catholic Renewal Retreat-Conference, May 1983* (Melbourne, 1983).

attended avowedly Anglo-Catholic churches or joined 'Catholic' societies was quite small. The influence of Anglo-Catholicism, however, was far wider, extending to many Anglicans who did not see themselves as members of a Church party. A moderate Anglo-Catholicism, based upon a Tractarian interpretation of the Book of Common Prayer and claiming continuity with the pre-Reformation English Church, provided the basis for a confident Anglican identity in a religiously mixed society.

CHAPTER 7

The Oxford Movement and the United States

Peter B. Nockles

The prolonged but unsuccessful campaign for a resident Anglican bishop in the North American Colonies was a contributory cause of the American Revolution. For dominant Whig, nonconformist and latitudinarian opinion, the move to introduce a native episcopacy, though supported by such native high churchmen as Samuel Johnson (1696–1774), first president of King's College, New York,[1] was presented as part of a plot to subvert American liberties and impose the kind of 'Laudian' despotism and sacerdotal aggression that had induced their Puritan forebears to flee to North America in the 1620s and 1630s. The Church of England in America and, in particular, the high church understanding of the Church was tarnished by associations with Toryism and eventually Loyalism. Anglican Loyalists such as Jonathan Boucher (1738–1804), Myles Cooper (*c.* 1737–85) and (for a time) Thomas Bradbury Chandler (1726–90), retreated to the mother country and inveighed against rebellion.[2] Thus the American Church lost many of her best clergy and laity, for a time was without government or discipline and was weakened by internal division. Although Samuel Seabury (1729–96), the first bishop in the United States, was a high churchman and owed his consecration

[1] See E. E. Beardsley, *Life and Correspondence of Samuel Johnson* (New York, 1874). Johnson was a staunch opponent of latitudinarianism and a close friend of contemporary English high churchmen such as the dominant Oxford 'Hutchinsonians' George Horne (1730–92), president of Magdalen College, Oxford, 1768, and bishop of Norwich 1792; William Jones of Nayland (1726–1800); and George Berkeley. He was highly critical of the 'ill-effects' of the popularity in North America of the sermons of Archbishop Tillotson. *Ibid.*, p. 231.

[2] R. Ingram, *Religion, Reform and Modernity in the Eighteenth Century: Thomas Secker and the Church of England* (Woodbridge, 2007), pp. 209–59; P. M. Doll, *Revolution, Religion, and National Identity. Imperial Anglicanism in British North America, 1745–95* (London, 2000), chap. 5; C. D. Loveland, *The Critical Years. The Reconstruction of the Anglican Church in the United States of America, 1780–1789* (Greenwich, CT, 1956); J. Boucher, *Reminiscences of an American Loyalist, 1738–1789*, ed. J. Bouchier (Boston, 1925). Boucher, who became vicar of Epsom, was the author of *A View of the Causes and Consequences of the American Revolution in Thirteen Discourses* (London, 1797), in which he blamed the American Revolution on the failure to establish episcopacy in the thirteen colonies.

to Scottish Episcopalian Nonjurors, the model of American episcopacy ultimately adopted was a latitudinarian one with the principle of popular election.[3]

As old wounds healed, a high church revival ensued in New York inspired by Connecticut churchmanship[4] under the leadership of John Henry Hobart (bishop of New York, 1811–30).[5] There was an emphasis on the divine constitution of the Church and on the primitive Church as the model for ecclesiology and apostolic order.[6] As Bishop Hobart explained to his Presbyterian critics who had accused him of urging 'extravagant and arrogant pretensions' on behalf of his communion, this was part of a concerted need to re-educate American Episcopalians in the principles of their own church; principles which Hobart himself, as he candidly admitted, had violated 'through the want of correct information'.[7] A renewed sense of affinity with the mother Church of England developed: Hobart's writings owed a debt to his English high church contemporary Archdeacon Daubeny (1745–1827),[8] while both Bishop Hobart and his 'low church' rival, Philander Chase, bishop of Ohio (from 1819) made fund-raising visits to England in 1823–4.[9] These visits helped raise the English as well as Scottish profile of the American Church.[10] Bishop Hobart was courted

[3] F. V. Mills, Sr, 'Mitre without Sceptre: An Eighteenth-Century Ecclesiastical Revolution', *Church History*, 39 (1970), pp. 365–71, at p. 371.

[4] The tradition of Connecticut high churchmanship can be dated back to 1722, when seven Congregationalist theologians of Yale University, led by its president, Samuel Cutler, read themselves into a conviction that their orders were invalid and made the hazardous voyage to England to gain episcopal ordination. Samuel Johnson, born in Guildford, Connecticut in 1696, was one of the seven Yale 'apostates' of 1722. He modelled King's College, New York, on an Oxford college. He, along with Myles Cooper, Johnson's Oxford-educated successor, Thomas Bradbury Chandler, and Samuel Seabury, the first American bishop, consecrated by nonjuring Scottish bishops in 1784, served as transmitters of this high church tradition to a later generation. For Bishop Seabury, see E. E. Beardsley, *The Life and Correspondence of Samuel Seabury* (Boston, 1882); B. Steiner, *Samuel Seabury 1729–1791. A Study in the High Church Tradition* (Oberlin, 1971).

[5] J. McVickar (ed.), *The Early Life and Professional Years of Bishop Hobart ... with a preface containing a history of the Church in America, by W. F. Hook* (Oxford, 1838).

[6] See P. Doll, 'The Idea of the Primitive Church in High Church Ecclesiology from Samuel Johnson [of New York] to J. H. Hobart', *Anglican and Episcopal History*, 65 (1996), pp. 6–43.

[7] J. H. Hobart, *An Apology for Apostolic Order and Its Advocates* (New York, 1807), p. 32.

[8] W. Berrian (ed.), *The Posthumous Works of the late Rt Rev John Henry Hobart, bishop of the Protestant Episcopal Church in the United States, with a memoir of his life*, 3 vols. (New York, 1833). It has been claimed that Daubeny's writings were first introduced to North America by John Bowden, head of an Episcopal academy in Connecticut in 1801. R. B. Mullin, *Episcopal Vision/American Reality. High Church Theology and Social Thought in Evangelical America* (London, 1986), p. 22.

[9] Hobart spent two years in Europe from September 1823 to October 1825. J. C. Emery, *John Henry Hobart* (August, 1921), p. 13.

[10] For evidence of the interest aroused in Britain, even prior to the visits, see 'State of the Episcopalian Church in the United States', *British Critic*, 17 (1822), pp. 540–55, 579–95.

by English high churchmen, notably those of the so-called 'Hackney Phalanx' such as Joshua Watson (1771–1855) and Henry Handley Norris (1771–1850).[11] On the other hand, Bishop Chase, who gave flattering accounts of attending divine worship in Manchester's Collegiate Church and Oriel College, Oxford (where he stayed as the guest of the provost, Edward Copleston), during this visit,[12] was lionised primarily by Anglican Evangelicals, and attracted criticism from English high churchmen,[13] a pattern that was replicated on Bishop Chase's later visit to England in 1835, when he failed to impress the Oxford Tractarians.[14] There were some notable exceptions such as Alexander Veits Griswold, bishop of the Eastern Diocese from 1811,[15] but the American Church never had a strong Evangelical component. It was later maintained, partly because of the opposition of the Episcopal Church to 'the Puritanism of revolutionary times', that it always had 'an anti-evangelical stamp and tendency'.[16]

This American high church revival spread, and by the early 1830s, partly in consequence of its separation from the state and the entanglements of establishment,[17] and its need to define itself against the dominance of protestant sects, the American Church was more considered catholic in feeling and teaching than the Church of England; one scholar has claimed that it

11 G. Best, 'Church Parties and Charities: The Experience of Three American Visitors in England 1823–1824', *EHR*, 78 (1963), pp. 243–67.

12 *Bishop Chase's Reminiscences: An Autobiography*, 2 vols. (Boston, 1848), vol. I, pp. 218–21. Chase made later fund-raising visits, such as in 1836, attracting further Anglican Evangelical support. M. Holroyd (ed.), *Memorials of the Life of George Elwes Corrie* (Cambridge, 1890), p. 43.

13 The 'Hackney Phalanx' high churchman William Van Mildert, bishop of Durham, described Bishop Chase as 'vain & pragmatical, & perhaps fanatical'. Bishop William Van Mildert to H. H. Norris, 8 May 1824, Norris Papers, Bodleian Library, Oxford, Ms Eng. Lett. c. 789, fol. 120.

14 See n. 73 below.

15 J. S. Stone, *Memoir of the Life of the Rt. Rev Alexander Griswold* (Northampton, 1854).

16 J. S. Stone, *A Memoir of the Life of James Milner* (New York, [1870]), pp. 625–6. For evidence from 1811 of the growth of Evangelicalism (partly as a result of the influence of Bishop Griswold), and of Evangelicalism's delicate relation to high churchmanship within the Protestant Episcopal Church, see D. H. Butler, *Standing against the Whirlwind: Evangelical Episcopalians in Nineteenth-Century America* (Oxford, 1995); Mullin, *Episcopal Vision/American Reality*.

17 Bishop Hobart upset his English high church friends, after his fund-raising visit to England in 1823–4, by his controversial assertion of the superiority of the American Episcopal Church over its English mother on account of its freedom from the limitations imposed by a state connection and religious establishment. See J. H. Hobart, *The United States of America compared with some European countries, particularly England*, 2nd edn (New York, 1826), esp. pp. 31–3. For all their admiration of Hobart's theological principles, English high churchmen, especially those 'Hackney Phalanx' churchmen who had had contact with the residual tradition of Anglican Loyalism represented by Jonathan Boucher, were puzzled by Hobart's combination of high churchmanship and 'republican' principles. Joshua Watson was critical of the American Episcopalian ecclesiastical model and even tried to win over Bishop Hobart to the merits of the Church of England's Church–state model. E. Churton, *Memoir of Joshua Watson*, 2 vols. (London, 1861), vol. II, p. 155.

'needed the Oxford Movement less than did the Church of England'.[18] It was precisely the independence of the American Church and its freedom from state control which in the mid 1820s impressed the influential fellow of Oriel College, Oxford and mentor of John Henry Newman, Richard Whately (1787–1863), future archbishop of Dublin. The anti-Erastian anonymous *Letters of an Episcopalian* (1826), almost universally attributed to Whately, apparently owed something to the successful example of the disestablished American Episcopalian Church: Whately even referred to his Episcopalian pamphlet as 'the address to the American episcopalians'.[19] By the mid 1830s, the expanding episcopacy in North America was attracting admiring notice from all parties in the Church of England.[20]

Circumstances had already forced American churchmen to address the questions – the divine origin of the Church, apostolical succession, baptismal regeneration, the real presence and Eucharistic sacrifice, the value of tradition – which the *Tracts for the Times* propounded.[21] Many believed that the tenets first presented in the *Tracts* 'contained nothing more than American high churchmen had taught'.[22] Bishop Hobart was hailed not only as 'the father of American High Churchmanship' but also as in many ways 'the foster father of the Oxford Movement'.[23] Bishop Hobart, who proudly claimed the title of 'high churchman',[24] had a considerable influence upon the Oxford Tractarians, partly through the publication in Oxford of McVickar's biography and the English high

[18] H. Caswall, *America and the American Church* (London, 1839), p. 334; J. T. Addison, *The Episcopal Church in the United States* (New York, 1951), p. 156; G. E. DeMille, *The Catholic Movement in the American Episcopal Church*, 2nd edn (New Brunswick, 1950), p. 40.

[19] P. Corsi, *Science and Religion. Baden Powell and the Anglican Debate, 1800–1860* (Cambridge, 1988), pp. 86–8, esp. p. 88n.7. Whately probably met Bishop Hobart on his visit to Oriel College in 1824, when Hobart was entertained by Provost Copleston.

[20] Holroyd (ed.), *Memorials of… George Elwes Corrie*, p. 43.

[21] W. F. Cread, *A Discourse in Commemoration of William Rollinson Whittingham, Bishop of Maryland* (New York, [1879]), p. 22.

[22] W. F. Brand, *Life of William Rollinson Whittingham, fourth Bishop of Maryland*, 2 vols. (New York, 1886), vol. 1, p. 363.

[23] It was argued by a contemporary following Hobart's death in 1832 that Hobart's publications had led to there being 'a more general and correct knowledge … among the people of our communion in the United States, respecting the government of the Church, the beauty and excellence of her forms, the purity of her principles, and the spirituality of her devotions, than even in England'. [J. Strachan], *A Letter to the Rev. Thomas Chalmers … on the life and character of the Right reverend Dr Hobart, Bishop of New-York* (New York, 1832), p. 9. See also E. de Waal, 'John Henry Hobart and the Oxford Movement', *Anglican Theological Review*, 65 (1983), pp. 324–31. J. W. Burgon singled out Hobart and the American Church for 'preparing the way' for the Oxford Movement. J. W. Burgon, *Lives of Twelve Good Men*, 2 vols. (London, 1888), vol. 1, p. 154.

[24] *A Word for the Church: consisting of "The Churchman", and "The High Churchman Vindicated". Two Episcopal Charges by the Rt. Rev. John Henry Hobart* (Boston, 1832), p. 4.

churchman W. F. Hook's sympathetic history of the American Church.[25] In number 81 of the *Tracts for the Times*, Pusey made favourable mention of the American liturgy. Moreover, English editions of a few American Episcopalian publications in the 1830s were readily welcomed by English high churchmen as 'the offerings of the daughter to the mother' and proof of 'her not unworthy parentage'.[26] On the other hand, the ecclesiastical ties between the mother and daughter Church remained fragile. During his stay in England in 1823–4, Bishop Hobart was not allowed to preach or assist at Anglican services, since the Act that had authorised the consecration of bishops for America had also prohibited their being beneficed or officiating in the mother country.[27]

Tractarian teaching certainly found a fertile soil in the United States,[28] though the first edition of the *Tracts for the Times* was only published in New York in 1840.[29] A recent historian of the nineteenth-century Episcopal Church has suggested that the *Tracts for the Times* and other Tractarian publications were more talked about than read.[30] None the less, even some American critics of the movement conceded that most churchmen in the United States initially welcomed the teaching contained in them.[31] The General Theological Seminary in New York, with figures such as Clarence Walworth, Isaac Hecker and James McMaster, had become a hotbed of Tractarianism by the early 1840s,[32] while the Episcopal Church had several leading supporters of the movement such as Dr Samuel Seabury (1801–72), editor of *The Churchman*, George Washington Doane

[25] G. E. DeMille, *The Catholic Movement in the American Episcopal Church* (Philadelphia, 1941), p. 60; *The Oxford Movement in America by the Rev. Clarence Walworth. Reprinted from the edition of 1895, with an introduction by J. N. O'Brien* (1974), p. vi; McVickar (ed.), *Early Life and Professional Years of Bishop Hobart.*

[26] Henry Melville's preface to J. H. Hopkins, *The Church of Rome in her primitive purity, compared with the Church of Rome at the present day*, 1st London edn (London, 1839), p. xvi.

[27] Emery, *John Henry Hobart*, p. 13.

[28] It was observed in 1839 that a 'great, and it is believed, an increasing number of the clergy, are strong in the assertion of the Apostolical succession'. Caswall, *America and the American Church*, pp. 330–31.

[29] I. Warren, *The causes and the cure of Puseyism* (Boston, 1847), p. 10; E. C. Chorley, *Men and Movements in the American Episcopal Church* (New York, 1946), p. 197. An American anti-Tractarian critic asserted in a letter to the English evangelical Daniel Wilson in 1842: 'It is evidence of the limited circulation of the "Tracts" among our churches, that there has been but one American edition of them, and that this resulted in the ruin of its publisher.' J. Milner to Bishop Daniel Wilson, 2 July 1842, quoted in Stone, *Memoir of the Life of James Milner*, p. 559.

[30] Mullin, *Episcopal Vision/American Reality*, pp. 153–4. This was the view of some Episcopalian Evangelicals, see n. 67 below.

[31] Warren, *Causes and the cure of Puseyism*, p. 10.

[32] *The Oxford Movement in America*, p. ix. Clarence Walworth's title to the original 1895 New York edition of his work was subtitled: *Glimpses of Life in an American Seminary.*

(1799–1859),[33] bishop of New Jersey, William Rollinson Whittingham, bishop of Maryland,[34] Henry Ustick Onderdonk (1789–1858), bishop of Pennsylvania, and Edgar P. Wadhams.[35] Bishop Doane, editor of the first American edition of Keble's *The Christian Year*, became a close confidant of Keble and Pusey.[36] He made an extended tour of England in 1841 and gave moral support to the Tractarian cause. This included preaching for W. F. Hook, vicar of Leeds, at the consecration of his new parish church of St Saviour's on 2 September 1841 – which Doane called a 'Catholic occasion'.[37] By 1846 at least one Episcopal clergyman in New York was receiving 'confessions, after a form furnished by Dr Pusey'.[38]

The Episcopal Church even had its Hurrell Froude parallel in the figure of the youthful Arthur Carey (1822–44), an assistant minister to Samuel Seabury at the Church of the Annunciation in New York City and one-time seminary student at the General Theological Seminary. Carey's examination and ordination in St Stephen's church, New York, in July 1843 provoked an outcry among more Protestant elements within the Episcopal Church on account of his 'Romanising' views.[39] It was claimed that Carey's ordination showed that the 'aim and intention of the Puseyites in America' was 'the same as that of the Puseyites in England – TO UNPROTESTANTISE THE CHURCH'.[40]

[33] Doane was one of the first students of the General Theological Seminary at New York under Bishop Hobart. Doane succeeded John Croes as bishop of New Jersey and became the acknowledged leader of the high church party in America.

[34] W. C. Doane. *A Memoir of the life of George Washington Doane* (New York, 1860); Brand, *Life of William Rollinson Whittingham*, vol. I, esp. pp. 238–9, 363; Cread, *Discourse in Commemoration of William Rollinson Whittingham*, p. 22. Bishop Whittingham was the editor of an American edition of William Palmer's *Treatise on the Church of Christ* (1838).

[35] C. A. Walworth, *Reminiscences of Edgar P. Wadhams, first bishop of Ogdensbur* (New York, [*c*.1893]).

[36] Bishop G. W. Doane to Sir J. T. Coleridge, Feast of St John the Evangelist, 1845, BL, Coleridge Papers, Add. Ms. 86229.

[37] Keble noted in a letter from Hursley: 'We have had Bishop Doane here, and liked him very much.' J. Keble to J. H. Newman, 19 July 1841, *LDN*, vol. VIII, p. 225. For Doane's reference to his visit, see Doane, *Life of George Washington Doane*, p. 283. Doane had published a first American edition of Keble's *The Christian Year* in Philadelphia in 1834. A second edition appeared in 1840 and a third in 1842. For Doane's acceptance of Hook's invitation to preach at Leeds, see W. F. Hook to J. H. Newman, 17 February 1841, *LDN*, vol. VIII, p. 37. The occasion was described by Florence Nightingale, who attended, as 'quite a gathering of Puseyites from all parts of England'. *LDN*, vol. VIII, p. 299.

[38] E. P. Wadhams to J. McMaster, 6 July 1846, McMaster Papers, University of Notre Dame Archives, South Bend, Indiana, Box II, Folder 4, no. 9, 1 l–m.

[39] *Letters to the Laity of the American Episcopal Church. By a Protestant Episcopalian* (Philadelphia, 1843), pp. 5–6; *A full and true statement of the examination and ordination of Mr Arthur Carey taken from "The Churchman"* (New York, 1843). Born in London, Carey had moved with his parents to the United States in 1830 when aged eight.

[40] [J. Jay], *The Progress of Puseyism. A Review of the Apologies of Dr Seabury and Mr Haight, for the ordination of Mr Arthur Carey; with remarks on the attempts now making to unprotestantise the*

The Carey ordination even attracted critical notice among anti-Tractarians in the Church of England. Edward Copleston, bishop of Llandaff and formerly provost of Oriel, was only too aware of the challenge posed by Tractarianism. He privately criticised Carey's ordination and its justification by an American bishop in a letter to his old pupil, Richard Whately, archbishop of Dublin, observing that it seemed to him 'decisive of the point that the American Episcopal Church is no longer Protestant, but Popish'.[41]

Carey corresponded with Newman, whose interest in the American Church had been evident in an article which he published in the *British Critic* in October 1839.[42] In November 1843, writing from New York, Carey urged Newman to remember him and 'a little band who are very lonely and who think that if you did but know of our existence, you would not forget us'.[43] He confided to Newman that he and his young friends from the General Theological Seminary were 'exposed to the temptation of shrinking from those points, which will make us suspected by the High Church party (the dominant one) in order to justify them in defending us'.[44] (This will have a struck a chord with Newman and his Littlemore circle, who had for some time been in a similar position in relation to such high church supporters of the movement as William Palmer of Worcester College and Edward Churton.)[45] Carey concluded his letter by a forthright avowal of the closeness that he and his like-minded friends in New York felt to Newman and his Littlemore community: 'The call on your disciples to pray for their teacher has thrilled through our hearts, and made us feel more near to you, than we are to our friends in this country.'[46]

Shortly after sending this letter, Carey, like Froude,[47] died tragically young (in Carey's case on board ship off Havana on 4 April 1844 at the age of twenty-one). Newman was approached by Tractarian supporters,

Protestant Episcopal Church (New York, 1843); C. C. Tiffany, *A History of the Protestant Episcopal Church in the United States of America* (New York, 1846), p. 475.

41 R. Whately (ed.), *Remains of the late Edward Copleston* (London, 1854), p. 75.

42 [J. H. Newman], 'The American Church', *British Critic*, 26 (1839), pp. 281–343.

43 A. Carey to J. H. Newman, 13 November 1843, *LDN*, vol. x, p. 57.

44 *Ibid.*

45 P. B. Nockles, *The Oxford Movement in Context. Anglican High Churchmanship 1760–1857* (Cambridge, 1994), esp. chap. 6.

46 A. Carey to J. H. Newman, 13 November 1843, *LDN*, vol. x, p. 57.

47 *American Catholic Quarterly Review*, 7 (1884), p. 260. 'Like Hurrell Froude in the English Oxford Movement, he took on, for the friends who outlived him, the mantle of a martyr to fearless religious truth seeking.' P. Allitt, *Catholic Converts: British and American Intellectuals Turn to Rome* (New York, 1997), p. 63.

such as Carey's seminary tutor, James McMaster (1820–74), in the General Theological Seminary in New York, to write a memoir of Carey and edit his writings.[48] The intention was to produce an American equivalent of Froude's *Remains* (1838–9). Newman, who was much affected by Carey's premature death and who always took the greatest interest in the cause of 'Apostolical' principles in North America, reluctantly declined the invitation.[49] Newman's reasons reveal a deep respect for the independence and self-identity of the high church revival in the United States. As he explained to Dalgairns:

> [I]t is plain that though Mr Carey was born on this side of the Atlantic, he is the property of America, and we must not take what is not ours. It would be a great disrespect to our American Fathers and brethren, and unjust.[50]

In a remarkable passage in the same letter, while explaining almost to himself why he was 'the last person' who should write Carey's memoir, Newman appeared to envy Carey's fate and to compare it favourably with his own embattled situation:

> He is taken away to the regret of all men, high in the favour, affection, and confidence of his church, whatever opponents he might have had besides. With me it is quite the reverse. There may be many individuals who think kindly of me, but my own church has no confidence in me, and has with great unanimity through its various organs reprobated what I have published, when it has not kept silence.[51]

McMaster and his friends, however, could only see affinities between how Newman and they were regarded in their respective churches. The feeling of desolation experienced by Newman and his followers over the premature death of Froude was replicated across the Atlantic in the anguish felt by McMaster and his friends following Carey's no less premature demise. McMaster gave expression to the sense of loss which the American Church had been dealt by Carey's demise in a letter to his friend Edgar Wadhams:

48 J. McMaster to E. P. Wadhams, 10 August 1844, McMaster Papers, University of Notre Dame Archives. For James Alphonsus McMaster (1820–86), see 'McMaster, James Alphonsus', *Catholic Encyclopaedia*, www.catholic.org/encyclopaedia/view.php.

49 Newman asked his friend, disciple and fellow resident in the community at Littlemore, Dalgairns, to inform McMaster that: 'It would be a great privilege, to be concerned in giving to the world the remains of such a man' but that he was 'not the man to do it'. J. H. Newman to J. D. Dalgairns, 7 June 1844, McMaster Papers, University of Notre Dame Archives.

50 *Ibid.* Carey's brother, perhaps mindful of the prospect of an American equivalent of Froude's *Remains*, prevented Carey's papers from being released to Dr Seabury for publication. J. McMaster to E. P. Wadhams, 8 June 1844, McMaster Papers, University of Notre Dame Archives.

51 *Ibid.*

What remains for us, dear Wadhams, but to drag out the rest of our life, remembering and acting on what we once gladly learned from him? As to doing anything in our miserable church, I am almost out of hope.[52]

It was a time to look more closely for support from the inner Tractarian coterie in Oxford itself. Newman's friend and principal disciple in the Littlemore community, John Dobree Dalgairns (1808–76) of Pembroke College, Oxford, acting as his mentor's respondent, reassured McMaster, who had already visited Newman in Oriel and in Littlemore:

You seem in some places of your letter to doubt whether I feel an interest in the Anglo-American church. You may however be quite at rest on the subject, for we all feel the greatest interest in persons who have in a great measure the same trials and temptations.[53]

Dalgairns was explicit in drawing out the analogy between the premature deaths of Carey and Froude, suggesting that the memory of the two lost prophets would serve to guide the course of the religious movement on both sides of the Atlantic. Thus, Dalgairns reminded McMaster:

Perhaps it may be of some comfort to you to recollect that in the outset of the movement in England Mr Newman and Mr Keble lost their most intimate friend Froude, and that his memory has had a great, perhaps the greatest effect on the course of the movement.[54]

In 1836 Newman informed Hook that he had 'for some time thought that a greater service could not be done to the Church, than for two or three men who agree with us to go over to New York and make it their head-quarters for several years'.[55] Newman had even wanted his one-time Oriel pupil and disciple Frederic Rogers (later Lord Blachford) to act as what Rogers facetiously called a kind of 'Apostolical bagman' who would facilitate lines of communication between Oxford and the Episcopal Church in the United States.[56] The correspondence between Dalgairns and McMaster exemplified this close communication, with Dalgairns keeping McMaster and his like-minded friends and students at the General

[52] J. McMaster to E. P. Wadhams, 25 April 1844, McMaster Papers, University of Notre Dame Archives.

[53] J. D. Dalgairns to J. McMaster, 7 June 1844, McMaster Papers, University of Notre Dame Archives.

[54] *Ibid.*

[55] J. H. Newman to W. F. Hook, 21 December 1835, *LDN*, vol. v, p. 180.

[56] 'I was a good deal amused at your American project for me … Apostolical bagman would certainly be an amusing trade.' F. Rogers to J. H. Newman, 24 February 1834, in G. E. Marindin (ed.), *Letters of Frederic Lord Blachford, Under-Secretary of State for the Colonies, 1860–1871* (London, 1896), p. 47.

Theological Seminary closely informed of events and theological developments and realignments at Oxford. Thus Dalgairns told McMaster of the condemnation of Pusey by the Six Doctors for his controversial sermon on the Eucharist in the university church of St Mary's in 1843, of the first moves to condemn W. G. Ward's *Ideal of a Christian Church* in 1844 and of the heterogeneous elements ('I do not know whether America can furnish specimens of each class') that were beginning to direct official opposition to Tractarianism within the University of Oxford.[57] By the mid 1840s, amid the growing difficulties for the movement, a common bond of sympathy united both groups on their respective sides of the Atlantic. The bond was particularly close between apparent 'Romanisers' such as Dalgairns and McMaster as they both pondered the ultimate step of joining the Roman Catholic Church. Dalgairns's comment in a letter of August 1844 to his American friend expressed this sense of common destiny: 'I am so much in the same situation as yourself that I can well appreciate the pain suffered by a person on his way to Rome, as you are.'[58]

It was appropriate that McMaster, who visited and stayed at Littlemore from 1 September until 2 September 1845,[59] should be one of the first to receive from Dalgairns in October 1845 the news 'that all those whom you saw at Littlemore have now the ineffable joy of being Catholics'.[60] There were others in the Protestant Episcopal Church deemed to be 'shaky' in their allegiance by 1845. On 28 May 1845, for example, writing from

57 J. D. Dalgairns to J. McMaster, 29 October 1844, McMaster Papers, University of Notre Dame Archives.

58 J. D. Dalgairns to J. McMaster, August 1844, McMaster Papers, University of Notre Dame Archives. McMaster's advanced Tractarian credentials are revealed by his approval of Pusey's published translations of Counter-Reformation spiritual and devotional classics at this time. J. McMaster to E. G. Wadhams, 16 April 1845, McMaster Papers, Notre Dame University Archives. In May 1845 Newman related that Frederick Oakeley had heard from McMaster that McMaster was about to go over to Rome 'at once', but noted that McMaster was 'evidently not a man to be trusted much'. J. H. Newman to J. D. Dalgairns, 28 May, 1845, *LDN*, vol. x, p, 676. McMaster duly converted to Catholicism in the summer of 1845 and accompanied fellow converts Isaac Hecker and Clarence Walworth from the General Theological Seminary to the Redemptorist novitiate in Louvain, calling on Newman at Littlemore in September 1845 on their way to Belgium. In the end, McMaster did not find the life of a religious to be suitable for him and returned to New York and became a prominent Catholic journalist and editor. Isaac Thomas Hecker (1819–88) had been baptised a Catholic somewhat earlier, in January 1844. After serving his Redemptorist novitiate, he was ordained priest by Bishop Wiseman in England in 1851 before returning to New York and later founding the Paulists. Clarence Augustus Walworth (1820–1900) became a Redemptorist priest and missionary in the United States, after his novitiate in Belgium.

59 Newman's diary entries for Monday 1 September and Tuesday 2 September 1845, *LDN*, vol. x, pp. 754–5.

60 J. D. Dalgairns to J. McMaster, 12 October 1845, McMaster Papers, Notre Dame University Archives.

Littlemore, Newman had noted that 'A Mr Forbes of New York, a very pleasing man … was here the other day, and appeared very shaky indeed, but Pusey has since steadied him.'[61]

These individuals represented an advanced wing among American churchmen and were in tune with the most advanced Tractarians in England. According to McMaster, even Dr Seabury, editor of *The Churchman*, was 'sick and tired' of traditional high churchmen in the Episcopal Church and 'goes about as far as I do'.[62] Moreover, Newman's 'in-tray' correspondence at Littlemore included letters from other American Episcopalians imbued with the principles of the Oxford Movement but which dealt primarily with practical matters of school education and discipline rather than the immediate issues of theological controversy.[63]

It was not only Newman's 'Romanising' circle that was in close contact with American Episcopalians in the 1840s. The ties between more moderate Tractarians of the so-called 'Bisley school' (such as Isaac Williams and Thomas Keble) and high churchmen in the United States were no less significant. For example, a Dr Henry Potter of Albany, New York, was in regular correspondence with Isaac Williams. During a visit to England in September 1845, Potter met with him and other old-fashioned Anglican high churchmen, such as Henry Handley Norris (1779–1850) and Thomas Bowdler, as well as Tractarians such as Pusey, in Christ Church, Oxford,[64] and William Dodsworth (whom he heard preach) in London[65] Potter waxed lyrical about his stay at Bisley as the guest of the vicar, John Keble's brother, Thomas.[66]

Nonetheless, for all its freedom from the limitations imposed by a religious establishment, and all the assertions that the Oxford Movement

[61] J. H. Newman to J. D. Dalgairns, 28 May 1845, *LDN*, vol. x, p. 676. According to Forbes, McMaster was 'forward and likes distinction'. Forbes regarded the high church American Episcopalian J. McVickar, Bishop Hobart's first biographer, more highly. It was said of McMaster that he 'spared no one, high or low, who differed from him, and his invective was as bitter as an unlimited vocabulary could make it'. 'McMaster, James Alphonsus', in *Catholic Encyclopaedia*.

[62] J. McMaster to E. P. Wadhams, 16 April 1845, McMaster Papers, University of Notre Dame Archives.

[63] For example, J. W. Williams wrote from Schenectady, New York, in November 1844, asking for an 'account of the training and system used at Littlemore' in the school there, but also proudly relating that his school chapel was 'Catholic': 'It is I believe the only Church in America, all the windows of which are stained, and I am glad to say that stone crosses, surmount the eastern gable, and the southern porch.' J. W. Williams to J. H. Newman, 4 November 1844, *LDN*, vol. x, pp. 385–6.

[64] H. Potter to I. Williams, 20 September 1845, LPL, Ms 4475, fol. 141.

[65] H. Potter to I. Williams, 3 September 1845, LPL, Ms 4475, fols. 137–8.

[66] H. Potter to I. Williams, 10 September 1845, LPL, Ms 4475, fol. 140.

consequently found 'fewer obstacles in that republic than in this kingdom',[67] certain factors ultimately restrained the progress of the Oxford Movement in the United States[68] and made English Tractarians somewhat ambivalent about their American Episcopal brethren. As Newman once observed: 'they have a great gift and do not know how to use it'.[69] John Keble and his brother Thomas shared the widespread perception that the American Church was a somewhat flawed model to follow. Thomas Keble noted that English latitudinarians could refer to the American Church as setting 'a good example in omitting the Athanasian Creed', that 'Socinianism & Arianism have flourished of late years more than in any Christian country' and that the theological opinions of Archbishop Whately (by then the great *bête noire* of the Tractarians) were 'astonishingly admired by the clergy (or some of them) in America'.[70] By the mid 1830s, W. F. Hook, one of the first English high churchmen to take up their cause, while still 'anxious to assist the Brethren in America', was lamenting to Newman that

> though they have a Catholic church, there prevails among its members very little genuine Church principle. I have watched their progress for some years, and have seen with sorrow that there has always been an inclination even among their best men to yield to the prevailing opinions of the age.[71]

Hook highlighted the example of the American Church's introduction of a rubric on regeneration which appeared to compromise the Catholic doctrine of baptismal regeneration. For his part, Newman informed Hook that Pusey believed there was a great fear that the American Church would split into two over the issue of baptismal regeneration, 'the Western taking the ultra protestant view, the New York connexion the Catholic'.[72] Newman was unimpressed by Philander Chase, now bishop of Illinois, when he called upon him in Oriel in 1835, noting disapprovingly that Chase had appeared ignorant of Hook's endeavours on behalf of his Church.[73] Hook concluded his American reflections to

[67] *Recent Recollections of the Anglo-American Church in the United States. By an English layman*, 2 vols. (London, 1861), vol. I, p. xxii.

[68] *A Letter to the Hon. and Rev. George Spencer on the Oxford Movement in the United States. By Americano-Catholicus* (New York, 1842), p. 3.

[69] J. H. Newman to W. F. Hook, 21 December 1835, *LDN*, vol. v, p. 180.

[70] T. Keble to J. Keble, n.d., Keble College Archives, Keble College, Oxford, '19. Thomas Keble to John Keble (1826–1842)', no. 6.

[71] W. F. Hook to J. H. Newman, December 1835, *LDN*, vol. v, p. 181.

[72] J. H. Newman to W. F. Hook, 21 December 1835, *ibid.*, p. 180.

[73] Writing from Oriel College, Newman informed Hook: 'Bishop Chase, now of Illinois, has lately been here – and called on me. I asked him if he knew you. He was very unsatisfactory, and Pusey says he is one of the ultra Protestants.' *Ibid.*

Newman with a telling comment: 'I fear that our American Fathers and Brothers are too apt to consider that, if they maintain the one doctrine of Episcopacy, sadly curtailed as the jurisdiction of Bishops is, nothing more is required.'[74]

Anti-Erastianism in itself was ultimately not enough. English high church advocates of establishment were not deficient in their sacramental theology or ecclesiology in comparison with those American high churchmen in the Hobartian tradition who disavowed the Church–state connection on principle. In fact, argued English high churchmen, in the United States there were other (perhaps less overt) restrictions on the independence of the Church such as the overweening popular lay and 'national' influence, and the limitations of a purely voluntary system of church support that had forced American churchmen to seek subscriptions in England to meet the most basic needs of theological education and learning, and to depend on the supply of books of divinity from W. F. Hook and other English benefactors.[75] English high churchmen in the 1830s still regarded a learned clergy in America as a noble aspiration but not yet, with notable exceptions, a reality. According to Hook in 1835, 'the Divinity of most of our brethren and many of our Fathers in that part of the world is somewhat crude'.[76] In short, there were features in the American church polity (such as its elective legislative framework) and in American liturgical and ecclesiological arrangements which English Tractarians found wanting. The latter were no more impressed than pre-Tractarian high churchmen had been, by the fact that American episcopacy was republican and popular and defended as such even by those in the Hobartian tradition, who insisted on it as a divine institution. Newman's review article on Henry Caswall's history of the American Church in the Tractarian *British Critic* in 1839 hinted at this. Newman combined praise for some features, such

[74] W. F. Hook to J. H. Newman, December 1835, *ibid.*, p. 181. For differences between the two churches over the nature and character of episcopal jurisdiction, see C. Podmore, 'A Tale of Two Churches. The Ecclesiologies of the Episcopal Church and the Church of England Compared', *Ecclesiastical Law Journal*, 10 (2008), pp. 34–70.

[75] [W. F. Hook], 'Preface', in McVickar (ed.), *Early Life and Professional Years of Bishop Hobart*, p. iii; [S. Wilberforce], 'Ecclesiastical History of the United States', *British Critic*, 20 (1836), p. 272. Newman asked A. P. Perceval as late as 1836, 'Do you think you could promote among your friends Hook's excellent project of presenting the New York Seminary with a set of the Fathers? The cost of the whole would be about £300.' J. H. Newman to A. P. Perceval, 6 August 1836, *LDN*, vol. v, p. 330.

[76] At this time, Hook was still pressing for the establishment of a 'good Theological library in New York' and proposed 'to raise a subscription for the purpose of presenting the institution at New York with a complete set of the Fathers'. W. F. Hook to H. H. Norris, 8 April 1835, Norris Papers, Bodleian Library, Oxford, Ms Eng. Lett. c. 789, fols. 63–4.

as the writings of Bishops Samuel Seabury and John Henry Hobart, with some pointed criticism tinged with sarcasm such as the following:

> Let the visible be a type of the invisible. You have dispensed with the clerk, you are spared the royal arms; still who would ever recognise in a large double cube, with bare nails, wide windows, high pulpit, capacious reading desk, galleries projecting, and altar obscured, an outward emblem of the heavenly Jerusalem, the font of grace, the resort of angels?[77]

The slightest liturgical innovations could be condemned by American bishops. For example, as Henry Potter of Albany informed Isaac Williams in late 1845, the 'Bishop of Massachusetts has just denounced one of his clergy for having a Holy Table like an altar'.[78]

While American Episcopalian sympathisers with the Oxford Movement remained confident at least until the mid 1840s that 'Catholic Truth is insensibly winning its way' and that many were joining the Episcopal Church, the fear was expressed that 'we find it hard to assimilate all the new material', and that 'many of our Bishops are Ultra Protestant'.[79] Vocal resistance to Tractarianism emanated from leading figures in the Episcopal Church such as the evangelical Charles Petit McIlvaine (1799–1873), bishop of Ohio from 1832, and the evangelical William Meade, bishop of Virginia from 1841, while a more muted and nuanced refutation came from John Henry Hopkins (1792–1868), first bishop of Vermont, who has been described as an old-fashioned American high churchman of the 'Connecticut–Hobartian school' and who fell out with Newman during a visit to England in 1839.[80] As has been recently argued, Hopkins

77 [Newman], 'The American Church', p. 324. Newman admitted to being flippant in his *British Critic* article on the American Church, conceding: 'I respect her members too much to mean to be so.' J. H. Newman to Mrs John Mozley, 8 September 1839, *LDN*, vol. v, p. 138.

78 H. Potter to I. Williams, 30 December 1845, LPL, Ms 4475, fol. 144.

79 *Ibid.*

80 Bishop McIlvaine, who was a favourite divine among Anglican Evangelicals in the Church of England, visited Oxford in April 1835 and lodged with the Evangelical principal of St Edmund Hall, John Hill. P. Toon, *Evangelical Theology 1833–1856: A Response to Tractarianism* (London, 1979), pp. 33–4. In his provocatively entitled treatise *Oxford Divinity Compared with that of the Romish and Anglican Churches* (Philadelphia, 1840) and in later Episcopal Charges, McIlvaine vehemently condemned Tractarian teaching on justification. Newman's *bête noire* in Oxford, the anti-Tractarian Charles Portales Golightly, in one of his many pestering letters to the bishop of Oxford, made much of Bishop McIlvaine's Charge and McIlvaine's view 'that the spread of Tractarian opinions in the Protestant Episcopal Church in America will enfeeble the Church's testimony and arrest its progress'. C. P. Golightly to the bishop of Oxford [S. Wilberforce], 15 February 1844, *LDN*, vol. x, p. 122. McIlvaine's sternly Protestant credentials were also displayed in his refusal to consecrate a church in Columbus, Ohio, in 1846, 'because it featured a stone altar instead of a modest table for the use in the communion service'. For Bishop Meade's critique, see W. Meade, *Sermons preached at the consecration of the Rt. Rev. Stephen Elliott* (Washington, 1841). For Bishop Hopkins's eventual opposition to Tractarianism, see J. H. Hopkins, *The Novelties which disturb our peace* (Philadelphia, 1844); J. H. Hopkins, Jr, *The Life of the Late Reverend John Henry*

was critical of Tractarian 'novelty' from a high church standpoint, fearing that the Tractarian emphasis on the indefectibility of the Church actually undermined the ground of certainty which the high church appeal to primitive record had seemed to provide for Bishop Hobart and his school in the American context.[81]

Prior to the impact of the Oxford Movement, the dividing lines between high church and evangelical elements within the Protestant Episcopal Church were somewhat indistinct or muted,[82] though English Tractarians, as we have seen, perceived a clear West–East division in the American Church as early as the mid 1830s. However, the reaction to Tractarianism drew the evangelicals within the Episcopal Church increasingly apart from their high church brethren, ultimately convincing some of them to found a new church.[83] Episcopalian evangelicals questioned whether Episcopalian high church supporters of the Tractarians had really read the *Tracts for the Times* or understood their tendency.[84] It has also been argued that the initial favourable responses to Tractarianism from high church American Episcopalians had resulted largely from appreciation of the Tractarian emphasis on the beauty of holiness in liturgy and worship, but that, as the example of Bishop Hopkins showed, many of their responses became less favourable as the Tractarian exaltation of catholicity became apparent.[85] In the case of Hopkins, English Tractarians would have been puzzled by his combination of a robust defence of 'the

Hopkins (New York, 1875). For discussion of Hopkins's Charges, see R. H. Fuller, 'The Classical High Church Reaction to the Tractarians', in G. Rowell (ed.), *Tradition Renewed* (London, 1986), pp. 56–62. Newman's article on 'The American Church' in the *British Critic* in 1839 included reviews of earlier publications by Bishop Hopkins. Notwithstanding later theological opposition, Bishop Hopkins visited Newman in Oriel on more than one occasion and presented him with books for Oriel College Library. See J. H. Newman to Bishop J. H. Hopkins, 21 February 1839, *LDN*, vol. VII, pp. 39–40; J. H. Newman to E. Hawkins, 31 March 1839, *LDN*, vol. VII, p. 58. The purpose of Bishop Hopkins's visit had been to solicit funds for the Vermont Episcopal Institute. Newman's relations with Hopkins, however, soured once Newman had had reports of the bishop's attendance at ill-constituted and Evangelical-dominated meetings of the Irish Home Mission in Dublin. For the exchange of letters between them on the subject, see *LDN*, vol. VII, pp. 67–71. Newman effectively curtailed this particular American Episcopal contact by maintaining that a further meeting would not remove 'as you suppose the embarrassments of the particular subject to which my late letters have related'. J. H. Newman to Bishop J. H. Hopkins, 7 May 1839, *LDN*, vol. VII, p. 74. However, for evidence of Bishop Hopkins's continuing high church credentials, see his later support for ritualism, 'so long as the great doctrines of the Reformation are faithfully preached by the clergy'. J. H. Hopkins, *The Law of Ritualism* (London, 1867), p. 64.

81 Mullin, *Episcopal Vision/American Reality*, pp. 158–9.

82 J. Bristed, *Thoughts on the Anglican and American-Anglo Churches* (New York, 1822); Tiffany, *History of the Protestant Episcopal Church in the United States of America*, pp. 461–2.

83 Butler, *Standing against the Whirlwind*, p. 211.

84 C. P. McIlvaine, *The Chief Danger of the Church in these times. A Charge delivered to the Clergy of the Diocese of Ohio* (London, 1843), p. 27.

85 Mullin, *Episcopal Vision/American Reality*, pp. 155–8.

great doctrines of the Reformation' with support for ritualism. These divisions within the Episcopal Church over Tractarianism were exploited by American Presbyterians.[86]

High church Episcopalians in the United States were also forced onto the defensive in 1845 by the suspension of Henry Onderdonk, bishop of Pennsylvania, for alleged moral misdemeanours.[87] As in the Church of England, the dominant high church position within the Episcopal Church as expressed by Bishop Whittingham and even Bishop Doane (who had personal battles with Rome[88] and personally strove hard to hold Newman within the Church of England[89]) became one of reaction against the 'excesses' of the movement and a reassertion of anti-Romanism. This trend was encouraged by Newman's conversion to Rome and his abandonment of his earlier *via media* position, with which high church Episcopalians identified, in favour of a theory of the development of doctrine. Stunned by Newman's defection, Henry Potter took comfort from claiming that Newman 'cannot slide from his former position into his present one. His former principles do not lead to his new ones. He is obliged to retract the former.'[90]

It was a trend also exacerbated by the lively interest that American Roman Catholic bishops such as Francis Patrick Kenrick and many clergy took in the progress of the Oxford Movement on both sides of the

[86] For example, [C. van Renssaleer], *"One Faith"; or, Bishop Doane vs. Bishop McIlvaine on Oxford Theology*, 2nd edn (Burlington, NJ, 1843). The point was made forcefully by the evangelical Bishop Griswold: 'The cry of Popery against us has hitherto caused our Church to be small in this country. This prejudice was fast being removed, when a really backward tendency towards Popery arose, and is now likely to revive and strengthen it.' Cited in Stone, *Memoir of ... Alexander Griswold*, p. 442.

[87] Mullin, *Episcopal Vision/American Reality*, p. 165.

[88] Doane recounted how he had personally 'saved' an Episcopal clergyman, Benjamin Winslow, from the 'snares' of 'Romish craft'. G. W. Doane, *Memoir of the Rev. Benjamin Winslow* (London, 1848), pp. 20–22; G. W. Doane (ed.), *The Catholic Churchman, in his life, and in his death. The Sermons and poetical Remains of the Rev. Benjamin Davis Winslow* (Oxford, 1842).

[89] As late as November 1844 Bishop Doane wrote to Newman expressing his intention of seeing him in Oxford on a visit to England commencing in June 1845 and urging him: 'You do, you must, you cannot but fight with us the good fight of the Holy and Apostolic Church.' 'I shall count much on seeing Oxford and shall hope to find you once more *fighting zealously*.' Bishop G. W. Doane to J. H. Newman, 14 November 1844, *LDN*, vol. x, p. 440.

[90] H. Potter to I. Williams, 30 December 1845, LPL, Ms 4476, fol. 144. On the other hand, other American high churchmen now adopted a face-saving formula. Thus, Bishop Whittingham sought to make light of Newman's pending loss to Rome as having little bearing on the Episcopal Church: 'But have we to do with Newman, Pusey, Keble or Williams? It is very absurd thus suffering ourselves to be disquieted about what they have done, do, or may do ... I should be vastly more disquieted about the Diocese of New York than about Oxfordism in England.' W. R. Whittingham to the Revd Dr Kerfoot, 10 September 1845, in Brand, *Life of William Rollinson Whittingham*, vol. 1, p. 347.

Atlantic as an opportunity for conversions to Rome,[91] an interest encouraged by Nicholas Wiseman, who kept Catholic bishops in the United States informed of Oxford news.[92] This interest, when coupled with American Catholic rebuttals of Tractarian claims of Anglican apostolical succession,[93] aroused suspicion and jealousy even among elements in the Protestant Episcopal Church most favourable to the movement.[94] All this would have longer-term implications for Anglo-Roman relations.[95] Although there were notable conversions to Rome from among the Episcopal clergy such as, in 1852, Levi Silliman Ives (1797–1867), bishop of North Carolina,[96] and, in 1855, Bishop Doane's own eldest son, whom the bishop had himself ordained,[97] and in spite of a significant crop of converts in 1845 such as James McMaster and Clarence Walworth from the General Theological Seminary in New York, it was clear by 1846 that the number of converts to Rome from the Episcopal Church in the United States was proportionally lower than those from the Church of England.[98] Moreover, some American converts to Rome in this period were not from the Protestant Episcopal Church; for example, one of Newman's sternest critics, Orestes Brownson, passed through from Unitarianism and Transcendentalism on his way to Rome.[99]

The Anglo-Catholic movement within the Episcopal Church continued to flourish, and standards of worship and liturgical observance

[91] Bishop John Joseph Chanco to Bishop J. B. Purnell, 9 December 1845, University of Notre Dame Archives.

[92] For example, see Bishop N. Wiseman to Bishop J. B. Purnell, 28 October 1841, 'Cincinnati Packet', University of Notre Dame Archives.

[93] For example, [H. D. Evans], *Essays to prove the Validity of Anglican Ordinations* (Baltimore, 1844); P. R. Kenrick, *The Validity of Anglican ordinations and Anglican claims to Apostolical Succession examined* (Philadelphia, 1848).

[94] W. R. Whittingham, *A Letter to the Right Rev. Francis Patrick Kenrick* (New York 1841), p. 3.

[95] K. L. Parker and D. Handschy, 'Eucharistic Sacrifice, American Politics, the Oxford Movement and *Apostolicae Curae*', *JEH*, 62 (2011), pp. 515–42.

[96] On Bishop Ives's path to Rome, see L. S. Ives, *The Trials of a mind in its progress to Catholicism. A Letter to his old friends* (Boston, 1854).

[97] Doane, *Life of George Washington Doane*, p. 507.

[98] E. P. Wadhams to J. McMaster, 6 July 1846, McMaster Papers, Notre Dame University Archives. G. P. Curtis, *Some Roads to Rome in America* (St Louis, 1910). It has been calculated that between 1817 and 1858, a total of thirty Episcopalian ministers seceded to the Roman Catholic Church.

[99] P. Sveino, *Orestes A. Brownson's Road to Catholicism* (New York, 1970). Brownson challenged Newman with a highly critical review of his *Development of Christian Doctrine* (1845) soon after its publication. Brownson was as forthright as any of Newman's Protestant critics, opening his review with this salvo: 'We felt, on reading the famous Tract 90, that the man who could write such a tract would never want ingenious reasons to justify himself any course he might choose to adopt.' [O. A. Brownson], 'Newman's Development of Christian Doctrine', *Brownson's Quarterly Review*, 4 (1846), pp. 342–68, at p. 343. On Brownson, see Allitt, 'Tractarians and Transcendentalists', in *Catholic Converts*, pp. 61–85.

improved; in the Midwest, it took an evangelistic and missionary form with the founding of Nashotah House in Wisconsin in the early 1840s.[100] However, as in the Church of England, the high church party was forced onto the defensive, and even evangelicals in the Episcopal Church felt challenged by Presbyterian and other non-Episcopalian evangelicals. Fears of episcopal despotism and 'priestcraft', dating back to the colonial era, resurfaced. Significantly, the number of high church clerics raised to the American episcopate declined after the 1840s.

The progress of the Oxford Movement in North America demonstrated the enduring residual ties between the mother country and her former colonies in religious and theological terms. The 'wider world' of our volume title in this case was English-speaking, 'Anglo-Saxon' and closely linked culturally (even if widely separated geographically). None the less, the lack of a formal communion between the Church of England and Episcopal Church was an obstacle which high churchmen on both sides of the Atlantic had to overcome.[101] Moreover, the impact of the Oxford Movement proved to be a mixed blessing in theological terms for the Protestant Episcopal Church of the United States and can be cited as one of several components in a process of a certain cultural divergence between England and Anglo-America that has been shown to characterise the period.[102] Just as British and American Methodisms grew apart,[103] so to an extent did British and American forms of high church Anglicanism. Although American Episcopalians made a virtue of the voluntary principle, the lack of state financing for the Episcopal Church was a source of weakness and rendered Episcopalians dependent on the mother Church and this in turn exacerbated church party rivalry. Without the Oxford Movement, the progress of American high churchmanship might well have been smoother and have remained better adapted to the realities of American politics and culture than it proved to be,[104] but it would not and could not then have been the same phenomenon.

[100] T. C. Reeves, 'James Lloyd Breck and the Founding of Nashotah', *Anglican and Episcopal History*, 6 (1996), pp. 50–81; D. H. V. Hallock, 'The Story of Nashotah', *Historical Magazine of the Protestant Episcopal Church*, 11 (1942), pp. 3–17.

[101] As part of a wider revival of church principles in the mid 1830s Newman advocated 'formal communion with the American Church'. J. H. Newman to H. J. Rose, 23 May 1836, *LDN*, vol. v, p. 304.

[102] R. A. Burchill (ed.), *The End of Anglo-America. Historical Essays in the Study of Cultural Divergence* (Manchester, 1991).

[103] L. Billington, 'British and American Methodisms Grow Apart', *ibid.*, pp. 113–36.

[104] DeMille, The Catholic Movement in the American Episcopal Church, 2nd edn, p. 88.

PART II

The Oxford Movement and continental Europe

CHAPTER 8

Europe and the Oxford Movement

Geoffrey Rowell

With his recent *God and Mystery in Words*, David Brown concluded a series of five books on the relationship between theology and imagination, reclaiming areas of human experience that were once matters for theological reflection but have in recent years been neglected. At the end of this book, David Brown comments that 'very dissimilar forms of change may be seen to stem from common wider roots'. He goes on to reflect that 'in the case of the changes effected within the nineteenth-century Church of England, it is impossible to divorce the Oxford Movement from the literary and artistic movement known as Romanticism'.

> So, in spite of its familiar doctrine of reserve, the desire for a more experiential faith lies at its roots. This is evident in Newman's own origins as an evangelical. But conjoined in Romanticism with its new emphasis on experience was nostalgia for the past in the face of growing industrialization and other change. It was that potent mix that ensured that a movement initially uninterested in liturgical change eventually came to champion so many controversial practices that divided the Church of England in the later nineteenth century. The fact that during this period Anglicanism replaced Lutheranism as the branch of the Church nearest to Roman Catholicism is thus not simply a function of intellectual argument, it also reflects the fact that changes in liturgy were profoundly affected by a wider cultural context.[1]

This wider cultural context had European dimensions. Although in many ways the Oxford Movement belongs primarily and most importantly to the Church of England – and especially to the very particular Oxford context – there are important ways in which it needs to be seen within a wider European setting. Owen Chadwick, in his sympathetic exposition of 'The mind of the Oxford Movement', has commented that 'though the leaders were not so extreme in their antagonism to Reason as their opponents sometimes believed, the Oxford Movement was one part of that

[1] David Brown, *God and Mystery in Words: Experience through Metaphor and Drama* (Oxford, 2008), pp. 262–3.

great swing of opinion against Reason as the Age of Reason had understood it and used it. Through Europe ran the reaction against the aridity of common sense, against the pride of rationalism.' As Chadwick rightly notes, there is little in common between the religion of Keble and Goethe, or of Pusey and Victor Hugo; indeed, there are clearly many differences between the complex strands of reaction to the Enlightenment. However, Chadwick observes, in the broadest sense the Oxford Movement was part of that larger reaction. 'The leaders wanted to find a place for the poetic or the aesthetic judgement; their hymnody shared in the feelings of the evocations of the romantic poets; they wished to find a place and value for historical tradition, against the irreverent or sacrilegious hands of critical revolutionaries for whom no antiquity was sacred; they suspected the reason of common sense as shallow; they wanted to justify order and authority in Church as well as State.'[2] In a later essay on Dean Church's classic account of the Oxford Movement, Chadwick notes that Church had offered four contemporary diagnoses of the movement – political theory, ecclesiastical reaction, anti-Calvinism and romantic imagination – all of which had more than a breath of truth. But Church, he adds, brought a longer and deeper perspective to understanding the movement, the perspective of one who had an understanding of the pre-Reformation centuries – not least through his appreciation of Dante.[3]

Much earlier, in 1933, Archbishop Yngve Brilioth, writing from a Swedish perspective, noted the kinship between the Oxford Movement and contemporary movements in France and Germany.[4] In the case of France, Brilioth cited Chateaubriand and de Maistre as representative figures.

François de Chateaubriand (1768–1848) lived in exile in England from 1793 to 1800, during which time he read much English literature, including Milton's *Paradise Lost*, which he translated into French. Chateaubriand is known above all for his *Génie du christianisme; ou beauté de la religion chrétienne* (1802), published coincidentally with the Concordat celebrating the Peace of Amiens, which was marked by a Solemn *Te Deum* in Notre Dame restoring public worship. Chateaubriand's romantic defence of Christianity as the main source of art and civilisation in Europe found in 'the marvels of Nature proof of the existence of God', claiming that the existence of conscience in mankind was the best evidence of immortality.[5] He stressed the importance of poetry and provided a Christian

2 Owen Chadwick, *The Spirit of the Oxford Movement: Tractarian Essays* (Cambridge, 1990), p. 2.

3 *Ibid.*, p. 148.

4 Yngve Brilioth, *The Anglican Revival: Studies in the Oxford Movement*, 2nd edn (London, 1933), p. 57.

5 Edward Boyle, *Biographical Essays, 1790–1890* (London, 1936), p. 19.

apologetic of feeling, expressed in powerful and evocative language. (John McManners cites his vivid description of his *vicaire* uncle, the abbé de Chateaubriand de la Guéronde: 'hefty, red-faced, with an unkempt wig, torn cassock, dirty shoes, holed stockings, plodding along with his big stick and muttering his matins; he was just a vicaire, but he had blown up the prince de Condé for insulting him by the offer of a tutorship in a ducal household.')[6] When Newman said of Keble that 'he did for the Church of England what only a poet could do, he made it poetical', Chateaubriand would have agreed with this recognition of the primacy of the poetical and its link with religion. Or, to take another example – Newman's sense that just as poetry provides a cathartic channel for raw human emotion, so the apogee of what poetry provides is found in the faith, order and worship of the Church:

> Now what is the Catholic Church, viewed in her human aspect, but a discipline of the affections and passions? What are her ordinances and practices but the regulated expression of keen, or deep, or turbid feeling, and thus a 'cleansing', as Aristotle would word it, of the sick soul? She is the poet of her children; full of music to soothe the sad and control the wayward, – wonderful in story for the imagination of the romantic; rich in symbol and imagery, so that gentle and delicate feelings, which will not bear words, may in silence intimate their presence or commune with themselves. Her very being is poetry; every psalm, every petition, every collect, every versicle, the cross, the mitre, the thurible, is a fulfilment of some dream of childhood, or aspiration of youth. Such poets as are born under her shadow, she takes into her service; she sets them to write hymns, or to compose chants, or to embellish shrines, or to determine ceremonies, or to marshal processions; nay, she can even make schoolmen of them, as she made St Thomas, till logic becomes poetical.[7]

The other French figure cited by Brilioth was Joseph de Maistre (1753–1821), who, having turned from revolutionary to reactionary, became the ultramontane apologist of the spiritual authority of the Church as the basis of society and set that out in his most celebrated work, *Du Pape* (1819). De Maistre read and appreciated Edmund Burke's *Reflections on the French Revolution* and found Burke's reverence for established institutions, distrust of innovation and defence of prejudice, aristocracy and an established Church congenial. Like Burke he was appalled by the violence, 'immorality' and 'atheism' of the Revolution, the only bulwark against revolutionary ideas was traditional Roman Catholicism and papal authority.

[6] John McManners, *Church and Society in Eighteenth-Century France*, 2 vols. (Oxford, 1998), vol. i, p. 392.

[7] J. H. Newman, *Essays Critical and Historical*, 3rd edn, 2 vols. (London, 1873), vol. ii, pp. 242–3.

For Germany Brilioth points to four leading figures – Johann Joseph von Görres (1776–1848), Friedrich Schlegel (1772–1829), Novalis (the pseudonym of Georg Philipp Friedrich Freiherr von Hardenburg) (1772–1801) and Friedrich Stolberg (1750–1819). Görres, the longest-lived of the four, followed the not-unusual trajectory of moving from being an early supporter of the French Revolution to reacting against its ideals. Having returned to the practice of the Catholic faith in 1824 he was appointed Professor of History in the University of Munich by King Ludwig of Bavaria, where he published in his *Christliche Mystik* a series of biographies of the saints and medieval mystics. In his *Athanasius* (1838) he protested against the deposition and imprisonment of the archbishop of Cologne, Clemens August von Droste-Vischering, by the Prussian government. Droste-Vischering, characterised by Owen Chadwick as 'an ox-like Becket with a sense of mission to fight the government to the point of martyrdom',[8] had taken action against the theological school of Hermesianism, which followed the teaching of Georg Hermes, who had sought to adapt traditional Catholic theology to Kantian principles. As Chadwick summarises his teaching:

> Unlike the great school tradition that believed that the human reason could prove the existence and being of God and so could move on to show the reality of revelation, Hermes taught that theology must begin with critical doubt and that the only initial certainty was the consciousness of reality in oneself; so that doubt is the source of faith; and no one may take as 'supernatural truth' what is contrary to the common rational judgement of humanity.[9]

Gregory XVI condemned this teaching in 1835, one of a number of examples, as Chadwick comments, 'where the Pope intervened personally, and with ... vagueness', condemning books though not the author.[10] When Droste-Vischering opposed the Prussian government on the matter of mixed marriages and was deposed, Görres's *Athanasius* depicted this contemporary Church–state conflict as though it were Athanasius fighting for the foundations of the Christian faith. There are echoes, though in a very different context – of Rhineland Catholics finding themselves under a Protestant government as a result of the Napoleonic redrawing of German boundaries – of Keble's Assize Sermon on National Apostasy and of the challenge of the *Tracts* as to the ground on which Anglican

[8] Owen Chadwick, *A History of the Popes 1830–1914* (Oxford, 1998), pp. 37–8. Chadwick adds: 'He was an unintelligent autocrat who stayed in his study rather than go out into his diocese. He listened to no advice, avoided public ceremonies, and was half inclined to the life of the solitary.'

[9] *Ibid.*, p. 42. [10] *Ibid.*

ministry stood. Görres, teaching at Munich, was not only as concerned as Newman and the Tractarians with holiness and transforming grace as the mark of the supernatural life of the Church – hence his lives of the saints and interest in the medieval mystics – he also became the centre of a circle of notable Catholic scholars. This circle included Johann Joseph Ignaz von Döllinger, Professor of Church History at Munich from 1826, and Johann Adam Möhler, who taught at Tübingen from 1826 to 1835 and then at Munich until his early death in 1838. Of the latter, Newman wrote to Mary Holmes, a governess with whom he had considerable correspondence, that 'Moehler's works are, I believe, very interesting – e.g. his Symbolique – (of course it is theological) – Essay on Unity – Athanasius.'[11] Möhler's pneumatological ecclesiology may have had some influence on Newman's own work on the development of doctrine. As Newman wrote in the introduction to his *Essay*: 'The view on which it is written has at all times, perhaps, been implicitly adopted by theologians, and, I believe, has recently been illustrated by several distinguished writers of the continent, such as De Maistre and Möhler.'[12]

The other three names mentioned by Brilioth are all earlier figures of German Romanticism. Friedrich Schlegel, the younger brother of August Wilhelm Schlegel (the German translator of Shakespeare), who after early work on philosophy and art, and a later study of Hinduism, converted to Catholicism in 1808. Once again there was a tension between the earlier, radical free-thinker and the later conservative advocate of Catholic principles defending the medieval imperial idea against the Napoleonic state – and likewise we must always keep in mind the political situation and recent history of Germany. Novalis, who was part of the same group of late eighteenth-century Romantic philosophers, wrote of the 'ungraspability' of the absolute or unconditioned: 'everywhere we seek the unconditioned [*das Unbedingte*] but find only things [*Dinge*]'.[13]

Friedrich Stolberg also belonged to German poetical circles and was a friend of Goethe. His early religious ideas were described as 'misty

[11] J. H. Newman to Miss Holmes, 8 March 1843, *LDN*, vol. IX, p. 275.

[12] J. H. Newman, *An Essay on the Development of Christian Doctrine* (London, 1845), p. 27. Owen Chadwick comments that this is 'a passing phrase which proves that he had not read him. Newman did not read German, but Möhler's *Unity* had been translated into French in 1836, and his *Symbolik* into English in 1843.' Owen Chadwick, *From Bossuet to Newman: The Idea of Doctrinal Development* (Cambridge, 1957), p. 111. The reference in the letter to Mary Holmes would not have been available to Chadwick at the time he wrote his study of doctrinal development, but may well have been stimulated by Newman reading a review of the newly translated *Symbolik*.

[13] Novalis, 'Pollen' Fragments, 1.

and confused', though he was introduced by his parents to a range of Christian authors – Augustine and Luther, Fénélon, the Moravian Zinzendorf and Edward Young, the author of *Night Thoughts*. When he joined the Catholic Church in 1800 he was attacked, like Newman, for having allegedly been a covert Catholic for some years. Significantly he was a close friend of Johann Michael Sailer, bishop of Ratisbon, whose moral theology and ecumenical spirit were later to make him so attractive to Bishop Edward King, who kept a portrait of him in his study at Lincoln. After his conversion Stolberg wrote a fifteen-volume history of Christianity from Old Testament times to St Augustine, as well as a life of Albertus Magnus.

As Brilioth notes, these French and German figures provide some interesting earlier and contextual parallels with Oxford Movement themes. The Church in danger, the spiritual independence of the Church as the bulwark against revolutionary ideas, the reaction against an arid rationalism in theology and a recovery of the importance of the imagination and the feelings, an interest in seeing Church history in a providential way – all of these have some resonances with themes that were important to the Oxford Movement. Brilioth notes that Kenelm Digby (1796–1880), a convert to Roman Catholicism, frequently quoted many of the continental Romantics in *The Broad Stone of Honour: Or the True Sense and Practice of Chivalry* (1822). Brilioth rightly acknowledged that 'the Oxford Movement and the tendency of which it is the expression, can only to a small extent be explained from the literary currents of the age. It was prepared for by these and appropriated some of their thoughts; but it was not evoked by them, nor can it, unless violence is done to the material, be classified only as part of the Romantic Movement.'[14] Recent scholarship would concur.

Pusey, as we know, encountered German Protestant theology early on, when he went to Germany in 1825 'for the critical and scientific part of Divinity', mastering the language and then returning a year later to spend a year studying Oriental languages, Syriac, Arabic and Hebrew dialects which would enable a fuller and more accurate understanding of the Scriptures. As Leighton Frappell has noted in his study of Pusey's early intellectual development, Pusey was shocked to discover that religious rationalism was so widely prevalent in the German universities.[15] 'He had left England naively confident of finding abroad Christian scholars employing their learning to uphold the complete range of revealed

[14] Brilioth, *The Anglican Revival*, pp. 57–8.

[15] P. Butler (ed.), *Pusey Rediscovered* (London, 1983), pp. 1–33.

truth and eager to learn at their feet, only to find that such eminent and supposedly orthodox men as Eichhorn and Pott scoffed at Balaam's ass and indeed rejected all scriptural miracles apart from the resurrection.'[16] It was Pusey who warned Newman, who had consulted him in relation to his early work on miracles in 1826, that it was an unsafe apologetic to distinguish apostolic from post-apostolic miracles on the ground that the former served uniformly moral ends whereas the latter did not. If one applied this maxim to Scripture, what was the status of the 'immoral' miracles of Elijah and Elisha?[17] We should, however, note that the use of scriptural miracles as evidences proving the truth of revelation depended in part upon the belief that the Spirit was given for miraculous evidences only in the apostolic age.[18] With reference to Pusey's comment to Newman, it may be that the seeds were then sown which would bear fruit in Newman's second essay *On Ecclesiastical Miracles*, in which he shifted his ground, allowing the possibility of miracles in the history of the Church, but arguing that each proposed miracle had to be judged by criteria of moral probability – not unlike his concern to find tests or notes of development in his *Essay on the Development of Doctrine.*

Frappell notes how Pusey shifted his own apologetic ground, 'withdrawing Christianity from the scrutiny of superficial reason' and 'calling to witness the hitherto despised testimony of religious sentiment and emotion'. Those who were important in this shift for Pusey were Friedrich Schleiermacher and August Tholuck, the latter becoming a close friend with whom Pusey corresponded until Tholuck's death in 1877. In their different ways they represented a regeneration of the Pietist strand of German Lutheran theology, with its stress on *Christus in nobis* rather than *Christus pro nobis* – an emphasis which, with its roots in the German mystical tradition, accords well with the powerful mystical strand we encounter in Pusey's sermons, and Pusey held up Arndt and Spener from the Pietist tradition as Christian examples to be followed. As Pusey put it in the preface to his *Parochial Sermons*, the whole aim of his preaching was 'the inculcation of the Great Mystery expressed in the words to be "*in* Christ", to be "Members of Christ", "Temples of the Holy Ghost"; that Christ doth dwell really and truly in the hearts of the faithful'.[19]

16 *Ibid.*, p. 9. 17 *Ibid.*

18 J. H. Newman, *Two Essays on Biblical and on Ecclesiastical Miracles*, ed. G. Rowell (Leominster, 2010), pp. xvi–xvii.

19 E. B. Pusey, *Sermons during the Season from Advent to Whitsuntide*, 2nd edn (London, 1848), p. iii. For further discussion of Pusey's sermons see G. Rowell, *The Vision Glorious: Themes and Personalities of the Catholic Revival in Anglicanism* (Oxford, 1983), pp. 80–91.

Frappell's essay analyses the German influences on Pusey and his own wrestling with the tensions arising from the critical study of the biblical texts, Christian orthodoxy and rationalism. In Pusey's first essay on the question, *An Historical Enquiry into the probable causes of the Rationalist Character lately predominant in the Theology of Germany* (1825), he optimistically looked forward to a 'new era of theology' energised by Schleiermacher, Tholuck and others which would provide a mediating position between a scholastic orthodoxy, rationalist reductionism and enthusiasm. However, his controversy with Hugh James Rose led Pusey to publish a second part of the *Historical Enquiry* to deal with Rose's criticisms. By 1839 he was writing to Tholuck that his prediction of a new era in theology 'may have been too sanguine'.[20] Pusey moved, as Frappell shows, to a discovery of the Fathers, whose principles of interpretation of Scripture bridged 'the gap which had always existed in his thought between his High Church orthodoxy and his Protestant scrupulousness in demanding that all doctrine be seen to arise from and find its warrant in the pure Word of God'.[21] In 1835, David Friedrich Strauss published his *Leben Jesu*, sceptically undermining the historical foundations of Christianity and making of the New Testament no more than an imaginative and mythological construction. Tholuck lamented to Pusey in 1836 that he could foresee that in Germany in a hundred years' time there would be 'only Pantheists and Faithful ... opposed to each other, Deists and the old Rationalists will entirely disappear'.[22] That same year Pusey delivered his *Lectures on Types and Prophecies*.

These lectures, which only exist in manuscript in the archives of Pusey House, were referred to by Newman in a letter to Pusey (in which Newman also commented that he had heard Strauss's views were doing great damage among students at Cambridge). In this letter of 1836, Newman observed that Pusey's lectures were a sound riposte that provided an effective orthodox defence against Strauss.[23] In an important paper delivered to the Oxford symposium on Newman in 1966 – a symposium made notable by the arrival of Archbishop Michael Ramsey coming from Rome after his historic meeting with Pope Paul VI when the Anglican-Roman Catholic International Conversations were announced – Donald Allchin portrayed Pusey's lectures as providing an important insight into the theological vision of the Oxford

[20] L. Frappell '"Science" in the Service of Orthodoxy: The Early Intellectual Development of E. B. Pusey', in Butler (ed.), *Pusey Rediscovered*, pp. 1–33, at p. 20.

[21] *Ibid.*, p. 23. [22] *Ibid.*, p. 21, quoting Tholuck to Pusey, 21 February 1836.

[23] J. H. Newman to E. B. Pusey, 1836, *LDN*, vol. v, pp. xx.

Movement.[24] Allchin noted the imaginative and romantic quality of the lectures. Like Newman, Pusey had reacted sharply against the rationalist theology of evidences. For him, as for Keble in his hymn for Septuagesima Sunday in *The Christian Year*, 'the natural world is an emblem of the spiritual'. Allchin summarised what he saw as the major themes of the lectures:

> There is the conviction that clarity and immediate intelligibility are qualities dearly purchased in reflection on divine things; that God reveals himself in images which strike us forcibly almost in proportion to our inability to capture or define them fully; that everything in this world can be a type or symbol of heavenly realities, and that the whole history of God's dealings with his people foreshadows and is prophetic of his revelation of himself in Christ. Finally there is the belief that to try to make a rationally intelligible and complete system of God's ways will inevitably lead to a narrowing and limiting of our apprehension of them. Clarity and intelligibility are of course in themselves good. Their danger in theology is that they should give us an external notion of things, that we should gain a wrong sort of objectivity, seeking to grasp divine truths from outside, when in fact they are realities which can only be understood in so far as we are entering into them and being grasped by them.[25]

As Pusey put it later, 'It is not in proportion to the clearness of our perception, that mysteries have their force.'[26]

In his contribution to the 1983 volume of essays on Pusey, David Jasper explored further the significance of Pusey's *Lectures on Types and Prophecies*, noting both his shared influences from the Romantics, particularly Wordsworth and Coleridge, and the points on which he differed from them. He notes that 'for Pusey, as for Coleridge, and in Germany Johann Herder (1744–1803) and Johann Eichhorn (1752–1827), it was fundamentally important to understand the particular historical circumstances of the Scriptures, and primarily of the Gospels, towards which the history of the New Testament was directed'.[27] In this working towards a theology of history Pusey quotes with approval the German writer J. D. von Braunschweig's *Umrisse einer allgemeinen Geschichte der Völker* published in Leipzig in 1833.[28] Braunschweig sought to identify within the sweep of human history

[24] A. M. Allchin, 'The Theological Vision of the Oxford Movement', in John Coulson and A. M. Allchin (eds.), *The Rediscovery of Newman: An Oxford Symposium* (London, 1967), pp. 50–75.

[25] *Ibid.*, p. 58. [26] *Ibid.*

[27] D. Jasper, 'Pusey's "Lectures on Types and Prophecies on the Old Testament"' in Butler (ed.), *Pusey Rediscovered*, pp. 51–70, at p. 60.

[28] Allchin notes that the Bodleian Library copy of this work was evidently used by Pusey. Allchin, 'Theological Vision', p. 67n.

another Divine institution … regulating all the phenomena in the life of nations, uniting things of this world with things beyond – which may be called 'the Divine Empire of the World', so far as it is visible and an object of history – 'the Kingdom of God' … The history of the Divine empire of the world is the marrow of the history of all nations on earth, around which everything takes its place, which supports and upholds all history, and it raises history to a science.[29]

None the less, Pusey's primary emphasis was not this attempt to construct a theology of history, but rather the conviction that biblical revelation is given through types, symbols and sacramental actions. Shaped by his Hebrew and Old Testament studies, and no less by Syriac writers like St Ephrem,[30] Pusey saw clearly that 'without an understanding of the essential role played by type and sacrament in the process of revelation, we shall be false to revelation itself, losing our awareness of it as a gift from God, into which we are called to enter, and instead transforming it into a mere conceptual scheme of our own devising'.[31] This is a theme which is stressed much later in Austin Farrer's Bampton lectures, *The Glass of Vision* (1948), and in a major recent work, Douglas Hedley's *Living Forms of the Imagination* (2008), which engages with a wide range of themes from the philosophy of mind and scientific accounts of the human person to the nature of symbol and the imaginative writing of Lewis and Tolkien.[32] Rowan Williams, in the preface to his *Dostoevsky: Language, Faith, and Fiction* (2008), reminds us of the necessary importance of imagination, symbol and metaphor in all human discourse, and not simply the religious:

Metaphor is omnipresent, certainly in scientific discourse … and its omnipresence ought to warn us against the fiction that there is a language that is untainted and obvious for any discipline. We are bound to use words that have histories and associations; to see things in terms of more than their immediate appearance means that we are constantly using a language we do not fully control to respond to an environment in which things demand that we see more in them than any one set of perceptions can catch. All of which is to say that no system of perceiving and receiving the world can fail to depend upon the imagination.[33]

Pusey's preoccupation with a world of imaginative, sacramental theology – a theology of mystery – is a reminder that the Tractarians were engaged in something more than a local, English religious movement.

[29] Quoted *ibid.*, p. 67.

[30] G. Rowell, '"Making the Church of England Poetical": Ephraim and the Oxford Movement', *Hugoye: Journal of Syriac Studies*, 2 (1999), http://syrcom.cua.edu/Hugoye/Vol2No1/HV2N1Rowell.html, accessed 12 January 2012.

[31] Allchin, 'Theological Vision', p. 68.

[32] Douglas Hedley, *Living Forms of the Imagination* (London, 2008).

[33] Rowan Williams, *Dostoevsky: Language, Faith, and Fiction* (London, 2008), p. x.

Pusey was certainly helped to that place by what he learned from his engagement with the theology of Germany.

One further intellectual engagement between the Tractarians and Europe is worthy of note – the exchanges between Newman and the Abbé Jager, which led eventually to Newman's *Lectures on the Prophetical Office of the Church* (1836). Fr Henry Tristram of the Birmingham Oratory was to comment on this in 1945 in his essay 'In the Lists with the Abbé Jager', included in the collection that he edited to mark the centenary of Newman's reception into the Roman Catholic Church.[34] A fuller study by Louis Allen appeared in 1975.[35] Allen notes Tristram's comment that this controversy, which Newman took over from his friend Benjamin Harrison, was somewhat exceptional because of 'the astonishing insularity of Tractarian Oxford'. That has a degree of truth, but, as Allen points out, it was not the complete truth. 'Oxford was not, in the eighteen-thirties, as insular as Fr Tristram thought, and European Catholics, for their part took a great interest in what has happening there.'[36] Anglicans visited continental Europe, and Tractarian sympathisers were acquainted with Paris, Rome, Louvain and other places. Newman and Hurrell Froude famously visited Rome and called at the English College to see Nicholas Wiseman, the rector, and to discover on what terms they would take them in. French priests living in England were a channel of information. John Rouse Bloxam, a friend of Newman, hosted both Montalembert and Lacordaire on their visits to Oxford and was a regular reader of *L'Univers*. Canon Hilaire Lorain of the seminary at Langre welcomed John Dobree Dalgairns.[37] English travellers on the Continent were fascinated by Catholic life and customs, many were surprised at the reverence and devotion they found in Catholic services in what they had often been taught to believe was mere mummery and idolatry. Others could import a whole raft of prejudice, as in Nicholas Wiseman's view did Mrs Trollope, whose *A Visit to Italy* he reviewed scathingly (along with Charles Dickens's *American Notes*) in a *Dublin Review* article of 1843 entitled 'Superficial Travelling'.[38]

[34] H. Tristram, 'In the Lists with the Abbé Jager', in Tristram (ed.), *John Henry Newman: Centenary Essays* (London, 1945), pp. 201–22.

[35] Louis Allen, *John Henry Newman and the Abbé Jager: A Controversy on Scripture and Tradition (1834–1836)* (London, 1975).

[36] *Ibid.*, p. 1. [37] *Ibid.*, pp. 2–3.

[38] N. Wiseman, *Works*, vol. VI, *Essays* (New York, 1873), pp. 161–83. Wiseman notes, 'She writes of the sacred temples of the living God: – *"The pleasantest morning lounges now are the churches."*… Manifestly she does not know that the mass is, nor what prayers are recited in it, nor what is the meaning of its ceremonial … Mass is to her a musical performance; and her judgements pronounced on it are whether it was long or short, and the music good or bad – that is according to *her* taste' (pp. 174–6).

The exchanges between Harrison and Jager, which were to lead eventually to Newman's *Lectures on the Prophetical Office of the Church*, arose from a chance meeting between Harrison and Jager, when Harrison was in Paris at Pusey's suggestion to further his study of Asian languages under the direction of Silvestre de Sacy, a renowned 'orientalist' and friend of Pusey, who was rector of the Sorbonne. Jean-Nicolas Jager, who was a few years later to be appointed to the chair of Ecclesiastical History in the University of Paris, had been a schoolmaster and an army chaplain, before taking up a chaplaincy at the Invalides which brought him to Paris.[39] Tristram notes that Jager was engaged in revising the Sixtine edition of the Septuagint with help from quotations from the Greek Fathers, when he met Harrison. The correspondence that ensued from that meeting seems at first to have been routed through William Cureton, an Oxford Syriac scholar who was in Paris at the time, another indication of the continental links of contemporary Oxford.[40]

The content of the correspondence with Jager, which Newman took over from Benjamin Harrison, has been analysed in detail by Louis Allen. We should simply note here that the issues of scripture, tradition and authority in the Church with which the correspondence was concerned, and which, through Jager's publication of the correspondence in *L'Univers*,[41] became known in French Catholic circles, played a significant part in the shaping of Newman's thought, certainly in the *Lectures on the Prophetical Office of the Church* and also, possibly, in *The Essay on Development*.

Continental contacts came from continental travel, as we have already seen with Pusey's visits to Germany, and Harrison's meeting with Jager, and of course the celebrated Mediterranean journey of Newman and Froude, culminating in Newman's illness in Sicily and the shaping effect that had on him. Tom Mozley reminds us of how novel continental travel was for English people in the 1820s because of the earlier difficulties as a consequence of the revolutionary and Napoleonic wars. 'At that time (1826) the Continent had not been opened more than ten years to the English tourist, who could scarcely be said to exist before 1815 ... Even in 1825 a Continental tour had its difficulties, and consisted chiefly of

[39] Tristram, 'In the Lists with the Abbé Jager', p. 206. [40] *Ibid.*

[41] There were two books that gathered the correspondence in French. Jager's *Le Protestantisme aux prises avec la doctrine catholique, ou Controverses avec plusieurs ministres anglicans, membres de l'Université d'Oxford* (Paris, 1836) and an edition published by de Lossy, *Controverse religieuse avec plusieurs anglicans, membres de l'Université d'Oxford, soutenue par M. l'Abbé Jager* (Paris, 1835). See Allen, *John Henry Newman and the Abbé Jager*, p. 8.

troublesome and costly incidents with vetturinos, guides, and hotel-keepers; road accidents, and brigands, real or imaginary.'[42] Robert Wilberforce on his 1826 journey, travelling with John Venn, the son of the Evangelical rector of Clapham, was deeply impressed by Cologne Cathedral, and the early art he saw at Munich. 'It is an illustration', Mozley tells us, 'of the turning of the tide, and one of the many smaller causes contributing to the "Movement," that in 1829 German agents, one of them with a special introduction to Robert Wilberforce, filled Oxford with very beautiful and interesting tinted lithographs of mediaeval paintings.' One such picture 'was a relief from the battle-scenes, sporting pictures and pretty female faces, which had been the chief subjects of English art now for a whole generation.'[43] By contrast Robert Wilberforce's earlier visit to Paris in 1824 evoked no such Romantic emotion; as he told his brother Samuel, 'I cannot speak French and the stupid dogs cannot understand English, which is a great bore. Paris is certainly a very entertaining place, but as dirty as sin in wet weather and there being no footpath, it is monstrous hard to get out of the way of the carriages.'[44]

Frederick William Faber, who went to the Continent in the early 1840s with the son of Benson Harrison of Ambleside, to whom he had been appointed as tutor, published an account of his tour, *Sights and Thoughts in Foreign Churches* (1842). They visited the tombs of Voltaire and Rousseau in Paris, and shuddered; they marvelled at the explosion of joy in Genoa for the Annunciation, and enthused: 'Lent seemed forgotten. The churches were thronged by men well dressed and women almost gorgeously apparelled. Bells ringing, chiming, and playing tunes without intermission all day.' In Milan, Faber lamented that it was 'an oppressive thing to be a priest in the city of St Ambrose and St Charles Borromeo, and yet a stranger'.[45] A later visit took him to Rome, where he 'prayed by moonlight at the Tomb of the Apostles, almost alone in the metropolitan church of the whole world'. He was moved by Rome, and, although at this time he found his 'attachment to the Church of England growing', at the same time he bewailed its position. 'In reality the one thing necessary to prove was, that adherence to the holy See was essential to the *being* of a Church; to the *well*-being of all Churches I admit it is essential.'[46] Another

[42] T. Mozley, *Reminiscences Chiefly of Oriel College and the Oxford Movement*, 2 vols. (London 1882), vol. 1, pp. 31–2.

[43] *Ibid.*, p. 32.

[44] D. Newsome, *The Parting of Friends: A Study of the Wilberforces and Henry Manning* (London, 1966), p. 72.

[45] R. Chapman, *Father Faber* (London, 1961), pp. 57–9.

[46] *Ibid.*, p. 78.

traveller and soon-to-be-convert to the Roman Catholic Church, the 'prickly and stubborn' T. W. Allies, incumbent of Launton near Bicester, caused a stir by publishing his *Journal in France*, an account of two visits to France, in which he said that for the Church of England to be united with Rome would be an incalculable blessing.[47]

Finally in this survey of aspects of the European influence on the Oxford Movement, we should note the French influence when rules were drawn up for new Anglican sisterhoods. More often than not it was to French models that Pusey, W. J. Butler and John Mason Neale turned. St Francis de Sales and St Vincent de Paul were inspirations, as was the latter to Charles Lowder in the founding of the Society of the Holy Cross. As Donald Allchin comments, 'they borrowed freely but not indiscriminately from such sources, and it would be almost impossible to underestimate the debt the Tractarians owed in the formation of their spiritual ideals to seventeenth-century French models'.[48]

As has been demonstrated in this chapter, it is clear that there are important continental parallels and influences on the Oxford Movement, which Yngve Brilioth, writing in Sweden many years ago, set out in *The Anglican Revival*. In the examples of French and German writers we have studied there are resonances of the same perspective that John Keble set out in the Advertisement to *The Christian Year*: 'Next to a sound rule of faith there is nothing of so much consequence as a sober standard of feeling in matters of practical religion.'[49] The French and German writers we have studied were in their different ways reacting against not only an arid rationalism in religion (in England represented by Paley's 'evidence theology') but also rediscovering the importance of image and symbol and the sacramental; of feeling – what might today be described as 'emotional intelligence' – mystery and the hiddenness of God, the apophatic dimension, the importance of poetry; and the significance of tradition and the historical. Pusey had a more immediate connection with Germany than Newman, yet Newman's correspondence with the Abbé Jager illustrates in a French context a similar European dimension. In some ways what John Coulson attempted in his book, *Religion and Imagination: 'In Aid of a Grammar of Assent'*, which linked Coleridge and Newman, the literary and the theological,

[47] For the controversy which drew in Samuel Wilberforce and Henry Manning, see Newsome, *The Parting of Friends*, pp. 343–6.

[48] A. M. Allchin, *The Silent Rebellion: Anglican Religious Communities 1845–1900* (London, 1958), p. 38.

[49] John Keble, *The Christian Year* (Oxford, 1827), Advertisement, p. v.

provides much of this common element.[50] It is significant that Newman thought Pusey's *Lectures on Types and Prophecies* were the best defence against the mythological reductionism of David Friedrich Strauss. Much more could be said on this theme – not least about the renewal of hymnody and worship under Oxford Movement influence and the extent to which this drew on European sources and parallels, and about the relationship between the Oxford Movement and the Gothic revival, which had its European counterparts with architects such as Viollet-le-duc, and sacramental worship. And in a very particular European Oxford Movement context, when the Diocese of Gibraltar was formed in 1842 it was not long before, in some places at least, churches were being erected and traditions of worship established which clearly affirmed that the Church of England in Europe had a catholic inheritance and a catholic identity. To study that development in detail is an important research topic for the future, for there are substantial archives of the diocese deposited in the Guildhall Library in London with rich and fascinating stories of continental ministries in the catholic tradition and the varying ecumenical relations which provided their setting.

[50] J. Coulson, *Religion and Imagination: 'In Aid of a Grammar of Assent'* (Oxford, 1963).

CHAPTER 9

Pusey, Tholuck and the reception of the Oxford Movement in Germany

Albrecht Geck

'I myself respect and love the Germans.'[1] This is a surprising statement, not only in itself, but because it was made by Edward Pusey as late as 1854; that is, long after his so-called 'German' period. A statement like this was by no means common in the nineteenth century, when nationalism gradually came to dominate all other discourses in both countries. For example, Friedrich Max Müller (1823–1900), the famous German Sanskrit scholar and Taylorian Professor of modern European languages in Oxford, stated that Anglo-German relations at the end of the century had become more difficult than half a century before.[2]

Many English and German people experienced a sort of culture clash when they visited the other country. On his first visit to England in 1825, for instance, Friedrich August Gotttreu Tholuck (1799–1877) was annoyed by the manner in which people dashing down the road would shout at him: 'Get moving, get moving!'[3] And when Robert Isaac Wilberforce went to an inn in Bonn he could hardly bear to see the Germans

I wish to thank Mark Chapman, vice-principal of Ripon College, Cuddesdon, who helped with the English version of this chapter. For background, see A. Geck (ed.), *Autorität und Glaube. Edward Bouverie Pusey und Friedrich August Gotttreu Tholuck im Briefwechsel (1825–1865)* (Osnabrück, 2009); A. Geck, 'The Concept of History in E. B. Pusey's First Enquiry into German Theology and Its German Background', *Journal of Theological Studies*, 38(2) (1987), pp. 387–408; A. Geck, 'Edward Bouverie Pusey. Hochkirchliche Erweckung', in P. Neuner and G. Wenz (eds.), *Theologen des 19. Jahrhunderts* (Darmstadt: Wissenschaftliche Buchgesellschaft, 2002), pp. 108–26; A. Geck, 'Friendship in Faith – Edward Bouverie Pusey und Friedrich August Gotttreu Tholuck im Kampf gegen Rationalismus und Pantheismus. Schlaglichter auf eine englisch-deutsche Korrespondenz', *Pietismus und Neuzeit*, 27 (2002), pp. 91–117.

1 E. B. Pusey, *Collegiate and professorial teaching and discipline in answer to Professor Vaughan's strictures, chiefly as to the charges against the colleges of France and Germany* (Oxford, 1854), p. 56.

2 Max Müller, *My Autobiography: A Fragment* (London, 1901), pp. 19–20.

3 Tholuck to Rudolf Stier, 4 September 1825, in G. N. Bonwetsch (ed.), *Aus A. Tholucks Anfängen. Briefe an und von Tholuck* (Gütersloh, 1922), pp. 102–3, at p. 102.

eating, as they ran their knives in and out of 'their monstrous Westphalian mouths'.[4]

These may be comic anecdotes, but people seriously believed that the English and the German peoples were different. For example, Pusey wrote: 'A German writes because he has something to say; an Englishman only because it is, or he thinks it is, needed.'[5] Pusey certainly did not mean that what the German said was not needed, and that the Englishman did not have much to say. The implication rather must have been that whereas English theology was practical, German theology tended to be speculative. This idea may also be later reflected in the twentieth-century saying: 'Theology was invented in Germany, corrected in England and corrupted in America.'[6]

According to Pusey, as a speculative nation Germany was more susceptible to the dangers of rationalism than was England. In general the English regarded the German theologians as excellent scholars – but also as staunch unbelievers. That was the view that Hugh James Rose preached from the university pulpit at Cambridge,[7] and that John Henry Newman adopted in his *Apologia pro vita sua*.[8] When Pusey became tutor at Oriel, it was understood that he 'should introduce no German Theology into [his] lectures'.[9] Later he was admired for his erudition, which was ironically attributed to his 'apprenticeship among divines of Germany'.[10]

I do not believe that theology should be understood in terms of national characteristics, antics or peculiarities. What, after all, would these be? The historian, however, has to acknowledge that the contemporaries of the Oxford Movement did rely upon some of these national stereotypes. Compared with what was thought and written around the turn of the twentieth century and afterwards, judgements in the 1830s and 1840s tended to be friendly in spirit and moderate in tone.

4 Robert Wilberforce to Samuel Wilberforce, July 1831, in D. Newsome, *The Parting of Friends: The Wilberforces and Henry Manning* (Leominster, 1993), p. 137.

5 In his report on the 'State of English Theology' in a letter to Tholuck, 24 May 1830, in Geck, *Autorität und Glaube*, p. 141.

A translation of Pusey's report was published in Germany; [E. B. Pusey,] 'Ueber den Zustand der neuern englischen Theologie. Ein Schreiben von einem englischen Geistlichen [aus dem Englischen ins Deutsche übersetzt von Tholuck]', in *Litterarischer Anzeiger für christliche Theologie und Wissenschaft überhaupt*, 2 (1831), cols. 348–52 and cols. 356–60.

6 Of unknown origin.

7 Hugh James Rose, *The State of the Protestant Religion in Germany* (Cambridge, 1825); Hugh James Rose, *The State of the Protestant Religion in Germany*, 2nd edn (London, 1829).

8 J. H. Newman, *Apologia pro vita sua*, ed. Martin J. Svaglic (Oxford, 1967), p. 45.

9 E. B. Pusey to J. H. Newman, 25 November 1826; quoted in H. P. Liddon, *Life of Edward Bouverie Pusey*, 4 vols. (London, 1893), vol I, p. 102.

10 R. W. Church, *The Oxford Movement: Twelve Years, 1833–1845* (London, 1909), p. 135.

THEOLOGICAL PLURALISM IN THE GERMAN 'VORMÄRZ' (1815–1848)

In German historiography the period from the Napoleonic wars up to the Great Revolution (1815–48) is referred to as the *Vormärz*. Following the Revolutions in America and in France, the peoples of Europe had to choose between two conflicting political systems, the republic and the monarchy. During and after the wars of liberation from Napoleonic domination, there had been a growing sense of national identity in Germany, which led to calls for a constitutional monarchy with greater national representation through a legislative assembly. The conservatives did their best to suppress these tendencies and to restore pre-revolutionary absolutism. Yet revolutionary movements in Europe in 1820 and the early 1830s, and a growing constitutional movement, indicated that this was no longer possible. The reform movement was supported by too many German intellectuals.[11] In March 1840, the orientalist Heinrich Georg August Ewald (1803–75), who was prosecuted in Germany as a constitutionalist, went to England to visit his old friend Pusey, whom he had first met in Bonn. The visit must have been difficult for both of them, because Pusey was no longer the young liberal figure whom Ewald had known.[12] According to Max Müller, the visit had not been easy to arrange, but Pusey would have been tolerant. To Müller he used to say 'with a sigh': 'I know you are a German!'[13]

The pluralism in politics tended to be mirrored in theology. When in March 1848 revolution broke out in Berlin, liberal theologians were more sympathetic to the movement than orthodox theologians.[14] Pusey knew about these affinities, and he distrusted them. He believed, for example, that Zwingli had deviated from orthodoxy so much, because 'as a member of a Republic, he was less impressed with the value of authority'.[15] And when revolution had convulsed Belgium in 1830 he had written to Tholuck: 'I fear that this political excitement will again awaken the dreams of human strength, & human capabilities from which Germany has suffered so much, & which are the most adverse to all the feelings & the whole frame of mind, necessary to embrace the doctrine of the cross.'[16]

[11] Miriam Saage-Maaß, *Die Göttinger Sieben – demokratische Vorkämpfer oder nationale Helden?* (Göttingen, 2007).

[12] Müller, *Autobiography*, pp. 287–8. [13] *Ibid.*, p. 288.

[14] J. F. Gerhard Goeters and R. Mau (eds.), *Die Geschichte der Evangelischen Kirche der Union* I (Leipzig, 1992), pp. 378–81.

[15] [E. B. Pusey], *Scriptural Views of Holy Baptism*, nos. 67–9 of *Tracts for the Times* (Oxford, 1835), p. 90.

[16] E. B. Pusey to F. Tholuck, 6 November 1830, in Geck, *Autorität und Glaube*, p. 153.

And yet it was impossible to turn back history. By the 1830s German Protestantism contained a large number of theological schools, Neo-Orthodoxy, Revival Theology, Mediating Theology, Speculative Theology, the Tübingen school and the various branches of Enlightenment theology, including the notorious rationalising school.[17] They all agreed on the *sola scriptura*, that 'the Bible contained all things necessary to salvation'. But they differed as to how the Bible should be understood, on whether historical methods, especially the instruments of higher criticism, should be applied or not and on whether confessions of faith should be used as the guide to and summary of biblical teaching.

It was a characteristic of the increasing pluralism in theology that journals sprang up like mushrooms. The neo-orthodox *Evangelische Kirchen-Zeitung* was founded in 1828.[18] In the same year the *Theologische Studien und Kritiken*, mouthpiece of Mediation Theology, saw the light of day.[19] Later Tholuck founded the *Litterarischer Anzeiger* to propagate the views of Revival Theology.[20] Pusey was asked to contribute to all three journals. Eventually he wrote a lengthy report on the 'State of Theology in England' for Tholuck's journal and turned down the others.[21] When he was taken ill in 1833 Pusey immersed himself in the *Litterarischer Anzeiger*, which to him was a sign that the dark days of rationalism were finally over.[22] When the controversy over the Jerusalem bishopric was raging in 1841, these and other journals published contributions on the Oxford Movement.

THE JERUSALEM BISHOPRIC AND GERMAN INTEREST IN THE OXFORD MOVEMENT

Until the foundation of the Jerusalem bishopric,[23] German scholars and Church leaders had not paid much attention to the developments associated with the Oxford Movement. There had been scattered references, but

[17] For a description of the various Protestant schools see F. W. Graf, *Profile des neuzeitlichen Protestantismus*, vol. 1 (Gütersloh, 1990), pp. 11–70.

[18] *Evangelische Kirchen-Zeitung*, ed. E. W. Hengstenberg, 1–92 (Berlin, 1827–1919).

[19] *Theologische Studien und Kritiken, eine Zeitschrift für das gesammte Gebiet der Theologie*, ed. C. Ullmann and F. W. C. Umbreit, 1–106 (Hamburg, 1828–1934/5).

[20] *Litterarischer Anzeiger für christliche Theologie und Wissenschaft überhaupt*, ed. F. A. G. Tholuck, 1–20 (Halle, 1830–49).

[21] Geck, *Autorität und Glaube*, pp. 71–2.

[22] E. B. Pusey to F. Tholuck, 4 August 1834, in Geck, *Autorität und Glaube*, 156.

[23] M. Lückhoff, *Anglikaner und Protestanten im Heiligen Land. Das gemeinsame Bistum Jerusalem (1841–1886)*, Abhandlungen des Deutschen Palästina-Vereins 24 (Wiesbaden, 1998), and Kurt Schmidt-Clausen, *Vorweggenommene Einheit. Zur Gründung des Bistums Jerusalem im Jahre 1841*, Arbeiten zur Geschichte und Theologie des Luthertums 15 (Berlin/Hamburg, 1965).

no substantial discussion of fundamentals. Ernst Wilhelm Hengstenberg (1802–69) gave the movement some detailed attention as early as 1839,[24] and in January 1840 Tholuck asked for an elaborate account of the 'old-orthodox party which tends towards Catholicism'. It is important to note that Tholuck, who personally knew John Keble, Newman, Richard Hurrell Froude and Pusey, wrote that these men should 'command the utmost personal respect'.[25]

The German interest in the Oxford Movement grew after the Jerusalem bishopric was made public. I say 'made public' because from a German point of view negotiations had at first been conducted in secret. The Prussian king, Frederick William IV (1795–1861), wanted to avoid political repercussions and theological complications. He was particularly interested in his vision of a united Christianity centred on the place of Christ's death and resurrection. The project should be seen in the line of the chiliastic tradition, which expected that the conversion of the Jews would be the beginning of the eschatological time of salvation.[26]

Yet even after the Jerusalem Bishopric Act of October 1841 the authorities hesitated to make the project public. Official papers mentioned a new bishopric in Jerusalem – but said nothing about the Prussian role.[27] Then in November it was announced that the government would donate £15,000 to the said bishopric.[28] People did not understand why and marvelled at such an act of apparent generosity.

In England there was heated debate over whether this co-operation of the Church of England with the Protestant Churches on the Continent was acceptable. Rose, who is sometimes regarded as the initiator of the Oxford Movement, was proud to call himself a Protestant.[29] Newman, on the other hand, regarded himself as a catholic and viewed the Jerusalem bishopric as a scheme to un-church the Church of England. Against the wishes of Keble, who wanted to protect the archbishop of Canterbury,

[24] 'Zur Charakteristik der Oxforder hochkirchlichen Partei', *Evangelische Kirchen-Zeitung*, 12 (1839), cols. 164–5, 175–6, 181–3, and 13 (1840), cols. 85–8, 96, 100–4, 181–4, 187–91, 220–24, 318–20, 323–8.

[25] F. A. G. Tholuck, 'Vorwort des Herausgebers zum zehnten Jahrgange', *Litterarischer Anzeiger für christliche Theologie und Wissenschaft*, 10 (1840), cols. 1–11, at col. 8 [my translation].

[26] M. Friedrich, 'Das evangelische Bistum zu Jerusalem. Fallstudie eines ökumenischen Prozesses', *Berliner Theologische Zeitschrift*, 13 (1996), pp. 267–84, at p. 269.

[27] For example, *Berlinische Nachrichten von Staats- und Gelehrten Sachen* (from 15 October 1841), as mentioned in Friedrich, 'Evangelisches Bistum zu Jerusalem', p. 270.

[28] For example, *Berliner Allgemeine Kirchenzeitung* (from 3 November 1841), as mentioned in Friedrich, *Evangelisches Bistum zu Jerusalem*, p. 270.

[29] Hugh James Rose, *Letter to the Lord Bishop of London in reply to Mr. Pusey's work on the causes of rationalism in Germany comprising some observations on Confessions of Faith and their advantages* (London, 1829), p. 40.

and Pusey, who did not want the Lutherans to be publicly called 'heretics', Newman published his views.[30] The ensuing uproar was such that in December 1841 the archbishop of Canterbury, William Howley, issued a declaration in which he described the continental Churches as 'less perfectly constituted'.[31] This may have been less than the Tractarians wanted to hear, but was certainly more than the German public would tolerate.

In Germany, the badly handled press campaign gave rise to suspicions that something unpleasant was going on, that there was some kind of conspiracy against the integrity of the Prussian Church. Eventually the Prussian government took three steps: first, Johann Albrecht Friedrich von Eichhorn (1779–1856), minister of culture, education, and church affairs, issued a statement in November 1841 to say that the English side was willing to respect 'the independence and national dignity of the German-Evangelical Church'.[32] Secondly, Christian Karl Josias von Bunsen (1791–1860) asked Johann Heinrich Künzel (1810–73), a German writer returning from a trip to England, to defend the bishopric against its critics.[33] Künzel published an article in the *Darmstädter Allgemeine Kirchen-Zeitung*, which used material from Bunsen's letter almost word for word.[34] Thirdly, Hengstenberg's *Kirchen-Zeitung* was drawn into the controversy. Hengstenberg's article was partly based on internal documents. He assured his readers that the Church of England respected the identity and integrity of the Prussian Church and that there were no plans to give it an episcopacy.[35]

Yet all this was too late and failed to dispel worries and fears. When the Prussian king sent Adolf von Sydow (1800–82) and Alexander von Uhden (1798–1878) to England to study the ecclesiastical situation, there was a widespread rumour that they would be consecrated as bishops and bring episcopacy to Prussia.[36] This apprehensive reaction shaped the frame of

30 Lückhoff, *Anglikaner und Protestanten*, p. 110.

31 'The Archbishop's Statement of Proceedings' (9 December 1841), quoted in Friedrich, 'Evangelisches Bistum zu Jerusalem', p. 273.

32 *Berliner Allgemeine Kirchenzeitung* (20 November 1841), quoted in Friedrich, 'Evangelisches Bistum zu Jerusalem', p. 270.

33 W. Fischer, *Des Darmstädter Schriftstellers Johann Heinrich Künzels (1810–1873) Beziehungen zu England* (Gießen 1939).

34 *Darmstädter Allgemeine Kirchen-Zeitung* (20 November 1841), quoted in Friedrich, 'Evangelisches Bistum zu Jerusalem', pp. 271–2.

35 *Evangelische Kirchen-Zeitung* (8–18 December 1841), quoted in Friedrich, 'Evangelisches Bistum zu Jerusalem', p. 271.

36 Martin Friedrich, '"Ich bin dort kirchlicher geworden und zugleich viel freier". Adolf Sydow in England und Schottland 1841–1844', *Jahrbuch für Berlin-Brandenburgische Kirchengeschichte*, 60 (1995), pp. 137–54, at p. 138.

mind in which the Oxford Movement came to be discussed in theological journals in Germany.

GERMAN THEOLOGICAL PLURALISM REFLECTED IN THE RECEPTION OF THE OXFORD MOVEMENT

The criticism of Anglo-Prussian co-operation naturally attracted attention in Germany. Summaries of books by Newman and Pusey were published in the journals, as were compilations of extracts interspersed with comments to direct the readers' attention to critical issues. The label 'Oxford Movement' was not used. Instead it was referred to as the 'high church' (*hochkirchlich*),[37] 'old-orthodox' (*alt-orthodox*)[38] or 'strictly Anglican' (*streng anglikanisch*)[39] party. This language indicates that the difference between the traditional high church party and Anglo-Catholicism was sometimes not clearly recognised. Yet some authors also used the adjective 'catholic'[40] or the term 'English catholicism'.[41] The article in the *Theologische Studien und Kritiken* was entitled 'Anglo-catholicity'.[42] Often the Oxford Movement was simply called 'Puseyism'.[43] Pusey, of course, disliked the term, because he did not want to be the head of a party, let alone a 'school'. In Germany 'Puseyism' may have reminded many of the man who had once defended German liberal theology against high church attacks from Cambridge.[44] This meant that the word became quite popular.

It goes without saying that the theology of the Oxford Movement challenged the identity of continental Protestants. I will consider three distinct approaches in this chapter: 'Neo-Orthodoxy', 'Revival Theology' and the 'Tübingen school'. While they all had reservations about episcopacy, it was only Neo-Orthodoxy that made it the primary *focus* of its discussion. It was typical of Tholuck's revivalist approach that he should take particular interest in the treatment of the doctrine of justification

37 'Zur Charakteristik der Oxforder hochkirchlichen Partei'.

38 Tholuck, 'Vorwort des Herausgebers zum zehnten Jahrgange', col. 8.

39 Tholuck, 'Eine Mittheilung aus Oxford über die Entstehung der streng anglikanischen mit dem Namen Puseyismus belegten Richtung der Englischen Theologie und Kirche', *Litterarischer Anzeiger*, 14 (1841), cols. 289–94, 301–4.

40 Heinrich Thiersch, 'Mittheilungen über das katholische System der Theologen zu Oxford', *Zeitschrift für Protestantismus und Kirche*, 2 (1842), pp. 341–78.

41 Eichler, 'Die Universität Oxford und der englische Katholicismus', *Allgemeine Kirchen-Zeitung*, 22 (1841), cols. 1278–90.

42 G. V. Lechler, 'Anglo-Katholizität. Zur Kirchengeschichte der neuesten Zeit', *Theologische Studien und Kritiken*, 14 (1841), pp. 1027–71.

43 Tholuck, 'Eine Mittheilung aus Oxford'.

44 Geck, *Autorität und Glaube*, pp. 39–48.

by faith. And the Tübingen school reflected on the implications of the Oxford Movement for the history of the Church of England.

NEO-ORTHODOXY AND 'EPISCOPACY': HEINRICH LEO'S ARTICLES IN THE *EVANGELISCHE KIRCHEN-ZEITUNG*

In 1825 Ernst Wilhelm Hengstenberg published a book on *Die Ueberordnung des äußeren Wortes über das innere* (Superiority of the external over the internal Word).[45] Hengstenberg argued that in order to comprehend God fully, one had to submit to the letter of the Bible. What this meant became most evident when in 1829 his *Christologie des Alten Testaments* (Christology of the Old Testament) appeared.[46] Here Hengstenberg insisted on the literal understanding of the messianic prophecies of Genesis 3:15 and other Old Testament texts. He re-established the old-orthodox doctrine of plenary inspiration. Thus he wanted to put an end to the arbitrariness of 'private judgement', and what he perceived as the disintegration of Church and theology. In the *Evangelische Kirchen-Zeitung* he repeatedly asked for the control of theological enquiry by state law.[47]

In 1842 the conservative professor of history at Halle, Heinrich Leo (1799–1878), published two articles in the *Evangelische Kirchen-Zeitung*.[48] He vigorously defended the Jerusalem bishopric and ridiculed those who feared that 'the German Michel[49] might one day wake up with an English wig on his head'. Leo took it for granted that only the liberals would be against the project, claiming that they feared the possible introduction of episcopal government in the Prussian Church would put an end to the freedom of theological enquiry. Leo assured his readership that no such thing was planned, but he also more than once praised the 'salutary effect of the monarchic element' in episcopacy: 'Only episcopacy enables any

[45] E. W. Hengstenberg, *Einige Worte über die Nothwendigkeit der Ueberordnung des äußeren Wortes über das innere: nebst Stellen aus Luthers' Schriften* (Berlin, 1825).

[46] E. W. Hengstenberg, *Christologie des Alten Testaments, und Commentar über die messianischen Weissagungen der Propheten*, I–III (Berlin, 1829–35).

[47] See the controversy surrounding the so-called 'Halle-Denunciation': *Urkunden betreffend die neuesten Ereignisse in der Kirche und auf dem Gebiete der Theologie zunächst in Halle und Berlin*, I–II (Leipzig, 1830).

[48] Heinrich Leo, 'Das Anglo-Preußische Bisthum zu St. Jakob in Jerusalem und was daran hängt', *Evangelische Kirchen-Zeitung*, 15 (1842), cols. 473–6, and Heinrich Leo, 'Über das Verhältniß der Bischöflichen Kirche von England zu der ursprünglichen apostolischen', *Evangelische Kirchen-Zeitung*, 15 (1842), cols. 481–3.

[49] The 'The German Michel' is a personification of the German nation, as John Bull is of the English nation.

Church to fight the world as *one* man.'[50] To claim that there was only one true form of Church government, Leo believed, would close the ranks of the Church and exclude all those who cannot accept that form of government. It would also lead to a frame of mind that would explicitly cut off communication and deny dialogue. In such a Church, he concluded, the gifted Hegelian theologian Bruno Bauer (1809–1882) would simply be excommunicated.[51]

Leo's understanding of the unifying tendencies of episcopacy was in some ways similar to Hugh James Rose's recipe for a more uniform church. In his 'State of the Protestant Religion in Germany', Rose had bemoaned the divisions among the German schools and asked for a 'control over the religious speculation' and an episcopal Church government, 'which shall diligently repress every tendency to carelessness, and every attempt at innovation'.[52]

Rose's high church view of episcopacy differed somewhat from the Tractarian understanding. He did not dwell upon the apostolic succession through the laying-on of hands as did Newman, for example in Tract 1, *Thoughts on the Ministerial Commission*. Instead, for Rose, there was a sense in which the continental Church constitutions were imperfect, but not invalid.[53] This was also Pusey's view in his 'Enquiry into Theology',[54] although he later changed his mind. In annotations to his wife's copy of Pusey's *Tracts 67–9, Scriptural Views of Holy Baptism*, he carefully and systematically un-churched the continental Churches. The term 'Lutheran church' in the first was replaced by 'Lutheran bodies' or simply 'the Lutherans' in following editions.[55] Pusey now believed that the Germans should receive historical episcopacy – 'not from us, but from the Apostles'.[56]

50 Leo, 'Anglo-Preußisches Bistum', col. 472.

51 Leo, 'Über das Verhältniß', col. 483.

52 Rose, *The State of the Protestant Religion in Germany*, pp. 14–15.

53 Compare the second with the first edition of Rose's *State of the Protestant Religion*. In the first, he said Episcopal Church government guaranteed the '*preservation* of any church', implying that episcopacy was of the *esse* of the Church. In the second, however, he replaced 'preservation' with 'well-being', which in turn means that it was only of the *bene esse* of the Church: Rose, *The State of the Protestant Religion in Germany*, p. 14 (1st edn); p. 8 (2nd edn).

54 E. B. Pusey, *An historical enquiry into the probable causes of the rationalist character lately predominant in the theology of Germany*, part II (London, 1830), p. 17. Here Pusey does not make any difference between Anglican bishops and Lutheran 'General-Superintendents': 'whether bishops or General-Superintendents'.

55 R. Imberg, *In Quest of Authority. The 'Tracts for the Times' and the Development of the Tractarian Leaders (1833–1841)*, Bibliotheca historico-ecclesiastica Lundensis 16 (Lund, 1987), pp. 159–77 and also Geck, *Autorität und Glaube*, pp. 91–4.

56 E. B. Pusey to F. Tholuck, July 1836, in Geck, *Autorität und Glaube*, p. 165.

Leo, it must be said, did not believe in any *elevated* concept of episcopacy and was therefore not interested in receiving it from the Church of England. This was even more true of the other German theological schools. Philipp Konrad Marheinecke (1780–1846), who wrote in the *Jahrbücher für wissenschaftliche Kritik* (the mouthpiece of Speculative Theology), argued that in England episcopacy only served as a cover for the Church's dependence on the state.[57] In the *Theologische Studien und Kritiken*, Gotthard Victor Lechler (1811–88) asked rhetorically, 'who among us would want to introduce Episcopal succession?'[58] And Tholuck wrote to Pusey: 'I very much sympathize with the noble Episcopal church, but should its present form be changed, console yourself with the thought that with a healthy substance God through all changing forms will create a new healthy form.'[59] In turn, the rationalists recklessly made fun of the English love of tradition and ritual. Karl Gottlieb Bretschneider (1776–1848) wrote:

> An Englishman easily regards the *form* as if it were the *substance*; and therefore fancies that if the form were to be changed, the substance would be destroyed. A true Englishman would persuade himself ... that the constitution of his country would go to ruin if the Lord Chancellor did not sit in parliament upon the *woolsack*.[60]

Neo-Orthodoxy agreed with all these schools in that it did not believe in historical episcopacy. But it differed from the other schools in its high estimation of the bishop as the monarch of the Church. This political analogy reveals that episcopacy was envisaged, at least by some, as a means to turn back the tide of theological pluralism.[61]

REVIVAL THEOLOGY AND JUSTIFICATION BY FAITH ALONE

Hengstenberg and Tholuck were friends. Tholuck wrote for the *Evangelische Kirchen-Zeitung*, but then founded his own journal, the *Litterarischer*

57 Philip Marheinecke, 'Ueber das Verhältniß der bischöflichen Kirche von England etc.' (reviews), *Jahrbücher für wissenschaftliche Kritik*, 16 (1842), cols. 921–33, at col. 926.

58 Lechler, 'Anglo-Katholizität', p. 1071.

59 F. Tholuck to E. B. Pusey, 19 July 1836 [my translation], in Geck, *Autorität und Glaube*, p. 161.

60 C. T. Bretschneider, *A Vindication of the modern theology of Lutheran Germany, against the recent accusations brought against it, or the judgement pronounced in the discourses of the Rev. H. J. Rose* (London, 1827), p. 79.

61 For the political implications of church constitutions see Mark D. Chapman, 'Bischofsamt und Politik. Zur Begründung des Bischofsamtes in der anglikanischen Kirche', *Zeitschrift für Theologie und Kirche*, 97 (2000), pp. 434–62.

Anzeiger. He was sympathetic to Hengstenberg's neo-orthodox views, but later described his own approach as 'modern-orthodox'.[62] What was the difference?

First, Tholuck's approach was much more subjective and practical. 'Experience – experience – experience' were his watchwords.[63] Tholuck's *Pektoraltheologie* sprang from the heart. It began with the individual's awareness of utter sinfulness and need for salvation. As he used to say: 'The descent into hell which is knowledge of oneself is the presupposition for the ascension into heaven which is the knowledge of God.'[64] Thus the individual's summons to the Christian faith, the personal relation of the redeemed soul to its redeemer became the primary focus of attention, rather than submission to the *letter* of the Bible. Tholuck criticised the higher criticism because it opened the door to the philosophical destruction of the presence of the personal Christ in the Scriptures. But he rejected the dry intellectualism of the neo-orthodox revitalisation of the old-orthodox doctrine of inspiration. In a letter to Pusey he wrote about Hengstenberg: 'Tell me your opinion about Hengstenberg's *Christologie*; I can't believe that we are under some sort of compulsion at least where the Old Testament is concerned to go back to the standpoint of the seventeenth century.'[65] Pusey agreed: 'I am very sorry to hear what you say about Hengstenberg's work. It has not yet arrived here, but from what I knew of the direction which his theology had been taking, I feared it would be so. The returning to the theology of the 17th century seems like wilfully throwing away our experience.'[66]

Second, Tholuck wanted to engage the whole individual – not just the heart and soul, but also the understanding. He sought to substantiate religious experience intellectually. He consequently indulged in scientific research and literary controversy to defend faith against historical and philological criticism. However conservative it may have been, it is still possible to describe Tholuck's 'modern orthodoxy' as a kind of mediating theology. He firmly believed that science and faith would eventually coexist harmoniously, and was therefore critical of Hengstenberg's *Christologie*. And, as we have already seen, Pusey was critical, too. In his *An historical enquiry into the probable causes of the rationalist character lately*

[62] F. A. G. Tholuck, 'Gespräche über die vornehmsten Glaubensfragen der Zeit', in *Dr. August Tholuck's Werke* (Gotha, 1865), vol. VIII, pp. 93–280, at p. 258.

[63] F. A. G. Tholuck, *Guido und Julius. Die Lehre von der Sünde und vom Versöhner, oder: Die wahre Weihe des Zweiflers* (Hamburg, 1823), p. 29.

[64] *Ibid.*, p. 12–13 [my translation].

[65] Tholuck to Pusey, 3 June 1829, in Geck, *Autorität und Glaube*, p. 128.

[66] Pusey to Tholuck, 29 June 1829, *ibid.*, p. 131.

predominant in the theology of Germany, part II (1830), Pusey wrote that religious truths were 'not abstractedly proposed as a sum of credenda … but blended with the circumstances of life'.[67] Hence every age had 'to re-translate Scripture' in order 'to influence the heart by the occupation of the understanding'.[68] This was very liberal language indeed, and it is difficult to concur with Colin Matthew's view that Pusey wrote this second *Enquiry* with only 'faint resolve'.[69] To him, conservatives like Hengstenberg and Rose were not orthodox, but 'orthodoxistical'.[70]

But where Pusey in the years that followed changed his views – Tholuck might have said that he had moved backwards – Tholuck retained his modern-orthodox views. He wrote in the *Litterarischer Anzeiger*:

> [Puseyism] tends to mould the subjectivity of thought and life in the objectivity of the apostolical tradition so that the pious subject will look for God's blessing and mercy primarily in the sacraments. This means that the apostolical succession of the ordained clergy is held in high regard, that regeneration happens only in baptism, that all Christian life outside of this church is imperfect … Sanctification happens by means of moral discipline rather than by means of the gracious love of God. Hence the main criticism is that this theology no longer possesses St Paul's priceless … doctrine of justification by faith alone in its purity.[71]

Pusey's objections to the doctrine of justification by faith alone were twofold. First, like Newman in Tract 45, *The Grounds of Our Faith* (1834), Pusey believed that this doctrine was the real reason behind modern rationalism and subjectivism. He argued in the 1836 foreword to his *Tracts 67–9*, *Scriptural Views of Holy Baptism* (1835), that the *sola fide* linked the communication of divine grace exclusively with faith, and as 'faith' was an operation of the human mind, the human mind consequently became the Archimedean screw of theology.[72] 'Truth must become objective', Pusey seemed to believe,[73] and he located religious truth in the 'objectivity' of the sacraments, the 'objectivity' of historical succession and the

67 Pusey, *Historical enquiry into … the theology of Germany* II, p. 38. 68 *Ibid*., p. 39.

69 H. C. G. Matthew, 'Edward Bouverie Pusey: From Scholar to Tractarian', *Journal of Theological Studies*, 32 (1981), pp. 101–24, at p. 111.

70 Peter B. Nockles, *The Oxford Movement in Context: Anglican High Churchmanship 1760–1857* (Cambridge, 1994), p. 33.

71 Tholuck, in his introduction to 'Eine Mittheilung aus Oxford', col. 291 [my translation].

72 E. B. Pusey, *Scriptural Views of Holy Baptism*, nos. 67–9 of *Tracts for the Times* (London, 1836), pp. ix–x.

73 He actually wrote: 'The Ultra-Protestants … deny this necessity of submission, & assert that to be truth which each individual himself derives from Holy Scripture; & yet they must set up a standard somewhere, else truth must become subjective only, not objective.' E. B. Pusey to F. Tholuck, 19 November 1839, in Geck, *Autorität und Glaube*, p. 177.

'objectivity' of a system of moral rules. Submission to the authority of the Church became the key to salvation.[74]

Pusey's second objection to justification by faith was deeply rooted within his own family tradition. His father used to say that when the sixteenth-century Reformers had propagated justification by faith alone they had in fact meant justification *exclusive* of works.[75] This helps explain why as a Tractarian Pusey emphasised practical Christianity so much. In his Tract 18, *On the Benefits of the System of Fasting Prescribed by Our Church* (1834), he endeavoured to revitalise the ancient practice of systematic fasting. His aim was to show that the demands of Christianity were not on our intellect to *understand* authority, but rather on our will to *submit* to authority.[76] The doctrine of post-baptismal sin which he outlined in his three *Tracts* on the *Scriptural Views of Holy Baptism* served to undermine the security of Christians who indulged in the safety of their justifying faith. As Tholuck said in the *Litterarischer Anzeiger*, this emphasis on sanctification was impressive: the protagonists of the Oxford Movement should indeed command the utmost personal respect.

Yet for a Lutheran that seemed a risky path. Faith without good works was not faith. That was true. But it was also true that good works without faith were not good works. Good works for the Lutheran presupposed the liberating faith in justification without works. Good works would then come naturally, even if all too often this did not happen because the faith was weak and because a weak faith was often used as an excuse for passivity. And yet, are there not indications that for Pusey the demands of Christianity on his soul and practical life sometimes took the form of a burden which seemed hard for him to bear? Here the doctrine of justification by faith alone, which, according to Tholuck, the Oxford Movement did not possess in its pure form, might have had a soothing effect.

THE TÜBINGEN SCHOOL AND THE HISTORY OF THE CHURCH OF ENGLAND

For many Protestants on the Continent the Oxford Movement represented a tendency towards Roman Catholicism. Pusey was right when he assumed

[74] E. B. Pusey to F. Tholuck, 19 November 1839, in Geck, *Autorität und Glaube*, p. 177. Pusey wrote: 'I think that there is a very important difference of ηθος; and it is, whether people must submit to authority or no.'

[75] Liddon, *Life of Pusey*, vol. 1, p. 4.

[76] [E. B. Pusey], *Thoughts on the benefits of the system of fasting, enjoined by our Church*, no. 18 of *Tracts for the Times* (London, 1834).

that Tholuck's friends would regard the movement as 'katholisch … we would be Katholiken'.[77] Marheineke wrote in the *Jahrbücher für Wissenschaftliche Kritik*: 'If the Puseyites were able to lure out popery from Anglicanism then it must have already been inside.'[78]

In 1844 Otto Heinrich Friedrich Fock (1819–72) published an article in the *Jahrbücher der Gegenwart*, in which he gave a detailed history of the Church of England.[79] The *Jahrbücher* had only recently been founded by Albert Schwegler (1819–57) as the mouthpiece of the Tübingen school. Schwegler was one of the most influential pupils of the New Testament scholar Ferdinand Christian Baur (1792–1860), who had applied Hegelian dialectic philosophy to Christian history. Baur had tried to show that Christianity developed as a synthesis of the conflict between St Peter and St Paul (who represented thesis and antithesis respectively).[80] In his article 'Puseyism, the English State Church and Protestantism', Fock used this Hegelian model to describe the history of the Church of England. Pre-Reformation Catholicism (Romanism) was the thesis and Reformation Protestantism the antithesis, which then led to the synthesis of the Elizabethan Settlement. However, because of the shortcomings of the English national character this outcome had proved unsatisfactory. It combined Protestant and Roman elements in a 'hermaphrodite form':

> The English National character is too proud to receive laws from the Pope in Rome; but it also sticks too much to the outer appearance of things, to the visible, the concrete, to feel comfortable in the Protestant world of ideas. So the Church of England stopped half-way.[81]

As a result, after Elizabeth's death there was an aimless swirling between the Scylla of Catholicism and the Charybdis of Protestantism, and Puseyism was described as the latest manifestation of the catholic tendencies. According to Fock, this history showed that either the catholic or the Protestant elements had to be eliminated before the Church of England could exist in peace.[82] The question now was would England be Protestant or Roman Catholic?

[77] E. B. Pusey to F. Tholuck, 6 March 1837, in Geck, *Autorität und Glaube*, p. 169.

[78] Marheinecke, 'Ueber das Verhältniß der bischöflichen Kirche von England', col. 928.

[79] O. H. F. Fock, 'Der Puseyismus, die englische Staatskirche und der Protestantismus', *Jahrbücher der Gegenwart*, 2 (1844), pp. 743–88.

[80] F. C. Baur, 'Die Christusparthei in der korinthischen Gemeinde, der Gegensatz des petrinischen und paulinischen Christenthums in der ältesten Kirche, der Apostel Petrus in Rom', *Tübinger Zeitschrift für Theologie*, 4 (1831), pp. 61–206.

[81] Fock, 'Der Puseyismus', p. 747 [my translation].

[82] *Ibid.*, p. 786.

Any answer to this question was bound to be contentious. Roman Catholics in Germany tended to point to a 'retro-progressive tendency of Protestantism' in England. This was the title of an article which appeared in the *Theologische Quartalschrift* in Tübingen in 1844.[83] Fock did not have high hopes for the future progress of Protestantism in England, either, and his doubts about the national character of the English made him still more sceptical. Were they capable, in the end, of finding their way in the 'world of ideas'? He believed that Roman Catholicism, which was authoritarian, suited the English more than the Protestant striving for freedom in the realm of ideas. The Roman Catholic sought submission to some higher authority outside himself. The Protestant, however, sought the identity of subjectivity and objectivity, of the will and the moral law, of *Wollen* und *Sollen*, within the individual human mind. To establish this identity was the ultimate meaning of history, and Protestantism was a decisive step in this process. It was, so to speak, the ideology of the day: 'Freedom! is the great watchword of our times; freedom! also in religion!'[84]

Now this was pure Hegelianism. The history of Christianity, the history of the Church and the history of Protestantism as its most developed branch – all became symbolic of the overall historical process. Tholuck had always feared this kind of historical 'pantheism' as he called it. As a reaction he wrote a book on the *Credibility of the Gospels*,[85] which was very much in the tradition of Nathanael Lardner's (1684–1768) monumental work.[86] Tholuck wanted to safeguard the scriptural ground for the encounter with the personal Christ.

Where did Pusey stand in this debate? After a break of twenty-five years in their correspondence, he wrote to Tholuck in 1865: 'I watched with deep interest and great hopefulness the early stages of revival of religious earnestness among you; then ... I turned heart-sick.'[87] Around this time the regular correspondence between the two apparently ended. Pusey now started to exchange letters with a member of the Roman Catholic Church in Germany: Johann Joseph Ignaz von Döllinger (1799–1890).

[83] J. S. von Drey, 'Die rückläufige Bewegung im Protestantismus und ihre Bedeutung', *Theologische Quartalschrift*, 26 (1844), pp. 3–56.

[84] Fock, 'Der Puseyismus', p. 787.

[85] F. A. G. Tholuck, *Die Glaubwürdigkeit der evangelischen Geschichte, zugleich eine Kritik des Lebens Jesu von Strauß, für theologische und nichttheologische Leser dargestellt* (Hamburg, 1838).

[86] N. Lardner, *The credibility of the gospel history, or, the facts occasionally mention'd in the New Testament confirmed by passages of ancient authors*, I–XIV (London, 1727–57).

[87] E. B. Pusey to F. Tholuck, 24 March 1865, in Geck, *Autorität und Glaube*, p. 180.

CONCLUSION

What I have discussed in this chapter represents only a few snapshots of the rich tradition of Anglo-German relations in Church and theology. While a great deal of work has already been done, there is still much that awaits systematic exploration: this includes more detailed studies of correspondence, travel diaries and books that were published in many different places. It is remarkable that, although there are and have been comparatively few Anglicans residing on the Continent, developments in the English Church have always been of some interest to German Protestants. Obviously there are affinities between the two nations and their respective cultures and, as the history of late nineteenth and the early twentieth centuries shows, political interests also contributed greatly to this awareness of the other self. With respect to this the English and the Germans have rightly been described as 'cousins at one remove',[88] related to each other but also strangers – *fremde Freunde*, so to speak.

As far as the Church of England and the Protestant Churches in Germany are concerned, relations have seldom been as unencumbered as they are now after the Meissen Agreement. So why should scholars engage in painstaking historical research and uncover the old stories? First of all, because any English person who is interested in Germany and any German person who is interested in England will find such research deeply rewarding. And second, because in the Meissen Agreement the Churches committed themselves 'to strive together for full, visible unity'.[89]

The knowledge of our common and distinct histories is undoubtedly an important aspect of that striving: the reception of the Oxford Movement in Germany proves particularly interesting in this respect. It offers a striking example of the respective theological traditions in action and thus reveals the nature of the relationship between the Churches in general. This, of course, would need a much broader and deeper enquiry than can be undertaken in a chapter of this length. It is clear, however, that the differing understandings of true Church government still remain the main stumbling block of 'full, visible unity' between Anglican and Continental Protestant Churches. As a movement within the walls of Protestant theology the Oxford Movement brought to mind the rich catholic – as distinguished from *Roman* Catholic – tradition sometimes too readily

[88] R. Byrn (ed.), *Cousins at One Remove* (Leeds, 1998).

[89] 'The Meissen Declaration/Die Meissener Erklärung', *Die Meissener Erklärung. Eine Dokumentation, bearbeitet von Klaus Kremkau, EKD-Texte 47* (Hannover, 1993), pp. 46–55, at pp. 46–7.

abandoned by Protestants on the Continent. In addition German scholars will be impressed that Pusey, who followed Newman as the leader of the Oxford Movement, had been one of England's leading experts in German theology.

That the Oxford Movement emerged at a particular point in history also shows that Anglo-Catholicism was not simply a timeless phenomenon, but was the product of historical circumstances. It was a response to one of the key problems of the age, namely the struggle for certainty in the face of theological diversity (a diversity which was evident in the different reactions of the various German theological schools to Anglo-Catholicism). This insight is important, since it may serve to soften harsh views of objective authority where and whenever these present a stumbling block to ecumenism in the twenty-first century. Indeed, one day Pusey's hope may be fulfilled: 'One wants to be united not only to individuals, but Church to Church; & it is unnatural to be united to an individual, and yet separated from his Church.'[90]

[90] E. B. Pusey to F. Tholuck, July 1836, in Geck, *Autorität und Glaube*, p. 164.

CHAPTER 10

The Oxford Movement: reception and perception in Catholic circles in nineteenth-century Belgium

Jan De Maeyer and Karel Strobbe

That the Oxford Movement aroused interest in nineteenth-century Belgium may come as a surprise. Yet our research indicates that the interest was both enthusiastic and intense, although it also requires some interpretation. This chapter consists of three sections. In the first section we outline the background in Belgian cultural and Church history to this remarkable interest. We then reflect briefly on the methodology used in our research of this reception. The third and main section explores the shifting representations of the Oxford Movement.

THE BACKGROUND: THE NINETEENTH-CENTURY REVIVAL OF INTEREST IN THE UNITED KINGDOM IN BELGIUM

Cultural history

The revival of interest in the United Kingdom in nineteenth-century Belgium is not surprising, given the long-term, sometimes intense but often latent cultural interaction between the two countries. That interest intensified during the first half of the nineteenth century for a variety of reasons: the French Revolution and the flight of some French aristocrats to England; the tensions between Napoleon Bonaparte's empire and Albion; and the fact that the post-Waterloo United Kingdom of the Netherlands (1815–30) was a British creation. Interest peaked after the Belgian Revolution of 1830, when the United Kingdom stood guarantor for the new independent nation, which had the most modern and liberal constitution on the Continent at the time. The highpoint was reached with the election of Prince Leopold of Saxe-Coburg-Gotha as first king of the Belgians. The widower of Crown Princess Charlotte Augusta (who had died at a young age and was the only daughter of George IV), this German-born prince was a frequent visitor to the English court and would maintain a very close relationship with Queen

Victoria throughout his life. It is hardly surprising then that a sort of Anglophilia developed among the Belgian elite and that Great Britain became a source of inspiration for numerous movements, including the restoration of the aristocracy, historicism in the arts and the conservation of historical monuments.[1]

Moreover, the new elites – industrialists, engineers and bankers – also looked to the example of the United Kingdom, and even went so far as to carry out industrial espionage, as the story of the Ghent textile industrialist Lieven Bauwens illustrates.[2] It was not coincidental that in 1835 one of the first three Belgian steam locomotives was named for the British engineer George Stephenson. Until the end of the nineteenth century, final-year engineering students were invariably sent for work placements at one of the large British industrial cities.[3]

Was this interest reciprocated? It was certainly evident in the numbers of English battlefield tourists who came to visit Waterloo after 1815, or who made a cultural tour of the old medieval cities in Belgium and/or the popular Rhineland.[4] Another important reason for the growing contact and interaction was the relatively large community known as the 'English Colony', which had settled in Bruges, especially in the years after 1815. By 1850 the English Colony had developed into a community of more than 500 inhabitants, with everything from their own schools (primary and secondary), shops with typical British goods and tea rooms to both an Anglican and a Roman Catholic church, each with its own clergy and a lively parish life. Needless to say, the newspapers and magazines circulating in the English Colony were a source of interest and news-gathering for the Belgian papers.[5]

[1] For the background to this, see J. C. H. Blom and E. Lamberts, *History of the Low Countries* (New York, 1999), pp. 313–27; V. Viaene, *Belgium and the Holy See from Gregory XVI to Pius IX (1831–1859). Catholic Revival, Society and Politics in 19th-Century Europe*, KADOC Studies 26 (Leuven, 2001), pp. 137–56; L. Van Biervliet, *Leven en werk van W. H. James Weale, een Engels kunsthistoricus in Vlaanderen in de 19de eeuw* (Brussels, 1991), pp. 21–4.

[2] Around 1798, Lieven Bauwens (1769–1822) had parts of a 'Mule Jenny' smuggled from England to the Continent. He first used them in his own factory near Paris, and then in 1800 he also started a clothing factory in Belgium.

[3] J. De Maeyer, *De rode baron. Arthur Verhaegen, 1847–1917*, KADOC Studies 18 (Leuven, 1994), pp. 61–2.

[4] See, for example, Robert Hills, *Sketches in Flanders and Holland, with some account of a tour through parts of those countries, shortly after the Battle of Waterloo, in a series of letters to a friend* (London, 1816).

[5] L. Van Biervliet, '"Dear old Bruges". The English Colony in Bruges in the Nineteenth Century', *The Low Countries: Arts and Society in Flanders and the Netherlands*, 6 (1998), pp. 52–9; Van Biervliet, *Leven en werk van W. H. James Weale*, pp. 23–4.

Church history

The Belgian interest in the Oxford Movement can also be placed within a specific context in church history and ecclesiology. The nineteenth century heralded a revival of interest in Church history and its development as an academic subject. This increasing interest in the past led many to recognise that the Christianisation of the Continent had received an important impetus from the British Isles, which were expressively referred to as '*les îles des saints*'. This in itself only further deepened the affinity with everything Anglo-Saxon. Another significant factor in Belgium, especially in Flanders among the Flemish-speaking clergy, was the realisation that there were linguistic and cultural connections between the Flemish and Anglo-Saxon peoples. These perceived bonds must be seen in the context of the emergence of the strongly Romantic and socially oriented Flemish cultural movement.[6]

It was also in Flanders that around 1850 the archaeologically and liturgically based, even purified, gothic revival began to gather an enthusiastic following in Catholic circles on the Continent. This interest originated in the ultramontane circles centred on the Courtrai Baron Jean-Baptiste Bethune and his friendship with the English architect, designer, thinker and writer, Augustus Welby Northmore Pugin.[7]

But *the* decisive reason for the interest of Belgium's Roman Catholics was the revival of Catholicism in England after 1829 (following the Act of Emancipation), and the subsequent restoration of the hierarchy in 1850. Notice was taken in Belgian dioceses and leading journals of the increasing number of English Catholics, of changes in English Church practice (including greater participation in the rites, and in the numbers taking communion), of English religious vocations and in ordinations to the priesthood. No detail escaped mention. After the restoration of the Roman Catholic hierarchy in England in 1850, this interest even became institutionalised, with, for example, a structural cooperation being set up between the diocese of Bruges and some English dioceses. It was in that context that the English baronet John Sutton founded the English

[6] L. Vints, 'De Belgische katholieke missiebeweging in de negentiende eeuw ten tijde van Gezelle', in L. Vandamme (ed.), *'Reizen in den geest'. De boekenwereld van Guido Gezelle* (Bruges, 1999), pp. 39–40 and *passim*.

[7] J. De Maeyer, 'The Neo-Gothic in Belgium: Architecture of a Catholic Society', in J. De Maeyer and Luc Verpoest (eds.), *Gothic Revival: Religion, Architecture and Style in Western Europe*, KADOC-Artes 1 (Leuven, 2000), pp. 19–34, and R. O'Donnell, '"An Apology for the Revival": The Architecture of the Catholic Revival in Britain and Ireland', *ibid.*, pp. 35–48.

Seminary, the Seminarium Anglo-Belgicum, in Bruges in 1859 with a view to training young priests for the United Kingdom mission. Between 1859 and its closure in 1873, 180 English, Scottish and Flemish seminarians were trained there.[8]

Of course, this lively cultural and religious interest in England must also be seen against the background of a latent and sometimes virulent anti-Protestantism. Although continental Anglophilia was mostly heartfelt and sincere, it was often accompanied by a certain ambivalence in the minds of many Catholics. England aroused admiration but also dislike. In his book, *Du mouvement religieux en Angleterre ou les progrès du catholicisme et le retour de l'Eglise anglicane à l'unité*, published in Leuven in 1844, the writer Jules Gondon – probably the first Catholic on the Continent to have seriously studied the Oxford Movement – argued that almost everything wrong in English society could be attributed to religion and that England's ills were a direct consequence of the Reformation. Since Henry VIII's decision to break with Rome, England had in the eyes of many Catholics become the embodiment of egoism. Catholic writers invariably set the allegedly negative influence of Protestantism in sharp contrast with 'the Catholic principle', the fountain of virtuousness, well-being and justice.[9]

Thus, interest in the Oxford Movement belongs to a long cultural tradition, as well as to a very specific tradition in Church history and ecclesiology. In this context one would expect that the movement's more hopeful signs, suggesting that England might soon again lay claim to the title of the 'island of saints', would be received with great excitement.

METHODOLOGICAL CONSIDERATIONS

This chapter is based on a thorough study of the reception and perception of the Oxford Movement in a number of leading Roman Catholic general cultural and Church periodicals and a number of tracts and occasional publications. Some of these journals – all in French – were also distributed outside Belgium. Our research draws particularly on *L'Ami de la Religion*, a French Catholic news magazine produced by laymen but with close ties to the clerical hierarchy. It first appeared in 1814; its last issue

[8] Vints, 'De Belgische katholieke missiebeweging', pp. 39–42.

[9] J. Gondon, *Du mouvement religieux en Angleterre ou les progrès du catholicisme et le retour de l'Église anglicane à l'unité* (Leuven, 1844), pp. 1–24.

was 14 June 1862. *L'Ami* considered itself to be 'designed for the clergy', but it addressed itself also to Christian male heads of families and 'to friends of the arts as well as of religion'. The magazine was immensely popular among the Belgian clergy. *L'Ami* reported mainly on ecclesiastical news, political news and literature.[10]

The *Journal Historique et Littéraire* first appeared in 1834, replacing *Le Mémorial du Clergé*, a magazine brought out by professors at the seminary of the diocese of Liège. It was a moderately ultramontane monthly with a deep interest in social, cultural and religious affairs at home and abroad. The magazine continued to be published until 1864 and can be seen as representative of the mental outlook of the clergy and of the Catholic 'hommes d'oeuvres' of the time.[11] A third relevant periodical was the authoritative *Revue Catholique*, a general interest journal dealing with religion and theology published by Louvain University, which appeared monthly between 1843 and 1884. It consisted of numerous, often anonymous, contributions on theological, ecclesiastical and religious issues.[12]

A study such as this demands a methodological framework consisting of separate sections on reception and perception. The study of reception is a quantitatively supported section, which examines the timing (at what point?), the intensity or frequency, the importance (the place, prominent or marginal?) and the nature or length (article or short notice?) of interest in the Oxford Movement. It was immediately obvious from our research that in the years 1841 to 1845, interest was intense, often very quickly becoming front-page news. In total we counted ninety-four contributions and notices, of which fifty-five appeared in the *L'Ami de la Religion*, thirteen in the *Journal Historique et Littéraire* and twenty-six in the *Revue Catholique*. Of interest is the fact that many of the notices came from the English College in Rome, the *Annales des Sciences Religieuses* (Rome), the *Feuilles Historiques et Politiques de Munich*, *L'Univers* and the *Journal de Bruxelles*.

The study of perception can be best described as a qualitative analysis of how the Oxford Movement was seen. This study considers perceptions both of the substantive characteristics of the movement and of the people who were considered the foremost players. What is most fascinating here are the shifts between various perceptions, although it is important to emphasise that these shifts were not at all radical, but rather that they interweave.

[10] See Viaene, *Belgium and the Holy See from Gregory XVI to Pius IX (1831–1859)*, pp. 25–135.
[11] *Ibid.*, pp. 32–3. [12] *Ibid.*, 80–81.

SHIFTING REPRESENTATIONS

1838–1840: a sympathetic but critical interest

Until 1838 events in Oxford were not reported in the periodicals we investigated. This silence undoubtedly reflects the relative calm in Oxford itself up till that time. The years after Keble's sermon on National Apostasy (14 July 1833) were for the Oxford Movement a time of the development and maturing of ideas. It is not surprising therefore that the overseas Catholic press had not yet received any signals from Oxford. However, as noted above, interest in England was already evident before 1838. Though Catholic readers were still ignorant about '*les puséystes*', they had already read many articles on 'l'état des catholiques en Angleterre', the building of new Catholic churches and chapels and the growing number of Catholic adherents.[13] Even before 1838, *L'Ami de la Religion* had an interest in Anglicanism. However, it was far from being a positive interest: one article dealt with the crisis in the Anglican Church in England,[14] another with the allegedly excessive income of Anglican bishops.[15]

The first news about the Oxford Movement came to the journals we investigated in a roundabout way. In January 1838, *L'Ami de la Religion* reproduced an interesting article from the *Annales des Sciences Religieuses*, a journal published in Rome by Antonio Saverio De Luca, later to become a cardinal.[16] The article in question, 'Sur l'état actuel du protestantisme en Angleterre', was written by the then 35-year-old rector of the English College, Dr Nicholas Wiseman. Wiseman's article was quickly picked up by the *Journal Historique et Littéraire*, which published it in its entirety in March 1838. This marked the introduction of the movement to Belgium. However, this first news about developments in Oxford did not immediately lead to a stream of notices in Belgium and France; on the contrary, there were remarkably few articles about the movement in the early years.

[13] This is especially true for the *JHL*. For examples, 'Sur l'état des catholiques en Angleterre', *JHL*, 2:18 (1836), pp. 323–5; 'Progrès de la religion catholique en Angleterre', *JHL*, 3:25 (1837), pp. 580–82; 'Sur l'église catholique d'Angleterre', *JHL*, 4:38 (1837), pp. 80–82.

[14] 'Sur la crise de l'église anglicane', *AR*, 80 (1834), pp. 350–52 (19 June 1834).

[15] 'Revenu des évêques anglicans', *AR*, 91 (1836), p. 329 (17 November 1836).

[16] 'Sur l'état actuel du protestantisme en Angleterre', *AR*, 96 (1838), pp. 81–4 (13 January 1838). Antonio Saverio De Luca (1805–83) was ordained a priest in the archdiocese of Monreale (Italy) in 1839, and in 1845 became bishop of Aversa (Italy). In 1853 he was appointed titular archbishop of Tarsus. He occupied nuncio positions in Germany and Austria from 1853 until 1863, when he was made a cardinal. During the last five years of his life he was Prefect of the Sacred Congregation for the Roman Universities.

Readers of the *Journal Historique et Littéraire* had to wait until October 1839 for a second article on the subject.[17]

Although this first introduction to the movement – described variously as '*les nouveaux théologiens d'Oxford*', '*docteur Pusey et son parti*' and '*le haut clergé représenté par le docteur Pusey*' – was a somewhat delayed one, it was thorough. Wiseman explained a number of the central ideas of the *Tracts*, their stance towards the *regula fidei*, the sacraments (confession and absolution, baptism, the Eucharist) and the liturgy. He then went on to give considerable attention to a number of events, including the various reactions to the *Tracts*, the false letter from Rome, the appointment of Dr Hampden and an address by Keble in Winchester. In this early account, then, we find a number of elements that would continue to characterise later accounts over a long period. From the beginning, Catholic commentators had held ambivalent attitudes towards the movement and their periodicals constantly alternate between positive and negative views. Since the Anglican Church, of all the Protestant sects, was the closest to the Church of Rome, Catholic commentators were charmed by the Anglicans' rediscovery of their origins and made no secret of their affinity with and admiration for the reform-minded theologians from Oxford. Yet, from the beginning, there was also criticism of the *Tracts*' authors (who were not yet called 'Tractarians'). The adoption of Catholic principles by the Anglican Church was seen as 'a strange inconsistency'. According to Catholic writers, the use of the concept 'Catholic' outside the Church of Rome was inappropriate. The Anglican Church had to choose: either it continued the Reformation line or else it opted for a clear and indisputable source of ecclesial authority. The question of what the movement might mean for Anglicanism itself did not arise for the commentators, and even less so in the succeeding years. From the beginning the movement was measured according to the yardstick of Roman Catholic doctrine.

1841–1843: hope for rapprochement

Following a brief and inexplicable silence in 1840, the subject was again taken up in 1841 in *L'Ami de la Religion* with a front-page article on the 'Retour de l'église anglicane à l'unité'.[18] Only in 1842 did the *Journal Historique et Littéraire* resume its coverage of the movement.[19] For the

[17] 'Sur l'état de la religion en Angleterre', *JHL*, 6:66 (1839), pp. 287–91.

[18] 'Retour de l'église anglicane à l'unité', *AR*, 111 (1841), pp. 17–19 (5 October 1841).

[19] In 1841 the journal included Wiseman's call for Catholic unity: 'Lettre sur l'unité catholique, adressée au très-honorable Comte Shrewsbury, par Nicolas, évêque de Melipotamos', *JHL*, 8:91 (1841), pp. 338–43.

Belgian journal, the movement was still living up to Rome's expectations, because in September 1842 it again reported news about the rector of the English College. On 30 June, Mgr Charles Baggs[20] had given a lecture entitled, 'Observations historiques et critiques sur les opinions des anglicans dits puseystes'. From 1841 to 1843 the reports in the journals we examined became significantly more frequent. These were the years when the Tractarians were arousing growing unrest in Oxford and in England generally. Partly because of Pusey's sermon on the Eucharist[21] and partly because of the conversion of Charles Seager,[22] Catholic circles gradually came to realise that the movement was at a decisive juncture. In any case, Catholic reporters continued to keep their readers informed of ongoing developments.

At this time the word '*puséystes*' became current. In contrast to the situation in England, we have no reason to suppose that it was used by Catholic writers in a disparaging sense, but was probably chosen as the most suitable term. Even though Newman and other members of the movement were well known,[23] the figure of Pusey was nevertheless central in the reports of the years 1841–3. *L'Ami de la Religion* even included a short biographical sketch.[24] Interest in the Regius Professor of Hebrew grew after his sermon on the Eucharist ('The Holy Eucharist: A Comfort to the Penitent'), which was extensively quoted and critically discussed. The subsequent condemnation of the sermon by the Oxford authorities, the prohibition on Pusey's preaching, Pusey's protest, the petitions against the prohibition, the increasing frequency of communion in Exeter College as a consequence of the sermon – all this was

20 'Dissertation sur les Puséystes anglais', *JHL*, 9:101 (1842), p. 252. From 1824 onwards, Charles Michael Baggs (1806–45) studied at the English College in Rome and was ordained priest in 1830. In 1840 he followed Nicholas Wiseman as rector of the English College and in 1844 was appointed Apostolic Vicar of the Western District in England.

21 'Puséistes en Angleterre', *JHL*, 10:111 (1842), pp. 158–9; 'Sermon du docteur Pusey', *JHL*, 10:112 (1843), p. 211; 'Progrès du puséisme, notice sur le docteur Pusey', *JHL*, 10:113 (1843), pp. 261–2; *AR*, 117 (1843), pp. 432–3 (1 June 1843); *AR*, 117 (1843), p. 25 (10 June 1843); *AR*, 118 (1843) (8 August 1843); 'Sermon prêché devant l'université d'Oxford, par le R. Docteur E. B. Pusey', *RC*, 1:9 (1843), pp. 417–26; 'Sermon prêché devant l'université d'Oxford, par le R. Docteur E. B. Pusey', *RC*, 1:10 (1843), pp. 510–14; 'Sermon prêché devant l'université d'Oxford, par le Docteur Pusey', *RC*, 1:12 (1844), pp. 613–18.

22 'Conversion d'un docteur de l'université d'Oxford', *JHL*, 10:116 (1843), p. 417; 'Sermon prêché devant l'université d'Oxford, par le R. Docteur E. B. Pusey', *RC*, 1:10 (1843), pp. 510–14. Charles Seager (1808–78), an Orientalist, was ordained an Anglican priest in May 1837. From 1839 until 1843 he was an assistant lecturer in Hebrew under E. B. Pusey. On 12 October 1843 he was received into the Catholic Church at St Mary's College, Oscott, one of the first Tractarian converts.

23 'Sur M. Newman, l'un des chefs des Puseystes', *AR*, 117 (1843), pp. 17–18 (4 April 1843).

24 *AR*, 118 (1843), pp. 201–2 (29 July 1843).

followed with great interest by the Catholic press on the Continent. This interest in Pusey's address is actually very understandable; the sermon was about the article of faith that was most dear to Catholics, especially since the Reformation: the real presence of the body of Christ in the bread and wine.

Judgements about the movement continued to shift between positive and negative. On the one hand, the movement was called '*un grand mouvement*' and Catholic writers never raised a doubt about '*les brillantes qualités*' and '*les lumières*' of its members. When the objections of English critics were given a hearing, the Catholic journals opted invariably for Pusey's side. Indeed, 'étouffer le puséysme, ce seroit ôter à l'Eglise anglicane ce qui lui reste de vie et d'espérance'.[25] On the other hand, the alleged inconsistencies of the movement continued to be exposed. Catholic authors could not understand how Puseyites could renounce key elements of Anglicanism, and yet continue to refuse to acknowledge the 'indisputable truths' of Catholicism. Furthermore, in commentaries on Pusey's sermon, the points on which he was in conflict with Roman Catholic doctrine continued to be highlighted.

A number of shifts of emphasis became noticeable in this period. The hope grew stronger that the protagonists would move more and more in the direction of '*romanisme*' and would turn back to '*l'unité catholique*'. People wondered aloud about the *final result* of the movement. Some writers also saw the movement as an attempt to make overtures to Rome, an interpretation particularly taken up by *L'Ami de la Religion*. The titles of two articles are highly significant here: 'Retour de l'Eglise anglicane à l'unité',[26] and 'Tendance vers un retour à l'unité catholique en Angleterre'.[27] The first of these articles mentioned a Puseyite who was 'tout à fait catholique', and who had plans to unite the two Churches. The second article included the complete text of a letter from Francis Diedrich Wackerbarth[28] to Sir Robert Peel about the pacification of Ireland and the situation of the established Church there. According to Wackerbarth, peace in Ireland would be possible only through the unification of the two Churches.

[25] 'Conversion d'un docteur de l'université d'Oxford', *JHL*, 10:116 (1843), p. 417.

[26] 'Retour de l'église anglicane à l'unité', *AR*, III (1841), pp. 17–19 (5 October 1841).

[27] 'Tendance vers un retour à l'unité catholique en Angleterre', *AR*, III (1841), pp. 225–7 (4 November 1841).

[28] Francis Friedrich Wackerbarth (1813–84) studied in Cambridge and from 1837 was working as an Anglican priest in Peldom, Essex. A few years later he became a minor canon of Lichfield Cathedral. In 1841 he converted to Roman Catholicism. The letter in question appeared in 1841 and was entitled 'Tuba Concordiae, or a Letter to the future Prime Minister relative to the Pacification of Ireland and the Condition of the Church'.

Alongside this reporting of its events, the movement was increasingly being contextualised and interpreted. Information was given to readers about its origin and history. That this 'burgeoning historiography' could be very one-sided and simplistic is evident from a passage in *L'Ami de la Religion* on the origin of Puseyism.[29] According to the author, there was a forbidden reading room in Oxford University called 'Hell', which housed, alongside the works of the Church Fathers, numerous pre-Reformation manuscripts. As part of a discussion about authority within the Church of England, some academics went to the forbidden room in search of clarification. 'Or, dans cette salle, toute remplie de la pensée des Pères de l'Eglise et des plus saints écrivains du catholicisme, dont beaucoup avaient appartenu à l'Université d'Oxford, fondée par Alfred-le-Grand, est sorti le puseyisme!' The *Revue Catholique* also made efforts to clarify the history of the movement. In a series of two articles (reproduced from a German journal) about the history of the Church of England, attention was focused particularly on Romanising elements in the past (Laud, the Stuart Restoration, etc.).[30] Readers of the *Journal Historique et Littéraire* in September 1842 were informed of the difference between '*Eglise basse*', '*Eglise haute*' and '*puséystes*'.[31]

1844–1845: towards a climax: rumour and speculation

The enthusiasm of Catholic writers waxed still more during the years 1844–5. Some suspected the movement was nearing a climax, that it would soon reach its highpoint and then come crashing down. Others had high expectations. In the *Journal Historique et Littéraire* one writer described events in England as a 'spectacle', which people throughout the whole world were following with pleasure.[32] It was unique in the history of the Church that a sect – as this writer termed it – would renounce its own past and initiate the end of its own schism. Earlier, Catholic readers were convinced that the movement had moved more and more in the direction of Catholicism; the supporters of the Oxford Movement seemed to believe in almost all the Catholic dogmas and to have restored practically all Catholic practices. According to the writer in the *Revue Catholique*,

[29] 'De la réaction qui s'opère en Angleterre, dans le sens catholique', *AR*, 114 (1842), p. 194 (30 July 1842).

[30] 'Mouvement Catholique dans l'église Protestante d'Angleterre', *RC*, 1:3 (1843), pp. 128–35; 'Mouvement Catholique dans l'église Protestante d'Angleterre', *RC*, 1:7 (1843), pp. 319–27.

[31] 'Dissertation sur les Puséystes anglais', *JHL*, 9:101 (1842), p. 252.

[32] 'Un sermon du docteur Newman', *JHL*, 11:121 (1844), pp. 22–5.

the Puseyites had reached a point of no-return: 'Si Rome a raison, les puséystes ne vont pas assez loin, et si Rome a tort, ils sont déjà allés trop loin.'[33]

The Catholic press kept close track of the movement's expansion, and people seemed to derive pleasure from the way in which its advance struck terror into English Protestants. One reason cited for this panic was the fact that Puseyism appeared to have gained hold in Cambridge, evident in the decision of the clergy of Trinity College to abstain from celebrating Guy Fawkes Day.[34] The movement had even crossed the Atlantic, and according to one writer, 'American dissidents now deemed it an honour to call themselves *Catholic*, like their brothers in England.'[35] Having for long appealed only to a number of intellectuals, the movement was now exercising an influence over the general English public, with the press becoming closely involved in the debates and meetings being organised. The discussion was in fact not only about dogma, but also about rites and practices. One writer in the *Revue Catholique* cited the example of a few pastors who, under the influence of the Tractarians, wanted to introduce a number of changes in their parishes and met with opposition.[36] The same writer found these conflicts in England to be a good thing, as thereby, involuntarily and perhaps even unwittingly, the Puseyites were serving '*la cause catholique*', a cause that was in fact already their own.

Just as in England during the years 1844–5, reporting on the Continent about the Oxford Movement also consisted of much rumour and speculation. In particular, *L'Ami de la Religion* published quite a lot of material from the English rumour mill. On 21 November 1844 it reported the general view that Newman would leave the Anglican Church and that many would follow his example.[37] On 26 November came the news from Oxford that Newman had written to Isaac Williams saying he no longer wanted to be part of the Anglican Church.[38] On 7 December the *Oxford Chronicle* was said to have received numerous queries about the possible conversion to Rome of Pusey, Newman and others, but that it was difficult to answer all these questions. There were reports of a correspondence carried on between Newman, Pusey and Williams about joining Rome. There was also speculation that some days before a meeting had taken

33 'Du mouvement des esprits en Angleterre', *RC*, 2:9 (1844), pp. 493–5.

34 *AR*, 123 (1844), pp. 360–61 (21 November 1844).

35 'Du mouvement des esprits en Angleterre', *RC*, 2:9 (1844), p. 495.

36 'Du Puséysme', *RC*, 2:11 (1845), pp. 588–93.

37 *AR*, 123 (1844), pp. 360–61 (21 November 1844).

38 *AR*, 123 (1844), p. 394 (26 November 1844).

place between important Puseyites in which the question of a possible connection with Rome was discussed.[39]

The events and matters that received most attention in this period, however, were Newman's Tract 90 (which led to the attempt at censorship in February 1845), the W. G. Ward affair and of course the conversion of John Henry Newman. Once again Mgr Baggs was asked to write a critical discussion of Tract 90. Baggs exposed the alleged weaknesses of Newman's argument, and showed which of the Thirty-Nine Articles of Faith were seriously in contradiction with Catholic doctrine. For Baggs the conclusion was clear: Anglicans either had to distance themselves from the Thirty-Nine Articles, or abandon Catholic truth since 'Nobody can serve two masters.'[40] According to other Catholic authors, Tract 90 was too much in conflict with the past and with common sense to allow for the debate to be satisfactorily concluded.[41] The Ward affair was treated in two articles in the *Revue Catholique*[42] and received one mention in *L'Ami*.[43] The reasons for the condemnation of Ward's *Ideal of a Christian Church*, as well as a detailed report of the process and of the consequences of the affair, all were given due attention.

The report in June 1845 that John Henry Newman was preparing to publish an article about the motives for his approaching conversion came as no surprise to the writer in *L'Ami de la Religion*.[44] Indeed, according to this writer, anybody who had followed Puseyism in recent years could not be surprised. The Oxford school, known for considering that practice was always more important than knowledge, finally had to acknowledge a positive religion, a permanent cult and a Church that preserved the apostolic traditions. The *Revue Catholique* expressed amazement at the timing, and thought the renunciation was made earlier than originally intended. It added: 'Undoubtedly, grace took precedence over human plans, and God took possession of this privileged soul, before the day he himself had intended to give himself to Him.'[45] The commentator in the *Revue Catholique* made two striking observations about the many conversions taking place at that time. First, educated men, who had joined forces for the revival of the Anglican Church, had all come to the same conclusion

[39] *AR*, 123 (1844), p. 473 (7 December 1844).
[40] 'Du système des Anglicans, appelés Puséystes', *RC*, 2:5 (1844), pp. 252–65.
[41] 'Du mouvement des esprits en Angleterre', *RC*, 2:8 (1844), pp. 434–40.
[42] 'Condemnation de M. Ward par l'Université d'Oxford', *RC*, 2:1 (1845), pp. 42–6; 'L'université d'Oxford et l'Anglicanisme', *RC*, 3:2 (1845), pp. 99–102.
[43] *AR*, 124 (1845), pp. 410–11 (18 February 1845).
[44] *AR*, 125 (1845), pp. 711–12 (21 June 1845).
[45] 'La conversion de M. J.-H. Newman', *RC*, 3:9 (1845), pp. 493–7.

that the Roman communion was the only one where truth, grace and salvation were to be found; and second, the converts all displayed an extraordinary selflessness in the great material sacrifices they had made.

The conversion of Newman and others naturally elicited optimistic reactions from Catholic commentators: 'May his [Newman's] example be emulated by his colleagues who, like him, have had the courage to confess their faults and not to push truth to the side when it is revealed to them!'[46] The many conversions that preceded and succeeded Newman's conversion were an occasion for the *Journal Historique et Littéraire* to speculate about Pusey's (near) future: '[C]ombien de temps l'inconséquence d'une telle conduite pourroit-elle se maintenir dans une si haute intelligence?'[47] Even before Newman's conversion, the Catholic press had already begun to speculate more and more about the future of the movement. Where would all this lead? 'L'île des saints va-t-elle reprendre son noble titre?' was a question preoccupying many commentators. Some allowed themselves to be seduced into an excessive, almost naive optimism. So, according to the *Journal Historique et Littéraire*, only 'unfortunate circumstances' prevented the members of the established Church from uniting with the Catholic Church, but the authors still expected 'enormous results'.[48] Likewise, Jules Gondon (see above) was very optimistic that a complete return to Catholicism would come in the near future. The reviewer in the *Revue Catholique* sided with that optimism.[49]

Nevertheless, there were also more sober voices. The anonymous author of the introduction to Mgr Baggs's article ('Du système des Anglicans, appelés Puséystes') struck a strikingly realistic note. He adopted a wait-and-see attitude towards a total return of the 'island of the saints' to Catholicism. Moreover, he warned that false doctrines cannot be easily thrown off, unless the conversion is accompanied by great pain. Anglicans had been brought up on error for generations. The writer used images from both biology and classical mythology to make his point clearer:

> When people have imbibed error with their mothers' milk, they become one with it, like life itself; it becomes part of their being. What a dreadful mingling! It is like the garment steeped in the blood of the Centaur; it absorbs a poison that can hardly be removed despite great pain and when people try to free themselves from it, they shred that which they love the most. That is what error does.[50]

[46] *AR*, 125 (1845), p. 712 (21 June 1845).

[47] 'Nouvelles ecclésiastiques et politiques. Angleterre', *JHL*, 12:143 (1846), p. 410.

[48] 'Un sermon du docteur Newman', *JHL*, 11:121 (1844), p. 22.

[49] 'Du mouvement religieux en Angleterre, *ou les progrès du catholicisme et le retour de l'église anglicane à l'unité*, par un Catholique', *RC*, 2:4 (1844), pp. 222–3.

[50] 'Du système des Anglicans, appelés Puséystes', *RC*, 2:3 (1844), pp. 124–6.

However, hope and optimism on the one hand, and sober level-headedness on the other, could go together. A clear example of this was Mgr Baggs himself.[51] Having analysed Tract 90, his conclusion was sceptical: 'These principles unfortunately enough do not give much hope for a union of these writers with the Catholic Church.' On the other hand, he was also of the view that the movement would lead to a large number of conversions and ended his article with a moving call to his 'brothers' to give their 'hands and hearts to God and join with us, Catholics'.[52]

In the years 1844–5 readers were given more detailed information about the origins of the movement. We have already mentioned Jules Gondon, the first Catholic historian of the movement. In the *Revue Catholique* Mgr Baggs also began his discussion with a paragraph about the origin of Puseyism, in which he emphasised the decadence of the Anglican clergy, the rise of Methodism, the abolition of the Irish dioceses and the developing interest in scholasticism in Oxford.[53] The same journal also corrected some misconceptions about the origin of the movement: 'Pusey is neither the founder nor the head of this school; Newman has more right to that title than he.'[54] The movement was also examined in the light of what could be called 'Catholic historiography'. A writer in the *Revue Catholique* hazarded a reflection about his own century: in the nineteenth century people dared to entertain thoughts and ideas that were formerly unthinkable; never before had the crazy and vain imaginings of people gone so far. But God always allows people to return to the full truth and this was also true for Protestant thought. According to this Catholic writer, Protestantism in some countries was as good as dead, and the full extent of its sterility and defencelessness could be seen in contemporary England.[55]

Finally, God was explicitly implicated in all that happened. A writer in the *Journal Historique et Littéraire* saw the movement as an instrument used by Providence to free Protestants from their errors, and to prepare them for their conversion.[56] Providence was also implicated in the movement by two other journals. According to the *Revue Catholique*: 'They [the members of the Oxford Movement] now have to take only a few steps to arrive at the gates of the temple. Will they enter? Will they bow down respectfully at the feet of the holy old man who reaches out

[51] 'Du système des Anglicans, appelés Puséystes', *RC*, 2:5 (1844), pp. 252–65.
[52] 'Du système des Anglicans, appelés Puséystes', *RC*, 2:6 (1844), pp. 304–5.
[53] 'Du système des Anglicans, appelés Puséystes', *RC*, 2:3 (1844), pp. 124–33.
[54] 'Du mouvement des esprits en Angleterre', *RC*, 2:8 (1844), p. 434.
[55] 'Du système des Anglicans, appelés Puséystes', *RC*, 2:3 (1844), pp. 124–5.
[56] 'Un sermon du docteur Newman', *JHL*, 11:121 (1844), p. 25.

to them? Only Providence knows.'[57] For *L'Ami de la Religion*, 'Providence always achieves its goals.'[58]

From 1846 to the interbellum*: the idealisation of converts and the continuing dream of rapprochement*

After Newman's conversion, interest in Puseyism gradually declined, although the relationship between Anglicanism and Catholicism in England still sporadically aroused the interest of the Catholic press.[59] However, the person of Pusey himself continued to be followed with interest.[60] In the last months of 1845, *L'Ami de la Religion* and the *Revue Catholique* examined a number of letters that Pusey had written to friends, in which he returned to the events of the previous years and attempted to prevent his countrymen from following Newman's example.[61]

For a long time the Catholic press continued to hope for that which Pusey so ardently wished to avoid: a wave of mass conversions. In the months and years after 1845, the Catholic press on the Continent regularly published calls for prayer for the conversion of England, expressions of sympathy for their English brethren and of delight about the individual conversions that had occurred. Indeed, until long after the First World War, conversion stories of prominent English people were a much-loved genre.[62] In 1846 Jules Gondon published a book about the conversion of sixty Anglican ministers or English academics and fifty '*personnes de distinction*'.[63] The conversion of Henry Wilberforce in 1850 attracted special attention from the *Journal Historique et Littéraire*. Wilberforce had in fact come to his final decision in a retreat house run by the Jesuits in Brussels.[64]

[57] 'Du mouvement des esprits en Angleterre', *RC*, 2:8 (1844), p. 440.

[58] *AR*, 123 (1844), p. 473 (7 December 1844).

[59] 'Du mouvement puseyiste en Angleterre', *RC*, 4:5 (1846), pp. 260–62; 'Mouvement catholique en Angleterre. Attitude du parti puséiste', *RC*, 8:11 (1851), pp. 598–600.

[60] 'Le docteur Pusey entreprend une nouvelle traduction des Saintes Ecritures', *JHL*, 14:159 (1847), p. 148; 'Doctrine du Docteur Pusey', *JHL*, 14:167 (1848), pp. 566–7; 'Anglicanisme et catholicisme. Controverses nouvelles suscitées par le Dr Pusey', *RC*, 24:5 (1866), pp. 174–81; 'Anglicanisme et catholicisme. Suite de la controverse suscitée par le Dr Pusey', *RC*, 24:9 (1866), pp. 524–30.

[61] 'Mouvement religieux en Angleterre', *AR*, 127 (1845), pp. 309–12 (6 November 1845); 'La conversion de M. J.-H. Newman et lettres de M. Pusey', *RC*, 3:10 (1845), pp. 541–9.

[62] One example: A. Janssens, *Anglicaansche en protestantsche bekeerlingen: Stanton, Johnson, Delany, Orchard, Legio* (Brussels, 1933).

[63] J. Gondon, *Conversion de soixante ministres anglicans ou membres des universités anglaises et de cinquante personnes de distinction, avec une notice sur MM. Newman, Ward et Oakley* (Tournai, 1846).

[64] 'Conversion de M. Wilberforce', *JHL*, 27:198 (1850), pp. 304–6.

While in Brussels Wilberforce very possibly met the Jesuit Victor De Buck, a name that certainly cannot go unmentioned here.[65] Victor De Buck (1817–76) became a member of the Society of Jesus in 1835. From 1840 until the end of his life, he was directly involved in the critical historical work of the Bollandists. Through his numerous contacts with foreign hagiographers and his meetings with English Jesuits while studying in Leuven, De Buck became very interested in the religious situation in England and in the question of the reunification of the Churches. In the course of the 1850s De Buck expressed his budding ecumenical interest in various publications, including *Etudes Religieuses*, *La Civiltà Cattolica* and *Journal de Bruxelles*. A number of his contributions also appeared in *The Rambler*, thanks to his close contacts with Richard Simpson. Though De Buck's attention initially focused on the problems of the Russian Church, his interest in the Anglican Church dominated from 1860 onwards. De Buck commented extensively on Pusey's *Eirenicon* in *Etudes Religieuses* and he maintained a lively correspondence with Anglican priests and leaders such as Bishop Alexander Forbes as well as with Pusey himself.[66] In his journalistic work and his correspondence, De Buck adopted a very understanding attitude towards Anglicans. He cautiously attempted to point out Anglican difficulties with Catholic doctrines and practices and to correct misunderstandings, thereby attempting to bring both faith communities closer together. At the end of the 1860s, with an eye on the upcoming Vatican Council, he urged Anglican leaders to travel to Rome, in the hope that their presence would enhance mutual understanding. In the event the Council marked a disappointing end to De Buck's ecumenical activities. From the beginning most of De Buck's Anglican correspondents were very reserved and skeptical. And their greatest fear, the formulation of the dogma of papal infallibility, also came to pass.

De Buck's failure to bring about an actual reconciliation at the highest level is not surprising. His Anglican contacts were far from representative of Anglican opinion, and as a result, he was rather naive about attitudes within the Anglican Church. The same can be said of the expectations he harboured of the Roman Catholic hierarchy.

The most concrete result of De Buck's ecumenical relations came to fruition only some time after his death. In 1892 the French Lazarist

[65] For an extensive analysis of De Buck's relations with Anglicans, see J. Jurich, 'The Ecumenical Relations of Victor De Buck, S.J., with Anglican Leaders on the Eve of Vatican I' (unpublished doctoral thesis, University of Liège, 1988).

[66] With regard to his appreciation of Pusey's *Eirenicon*, De Buck was more in the line of Newman than of the ultramontane Manning.

Fernand Portal read an article by De Buck that had appeared in the *Union Review* in 1869. Portal, who was deeply interested in the reunification of the Roman Catholic and Anglican Churches, gave the article to his good friend Lord Halifax (Charles Lindley Wood). These two figures would play a significant role in the Roman Catholic–Anglican dialogue, the so-called 'Conversations of Malines', which forms an epilogue to our story.

Belgian interest in Anglicanism increased again when the question of the validity of Anglican ordinations had to be settled by Pope Leo XIII. Following his negative judgement in *Apostolicae Curae* in 1896 and a period of relative calm on the reporting level, the Conversations of Malines brought the idea of rapprochement again to the fore.[67] Between December 1921 and May 1925 meetings took place between Lord Halifax, Fernand Portal and the Belgian Cardinal Désiré Mercier. A variety of topics, both practical and dogmatic, were discussed. After the third meeting, at the end of 1923 and beginning of 1924, the Conversations came to public attention, partly because of a pastoral letter by Mercier. This attention and various manoeuvres by the opposition, both on the Catholic and the Anglican side, slowed the Conversations down. The fourth meeting in May 1925 was both a highpoint and at the same time a turning point. The final conversations, under the leadership of the new archbishop, Jozef Ernest Van Roey, ended on a minor key because of the deaths of Mercier and Portal in 1926 and a change in attitude in Rome. Interest in the Oxford Movement would thus be limited to the well-known converts, Newman primarily, and would so remain until the end of the twentieth century.

CONCLUSION

Belgium's interest in the Oxford Movement must be viewed against the background of the country's long-standing interest in the history and culture of the United Kingdom and its many ties with nineteenth-century Britain. The interest in the Oxford Movement also has to be seen in the context both of the revival and academic development of the discipline

[67] R. Aubert, *Les conversations de Malines: le cardinal Mercier et le Saint-Siège* (Brussels, 1967); B. Barlow, *A Brother Knocking at the Door: The Malines Conversations 1921–1925* (Norwich, 1996); A. Denaux (ed.), *From Malines to ARCIC: The Malines Conversations Commemorated* (Leuven, 1997); on the Mercier background, see also J. De Maeyer, 'L'Église se tourne vers le peuple, 1884–1926', in *L'Archidiocèse de Malines-Bruxelles. 450 ans d'histoire* (Antwerp, 2009), vol. II, pp. 161–2.

of church history, and of a traditional and at times virulent Catholic anti-Protestantism. Although continental Anglophilia was often heartfelt and sincere, it was often accompanied by a certain ambivalence in the minds of many Catholics. What is distinctive about the perceptions of the leaders of Catholic opinion in Belgium was the continual shifting between various interpretations: from a sympathetic but critical interest to hopes of a rapprochement with Rome, through the next phase of rumour and expectation to the idealisation of the converts *c.*1846 and the continuing dream of rapprochement in the second half of the nineteenth and the first decades of the twentieth century.

From this study of the reception and perception of the Oxford Movement in Belgium, a number of points come sharply into focus. First, the initial sympathetic interest evolved relatively quickly into a more antithetical approach. It was typical of the self-satisfaction of Rome at the time that when the conversions seemed to be too few or too slow in coming to completion, the blame was put on the inconsistency of the protagonists, the Puseyites. Once the story of Newman was concluded in 1845, the initial openly receptive attitude also disappeared.

The study of perception makes clear that the leading Catholic periodicals in Belgium had little or no understanding of the authenticity, the substantive richness and ecclesiological meaning of the Oxford Movement. They overlooked the depth of the liturgical and ecclesiological renewal and paid no heed to the social and monastic dimensions of the movement. In other words, theirs was a selective, ultramontane, almost strategic reading of the Oxford Movement. It was, therefore, a missed intellectual opportunity.

CHAPTER 11

'Separated brethren': French Catholics and the Oxford Movement

Jeremy Morris

According to the Catholic biographer Edmund Purcell, 'In those stirring and eager days of the revival of religion ... an extraordinary interest was taken by foreign Catholics in the Oxford Movement.'[1] Purcell had lived in Germany from 1837 to 1844, and may have drawn on his own memory in saying this, though it is equally likely that he was influenced by his friend Ambrose Phillipps de Lisle.[2] Most historians have simply not examined Purcell's suggestion in any depth. Gordon Roe's study of Lamennais and England – still impressive after forty years – is perhaps an exception, but as Roe himself acknowledged, it was really a study of Lamennais's reception in England.[3]

The reason why continental Catholics' interest in the Oxford Movement might have been noticed by nineteenth-century commentators, but virtually ignored by historians writing in the twentieth and twenty-first centuries, surely has much to do with the functional specialisation of national academic communities. It has had the unfortunate effect, however, of reinforcing the presumption of many British Church historians that, for almost any significant development in British ecclesiastical history in the nineteenth and early twentieth centuries, there was, in practical terms, 'fog in the Channel'.[4] A revision of this view is long overdue.

The main purpose of this chapter, however, is not so much to argue that French Catholicism exercised a hitherto unacknowledged influence over

[1] E. S. Purcell, *Life and Letters of Ambrose Phillipps de Lisle*, 2 vols. (London, 1890), vol. I, p. 137.

[2] S. Gilley, 'Purcell, Edmund Sheridan (1823–1899)', *ODNB*, vol. XLV, pp. 567–8; on Phillipps, see also M. Pawley, *Faith and Family: The Life and Circle of Ambrose Phillipps de Lisle* (Norwich, 1993), and M. Pawley, 'Lisle, Ambrose Lisle March Phillipps de (1809–1878)', *ODNB*, vol. XXXIII, pp. 961–3.

[3] W. G. Roe, *Lamennais and England* (Oxford, 1966), p. v.

[4] One persuasive instance is Donald Gray's study of the English liturgical movement, *Earth and Altar: The Evolution of the Parish Communion in the Church of England to 1945* (London, 1986); for a partial corrective, see R. W. Franklin, *Nineteenth-Century Churches: The History of a New Catholicism in Württemberg, England, and France* (New York, 1997).

Tractarianism – for which there is, nevertheless, some evidence[5] – as to observe and evaluate the reactions of French Catholics to what was happening in the Church of England. Three main strands will be explored here: first, the so-called 'Mennaisian' or 'liberal Catholic' circle, that is former followers of Felicité de Lamennais, including the lay theologian and politician Charles de Montalembert, and Jean-Baptiste Henri Lacordaire, the refounder of the Dominican order in France; second, the 'extreme ultramontane' circle of Louis Veuillot, editor of *L'Univers*, probably the most influential Catholic newspaper of the century; and third, one of the most influential Gallican organs, the newspaper *L'Ami de la Religion*, which by the early 1840s was under the influence of Félix Dupanloup, later bishop of Orléans and one of the leaders of the 'Inopportunists' at the First Vatican Council.

Many scholars have pointed out the inadequacy of the typology of Gallicans, liberal Catholics and extreme ultramontanes, given the substantial differences within as well as between these groups, and certainly many Catholics straddled these divisions awkwardly.[6] Dupanloup, for example, could be classed with either the so-called 'Mennaisian school' (a particularly weak designation) or with the Gallicans: neither designation seems wholly apposite.[7] Whatever their differences, however, they were mostly of a common mind when they commented on developments in the Church of England. Only in the case of some of Montalembert's circle was there a significant departure from central elements of this shared view. As a prelude to discussion of the three main groups, it is therefore helpful to pin down six key features of this overarching outlook.

First, and most obviously, there was a basic readiness to assert the papal primacy as a central, defining element of Catholicity. Even Montalembert

[5] Purcell claimed the descriptions of continental Catholicism by various travellers such as Frederick Faber and Thomas Allies came 'as a revelation' to the Tractarians: Purcell, *Phillipps*, vol. 1, p. 116. See T. W. Allies, *Journal in France* (London, 1849), and F. Faber, *Sights and Thoughts in Foreign Churches and among Foreign Peoples* (London, 1842). Inclusion of Allies was surely a little anachronistic. Purcell could have added the Tractarian sympathiser Christopher Wordsworth's *Diary in France, Mainly on Topics Concerning Education and the Church* (London, 1845), though unlike Allies and Faber, Wordsworth did not convert.

[6] See A. R. May's strictures on the conventional classification, in 'The Falloux Law, the Catholic Press, and the Bishops: Crisis of Authority in the French Church', *French Historical Studies*, 8 (1973), pp. 77–94; and Norman Ravitch's alternative typology contrasting a 'Catholicism of order' ('bourgeois Catholicism') and a 'Catholicism of change', in *The Catholic Church and the French Nation 1589–1989* (London, 1990), pp. 60–66.

[7] Philip Spencer, for example, saw him as a liberal Catholic, whereas Austin Gough marked him as a Gallican: P. Spencer, *Politics of Belief in Nineteenth-Century France: Lacordaire, Michon, Veuilliot* (London, 1954), p. 134; A. Gough, *Paris and Rome: The Gallican Church and the Ultramontane Campaign 1848–1853* (Oxford, 1986), p. 58.

could say with Manzoni against Protestants, that if the main point was denied, even the smallest deviation was a 'damnable heresy', and that the main point was the infallibility of the Church, or rather the pope.[8] Second, therefore, Protestantism was heresy, but it was not just a constitutional heresy, or a heresy of order; it was a developmental and moral heresy, which brought in its train the evils of rationalism, liberalism, socialism, moral decay and ultimately atheism.[9] Jules Gondon could describe Protestantism as leaning on rationalism, dividing the world into rationalists and Catholics.[10] Protestantism was inherently divisive: it provoked disagreement and disunity. To Catholics, the existence of a bewildering variety of dissenting sects in Britain was decisive proof of Protestantism's corruption, as was, moreover, the zeal with which Protestants seemed to want to intrude their doctrines into Catholic Europe via the Bible societies. London was, in Gondon's words, the arsenal whence the champions of Protestantism drew the weapons with which venal souls ('*âmes vénales*') had triumphed.[11]

On these first two points, some French Catholics subsequently shifted ground. They did not dissent substantially, however, from the remaining four. Third, then, their strongly critical view of Protestantism was contextualised by a sense not of the *vulnerability* of the Catholic Church, but rather of its astonishing revival in the early nineteenth century. Catholic writers spoke freely, by the 1830s, of the utterly changed religious situation in Europe since the fall of Bonaparte, noting the extraordinary growth in religious orders, and the revival of parish life, as well as a sea-change in the intellectual atmosphere. Lacordaire, for example, could write to a correspondent of how it was a marvellous thing that, in his view, the destiny of Europe could depend on a pope, Gregory XVI: all had changed since 1815.[12] Fourth, more specifically, all of these

[8] Le comte de Montalembert, *A Letter addressed to a Rev. Member of the Camden Society, on the Subject of Catholic Literary Societies, on the Architectural, Artistical, and Archaeological Movements of the Puseyites* (Liverpool, 1844), p. 10.

[9] As Christopher Wordsworth put it, describing his meeting with the Abbé Bautain of the seminary at Juilly: 'His frankness of language showed me the feeling with which the Church of England is regarded by Romish theologians; and however much they may wish for advances in their direction from England, certain, I think, it is that they are wholly indisposed to make any approaches whatever towards us, simply because in their minds we are not only heretics but are unworthy of the name of *Christians*': Wordsworth, *Diary*, p. 139.

[10] Jules Gondon, *Motifs de Conversion de Dix Ministres Anglicans, exposés par eux-mêmes, et Rétraction du Réverend J. H. Newman* (Paris, 1847), p. ix.

[11] *Ibid.*, p. vii. All translations from French publications here are my own.

[12] *Correspondence du R. P. Lacordaire et de Madame Swetchine, publiée par le Cte de Falloux* (Paris, 1864), p. 241: Lacordaire to Swetchine, 24 July 1840.

writers shared a fascination with, to their eyes, the miraculous revival of Catholicism in Britain, and a common assumption that the reconversion of Britain to Catholicism was imminent. Gondon could write of the 'last gasp' ('*la dernière pulsation*') of Anglicanism.[13] Lacordaire could claim in 1840 that England should be counted amongst the Catholic powers of Europe, because in fifty or sixty years 'it will be ours'.[14] If this was a shared assumption, nevertheless in time some divisions opened up on strategic lines: how best could this goal be achieved? Fifth, jubilation at the Catholic revival and imminent national reconversion in Britain ran alongside a more paradoxical view of the true state of British society. In a way eerily reminiscent of the arguments used by Christian supporters of slavery in the American South in *antebellum* America, many French Catholics identified the perils of industrialisation, mass poverty and urbanisation with the individualism in British society that had ostensibly produced the anti-slavery campaign, and then made the further connection, predictably, to the pervasive influence of Protestantism.[15] Hailing the restoration of the hierarchy in England, Veuillot could write in 1850 that this was a country in which Protestant barbarity over 300 years had created the widest possible gulf between rich and poor, a country of all countries in which the rich least knew their soul and the people were most despised, and whose capital had more prostitutes than any other city in Europe.[16] Finally, all these points were brought together and epitomised in Catholic views of Ireland. French Catholic writers almost universally saw Ireland as the great flaw in the British governmental system – a practical, governmental and religious tyranny. The French press carried frequent reports on Irish affairs. Daniel O'Connell was hailed as a hero of Catholicism, not nationalism. Veuillot typified widely shared views: before O'Connell, he wrote, Ireland was enslaved, more imprisoned by the Anglican despotism than by the seas around it; but now, thanks to this great citizen of the world, whose country was Rome ('*Rome était sa patrie en effet*'), she was free.[17]

[13] Jules Gondon, *Du Mouvement Religieux en Angleterre, ou Les Progrès du Catholicisme et le Retour de l'Église Anglicane à l'Unité; par un Catholique* (Paris, 1844), p. xix.

[14] *Correspondence du R.P. Lacordaire et de Madame Swetchine*, p. 24.

[15] See E. Fox-Genovese and E. D. Genovese, *The Mind of the Master Class: History and Faith in the Southern Slaveholders' Worldview* (Cambridge, 2005).

[16] L. Veuillot, 'Le Pape et l'Angleterre (rétablissement de la hiérarchie)', dated 12 November 1850, originally published in *L'Univers*, reprinted in Veuillot, *Mélanges Religieux, Historiques, Politiques et Littéraires (1842–1856)*, vol. VI (Paris, 1856), p. 17.

[17] L. Veuillot, 'Mort de M. O'Connell', dated 27 May 1847, originally published in *L'Univers*, reprinted in *Mélanges*, vol. III, p. 552.

Despite the shared nature of these assumptions about the world, there were significant differences between the various elements of the French Church on other issues, such as the liturgy, education, the monarchy and above all the scope and nature of papal primacy. But French reactions to the Oxford Movement demonstrated the tenacity and ubiquity of French suspicion of Britain. Just as one could encounter surprisingly critical views of the British monarchy amongst French monarchists – as when the comte d'Artois, the future Charles X, claimed he would rather earn his living as a wood-cutter than be king of England[18] – so too in Gallican ecclesiastical circles (as opposed to *civil* Gallicanism) there was very little sympathy for the constitutional position of the established Church of England.[19] Gallicans and ultramontanes alike simply wrote it off as Erastian.[20]

THE 'LIBERAL CATHOLICS'

The most significant shift away from this framework occurred amongst the so-called 'Mennaisian' or 'liberal Catholic' school, which generally showed the warmest French Catholic reaction to the Oxford Movement. It was not a particularly large group, and its influence on the French Church has perhaps been exaggerated. It was composed, at its core, of those who embraced Lamennais's intoxicating mixture of political liberalism and ultramontanism, and yet distanced themselves from Lamennais and submitted to the judgement and discipline of the Church after Gregory XVI's encyclical *Mirari Vos* (1832).[21] Admiration for British political and religious liberty predisposed many of this group towards sympathy with Anglicans. Yet papal condemnation of Lamennais, as well as French ecclesiastical politics, made this a highly sensitive matter.

This is evident in Charles de Montalembert's *Letter to a Rev. Member of the Camden Society on … the Puseyites* (1844), published in English by a Catholic publishing house based in Liverpool. Montalembert, who had

18 A. Cobban, *A History of Modern France*, vol. II, *1799–1871*, 2nd edn (Harmondsworth, 1965), p. 73.

19 On the distinction between civil and ecclesiastical Gallicanism, see Gough, *Paris and Rome*, pp. 22–33.

20 See *L'Ami de la Religion* on the corruption, nepotism, and subjection of the Church of England, drawing probably on John Wade's *Extraordinary Black Book*: 'Sur L'état de l'église Anglicane et des communions dissidents en l'Angleterre', *L'Ami de la Religion*, 11 October 1831, and a shorter report, 6 September 1831.

21 The most useful in English probably remains A. Vidler, *Prophecy and Papacy; A Study of Lamennais, the Church, and the Revolution* (London, 1954), but see also B. M. G. Reardon, *Liberalism and Tradition: Aspects of Catholic Thought in Nineteenth-Century France* (Cambridge, 1976).

been educated in England, was an ardent Anglophile.[22] Yet the pamphlet was provoked by the Camden Society's making him an honorary member without consulting him – something that could have played badly in France.[23] Its general tone therefore was hostile.[24] The Camden Society, he claimed, posed as a scientific society, but in fact aimed at identifying the Catholic Church of the Middle Ages with the 'Anglican schism'.[25] The Church of England had stolen the term 'Catholic'; not even the 'debased' Russian Orthodox Church recognised Anglicans as Catholic.[26] To dig out 'a small channel of your own … wherein the living truth will run … will no more be granted to you, than it has been to the Arians, the Nestorians, the Donatists, or any other triumphant heresy'.[27] The great luminaries of the medieval English Church, he continued, would be horrified to see married priests and English prayers in the now 'desecrated edifices' they had built.[28] In a passage which he must have regretted subsequently, Montalembert averred that the Anglican Church surpassed even continental Protestantism in its subservience to the state: 'Was there ever a Church, except perhaps the Greco-Russian since Peter I, which has so basely acknowledged the supreme right of secular power?'[29] The pretensions of the Puseyites to resurrect Catholic art and teaching within the Church of England were misplaced; even if they succeeded, they would not have taken a step nearer to true unity, and would have severed their Church from the rest of Protestantism, as Newman himself implied.[30]

[22] The most recent biography is B. Cattanéo, *Montalembert: un catholique en politique* (Chambray, 1990); there is also a relevant older study, É. Lecanuet, *Montalembert: sa jeunesse (1810–1836)*, 2nd edn (Paris, 1898).

[23] J. M. Neale, whom Montalembert had met at Madeira in 1843, is the likeliest addressee of the *Letter*. Michael Chandler mentions Montalembert's honorary membership of the Camden Society in his biography of Neale; Neale thought Montalembert was privately delighted, but Chandler does not appear to be aware of the *Letter* and of the public embarrassment the Society's action had would have caused Montalembert: M. Chandler, *The Life and Work of John Mason Neale* (Leominster, 1995), p. 128.

[24] Tellingly, the only English pamphlet (to my knowledge) to reply directly to Montalembert's was by an Evangelical who thanked him for his candour about Romanism and used it to criticize the 'moral dishonesty' of the Tractarians: [Anon.] 'An Enquirer', *A re-print of a letter addressed to a Revd Member of the Cambridge Camden Society … with a few remarks and queries* (London, 1845), p. 3.

[25] Montalembert, *Letter*, p. 3.

[26] *Ibid.*, p. 4. [27] *Ibid.* [28] *Ibid.*, p. 5.

[29] *Ibid.*, p. 8. Comparison of royal domination of the Anglican and Russian Orthodox Churches was a common trope of Catholic polemic; see for example *Le Guide des Curés*, as quoted by Christopher Wordsworth: 'Ce n'est qu'à Petersbourg et à Londres qu'un autocrate qui est Roi-pontife et qu'une femme à la fois Reine et Papesse peuvent s'ériger, en regulateurs du culte et en juges du Clergé, des sects grecques et protestantes': Wordsworth, *Diary*, p. 164.

[30] Wordsworth, *Diary*, p. 10. Montalembert referred to a passage in Newman's sermon on the 'Connexion between Personal and Public Improvement' in *Sermons on Subjects of the Day*

If these views were sincere – and by then Montalembert was well informed about the Oxford Movement – the intensity of his criticism nevertheless contrasts with the position he adopted by the mid 1850s. In a work that attracted some notoriety on both sides of the Channel, *The Political Future of England* (first published as articles in *Le Correspondant* in 1855), we find an altogether different view of English religion.[31] This book's main focus was political, endorsing British constitutionalism in almost extravagant terms.[32] But Montalembert also reviewed the condition of both the Catholic and Anglican Churches in England. He still had harsh things to say about Anglican 'greedy pride' in usurping the magnificent church buildings of medieval England.[33] And yet a more cautious note was there in his assessment of the Christian character of Britain. Though disfigured, he observed, Christianity in England had force and energy, and Catholics should not seek to import a foreign Catholic culture into England, but trust the Catholic Church's ability to adapt itself to national customs and traditions, including liberty.[34] Montalembert's French target was obvious. But far from disparaging Anglicanism in comparison with continental Protestantism, he now suggested that it had more vitality and strength: it was a 'positive, substantial religion, incomplete as it is and sovereignly illogic [*sic*]'.[35] He praised the faith and the influence of Anglican laymen and ministers, and admitted there had been a 'revival of religious feeling in England amongst Anglicans as well as amongst the Catholics'.[36] This had produced a general improvement in morality and public religious feeling.[37] Montalembert described the Anglican clergy as a branch of the aristocracy, and, being an aristocrat himself, he had a very high view of aristocracy.[38] The overthrow of the Anglican Church would not be a triumph for Catholicism, but would simply enlarge the ranks of rationalists and Socinians.[39] The Puseyites had opened the door to the serious study of ecclesiastical antiquity, and put many on the road to the unity of the Church; they had engendered 'a profound respect for religious

(London, 1843), pp. 149–50, where he warned against severing personal, spiritual unity from the external unity of the Church: 'We cannot hope for the recovery of dissenting bodies, while we are ourselves alienated from the great body of Christendom … Break unity in one point, and the fault runs through the whole body' (p. 150).

31 Charles de Montalembert, *The Political Future of England*, 2nd edn (London, 1856).

32 For example, 'England alone has created and for centuries maintained a system which oppresses and humiliates no one, and permits every Englishman to walk erect, and to say for himself, as well as the King [*sic*], *Dieu et mon droit*!': *ibid.*, p. 95.

33 Montalembert, *Political Future of England*, pp. 166–7.

34 *Ibid.*, pp. 176–8. 35 *Ibid.*, p. 193. 36 *Ibid.*, p. 194.

37 *Ibid.*, p. 195. 38 *Ibid.*, p. 197. 39 *Ibid.*, p. 200.

traditions, and consequently for Catholic authority'.[40] They had restored and built hundreds of churches, freed up sittings and made efforts to throw off the yoke of temporal power, including reviving Convocation.[41] In sum, the Anglican Church had a vital, though not exclusive, role to play in the Christian struggle against the social difficulties that threatened England.[42]

Why had Montalembert changed his mind? By the mid 1850s he was thoroughly disillusioned with the Second Empire, and a gulf had opened up between him and Veuillot on the relations of Church and state in France, marked by his praise of political liberty in *Les intérêts catholiques au XIXe siècle* (1852). *The Political Future of England* had a French audience in view: Montalembert was reminding the French of what they were lacking, and he idealised English society accordingly.[43] But he was also perhaps influenced by others in his circle of contacts, including Ambrose Phillipps de Lisle. Phillipps was a frequent correspondent of Montalembert. In 1840, for example, he wrote to Montalembert that the 'great mass of the English people are profoundly religious though heretical'.[44] Writing again, in 1841 he expressed a view on the Oxford Movement that casts more light on Montalembert's later change of heart: 'I am fully persuaded', Phillipps affirmed,

> that there is no point of the globe at the present moment in which a more important work is going on for the glory of the Catholick [*sic*] Church, than that which is in progress in Oxford . . . you can have no idea, excepting from personal intercourse, of the immense advance towards Catholicism, which these good men have made. In fact they are in every respect much more Catholick than half of those who have been born and bred Catholick.[45]

Phillipps was out on a limb amongst English Catholics on this; in the same letter he even accused his co-religionists of being 'stupidly perverse' for their sneers against the Tractarians.[46] Though his views echoed to some extent those of Nicholas Wiseman – a man himself of incalculable influence in interpreting Tractarianism to the wider Catholic world – they were expressed with much less discretion and realism. Montalembert too never went as far as Phillipps, either in his appreciation of the Tractarians, or in Phillipps' apparent extension of a notion of partial Catholicity to

[40] *Ibid.*, p. 201. [41] *Ibid.*, pp. 202–3. [42] *Ibid.*, p. 205.

[43] On this, see R. Aubert (ed.), *Correspondance entre Charles de Montalembert et Adolphe Dechamps 1838–1870*, Bibliothèque de la Revue d'Histoire Ecclésiastique 69 (Louvain, 1993), pp. 5–12.

[44] L. Allen, 'Letters of Phillipps de Lisle to Montalembert', *Dublin Review*, 228 (1954), pp. 53–64, at p. 59.

[45] *Ibid.*, p. 62. [46] *Ibid.*

include Anglicans.[47] Phillipps's role in the Association of Universal Prayer for the Uniting of the Anglican and Catholic Churches is probably well enough known, as is the fact that his Association for the Promotion of the Unity of Christendom was effectively condemned by the Vatican in 1864.[48] He was a risky associate. And yet his ceaseless networking drew Montalembert and his friends into the fringes of the Tractarian circle. In 1839 Montalembert was Phillipps' guest at Grace-Dieu, his country estate in Leicestershire, and he had previously met Gladstone in London.[49] In 1841 Phillipps was enthusing to J. R. Bloxam about the prospect of introducing 'some foreign Theologians, who ... thoroughly appreciate the Catholic movement [at Oxford]' to the Tractarian leaders, and this must surely have included Montalembert.[50] In 1852 Lacordaire was a guest at Grace-Dieu, from whence he made a brief detour to Oxford. His description to another associate, Madame de Swetchine, was almost rhapsodic: 'I do not remember having seen anything which has produced such a delightful impression ["*aussi douce impression*"] on me.'[51] The comte de Falloux, another associate, described Oxford in the 1830s similarly: 'It is a city crowded ["*toute peuplée*"] with catholic monuments and preserved by protestants, like a sort of national Pompei. The monasteries have become colleges where the teaching of Christian science is maintained.'[52] Lacordaire described the religious revival in England in terms similar to those of Phillipps himself: '[O]ne feels throughout this country that the era of religious liberty has here begun its reign and is producing its due effects: they are building, founding, creating an art for the Church.'[53] He explicitly repudiated the characteristic view of Protestantism encountered amongst French Catholics: Protestantism had its weaknesses, and did lead some people out of Christianity, but this was not its general effect. For Lacordaire, England had been Protestant for 300 years, but was hardly a pagan country. The Bible, taught by the clergy, encouraged Christian notions in the population at large, and a supernatural life properly

[47] '[T]he Roman Church is (to use the expression of the creed of P. Pius IV) the Mother and Mistress of ALL Churches, but She is only an integral though the principal part of the Church Catholick': *ibid.*, p. 60.

[48] M. Chapman, 'The Fantasy of Reunion: The Rise and Fall of the Association for the Promotion of the Unity of Christendom', *JEH*, 58 (2007), pp. 49–74; on Spencer, see J. V. Bussche, *Ignatius (George) Spencer, Passionist (1799–1864), Crusader of Prayer for England and Pioneer of Ecumenical Prayer* (Leuven, 1991).

[49] Allen, 'Letters', pp. 53–4.

[50] Purcell, *Phillipps*, vol. 1, p. 203; in the event, the meeting did not take place.

[51] *Correspondence du R. P. Lacordaire et de Madame Swetchine*, p. 507.

[52] Comte de Falloux, *Mémoires d'un Royaliste*, 2 vols. (Paris, 1888), vol. 1, p. 115.

[53] *Correspondence du R. P. Lacordaire et de Madame Swetchine*, p. 508.

so-called in many souls of good faith, in whom the Holy Spirit worked through grace and salvation.[54] If there are echoes there of Phillipps, there are surely also some of Newman himself.

THE VEUILLOT CIRCLE

Lacordaire's striking appreciation of the merits of Anglicanism would not have found much sympathy with Louis Veuillot (1813–83), the self-made journalistic genius of the 'extreme ultramontane' party, and editor of *L'Univers*. Montalembert had been a major shareholder in the newspaper in the late 1830s, but by 1842 Veuillot had taken it over completely, and turned it in a direction which 'openly disdained moderation and restraint'.[55] Yet commercially his policy was a success. The paper's circulation increased fourfold in just five years.[56] It out-sold all the other religious journals, and parish clergy snapped it up. Christopher Wordsworth, visiting Paris in 1844, found it 'now the principal organ of the church party in France'.[57] As Austin Gough put it, Veuillot in effect 're-educated the parish clergy, giving them a daily course in simplified theology and political doctrine, supported by a highly tendentious précis of Church history'.[58] Though welcoming English conversions, it was hardly likely that Veuillot would take a generous view of the Oxford Movement as a movement within Anglicanism: Anglicanism was simply another form of the general heresy of Protestantism, with all its dire effects.[59]

Nevertheless, *L'Univers* was an essential medium for those who wanted to communicate what was happening in England to a continental audience, and even those much out of sympathy with Veuillot – Phillipps, for example – used it.[60] Though he did not write all that much himself on

[54] *Ibid.*, p. 518, letter dated 21 September 1852.

[55] J. N. Moody, 'The French Catholic Press in the Education Conflict of the 1840s', *French Historical Studies*, 7 (1972), pp. 394–415, at p. 398.

[56] *Ibid.* [57] Wordsworth, *Diary*, p. 13.

[58] Gough, *Paris and Rome*, p. 96.

[59] See his judgement on the Gorham case: 'There are bishops in England who call themselves Christian and who tolerate the fact that one of their colleagues has been obliged to give to part of his flock a pastor who denies baptismal regeneration; and this bishop, after having vainly protested against this impiety, simply accepted it; that's what we call barbarousness': Veuillot, *Mélanges*, vol. VI, p. 18.

[60] Phillipps's letter to Bloxam, quoted above, referred to *L'Univers*'s approval of his letter to the *Tablet* rebutting its crude criticism of the Tractarians: Purcell, *Phillipps*, vol. I, p. 203; this was before Veuillot became editor-in-chief. Gondon claimed *L'Univers* was the only paper to keep continental readers informed of the progress of Catholicism in England, and of the Anglican Church; however, this was patently untrue, as a review of the contents of *L'Ami de la Religion* demonstrates (see below); but then Gondon was hardly an impartial witness.

England, Veuillot was an astute judge of what his readership wanted, and made a point of employing a specialist writer on English Church matters, Jules Gondon.[61] Gondon himself occupied a mediating position between Veuillot and (for example) Montalembert; he was on good terms with the latter, and with Phillipps. Veuillot himself doubted that Gondon 'was really one of us'.[62] Gondon's writing on Tractarianism and in particular on the motives of converts to Catholicism is extensive and worthy of a paper in itself.[63] Here I shall concentrate on the work which most directly addressed the Oxford Movement, *On the Religious Movement in England, or, the Progress of Catholicism and the Return of the Anglican Church to Unity* [my translation] (published in Paris in 1844), complementing it with his introduction to an anthology of translations from writings of converts.[64]

On the Religious Movement in England is a substantial work, constructed from Gondon's contributions to *L'Univers*, and based on firsthand acquaintance with the Oxford leaders. Gondon made three visits to England between 1838 and 1844, and in 1842 he met Pusey, Newman and others in Oxford.[65] Drawing on Cobbett's highly polemical *History of the Protestant 'Reformation'* (1824–7), he claimed that the strength of the English constitution derived not from its Protestantism, but from its origins at the hands of Catholic kings.[66] He devoted seven chapters to the Church of England, identifying three parties – (1) the evangelicals, (2) the 'political' high churchmen (who corresponded somewhat to Froude's 'Zs', the so-called 'High and Dry' school, or the high church 'Orthodox', in Peter Nockles's terminology) and (3) the Puseyites, or Anglo-Catholics.[67] The latter re-emphasised the Catholic roots of Anglicanism and rejected

[61] Apart from his writing on English Church affairs, Gondon was probably best known for his pamphlets on Italian politics, including *De l'état des choses à Naples en Italie* (Paris, 1855).

[62] Allen, 'Letters', p. 61; E. Veuillot, *Louis Veuillot*, 4 vols. (Paris, 1899–1913), vol. II, p. 429, as cited in Gough, *Paris and Rome*, p. 99.

[63] See also J. Gondon, *Conversion de soixante ministres Anglicans* (Sagnier, Paris, 1846), and *Notice biographique sur le R. P. Newman* (Paris, 1853).

[64] Gondon, *Mouvement*; Gondon, *Motifs*.

[65] Gondon refers to these meetings in *Mouvement*, p. viii. The introductory letter he brought with him from Fr James Jauch, a Catholic chaplain in London, is preserved amongst Newman's papers, and includes an interesting warning to Newman about Gondon, who was described as 'a good young man of sound catholic principles, but still rather belonging as yet more to this world ... You will wisely measure Your word, because redactors of newspapers take hold of every one fit to create sensation', *LDN*, vol. IX, pp. 101–2; see also p. 115. Christopher Wordsworth met Gondon in Paris in 1844; his *Diary* contains an extensive account of their conversations.

[66] Gondon, *Mouvement*, p. 33.

[67] *Ibid.*, pp. 224–6; see also P. B. Nockles, *The Oxford Movement in Context. Anglican High Churchmanship 1760–1857* (Cambridge, 1994), pp. 25–43.

state interference in the Church; in this, the sincerity of Pusey, Newman and others could not be doubted.[68] They had no desire to be leaders as such: '[T]hey limit themselves to engendering ["*à féconder*"] by their genius and their talent the marvellous renaissance of which Oxford was now the heart.'[69] They were not innovators; they merely sought to restore doctrines lost to the Anglican Church; '[I]n a word, the Catholic spirit is being rekindled ["*l'esprit catholique se rallume*"] gradually within the Anglican Church.'[70] Catholics should welcome this renewal, and encourage individual conversions, so that in time the whole Anglican Church might be drawn towards the centre of Catholic unity, Rome.[71]

This sounds not dissimilar to the views of Montalembert and Lacordaire, but whilst Gondon certainly showed a great deal of sympathy for the Tractarians, he conceded very little to their claims of Catholicity.[72] He strongly denied that unity with Rome would be gained more quickly if Catholics in England and Ireland rectified their own abuses – there were none.[73] There was no salvation outside the Roman communion.[74] There was nothing intrinsically Catholic about the Oxford Movement; all hung on its value as a means for leading people to Rome. His understanding of Protestantism savoured strongly of the degenerative view; in England, he said, all possible forms of Protestantism were to be found, and they were all breaking up, piece by piece.[75] He could hail the Roman Catholic Church as mother of true religious liberty – on that, of course, he came near to Montalembert, and one can see why Veuillot was a little ambivalent about him – but there was nothing intrinsically valuable about Anglicanism.[76] Moreover, Gondon's cast of mind shared with Veuillot's a predilection for sharply defined contrasts and oppositions. The world was divided simply into rationalists and Catholics; Protestants were in effect a subset of rationalism.[77] Anglicanism had lost its light and life, and so its sons walked in darkness, their spiritual life extinguished.[78] Even when he considered the temperance movement, he could only see that the efforts of the Protestant associations were sterile; only the approach of the Catholic agencies, and the influence of Fr Matthews, were fruitful.[79] Thus, Gondon's position overall had some elements of the constructive

[68] Nockles, *The Oxford Movement*, p. 227. [69] *Ibid.*, p. 232.

[70] *Ibid.*, pp. 233–4. [71] *Ibid.*, pp. 235–6.

[72] This was reflected in Christopher Wordsworth, *Letters to M. Gondon, author of 'mouvement religieux en Angleterre'* (London, 1847), a strongly worded rebuttal of Gondon's arguments.

[73] *Ibid.*, pp. 331–3. [74] *Ibid.*, p. 335. [75] *Ibid.*, p. xiv.

[76] *Ibid.*, p. xii. [77] Gondon, *Motifs*, p. ix.

[78] *Ibid.*, p. vii. [79] Gondon, *Mouvement*, pp. 210–19.

approach favoured by the Montalembert circle, and yet it also shared much with the polarised view of Veuillot himself.

L'Ami de la Religion

Despite the Gallican loathing of Veuillot, Gallican reactions to the Oxford Movement were much the same as his. Here, there is space only for a brief consideration of what was, by the 1830s, the most influential Gallican paper, *L'Ami de la Religion. L'Ami* never had the circulation of *L'Univers*; appearing three times a week, rather than daily, its influence lay in its popularity with the ecclesiastical hierarchy. Founded in 1796 and frequently suppressed under the Directorate and the Empire, by the 1830s it was moderately legitimist.[80] Later it was purchased by Félix Dupanloup, though its editorial policy did not change substantially.[81]

In contrast to *L'Univers*, *L'Ami* was moderate in tone and rather stuffy. It was a perplexing mixture of periodical and newspaper, carrying a handful of long articles along with columns of news. Its coverage was international: ransacking the foreign press for titbits of information, it maintained a consistently high level of interest in religious and political news about France's most powerful neighbours in particular. Almost every issue carried news and articles about England. Naturally news about Catholicism predominated, especially when, from the late 1820s, the paper began to comment on the remarkable efflorescence of Catholicism in Britain. Reports drawing on the *Laity's Directory* and other sources frequently enumerated new churches built, new monasteries opened and conversions made.[82] But Anglicanism featured too, and with increasing frequency in the late 1830s and early 1840s. In 1841, for example, *L'Ami* carried seventeen separate articles on Tractarianism; in 1842, sixteen; in 1843, no fewer than twenty. Often these were substantial articles, including long extracts from translations of Tractarian works.

L'Ami's editorial outlook on Tractarianism differed little from the main lines of the ultramontanes' view. It shared with other French Catholics abhorrence both for the English tyranny in Ireland and for the missionary work of the Bible societies.[83] Its references to Protestantism were always

80 Moody, 'The French Catholic Press', p. 397. Moody's assertion that by the 1840s the paper had moved to a 'rigid ultramontanism' makes little sense, in the light of Dupanloup's involvement.

81 May, 'The Falloux Law', p. 84.

82 In 1832 alone: 21 February, 28 July and 20 October.

83 See, for example, 'Sur la réforme de l'église anglicane en Irlande', *AR*, 12 March 1833, and the implied approval of Count Achille de Jouffroy's criticism of the Bible societies, in *AR*, 22 December 1832.

negative: Protestantism's existence was 'the most striking witness to the infirmity of human reason, which wraps itself up ["*qui s'isole*"] in its own pride'.[84] Anglicanism was a 'parliamentary religion', and certainly not a sister Church to Rome.[85] *L'Ami* could not resist quoting with approval the Abbé Genoude's letters on England, originally published in the *Gazette de France*: 'The English are all mad when they speak of religion. You have just been speaking with a man you have found perfectly reasonable – but you discover he won't even go to Rome; like Luther, he would rather see the devil than the Pope.'[86] Placing the characteristic prejudices about Protestantism alongside suspicion of British colonial policy enabled French Catholics to see Anglicanism as the handmaid of tyranny. Not only in Ireland, but also in India, Africa and, back on the doorstep of Europe, Gibraltar was there evidence of the English establishment's oppression of Catholics – the word almost always used for the Gibraltar government, for example, was 'junta'. On the Oxford Movement, the paper's line was not all that different from Gondon and Veuillot (and indeed Gondon almost certainly wrote for it as well as for *L'Univers* from time to time[87]). The movement was to be welcomed as a rejection of Protestantism, and for its recovery of elements of Catholic devotion and doctrine, but only because it assisted the movement of converts to Rome. So eager was *L'Ami* to see this goal fulfilled, that it was frankly credulous. Several times in the early 1840s it carried without question wildly exaggerated claims about the numbers of Anglican clergy who were Puseyites – 5,000 on one informed estimate, or half of the total, on another.[88] It quoted and apparently accepted a report from *The Examiner* that even Queen Victoria was tending to Puseyism, and that a Puseyite was to be private tutor to the Prince of Wales.[89]

L'Ami's naivety about such things is telling: by the early 1840s, the Catholic press in France was working within a hermeneutic of imminent national conversion. Stories about Tractarianism, however flimsy, were instantly seized on as proof of what was about to happen. But over the course of the 'twelve years', the coverage of the paper varied considerably. A narrative of the Oxford Movement from *L'Ami* alone would look oddly misshapen. Apart from some passing references, the first article directly on

[84] *AR*, 8 October 1840.

[85] 'De la reaction qui s'opère en Angleterre, dans le sens catholique', *AR*, 30 July 1842, and 'Sur le Puseysme (1)', *AR*, 19 September 1843.

[86] *AR*, 9 February 1841.

[87] An item on the divisions of Anglicanism in 1844, for example, was couched in terms closely matching those of Gondon's *Mouvement, AR*, 9 March 1844.

[88] *AR*, 29 July 1843, and 31 October 1843.

[89] *AR*, 8 October 1842.

Tractarianism did not appear until June 1835, when the paper covered the Abbé Jager's literary exchange with Benjamin Harrison and Newman.[90] There were several articles in the early and mid 1830s on the activity of the Catholic convert George [Ignatius] Spencer.[91] Not until 1838, however, was there a substantial assessment of the Oxford Movement. This was an article that drew heavily on Wiseman, and which for the first time placed Pusey before the paper's readership.[92] For the next five years, it was his name that dominated *L'Ami*'s coverage, and the terms 'Puséyste' and 'Puséysme' became the most common designations in French journalism to describe the movement. Much of the conventional narrative of the movement was scarcely touched on, if noticed at all, by *L'Ami*, until 1843. The controversies over Hampden's chair, Froude's *Remains*, the Jerusalem bishopric, even Tract 90, were largely ignored as they occurred. All that changed, however, in the early 1840s. The swelling number and scale of articles on Tractarianism marked a new phase in *L'Ami*'s coverage. A substantial article on Newman's retraction in April 1843 began a shift in emphasis away from Pusey.[93] Thereafter, the paper's coverage tracked the conventional narratives of the movement much more closely: Newman's resignation from St Mary's, Littlemore, Pusey's sermon and his inhibition from preaching, Ward's *Ideal* – these and other events were extensively reported and discussed, leading up to Newman's conversion. The paper's reporting of that event captured perfectly its impression of the movement's value and limitations: the news would rejoice all truly catholic hearts; Newman's reception had taken place in the chapel attached to the monastery he had built; some years ago Pusey had begun to lose the best part of his influence; his most enlightened disciples, and those most faithful to the principles he had adopted, had chosen another master, and now that master is one of our brothers; this, of all the graces God has given recently to English Catholics, is the most illustrious and the one likely to lead to the most abundant fruit.[94]

CONCLUSION

The readership of *L'Ami*, *L'Univers* and other Catholic papers and journals were gradually tutored to read the Oxford Movement not so much for

90 *AR*, 27 June 1835; see also L. Allen (ed.), *John Henry Newman and the Abbé Jager: A Controversy on Scripture and Tradition (1834–1836)* (London, 1975).

91 See *AR*, 4 June 1836.

92 'Rapport sur l'état actuel du protestantisme en Angleterre (1)', *AR*, 13 January 1838.

93 'Sur M. Newman, l'un des chefs des Puséystes', *AR*, 4 April 1843.

94 *AR*, 18 October 1845.

what it told them about the Church of England and the religious condition of England, as about the post-Napoleonic resurgence of the Catholic Church, and above all the imminent conversion of England. Their expectations were unrealistically high. But it is easy to understand why. It was hardly surprising that French Catholics tended to read Tractarianism in terms of their own preoccupations and struggles. The revolutions of 1830 and 1848 were in different ways catastrophes for the French Church that book-ended a period of deep tension between Church and state. The growing internal struggle of ecclesiastical Gallicans and ultramontanes over education and the Roman rite ran through a period that otherwise looked like one of remarkable revival for the Church. French Catholics identified readily with Catholics in England – whom they almost never differentiated into Irish and English constituents – when they saw them growing remarkably in numbers and struggling with the political and social challenges thrown at them by the state Church. Furthermore, apart from the practice of shadowing the English press, information about the Oxford Movement mostly came from a small group of people, some of whom were hardly likely to furnish impartial evidence. There were other French commentators on the Oxford Movement than those I have covered, including some travellers in England.[95] There were some Anglicans who did not convert, and were never likely to, who travelled in France and clearly acted as a source of information for the French – such as Christopher Wordsworth, whose published *Diary in France* itemised extensive conversations with a variety of French Catholics, including Gondon, in August 1844. But French commentators also did rely on a number of converts who were not reliable sources at all.[96] The ensuing distortion of perspective gradually unravelled after Newman's conversion, though not instantly: it was sustained by the restoration of the hierarchy in 1850, but the popular reaction to that in England almost certainly disillusioned many of those who had swallowed the idea that large swathes of the Church of England were only waiting for the opportune moment to cross over.

[95] *L'Ami* mentions the following: Count Achille de Jouffrey, *Adieux à l'Angleterre* (*c.*1832); J. F. M. Travern, *Discussion amicale sur l'église anglicane* (1817; translated by W. Richmond, 1828 and republished *c.*1835); Abbé Brajeul, *Lettres d'un catholique à un protestant de l'église anglicane* (1839); Abbé Robert, *Souvenirs d'Angleterre et Considérations sur l'Église anglicane* (*c.*1842).

[96] One was Francis Diedrich Wackerbarth, who, while still an Anglican, confided to a French contact that if O'Connell had secured the appointment of a Puseyite bishop during the Whig ministry, that bishop could have gone to Rome and secured the reunification of the Anglican and Catholic Churches, and the queen would not have been troubled about renouncing the Royal Supremacy: *AR*, 5 October 1841.

This brief discussion of French Catholic reactions to the Oxford Movement opens up some glimpses into deeper issues in Catholic ecclesiology and ecumenism. The clue is there in the terminology. Stephen Sykes observed that the word 'Anglicanism' referred at first only to the ecclesiological system advocated by Tractarianism.[97] Yet French writers used the term in the 1830s in the modern sense, for the whole Anglican 'system', as it was a handy enough derivation from '*l'église Anglicane*' and summarised a system of belief and practice distinct from Catholicism. But that raised a difficulty of description when dealing with Anglican claims to Catholicity, and especially with the terms 'Anglo-Catholic' and 'separated brethren'. Gondon, for example, did use the term 'Anglo-Catholic', but explained to his readers that he did not intend any concession to Anglican claims of Catholicity in doing so: in fact, he said, linking the words Anglican and Catholic 'implied a contradiction', but it was useful because it 'expressed perfectly the abnormal position ["*la position anormale*"] of the Church of England'.[98] Yet Gondon's view was evidently not quite the same as that of Lacordaire, for example, and the later Montalembert, for whom there did seem to be a sense in which it was not absolutely a contradiction to see some Catholic identity in the Church of England. What about the phrase 'separated brethren', however? It was a fairly common expression in Catholic discourse, and again did not necessarily concede anything to Protestant claims; it could be used in a heavily ironic way, with the emphasis on the 'separated'. More commonly, French observers used the phrase 'misled' or 'misguided', or even 'lost' brethren – '*frères égarés*'.[99] Yet increasingly the term '*frères separés*' also came into use to describe the Tractarians, particularly at the hands of people such as Spencer and Phillipps, when their letters and articles were translated into French.[100]

That terminological shift differentiated two different reactions to Tractarianism. One was strategic appreciation: from Gallican circles to extreme ultramontanes, French Catholics mostly watched the Oxford Movement with growing excitement, as they contemplated the overthrow of a state Protestant Church and the reconversion of England. The Church of England could not in any sense be called Catholic; but the so-called Catholic movement within it could well bring not just thousands of individuals, but a whole nation back to the See of Peter. To the extent

97 S. W. Sykes, *Unashamed Anglicanism* (London, 1995), p. xiv.
98 Gondon, *Mouvement*, p. vii.
99 For example, *AR*, 1 June 1844.
100 *AR*, 12 August 1841, citing a letter from George Spencer to *L'Univers*.

that it was likely to do so, the Oxford Movement could be welcomed, and the hand of friendship extended to its followers. But with a small, if influential, minority, a more subtle appreciation of the merits of the movement gained ground. Montalembert, Lacordaire and their circle shared a more positive evaluation both of the English constitutional settlement, and of Anglicanism as a religious tradition. Implicitly, they recognised a certain substantial, if attenuated, Catholicity within it. Their brothers were 'separated', but not thereby 'lost' altogether. Is it altogether fanciful to see a distant connection between their appreciation of their 'separated brethren' and the ecclesiology of 'separated brethren' in *Unitatis Redintegratio*?

CHAPTER 12

The Oxford Movement, Jerusalem and the Eastern Question

Mark Chapman

On 16 July 1842, John Henry Newman, who was already beset with doubts over the authority of the Church of England, wrote to James Cecil Wynter:

> While the Catholic Church is broken up into fragments, it will always be a most perplexing question, what and where is the Church? ... I consider that according to the great Anglican theory, (by which I mean the theory of Laud, Bull, Butler, etc upon which alone the English Church can stand as being neither Roman nor Puritan) the present state of the Church is like that of an Empire breaking or broken up. At least I know of no better illustration. Where is the Turkish Empire at this day? In a measure it has been and is no more. Various parts of it are wrested from it. Others are in rebellion, there is no one authority which speaks – individuals in particular localities know not whom to obey or how they shall be best fulfilling the duty of loyalty to the descendants of Ottoman – sometimes the truest allegiance is to oppose what seems to come with authority – In many cases there is only a choice of difficulties – For the most part a Turk speaking of Ottoman laws[,] precepts, prerogatives, powers[,] speaks but of Roman times – He appeals to history he means the earlier Empire when he speaks of Ottoman principles and doctrines. – In whatever degree this is true of the Turkish power at least it is true of the Church. Our Lord founded a kingdom, it spread over the earth and then broke up – Our difficulties in faith and obedience are just those

On the Eastern question more broadly, see P. E. Shaw, *The Early Tractarians and the Eastern Church* (Milwaukee, 1930); G. Florovsky, 'Orthodox Ecumenism in the Nineteenth Century', *St Vladimir's Seminary Quarterly* 4 (1956), pp. 2–11; E. C. Miller, Jr, *Toward a Fuller Vision: Orthodoxy and the Anglican Experience* (Wilton, 1984), chap. 5; H. R. T. Brandreth, *The Œcumenical Ideals of the Oxford Movement* (London, 1947), chap. 2; Brandreth, 'The Church of England and the Orthodox Churches in the Nineteenth and Twentieth Centuries', in S. Runciman *et al.*, *Anglican Initiatives in Christian Unity: Lectures Delivered in Lambeth Palace Library* (London, 1967), pp. 19–39; L. Litvack, *J. M. Neale and the Quest for Sobornost* (Oxford, 1994), chap. 1; T. Soloviova, 'Anglican–Orthodox Dialogue in the 19th Century and Gladstone's interest in the Reunion of Christendom', in P. Francis (ed.), *The Gladstone Umbrella* (Hawarden, 2001), pp. 50–72. See also P. E. Shaw, *American Contacts with the Eastern Churches, 1820–1870* (Chicago, 1937) and G. Rowell, 'Eastern Horizons: Anglicans and the Oriental Orthodox Churches', in N. Aston (ed.), *Religious Change in Europe, 1650–1914* (Oxford, 1997), pp. 381–97.

which a subject in a decaying Empire has in matters of allegiance. We sometimes do not know what is of authority and what is not.

The Catholic Church, splintered as it was into different communions, appeared to be like the collapsing Ottoman Empire, the 'sick man of Europe', which lacked both authority and power. For Newman, the coherence of the Church was thrown into doubt as it had split into a number of competing parts. Indeed, it was not clear precisely where the Church was to be found:

> Under these circumstances when we are asked 'Where is the Church?' I can but answer where it *was* – The Church only *is*, while it is one, for it is individual, as he who animates and informs it ... The Church has authority only while all the members conspire together – In such strange circumstances as those in which we find ourselves, we can but do what we think will best please the Lord and Master of the Church, what is most pious; we rule ourselves by what the Church did or said before this visitation fell upon her, we obey those that are set over us first because they *are* set over us – next because at least the apostolical succession is preserved ... We consider the local Church the type and deputy of the whole.[1]

For Newman, there was an obvious tension between the claims of the universal and the particular. Similarly, it was not clear precisely where authority is to be located. While he still claimed allegiance to the primitive Church and trusted in the authority of the successors to the apostles, he was evidently beginning to question the nature of this temporal version of catholicity – perhaps it would be better preserved in something like a new state that might replace the collapsing Ottoman Empire with a more efficient and coherent government?

While Newman was obviously speaking metaphorically in his comparisons between the collapse of the Ottoman Empire and the state of the Catholic Church, his analogy is of particular interest with regard to ecumenism. The 1830s had been a period of great unrest in the Ottoman Empire, especially in the Holy Land and Egypt where Mehmet Ali (1769–1849; pasha of Egypt from 1805 to 1849) had led a rebellion against the Ottomans.[2] The Eastern question had consequently become increasingly important in European politics through the 1830s. This would lead directly to greater interest in the Eastern Churches. The loose hold over

[1] Newman to Wynter, 16 July 1842, *LDN*, vol. IX, pp. 43–4. The correspondent of this letter had previously been identified as W. R. Lyall, archdeacon of Maidstone.

[2] For a fascinating account of the perception of the Holy Land in the nineteenth century, which includes a discussion of British reactions to the conflicts of the 1830s, see Eitan Bar-Yosef, *The Holy Land in English Culture* (Oxford, 2005), pp. 120, 140.

the Empire by its central power had been replaced by a far more volatile and complex situation which led to both the piecemeal modernisation of the Empire, as well as its gradual dismemberment as the great powers jockeyed for influence: the Christian nations of Russia, France, Prussia and Britain attempted to fill the emerging vacuum. At the same time as it reined in the powers of Mehmet Ali, the Treaty of London of 2 June 1841 greatly expanded the spheres of influence of the European powers in the Ottoman Empire.

Although it certainly did not begin in the 1830s,[3] interest in the Eastern Churches by the English Church was reawakened through this clamour for political influence in the Middle East. At the same time, while the breakdown of the Ottoman Empire in Europe and Asia Minor led to a vastly expanded knowledge of the Eastern Churches, it also provided the conditions for the expansion of ecumenism through the creation of the Anglo-Prussian Jerusalem bishopric,[4] which – perhaps ironically – Newman regarded as the beginning of the end of his Anglican existence: 'As to the project of the Jerusalem Bishopric', he wrote in his *Apologia*, 'I never heard any good or harm it has ever done, except what it has done for me; which many think a great misfortune, and I the greatest of mercies. It brought me on to the beginning of the end.'[5] The collapse of an Empire thus had quite momentous – albeit unforeseen – consequences for the Church of England and the Roman Catholic Church.

THE OXFORD MOVEMENT AND ECUMENISM

Before the creation of the Jerusalem bishopric in 1841, the same year as the Treaty of London, there was little interest by the members of the Oxford Movement in the Eastern Churches. References are sparse and – despite a common inheritance of patristic authority in the Anglican and Eastern Churches – there was very little questioning of the supremacy of

[3] J. Pinnington, *Anglicans and Orthodox: Unity and Subversion 1559–1725* (Leominster, 2003); P. Doll (ed.), *Anglicanism and Orthodoxy: 300 Years after the 'Greek College' in Oxford* (Oxford, 2006); G. Williams, *The Orthodox Church of the East in the Eighteenth Century Being the Correspondence between the Eastern Patriarchs and the Nonjuring Bishops* (London, 1868); Florovsky, 'Orthodox Ecumenism in the Nineteenth Century'; Miller, *Toward a Fuller Vision*.

[4] On the Jerusalem bishopric, see M. Lückhoff, *Anglikaner und Protestanten im Heiligen Land. Das gemeinsame Bistum Jerusalem (1841–1886)* (Wiesbaden, 1998), esp. chap. 6; S. M. Jack, 'No Heavenly Jerusalem: The Anglican Bishopric, 1841–83', *JRH*, 19 (1995), pp. 181–204; P. B. Nockles, *The Oxford Movement in Context: Anglican High Churchmanship, 1760–1857* (Cambridge, 1994), pp. 156–64; K. Curran, *The Romanesque Revival: Religion, Politics, and Transnational Exchange* (State College, PA, 2003), pp. 179–84.

[5] J. H. Newman, *Apologia pro vita sua* (1913) (repr., Whitefish, MT, 2004), p. 146.

the Western Church. This means that Charles Miller's bold assertion that the 'Oxford Movement was an ecumenical movement' needs to be treated with a degree of caution. Indeed, it was only some aspects of the Oxford Movement that ultimately led in an ecumenical direction, as Miller himself recognised:

> Though this was not the conscious intention of its first members, the movement's unequivocal assertion of the identity of Anglicanism with the continuing life of the universal church provided a theological impetus for contact and dialogue with the other churches of catholic Christendom.[6]

While the branch theory of the Church, which Miller presumably has in mind, led some towards an openness to ecumenism, for the most part the early Tractarians displayed either a complete indifference towards other Churches or even a resolutely unecumenical spirit. Despite what Peter Nockles calls its 'Froudean bravado and fighting talk',[7] the polemics of the Oxford Movement in general retained a high view of the alliance between throne and altar uniquely embodied – at least in England – by the National Church. This attitude was noted by William Palmer (1811–79) of Magdalen College, Oxford, one of the pioneers of ecumenical engagement with the Orthodox Churches and a close collaborator with the Tractarians. Explaining the Oxford Movement to the Russian theologian Khomiakoff, he wrote:

> It began in a spirit of the most loyal Anglicanism evoked by the successful attacks of the Protestant sectaries and the Roman Catholics, aided by a Liberalist Government, upon the Established Church. It proceeded up to a certain point, in a spirit of resolute hostility to Popery no less than to Sectarianism.[8]

Although it had its radical edge, the Oxford Movement can be seen at least in part as one of the many conservative responses in Europe to the collapse of the Holy Alliance in the period following the revolutions of 1830.[9] Although they might have located the catholicity of the Church in the period of the undivided Church of the ecumenical councils, the

[6] Miller, *Toward a Fuller Vision*, p. 61.
[7] Nockles, *Oxford Movement in Context*, p. 83.
[8] W. J. Birkbeck (ed.), *Russia and the English Church during the Last Fifty Years*, vol. 1, *Containing a correspondence between Mr. William Palmer, Fellow of Magdalen College, Oxford and M. Khomiakoff, in the years 1844–1854* (London, 1895), p. 22. On Palmer, see R. Wheeler, *Palmer's Pilgrimage: The Life of William Palmer of Magdalen* (Oxford, 2006). For Palmer's efforts to harmonise Anglican and Orthodox doctrine, see William Palmer, *A Harmony of Anglican Doctrine with the Doctrine of the Catholic and Apostolic Church of the East being the Longer Russian Catechism* (Aberdeen, 1846); and William Palmer, *Dissertations on Subjects Relating to the "Orthodox" or "Eastern-Catholic" Communion* (London, 1853).
[9] N. Aston, *Christianity and Revolutionary Europe, c.1750–1830* (Cambridge, 2002), chap. 8.

Tractarians did little to question the authority and superiority of their own Church as the legitimate successor of the primitive Church.[10] What they sought, above all, was a purification of all Churches by a return to the past. In his sermon on *Primitive Tradition*, for instance, Keble limited tradition solely to

> those rules, in which *all* primitive Councils are uniform, those rites and formularies which are found in *all* primitive liturgies, and those interpretations and principles of interpretation in which *all* orthodox Fathers agree ... genuine canons of the primitive Councils, and the genuine fragments of the primitive Liturgies, are reducible into a small space; even although we go so low down in both as the division of the Eastern and Western Churches, including the six first Councils general, and excluding image-worship and similar corruptions by authority.[11]

Such a conception of catholicity ruled out the contemporary Roman Catholic Church, which was developing a very different understanding of tradition, as well as the Orthodox Churches for whom 'image-worship' was a key component of their religious system.

Hostility to Rome characterised many of the writings of the Tractarians.[12] This is hardly surprising given the specific conditions of the emergence of the Oxford Movement as a response to the perceived end of Anglican hegemony in the repeal of the Test and Corporation Acts in 1828 and Catholic Emancipation the following year. Many of the *Tracts* were decidedly anti-Roman in their thrust, even though few went as far as the other William Palmer – of Worcester – (1803–85), who later sought to deny Nicholas Wiseman the right to exercise his episcopal ministry without a licence from his 'legitimate Diocesan, the Bishop of Worcester'.[13] Even though the branch theory of the Church would later become the basis for ecumenical encounter with the Churches of the East, in the hands of its first major exponent it was used to defend the sole claims of the Church of England within its national boundaries. It alone was the legitimate branch of the catholic Church in England. Unity was perceived more in mystical than in concrete terms. Indeed, for Palmer, visible division was not a sign of disunity. He wrote in his *Treatise of the Church*: 'the divisions in the Catholic Church of Greek, Roman, and Anglican, though

[10] Nockles, *Oxford Movement in Context*, chap. 2.

[11] J. Keble, *Primitive Tradition Recognised in Holy Scripture* (London, 1836), p. 40.

[12] R. H. Greenfield, 'The Attitude of the Early Tractarians to the Roman Catholic Church' (unpublished D.Phil. thesis, University of Oxford, 1956).

[13] William Palmer, *A Letter to N. Wiseman, D.D. (calling himself the Bishop of Melipotamus)* (Oxford, 1841), p. 4.

unfortunately they are the cause of interruption of communion, do not break up the unity of the Church of Christ'.[14] The Church of England did not 'by any voluntary act whatever, *separate herself from the communion of the universal* church'.[15] In short, Palmer claimed, members of the Church of England continued to 'acknowledge the catholic church, respect its authority, receive its faith, and have never been cut off from it'.[16]

In an 1840 article in the *British Critic* on 'The Catholicity of the English Church', Newman similarly advocated a branch theory of the Church even though his anti-Romanism was now more muted than Palmer's. Intercommunion, he held, was not a fundamental aspect of catholicity while the great branches of the church were divided. It was a fiction to suppose that the Roman Communion could spread its appeal across the 'vast spaces of Russia'.[17] Newman went on: 'The Anglican view, then, of the Church has ever been this, that its portions need not otherwise have been united together for their essential completeness, than as being descended from one original.'[18] Similarly, he noted: 'The Anglican theory of ecclesiastical unity, [is] that each church is naturally independent of every other; each bishop a complete channel of grace, and ultimate centre of unity; and all unions of see with see but matters of ecclesiastical arrangement.'[19] Descent from the early Church conferred an invisible unity which made visible unity a secondary and solely practical consideration: at least in this article, reunion was therefore not high on Newman's agenda.

Shortly before its publication, Newman had sent the draft article to Pusey to ask for his approval. While noting that he liked it, Pusey nevertheless had reservations about the lack of any discussion of the Greek Church. This had been merely alluded to, since Newman knew so 'little about it'. For the first time, Pusey showed some sympathy with the Eastern Orthodoxy. He wrote back to Newman:

> I like your article very much. I only wish you had dwelt more upon the case of the Greek Church; we make but a poor appearance against the Roman communion, but practically the question with people will be, Are we safe out of communion – not with the Catholic Church, but – with Rome? Here, then, I think we might take refuge under the shadow of the Greek Church; people who might doubt whether we were not schismatical, on account of the smallness of our communion, and might have misgivings about ourselves, would feel that the

[14] William Palmer, *Treatise on the Church*, 3rd edn, 2 vols. (London, 1842), vol. 1, part 1, chap. iv, section iii; section iv.

[15] *Ibid.*, vol. 1, part 1, chap. x; vol. 1, part 2, chap. ii, section vii, pp. 339–42.

[16] *Ibid.*, vol. 1, part 1, ch. x, section v.

[17] J. H. Newman, 'The Catholicity of the English Church', *British Critic* (January, 1840), p. 74.

[18] *Ibid.*, p. 54. [19] *Ibid.*, p. 6.

language of the Fathers would not apply, when it would cut off 90,000,000 in one Orthodox Church.[20]

According to Pusey, what had to be emphasised in any notion of catholicity was the idea of antiquity, which required acquaintance with the Fathers. What was key for the future was making available translations of the Fathers, which would help Churches purify themselves through knowledge of the past: 'the translation of their writings is the greatest boon which could be given to the Church; and if it were not presumptuous to say so, there would seem to have been some secret Providence directing you to the project of translation'.[21]

For the most part, opposition to Rome by the Tractarians was most usually expressed in terms of anti-Popery than in outright hostility to the Roman Catholic Church. Nevertheless, even at the end of the Tractarian period, there was still little sympathy among the leading figures with the practical system of the Roman Church. For instance, Newman – with only a few years left in the Church of England – was able to articulate the differences between Popery and Roman Catholicism in his open letter to Bishop Bagot of Oxford following the publication of Tract 90 in 1841:

I cannot speak against the Church of Rome, viewed in her formal character, as a true Church, since she is 'built upon the foundation of the Apostles and Prophets, Jesus Christ Himself being the chief Cornerstone'. Nor can I speak against her private members, numbers of whom, I trust, are God's people, in the way to Heaven, and one with us in heart, though not in profession. But what I have spoken, and do strongly speak against is, that energetic system and engrossing influence in the Church by which it acts towards us, and meets our eyes, like a cloud filling it, to the eclipse of all that is holy, whether in its ordinances or its members. This system I have called in what I have written, Romanism or Popery, and by Romanists or Papists I mean all its members, so far as they are under the power of these principles; and while, and so far as this system exists, and it does exist now as fully as heretofore, I say that we can have no peace with that Church, however we may secretly love its particular members … This view … presents her under a twofold aspect, and while recognizing her as an appointment of God on the one hand, it leads us practically to shun her, as beset with heinous and dangerous influences on the other.[22]

[20] Pusey to Newman, 31 December 1839, in H. P. Liddon, *Life of Edward Bouverie Pusey*, 4 vols. (London, 1894), vol. II, p. 152.

[21] The *Library of the Fathers* was published from 1838. The full title emphasises the temporal sense of catholicity: *A Library of the Fathers, anterior to the division of the East and West. Translated by members of the English Church.* See Liddon, *Life of Pusey*, vol. I, chap. 18; and R. W. Pfaff, 'The Library of the Fathers: The Tractarians as Patristic Translators', *Studies in Philology*, 70 (1973), 329–44.

[22] J. H. Newman, *A Letter to the Right Reverend Father in God, Richard, Lord Bishop of Oxford, on the Occasion of No. 90 in the Series called The Tracts for the Times* (Oxford, 1841), pp. 20–21.

Thus, according to Newman, like all other Churches Rome had to be purged of its excesses which expressed themselves in the system of Popery.

In his Tractarian period at least, Pusey was not overly concerned with other Churches. His principal interest was with internal reform of the Church of England rather than any prospect of what he regarded as premature reunion. Before there could ever be an outward and visible union of the Churches, he held, there would need to be a renewal within each Church. All Churches would be brought into line as they conformed ever more to the teachings of the primitive Church. This understanding of reunion was based on what I have called elsewhere Pusey's 'catholicism of the word'.[23] Such a form of catholicism was defined primarily not in terms of development and accretion nor even of episcopal authority, but on the basis of a return to the explicit teachings of the undivided Church. Like Keble, Pusey held that the tradition of the Church was something concrete and had been fixed in the first five centuries or so. In 1839, for instance, he had written a lengthy open letter to Bishop Bagot countering the charge of Romanism in the *Tracts*. Defending the primitive method, he clearly differentiated between general and ecumenical councils: 'We believe that (although Councils which have been termed "General," or which Rome has claimed to be so, have erred,) no real Œcumenical Council ever did; that is, no Council really representing the Universal Church.'[24] According to Pusey, doctrine was to be defined in terms of what had been taught in the period of the first six Councils. This was principally because the 'Church then was one, and it was to His one Church, and as being one, that our Lord's promise was made. And now, on that ground, her functions are, in this respect suspended; she cannot meet as one.'[25]

Although he refused to rule out the possibility of future reunion and a further ecumenical council, Pusey nevertheless held that so long as the state of disunity persisted, all that the Church could hope for was purification through returning to what was indisputably taught by the united Church of the ecumenical councils. This process of purification applied equally to all Churches, including the Roman Catholic Church: 'For the present', Pusey claimed, 'what has been bestowed in the period of unity;

[23] M. Chapman, 'A Catholicism of the Word and a Catholicism of Devotion: Pusey, Newman and the First *Eirenicon*', *Zeitschrift für neuere Theologiegeschichte/Journal for the History of Modern Theology*, 14 (2007), pp. 167–90.

[24] E. B. Pusey, *A Letter to the Right Rev. Father in God, Richard Lord Bishop of Oxford on the Tendency to Romanism imputed to Doctrines held of old, as now, in the English Church* (Oxford, 1839), p. 44.

[25] *Ibid.*, p. 44.

the main articles of the faith have been fixed and guarded by her, and we possess them in her Creeds ... With this, Rome is not content; *we* take the event, (as it is ever ruled to be) as the interpreter of prophecy; *she* would bind her Lord to accomplish it in her own way.'[26] In short, Pusey wrote:

> The Anglican view regards the promise as belonging to the universal Church, but restrained to those Articles of the faith which were delivered to her, and to which in her real Œcumenical Councils she has defined; one may add, the Ultra-Protestant view narrows the promise, like the Church of Rome, in extent, to a handful of believing Christians, and, like Rome also changes the subjects of the Faith, substituting a system of its own for Catholic truth; differing, as before, from Rome in this, that what Rome claims to the Churches of her own communion, it applies to individuals.[27]

Unlike these polar extremes, the Church of England was consequently the 'representative of the Universal Church' to which submission was owed. At the same time she had no right to add anything to the faith that could not be proved on the basis of the tradition of the primitive Church.[28]

Following the controversies surrounding Tract 90, Pusey continued to argue in a similar vein. He published a lengthy open letter to Richard William Jelf in which he claimed that 'there is ample scope for our Article in asserting that "General Councils may err, and sometimes have erred," without touching on the ecumenical'.[29] When applied to the process of renewal this meant that the excesses of all Churches – which included those matters that had been decided by erroneous general councils – would need to be removed through application of the ecumenical 'patristic' principle. For Pusey, this was to become something like the functional equivalent of the *sola scriptura* of the Reformation, which Nockles refers to as 'patristic fundamentalism'.[30] Indeed Pusey believed that the patristic principle had been retained through the English Reformation and provided the basis for the great Anglican apologists such as John Jewel in their critiques of Rome. He wrote to Jelf: 'We have remained since the Reformation, as before, a branch of the Church Catholic; we were placed on no new platform; our Reformers did not, like Luther, form for us any new system of doctrine, such as that which bears his name; they ever appealed to catholic antiquity; submitted their own judgement to hers.'[31]

[26] *Ibid.*, p. 45. [27] *Ibid.*, p. 49. [28] *Ibid.*, p. 52.

[29] E. B. Pusey, *The Articles treated on in Tract 90 reconsidered and their Interpretation vindicated in a Letter to the Rev. R. W. Jelf, D.D.* (Oxford, 1841), p. 27.

[30] Nockles, *Oxford Movement in Context*, p. 145.

[31] Pusey, *The Articles*, p. 8.

As Pusey's later controversies with Newman over his three-volume *Eirenicon* in the years leading up to the Vatican Council exemplify, such an approach to catholicism meant that there was a fundamental difference between them over what precisely could be held to be *de fide* by the catholic Church. Since catholicity was defined primarily in terms of a return to the teaching of primitive Church or what Pusey called the 'first deeds',[32] this meant that reunion was regarded by Pusey – as it had been for Newman in his Anglican years – as a second-order activity which could take place only after a cleansing process in all the Churches (including those Churches which embraced the apostolic succession).

THE OXFORD MOVEMENT AND THE EASTERN CHURCHES

By 1840 Pusey was becoming increasingly aware of the importance of the Churches of the East, in part through the efforts of the Coptic Patriarch of Alexandria to persuade the SPCK to print a copy of their liturgy 'as unmutilated by the Romanists'.[33] In response to the Cambridge Professor of Hebrew, William Hodge Mill, who had reservations about the use of monophysite language, Pusey wrote to his fellow Tractarian Benjamin Harrison, asking: 'What should hinder communion from being restored with the Orthodox Greek Church? Does it seem that we need insist on their receiving the *Filioque*, or that they would not enter into communion with us because we retain it?'[34] In a further letter written a few days later he continued:

> It will come as a painful question to many, and to some be a difficulty as to our Church (as they come to see the perfect unity of Antiquity), why are we in communion with no other Church except our own sisters and daughters?
>
> We cannot have communion with Rome; why should we not with the *Orthodox* Greek Church? Would they reject us, or must we keep aloof? Certainly one should have thought that those who have not conformed with Rome would, practically, be glad to be strengthened by intercourse with us, and to be countenanced by us. One should have hoped that they would be glad to be re-united with a large Christian Church exterior to themselves, provided we need not insist upon their adopting the *Filioque*.[35]

The following year, as the Jerusalem bishopric came to fruition, Pusey spoke of the renewal of different Churches across Europe as they

[32] *Ibid.*, pp. 181–3. [33] Liddon, *Life of Pusey*, vol. II, p. 148.
[34] E. B. Pusey to B. Harrison, 17 February 1840, in Liddon, *Life of Pusey*, vol. II, p. 148.
[35] E. B. Pusey to B. Harrison, 21 February 1840, *ibid.*, p. 149.

responded to the difficult times and began to purify themselves. In his *Letter* to Jelf, Pusey noted:

It may be long ere the issue comes; at present, the course pointed out to the several Churches seems to be to amend themselves, to become again what they once were, even though imperfect; to 'return to their first deeds'; so may they, through repentance and amendment of life, and keeping the commandments, be led to further knowledge of the truth, and in the end be restored to unity, if this blessing be yet in store for the Church. At least such seems the course which things, under God's guidance, are taking. Thus even the Greek Church is again become proselytizing; the Gallican Church is sending out missionaries and praying for our conversion, shewing her new life, in part, in seeking to extend her own communion; in Prussia, religion is reviving in connection with Lutheran doctrine; we are being guided back to the principles of our Church.

Here, for the first time in print, and in the same year as the Treaty of London, Pusey noted the importance of the Orthodox Churches, even if they were included along with Lutherans and Gallicans. At the same time, however, he suggested that reunion had to play second fiddle to internal reform: 'repentance and zeal must come first, union afterwards; union is to be looked for, as God's gift, to be prayed for, not compassed by man's device ... our duties then lie not now towards Rome; our present path and duties are plain; – with ourselves; to fit ourselves to be His instrument'.[36]

In a statement which would shortly afterwards become unthinkable, Pusey even claimed that 'it may be that our first office will be, not with Rome, but with those bodies which were separated from Rome at the same time as ourselves, but were not so signally blessed and preserved'. The Jerusalem bishopric might even allow for the purification of the Prussian Church through the restoration of episcopacy:[37]

[I]t may be, that through us what is lacking in them to the full gifts of a Church is to be supplied ... thus we may be reunited with the rest of Christendom, not alone nor selfishly, but decked with the rich jewelry of them whom we have won back to Primitive Faith and Discipline ... Our office then is with ourselves and within ourselves, ready to do acts of charity to those severed from us, as far as we may without compromise, but not seeking untimely union.[38]

As Pusey thought about the implications of the Jerusalem bishopric, so he contemplated a restoration of relations with the Eastern Churches which might be realised through the constructive presence of Anglicans

[36] Pusey, *The Articles*, pp. 181–3.
[37] See also Liddon, *Life of Pusey*, vol. II, p. 250.
[38] Pusey, *The Articles*, pp. 181–3.

in the Holy Land. Indeed, in a typically Orientalist approach to the Eastern Church, he claimed that the intellectual superiority of the English Church could assist in the renewal of Orthodoxy. In his *Letter* to Jelf he asked:

Why should we direct our eyes to the Western Church alone, which, even if united in itself would yet remain sadly maimed, and sadly short of the Oneness she had in her best days, if she continued severed from the Eastern? After a long separation, in which we have not much been known by name to the Eastern Church, much less our real character, God seems again to be opening to us ways of kindly intercourse, with some portions of her, which must increase love, which will also, under God's blessing, help her to restore the holiness and knowledge of her early years, and therewith make her wish to understand us better, and be united to us.[39]

By the following year, however, Pusey had begun to have serious reservations about the Jerusalem bishopric. In his open letter to the Archbishop of Canterbury of 1842, he noted that it had come at such a time when it could do nothing other than arouse suspicion among a 'Greek Communion which has just heard of us and is beginning to value us'.[40] What was little more than what he called an 'experiment' in union between very different communions, one protestant and one apostolic, and which, according to Pusey, had a membership of no more than four persons, could do little else but lead to resentment among the local Christians: 'What an outward and unspiritual view of a Church and of Episcopacy would it seem to imply us to hold, who could think that such a juxta-position [*sic*] of discordant elements under the – one cannot say government but the – presidency of our Bishop, could constitute a Church!'[41]

Newman, who had been opposed to the Jerusalem bishopric from the beginning, went even further than Pusey, seeing the scheme as little more than a piece of cynical politics. In October 1841, he wrote to his friend S. F. Wood:

Have you heard of this deplorable Jerusalem matter? I do dread our bishops will convert our men to Rome, Dr Wiseman sitting still. There is not a single Anglican at Jerusalem, but we are to place a Bishop (of the *circumcision, expressly*) there, to collect a communion out of Protestants, Jews, Druses and

[39] *Ibid.*, pp. 184–5. Others thought that a preoccupation with the Eastern Churches could distract attention from continued negotiations with the Roman Catholic Church. See, for instance, J. W. Bowden, 'The Anglican Church in the Mediterranean', *British Critic* (July 1841), pp. 135–63.

[40] E. B. Pusey, *A Letter to His Grace the Archbishop of Canterbury, on some circumstances connected with the present crisis in the English Church* (Oxford, 1842), p. 115.

[41] *Ibid.*, p. 116.

Monophysites, conforming under the influence of our war-steamers, to counterbalance the Russian influence through Greeks, and the French through Latins.[42]

He wrote in a similar vein a week later: 'What a miserable concern this Jerusalem Bishoprick is! We have not a single member of our Church there, except for travellers and officials. It is a mere political piece of business, to give our government influence in the country.'[43] He even claimed that the archbishop was 'doing all he can to unchurch us',[44] and that 'we join with Protestant Prussia to found a sect and put a bishop over it'.[45] However well versed in rabbinical learning the new bishop might be, Newman wrote to *The Times* in November 1841, 'this will not teach him the difference between Catholic and Protestant'.[46]

For both Newman and Pusey, even worse than joining with a Protestant body would be the possibility of conversion and proselytising of local Christians by the new joint Church.[47] While this had been explicitly ruled out by the Turkish civil authorities and had been upheld in the archbishop's letter to the local Christian leaders that had been given to Michael Solomon Alexander, the first bishop (which Newman called an 'afterthought'),[48] conversion remained a very real danger, especially since so many Protestant Christians regarded the Orthodox Church as engaged in little more than idol worship.[49] Newman wrote with more than a hint of irony about the real intentions behind the scheme:

I see it now professed that an understanding is to exist between our Bishop and the Greek orthodox body. This was an afterthought. The main object was, and I believe is, to negociate [*sic*] with the heretical Monophysites especially of Mesopotamia. Mesopotamia is the way to the Euphrates; the Euphrates is the way to India. It is desirable to consolidate our Empire. What is the Church worth if she is to be nice and mealy-mouthed when a piece of work is to be done

42 J. H. Newman to S. F. Wood, 10 October 1841, *LDN*, vol. VIII, p. 293.

43 J. H. Newman to M. R. Giberne, 17 October 1841, *ibid.*, p. 299; almost identical sentiments are expressed in letters from Newman to Thomas Mozley, 24 October 1841 and to H. A. Woodgate, 24 October 1841, *ibid.*, pp. 307, 309–10.

44 Newman to Mrs T. Mozley and Mrs J. Mozley, 17 October 1841, *ibid.*, p. 296.

45 J. H. Newman to J. Keble, 24 October 1841, *ibid.*, p. 306.

46 J. H. Newman to *The Times*, 1 November 1841 (unpublished), *ibid.*, pp. 314–16, 315.

47 George Williams, who had been chaplain to Bishop Alexander, in his introduction to *The Orthodox Church of the East*, published the correspondence of Archbishop Howley with the patriarchs (p. lxii).

48 Newman to *The Times*, 1 November 1841 (unpublished), p. 315.

49 See, for instance, Joseph Bardsley, *The Greek Church, her doctrines and principles contrasted with those of the Church of England* (London, 1870).

for her good lord the State. Surely, surely, in *such* a case, some formula can be found for proving heresy orthodoxy and orthodoxy heresy.[50]

Pusey moved in a quite different and far more hopeful direction than Newman, again expressing a degree of hope for reunion with the Eastern Churches. Indeed the bishopric of Jerusalem had provoked a sense of crisis for the future of the Church:

> But any attempts at 'conversion' or connivance in persons forsaking the Orthodox Communion in which they were baptized, besides encouraging sin, must immeasurably delay the prospect of union with that communion … We must either rigidly prescribe to ourselves our own bounds and remain with them, or give up the opening prospect of ultimate reunion. We cannot treat the Orthodox Greek Church as once Orthodox and heterodox; Orthodox, in that we think union justifiable, heterodox, since heresy alone can justify secession. The reopened intercourse with the East is … a crisis in the history of our Church. It is a wave which may carry us onward, or, if we miss it, it may bruise us sorely and fall on us, instead of landing on the shore. The union or disunion of the Church for centuries may depend on the wisdom with which this providential opening is employed.[51]

This meant that despite the reservations among the Tractarians, the Jerusalem bishopric, which was in part a response to political circumstances, ensured that the question of the Eastern Churches was firmly – if accidentally – on the agenda of the Church of England. Ecumenism with the Orthodox thus owed much to the ecclesiastical and political response to the Eastern Question.

CONCLUSION

The first serious studies of the Eastern Churches emerged shortly afterwards, even if those who undertook them, such as the 'ecclesiastical Don Quixote', William Palmer of Magdalen, were subject to ridicule and had to find support first in the Episcopal Church of Scotland and then in Rome.[52] Others became the objects of much suspicion, including J. M. Neale, the hymnologist and historian.[53] Nevertheless in the early 1840s an openness to the East began to emerge which meant that by the

[50] Newman to *The Times*, 1 November 1841 (unpublished), pp. 315–16.

[51] Pusey, *Letter to His Grace the Archbishop of Canterbury*, pp. 117–18.

[52] See William Palmer, *Notes of a Visit to the Russian Church in the years 1840, 1841*, ed. J. H. Newman (London, 1882), p. viii: 'Mr Palmer demanded communion, not as a favour, but as a right; not as if on his part a gratuitous act, but as his simple duty; not in order to become a Catholic, but because he was a Catholic already.'

[53] On Neale, see Litvack, *J. M. Neale*.

time of the crisis provoked by the First Vatican Council, which more or less put an end to ecumenical discussion with Roman Catholics for a generation, the Orthodox could participate as equal players around the ecumenical table, most importantly at the Bonn Conferences of 1874 and 1875.[54] The slow breakdown of the Turkish Empire consequently led in part to the desire for a new ecclesiastical settlement based on national catholic Churches – the power vacuum in the East created the conditions for the possibility for reunion discussions between the severed non-Roman Churches of the East and West.

From the perspective of the twenty-first century it is worth remembering that the replacement regimes for the crumbling Ottoman Empire have still not been finally settled: Iraq, the Holy Land and the Balkans are seldom off the political agenda. The impact of global politics in the Middle East, which began in earnest in the 1830s and has continued ever since, has shaped a contemporary political situation which admits of no easy answers. The successor states to the Ottoman Empire are products of recent political settlements, even if they are usually supported by competing and often incompatible historical myths and religious ideologies. Similarly – and despite a century and a half of ecumenical discussion – the unity of the catholic Church, which Newman compared to that Empire, remains equally unsettled, perhaps for similar reasons.

[54] M. Chapman, 'Liddon, Döllinger and the Bonn Conferences of 1874 and 1875: A Case Study in Nationalism and Ecumenism', *IKZ*, 92 (2002), pp. 21–59.

CHAPTER 13

Ignaz von Döllinger and the Anglicans

Angela Berlis

I dare say I do not tell you anything new when I mention that in Germany also all eyes – of Protestants as well as of Roman Catholics – are turned in fear and hope towards Oxford; it becomes more and more probable that your great and memorable movement will have essential influence also on the course of religious development in Germany.[1]

Ignaz von Döllinger (1799–1890) was one of the most significant theologians and Church historians of the nineteenth century. From the 1870s, his rejection of the First Vatican Council and his prominent role in the counter-movement made him known world-wide and at all levels of society. Throughout his life, Döllinger, who had learned English at an early age, had a great interest in and fondness for England and its churches. This interest was extensively explored for the first time a few years ago by the well-known Döllinger scholar Victor Conzemius in a valuable article on 'Döllinger and the Victorian Church'.[2] Conzemius, who also published editions of the correspondence between Döllinger and Lord Acton and between Döllinger and Lady Blennerhassett,[3] depicted not only Döllinger's Anglophilia but even his Anglomania.[4] We find a similar assessment made by one of Döllinger's contemporaries, Julian Joseph Overbeck (1820–1905), a Roman Catholic convert to

The translation of this chapter is by Joanne Orton, Croydon, and Martin della Valle, Berne (Switzerland). I would also like to thank the Royal Dutch Academy of Sciences, Amsterdam, for its financial support for the translation.

[1] I. von Döllinger to E. B. Pusey, 4 September 1842; original German letter in Pusey House, Oxford; English translation in H. P. Liddon, *Life of Edward Bouverie Pusey*, 4 vols. (London, 1893–7), vol. II, 295–6.

[2] V. Conzemius, 'Ignaz von Döllinger und die Viktorianische Kirche', in A. M. Birke and K. Kluxen (eds.), *Kirche, Staat und Gesellschaft im 19. Jahrhundert. Ein deutsch-englischer Vergleich* (Munich, 1984), pp. 121–52.

[3] V. Conzemius (ed.), *Ignaz von Döllinger, Briefwechsel 1820–1890: Ignaz von Döllinger – Lord Acton*, 3 vols. (München, 1963–71); *Ignaz von Döllinger – Lady Blennerhassett* (Munich, 1981).

[4] Conzemius, 'Viktorianische Kirche', p. 122.

Orthodoxy, who insisted that Döllinger was 'foolishly fond of what is English'.[5]

Döllinger's close relationships with prominent Anglicans are well known: these include his friendship with William Ewart Gladstone, who first visited him in Munich in 1845[6] and corresponded with him until just a few months before Döllinger's passing,[7] as well as various other Anglicans. His home in Munich (from 1839, Frühlingstrasse 11; later, after the Franco-German War, his rented accommodation at Tannstraße 11[8]) provided hospitality to English travellers even before the First Vatican Council (1869–70), and for decades he took in English lodgers (the best known was his student and friend Sir John Acton, who lived with him from 1850 to 1854). Among German theologians, Döllinger was certainly one of the best informed on the spiritual and cultural life in England, an expertise which he nurtured through personal contacts and also through his regular reading of English newspapers and journals.[9]

Thirty-eight years ago Conzemius pointed to the need for 'a more accurate investigation of Döllinger's attitude towards Anglicanism'.[10] Conzemius addressed this gap to some extent a few years later.[11] In England, Owen Chadwick also described Döllinger's relation to Anglicans, placing a special emphasis on his efforts towards Church reunion, in particular the Bonn Union Conferences of 1874 to 1875.[12] This chapter will explore

[5] J. J. Overbeck to Olga Novikoff, 14 November 1871: 'for I feared that Döllinger who is as foolishly fond of what is English, as he is foolishly hostile to what is Russian, would engage himself with the Anglican Church and thus compromise the whole movement'. Quoted in W. Kahle, *Westliche Orthodoxie. Leben und Ziele Julian Joseph Overbecks* (Leiden, 1968), pp. 132–3.

[6] J. Friedrich, *Ignaz von Döllinger. Sein Leben auf Grund seines schriftlichen Nachlasses*, 3 vols. (München, 1899–1901), vol. II, pp. 223–6. E. Steinsdorfer, 'Gladstone – gehörte mit Lord Acton zum Döllinger-Kreis', *IKZ*, 90 (2000), pp. 123–31; M. Chandler, 'The Significance of the Friendship between William E. Gladstone and Ignaz von Döllinger', *IKZ*, 90 (2000), pp. 153–67.

[7] Döllinger's thirty letters written between 1845 and 1889 are in the BL in London; Gladstone's forty-six letters written between 1862 and 1889 are at the Bayerische Staatsbibliothek Munich (hereafter BSBM). *Letters 1821–1890 by and to Johann Joseph Ignaz von Döllinger. Correspondence between Ignaz von Döllinger and William Ewart Gladstone*, transcribed by Hubert Huppertz (Alverskirchen: unpublished manuscript, 1995).

[8] Friedrich, *Ignaz von Döllinger*, vol. II, p. 154.

[9] Parts of Döllinger's estate, including a large collection of newspaper clippings, can be found in the Archives of the Catholic Diocese of Old Catholics in Germany at Bonn (BABo); the Döllinger Papers (*Döllingeriana*) stored at the BSBM contain many references to this expertise, e.g. in the 'Zeitgeschichtliche Notizen' (BSBM, *Döllingeriana*, VII).

[10] V. Conzemius, 'Ignaz von Döllinger: The Development of a XIXth-Century Ecumenist', *IKZ*, 64 (1974), pp. 110–27, at p. 118.

[11] Conzemius, 'Viktorianische Kirche'.

[12] Owen Chadwick, 'Döllinger and Reunion', in G. R. Evans (ed.), *Christian Authority. Essays in Honour of Henry Chadwick* (Oxford, 1988), pp. 296–34; P. Neuner, *Döllinger als Theologe der Ökumene* (Paderborn, 1979). Some of Chadwick's arguments require correction. He overemphasises Döllinger's concern that the Old Catholic movement might develop into a sect (Chadwick,

Döllinger's relations with members of the Church of England, giving particular attention to Döllinger's view of the Oxford Movement and Anglo-Catholicism, as well as to his contacts with Edward Bouverie Pusey.

DÖLLINGER AND THE OXFORD MOVEMENT

Döllinger was never satisfied with only reading about other countries and cultures; personal contacts were also extremely important to him. In engaging with Döllinger's view of the Church of England and especially the Oxford Movement, we must consider both his correspondence and published works. Döllinger's correspondence shows the wide extent of his circle of acquaintances. He knew many of his correspondents personally and developed these connections through mutual visits or academic exchanges. Among his correspondents was Edward Bouverie Pusey. In their correspondence, Pusey took the initiative when he addressed himself to Döllinger in a Latin letter, dated 30 March 1840, requesting that Döllinger send him excerpts from works of the Church Fathers that were held in the Munich libraries.[13] On 7 February 1842, Döllinger responded that he would send a collection of works by Cyril of Jerusalem, while adding that he had read most of Pusey's works and

> that an acquaintance with your writings has given me a very high idea of the importance of your vocation in the Church of God, and that I am persuaded that you are called upon to do great service not only to your own Church, but also to the Catholic Church in general. As I propose to undertake sooner or later a grand excursion to England I hope to enjoy the pleasure and honour of becoming personally acquainted with you at Oxford.[14]

Pusey thanked Döllinger in the second week following Easter 1842 'for the kind interest, which you express in us'.[15] However, Pusey also added several

'Döllinger and Reunion', pp. 299, 300 and 301). His statement regarding the Bonn Union conference of 1874 'as not an official Old Catholic meeting where the Old Catholics were the hosts' and his claim that 'it was Döllinger's conference' (Chadwick, 'Döllinger and Reunion', p. 313) are both only partially accurate. As chairman, Döllinger was the initiator of the 'Kommission für die Wiedervereinigung der getrennten Kirchen und Konfessionen' (Commission for Reunification of the Divided Churches and Confessions), which was created by the Cologne Old Catholics Congress in 1872 and which later continued its work in sub-commissions. Friedrich, *Ignaz von Döllinger*, vol. III, p. 648. Christian Oeyen, *Die Entstehung der Bonner Unions-Konferenzen im Jahr 1874* (unpublished *Habilitation* thesis, Faculty of Old Catholic – Theology, University of Berne, 1971).

[13] E. B. Pusey to Döllinger, Oxford, 30 March 1840, BSBM, *Döllingeriana*, II. For the handwritten texts in the *Döllingeriana* (BSBM) I made use of the following transcription: *Briefe 1821–1890 an Johann Joseph Ignaz von Döllinger, Döllingeriana*, II, transcribed by Hubert Huppertz, 15 vols. (Alverskirchen: unpublished manuscript, 1997–2003) [hereafter Huppertz, Transcription]; here, vol. XII, pp. 235–6.

[14] Pusey House, Oxford.

[15] BSBM, *Döllingeriana*, II; Huppertz, Transcription, vol. XII, pp. 236–7. Also published in Friedrich, *Ignaz von Döllinger*, vol. II, pp. 215–17.

comments to his thanks. For him, the 'saddest hindrance is disunion'.[16] Then Pusey commented on what he portrayed as the proselytism and obsessive expansiveness of the Roman Catholic Church. These comments included a claim that every Church should be concerned with its own affairs:

This proselytising is the greatest hindrance to the progress of the truth. It brings sorrow, mistrust, suspicion. Each individual who goes over from us to you throws back numberless others. Your communion here (you will not mind my speaking plainly) has too much the character of a rival communion, intent rather on its own aggrandisement than on our restoration. There surely are proofs enough that we are a Church, a Church (we confess ourselves) many ways in an imperfect condition, but still a Church, with strong reviving life, and evident tokens of our Lord's gracious Presence with us, both individually in the Sacraments and on a whole. Our duty then is within her; and that of others to work upon her as a Church, pray for her as one, long that she should be restored to perfect soundness, not try to withdraw her children, one by one, from her. Things will never go on well, until Churches too 'seek not every one their own things' their own enlargement, aggrandisement, but each also 'the things of others'.[17]

Johann Friedrich, Döllinger's biographer, believes that Pusey's candour in this letter convinced Döllinger that he should exercise restraint in their subsequent correspondence. Yet Pusey's assessment was largely borne out by events: when during the 1840s a number of Anglicans involved in the Oxford Movement converted to Catholicism, Roman Catholic circles, including the Munich Görres circle, celebrated 'every conversion of an English or Irishman as a win for the Catholic Church'.[18] Indeed, according to Conzemius, even Döllinger hoped during these years that the Church of England would fall into the Roman Catholic Church's lap as 'a ripe fruit'.[19]

At the end of 1841, Döllinger received from an English acquaintance (a Dr Cox) a pamphlet by Wiseman on 'Puseyism'.[20] Soon, certain circles in Germany qualified 'Puseyism' as 'an English phenomenon through and through', which was viewed as being in opposition to 'German indifferentism'.[21] Döllinger was by now impressed with the significance of the Oxford Movement; indeed, he would later write to Pusey on 4 September 1842 that

[16] Friedrich, *Ignaz von Döllinger*, vol. II, pp. 215–17. [17] *Ibid.*

[18] *Ibid.*, p. 231. On the relationship between the Görres circle and Roman Catholic scholars in England, see M. Bär, *Die Beziehungen des Münchener Görreskreises und anderer katholischer Gelehrter in das katholische England* (St. Ottilien, 2010).

[19] See Conzemius, 'Viktorianische Kirche', p. 133.

[20] N. Wiseman, 'The Catholic and Anglican Churches', *Dublin Review* 11 (1841), p. 240; Friedrich, *Ignaz von Döllinger*, vol. II, p. 218.

[21] See 'Der Puseyismus in England. Der deutsche Indifferentismus. Herrn v. Raumers Rede über Friedrich II', *Historisch-Politische Blätter* 11 (1843), pp. 329–46. The author of this article is probably Döllinger.

I dare say I do not tell you anything new when I mention that in Germany also all eyes – of Protestants as well as of Roman Catholics – are turned in fear and hope towards Oxford; it becomes more and more probable that your great and memorable movement will have essential influence also on the course of religious development in Germany. As a matter of course, and you will most likely not expect it otherwise, all the voices of German Protestantism express their most decided disapproval of your direction, while on the Catholic side a proportionally increasing sympathy is shown.[22]

Döllinger wrote several articles on English Church history for the journal *Historisch-Politische Blätter* (Historical Political Papers).[23] In the first of these, published in 1841, he described the theological developments in the Church of England up to the Commonwealth of Oliver Cromwell (though he did not mention the Oxford Movement in this essay).[24] Döllinger also contributed three articles in 1841–2 on the establishment of the Anglo-Prussian bishopric in Jerusalem – an initiative that was causing intense controversy in England.[25]

Döllinger made three visits to England: in 1836,[26] 1851 and 1858.[27] During his first visit (from September to mid October 1836), he met various Roman Catholics. In Oxford he also met the distinguished Hellenist and later Anglican bishop of Lincoln, Christopher Wordsworth, as well as John Sherren Brewer – both of whom sympathised with the Tractarian movement.[28] His second visit, in May 1851, when he was accompanied

[22] Döllinger to Pusey, 4 September 1842; original German letter in Pusey House, Oxford; English translation in Liddon, *Life of Pusey*, vol. II, pp. 295–6.

[23] Stefan Lösch attributed the contributions mentioned in the subsequent footnotes (and in n. 21) to Döllinger: S. Lösch, *Döllinger und Frankreich. Eine geistige Allianz 1823–1871* (Munich: C. H. Beck, 1955), pp. 522–6. Friedrich, *Ignaz von Döllinger*, vol. II, p. 134, considers Döllinger's authorship assured only for the articles on 'the Catholic movement' and the Jerusalem bishopric.

[24] [I. Döllinger], 'Die Katholische Bewegung in der protestantisch-bischöflichen Kirche von England', *Historisch-Politische Blätter*, 8 (1841), pp. 688–701; 9 (1842), pp. 65–79.

[25] [I. Döllinger], 'Das Anglo-Preussische Bisthum zu Jerusalem', *Historisch-Politische Blätter*, 8 (1841), pp. 621–37; 'Der Erzbischof von Canterbury und das neue Bisthum zu Jerusalem', *Historisch-Politische Blätter*, 9 (1842), pp. 178–92; 'Anglikanisierung des deutschen Protestantismus in Palästina', *Historisch-Politische Blätter*, 10 (1842), pp. 242–56.

[26] Conzemius indicates the year 1835, which seems unlikely. Friedrich mentions 1836 twice, and letters from the family archives also suggest 1836. See Fritz Döllinger to his brother Ignaz, 10 July 1837, BABo. Included in *Briefe 1821–1890 von und an Johann Joseph Ignaz von Döllinger aus dem Familiennachlaß*, transcribed by Hubert Huppertz (Alverskirchen: unpublished manuscript, 1994), p. 43.

[27] Letters from family members show that Döllinger had contemplated a visit to England (combined with a trip to France) as early as 1833. See Elisabethe Ladron to Ignaz Döllinger, 4 August 1833, BABo; Huppertz, *Briefe Familiennachlaß*, p. 120.

[28] Friedrich, *Ignaz von Döllinger*, vol. I, pp. 472–3. Conzemius, 'Viktorianische Kirche', p. 125. The encounter appears to have led to an exchange of books amongst scholars. See: Ignaz Döllinger to Christopher Wordsworth, Munich, 24 July 1837, LPL, MS 2141, fol. 235r.

by Lord Acton, brought him once again to Oxford. This time he met the recently converted Henry Manning,[29] with Cardinal Wiseman and twice with Pusey; he also travelled to Birmingham to meet John Henry Newman. On his last visit (from the end of August until the beginning of October 1858), Döllinger was once again accompanied by Lord Acton. From London, which he described as the 'King of Cities' ('the great Babylon where 2,300,000 people live together, more than half the population of the Bavarian kingdom'[30]), Döllinger wrote as follows to Anna Gramich about the English:

> Power, energy, restless activity, a tenacious, enduring will, as well as intelligence – in short one can see that these people possess exactly those characteristics, in which their calling lies to be the world-leading nation.[31]

At Aldenham, Acton's country estate in Shropshire, Döllinger again met various Oxford figures, including Pusey. These meetings did not result in particularly extensive correspondence between Pusey and Döllinger (only ten letters from Pusey to Döllinger survive in Döllinger's papers, and only five letters from Döllinger to Pusey). Nevertheless, each was interested in the other's writings and the development of the other's religious views. Moreover, the two men were also kept informed of each other's views and activities by third parties (including Henry Parry Liddon,[32] and from 1870, Alfred Plummer, whom Pusey himself had introduced to Döllinger[33]).

[29] Furnished with a letter of recommendation by Gladstone, Manning had visited him in Munich in 1847. Friedrich, *Ignaz von Döllinger*, vol. II, p. 231. At that point Manning had already decided to convert to Roman Catholicism. He denounced Döllinger in Rome in 1866. *Ibid.*, p. 233.

[30] Döllinger to Anna Gramich, 4 September 1858, quoted in H. Schrörs (ed.), *Ignaz Döllingers Briefe an eine junge Freundin* (Kempten, 1914), p. 57.

[31] *Ibid.*, p. 58.

[32] John Emerich Edward Dalberg, Lord Acton, *Letters of Lord Acton to Mary, Daughter of the Right Hon. W. E. Gladstone*, 2nd edn (London, 1913). It includes, in a letter by Acton dated 29 August 1884, Döllinger's views on Liddon and Pusey: 'He [Döllinger] hardly knows the better side of Liddon, as a preacher, and as a religious force. He sees that he is not a very deep scholar, and thinks his admiration for Pusey a sign of weakness, I think he once used the term fanatical – meaning a large allowance of one-sidedness in his way of looking at things. Indeed, Döllinger is influenced by nearly the same misgivings that I felt some months ago; and he has not had the same opportunities for getting rid of them. For instance, the Dean [R. W. Church] of St. Paul's assured me that Liddon, far from reclining on others, is masterful and fond of his own opinion. Moreover, Liddon's attitude in the question of Church and State is a matter which the Professor and I judge very differently, and it is a difference which is useless to discuss any more' (*ibid.*, pp. 152–3).

[33] See Pusey to Döllinger, 11 June 1870, BSBM, *Döllingeriana*, II; Huppertz, Transcription, vol. XII, p. 239. See also the letters in Pusey House, Oxford and in BSBM; and R. Boudens (ed.), *Alfred Plummer. Conversations with Dr. Döllinger, 1870–1890* (Louvain, 1985).

DÖLLINGER ON THE CHURCH OF ENGLAND

Döllinger's developing views on the Church of England found expression in his book *Kirche und Kirchen, Papstthum und Kirchenstaat*, published in 1861.[34] This book – translated into English in 1862 – 'more than any of his previous volumes made his name familiar in England'.[35] It was written as an elaboration of the so-called 'Odeon lectures' that Döllinger had delivered in 1861. In the first part of the book, Döllinger discussed (among other matters) Anglicans and English Dissenters, and the social consequences of the Reformation. He also considered the 'supposed'[36] (note the choice of wording) apostolic succession of the Church of England, as well as the main Anglican movements, including the Oxford Movement.[37] He characterised the Oxford Movement as a failed attempt to revitalise the theological and ecclesiastical principles of the reigns of Charles I and Charles II (1625–80).[38] According to Döllinger, the most important representatives of the Oxford Movement became Roman Catholics; many others rejected the Oxford Movement once the consequences of its principles grew clear, and they became once again 'ordinary Anglicans'.[39] Those who embraced the Oxford Movement but remained in the Anglican Church (Döllinger estimated them to be about 1,200 clergy) generally adhered, in his view, to the Roman Catholic Church spiritually and hoped that the established English Church would eventually be catholicised. All in all, Döllinger's assessments were acute, although harsh. For him, the Church of England lacked any 'settled dogmatic principles' and 'theological system'.[40] The established English Church had 'many heads (and every one with different "views") but very few hands'.[41] He was also vocal in his criticism of the Anglican clergy; for him, the average Church of England clergyman was 'quite satisfied with their Sunday reading exercises' and occupied himself during the rest of the week with his family life and social commitments.[42] Döllinger also pointed to the 'fiction of a general national

[34] I. Döllinger, *Kirche und Kirchen, Papstthum und Kirchenstaat. Historisch-politische Betrachtungen* (Munich, 1861), pp. 190–239; English translation: *The Church and the Churches, or, the Papacy and the Temporal Power. An Historical and Political Review* (London, 1862), pp. 143–73.

[35] H. B. Smith, Introduction, in *Dr. J. J. I. von Döllinger's Fables respecting the Popes in the Middle Ages*, trans. Alfred Plummer (New York, 1872), pp. i–xii, viii.

[36] Döllinger, *Kirche und Kirchen*, p. 223.

[37] See *ibid.*, pp. 225–7; Döllinger, *Church and Churches*, p. 163 (in English, the '"professed" apostolic succession').

[38] Döllinger, *Kirche und Kirchen*, p. 225; Döllinger, *Church and Churches*, p. 164.

[39] Döllinger, *Kirche und Kirchen*, p. 226; Döllinger, *Church and Churches*, p. 165.

[40] Döllinger, *Kirche und Kirchen*, p. 234; Döllinger, *Church and Churches*, p. 170.

[41] Döllinger, *Kirche und Kirchen*, p. 235; Döllinger, *Church and Churches*, p. 171.

[42] Döllinger, Kirche und Kirchen, p. 236; Döllinger, *Church and Churches*, p. 171. Statements of this kind regarding married priests and their family life are common in Döllinger's historical

religion', according to which millions in England were members of the established Church, although they were never visited by any clergy, rarely attended public worship and had scarcely heard the Saviour's name.[43]

Why this sharp criticism from a man who had himself by now experienced the flames of Roman criticism and who – as is clear from his letters – was privately reflecting with more subtlety on the Church of England? According to Conzemius, Döllinger's harsh and self-righteous criticism of Anglicanism in 1861 was rooted in information that he had collected over the previous forty years.[44] In his account of the Oxford Movement, Döllinger largely employed the same methods he had employed in an earlier book, on the Reformation; that is, he relied on the critical comments of those personally involved in the Oxford Movement.

Despite this criticism of the Church of England, the book's preface expressed Döllinger's emerging ecumenical reorientation. Milestones for this reorientation were the Erfurt Conference, where Roman Catholics and Protestants met (1860), Döllinger's contact and friendship with Anglicans and Protestants and his membership of the Bavarian Academy of Sciences (as the Academy's secretary, he came into frequent contact with such prominent Protestant historians as Ranke, von Sybel and others). His famous speech at the *Münchner Gelehrtenversammlung* (Munich Scholars' Convention, 1863), in which he argued that it should be the objective of German theology to overcome the Reformation divisions, reflects this new conciliatory perspective.[45]

Döllinger's growing ecumenical reorientation found expression in his *Lectures on the Reunion of the Churches*, published in English in 1872.[46] Here he conveyed a deeper understanding of the Reformation in England, emphasising the mistakes of the popes in their dealings with the English as a major cause of the ecclesiastical conflict. In these lectures, Döllinger also briefly discussed the Oxford Movement:[47] as in his earlier *Kirche und Kirchen*, he referred to the movement's historical roots, noting that it 'claims descent from the school of theologians of the seventeenth century'.[48] He observed that within Anglicanism suggestions for the reunification of Churches had arisen mainly from adherents of the

works, to point out the deterioration of a church. A. Berlis, 'Seelensorge verträgt keine Teilung. Ignaz von Döllinger (1799–1890) und die Frage des Zölibats', *Annali di studi religiosi*, 6 (2005), pp. 249–81.

43 Döllinger, *Kirche und Kirchen*, pp. 236–7; Döllinger, *Church and Churches*, pp. 171–2.

44 Conzemius, 'Viktorianische Kirche', p. 138.

45 *Ibid.*, pp. 138–9, mentions these as factors for a broadening of Döllinger's horizon.

46 J. J. I. von Döllinger, *Lectures on the Reunion of the Churches* (London, 1872). The German version was published almost two decades later: J. von Döllinger, *Ueber die Wiedervereinigung der christlichen Kirchen. Sieben Vorträge, gehalten zu München im Jahr 1872* (Nördlingen, 1888).

47 Döllinger, *Lectures on the Reunion of the Churches*, pp. 133–5.

48 *Ibid.*, p. 133.

Oxford Movement. He noted that Pusey had shown in his *Eirenicon* 'how comparatively easy a union would be, inasmuch as the doctrines in which both Churches agree are so many'.[49] Döllinger repeated here what he had already written in a personal letter to Pusey in 1866, following the publication of the latter's *Eirenicon* (which was published as a letter to Keble in response to Manning's attacks). According to Pusey it was not so much differences in doctrine but rather Roman exaggerations (in Mariology, the doctrine of purgatory and the practice of indulgences) that separated the Anglican and Roman Catholic Churches. In 1866, Döllinger, impressed with the *Eirenicon*, had even invited Pusey, who had planned a visit to Germany at that time, to be a guest in his home, where they might discuss further prospects for reunion:

> We can then have relaxed discussions about things that are of concern to both you and me. *I am convinced by reading your Eirenicon, that inwardly we are united in our religious convictions, although externally we belong to two separated churches. There can be no fundamental difference of opinion between us.* There is perhaps no one to give you better information than myself about the religious situation in Germany.[50]

This visit did not happen, and after 1870, according to Döllinger in his *Lectures*, the 'bridge for corporate union' of which Pusey had dreamed in his *Eirenicon*, had apparently collapsed.[51] Certainly for Pusey, the Vatican Council ended hopes for reunion. On the feast of the Conversion of St Paul in 1870, he wrote to Döllinger: 'I believe that I have expressed the mind of most Englishmen that the declaration of Papal Infallibility would make all reunion hopeless. I could only look upon it as a preparation of AntiChrist, by making faith more difficult.' [52]

DÖLLINGER AND ANGLO-CATHOLICISM AFTER 1870

Another factor that would define Döllinger's relationship with the Church of England had developed before and after the First Vatican Council.[53] This had less to do with ecclesiastical politics than with the increasing

[49] *Ibid.*, p. 135.

[50] Döllinger to Pusey, Munich, 30 May 1866, Pusey House, Oxford. Quoted in Liddon, *Life of Pusey*, vol. IV, p. 118. The original letter is in German; one sentence that was in English in the original is in italics.

[51] Döllinger, *Lectures on the Reunion of the Churches*, p. 135.

[52] Pusey to Döllinger, Conversion of Saint Paul, 1879, BSBM, *Döllingeriana*, II; Huppertz, Transcription, vol. XII, pp. 239–40, at p. 240.

[53] See R. Fitzsimons, 'The Church of England and the First Vatican Council', *JRH*, 27 (2003), pp. 29–46.

theological discussions between Döllinger and leading Anglican thinkers.[54] Döllinger's excommunication (by the archbishop of Munich, Gregor von Scherr) in 1871 broke many of his connections with Roman Catholics in England, but at the same time it expanded his contacts with Anglicans. In 1871, the University of Oxford awarded him an honorary doctorate.[55] (Döllinger did not travel to England to receive his degree; indeed, after 1860 he made no more trips abroad.)

Pusey, meanwhile, was critical of the Old Catholic movement.[56] He did not attend the Cologne Congress in 1872, where important issues were discussed regarding the ecumenical orientation of the Old Catholic movement. Pusey's comments to Döllinger expressed a hope that the Old Catholic movement would come to a clear theological agenda as soon as possible.[57] Pusey also hoped the Old Catholic movement would pursue a conservative agenda, and he opposed the liberal elements within Old Catholicism. Letters to the archbishop of Canterbury, Archibald Campbell Tait, show that other Anglicans were also interested, but at the same time cautious in their approach towards the Old Catholic movement. The Church of England as a whole kept its distance. While the bishops of Ely, Winchester and Lincoln attended the first Old Catholic conferences as representatives of the Anglo-Continental Society, they did not attend as official representatives of the Church of England.[58]

54 Conzemius, 'Viktorianische Kirche', p. 140, makes this reference but also indicates that an examination of Döllinger's reception in England was still pending (*ibid.*, n. 94).

55 Newspaper clipping from the *Daily News* (undated), BABo, Döllinger Papers, 5.266.17. For background, see the letters of Henry Nutcombe Oxenham to Döllinger, 9 and 23 May 1871, BSBM, *Döllingeriana*, II; Huppertz, Transcription, vol. XI, pp. 237–8; and Conzemius, 'Viktorianische Kirche', pp. 142–3.

56 Pusey to Döllinger, 6 September 1872, BSBM, *Döllingeriana*, II; Huppertz, Transcription, vol. XII, pp. 240–41. Regarding the emergence of the Old Catholic movement, see A. Berlis, *Frauen im Prozess der Kirchwerdung. Eine historisch-theologische Studie zur Anfangsphase des deutschen Altkatholizismus (1850–1890)* (Frankfurt a.M., 1998), pp. 86–232.

57 Pusey to Döllinger, 9 October 1872, BSBM, *Döllingeriana*, II; Huppertz, Transcription, vol. XII, pp. 241–2: 'We looked at one time to the Old Catholic movement very hopefully, as an instrument of re-union, when the decrees of the Vatican closed that door. I look very anxiously now. It has raised no standard; it seems to have no compass: it owns no one as pilot. One of the chief speakers said that they were "searching for the truth". To say this, is to own that they have not yet found it. I do not see how it can enlist others, when it cannot hold out any definitive haven, for which it is directing its course. One cannot anchor on a floating island. I hope on; but with an anxious and aching heart.'

58 Bishop Christopher Wordsworth of Lincoln to the archbishop of Canterbury, 13 July 1872, LPL, Tait Papers 185, fols. 98–98v: 'I feel it my duty to consult Your Grace with response to it. I would not be committing to be present at the Congress if there would be any danger of my incoming to compromise the Church of England by my presence. My mere inclination would be (in case I accepted the invitation) to state clearly the terms of the acceptance; via an adhesion on one

Anglican perceptions of the Old Catholic movement were very closely linked to their views of Döllinger, to whom they attributed great theological importance. This respect for Döllinger is made clear, for example, in one of Pusey's letters to Döllinger in 1872, when he expressed the hope that Döllinger, with the weight of his reputation, would involve himself in the debate that had broken out within the Church of England with regard to the Athanasian Creed.[59]

There have been diverse interpretations of the Bonn Union Conferences[60] and of Pusey's reaction to the second conference in 1875.[61] We will not go over this story again. But it is important to note that most Anglicans continued to view Döllinger as almost a personification of the Old Catholic movement. An anecdote from Döllinger's penultimate year illustrates how much the Anglicans perceived Döllinger as embodying the Old Catholic movement. Shortly before the Lambeth Conference of 1888, the Regius Professor of Divinity at Cambridge University, Brooke Foss Westcott (1825–1901), who would become bishop of Durham in 1890, wrote anxiously to John Eyton Bickersteth Mayor (1825–1910), classical scholar, Anglican clergyman and member of the Anglo-Continental Society:[62]

A rumour has been brought to me that Dr. Döllinger has recently said that Englishmen have received a certainly exaggerated impression of the importance

side, to all sempiternal [?] and Catholic doctrine and discipline, as received by the Church of England; and, on the other side a negation of all Romish errors, novelties and usurpations, as far as they are authoritatively projected by mere law.'

59 'A younger lay friend of mine, feeling about how to save the Athanasian Creed to us, writes to me: "Would not Dr. Döllinger write a letter to the Archbishop of Canterbury (on the value of the Athanasian Creed). His name would have great weight, and would tell on public opinion." He or I would publish it.' Pusey to Döllinger, 6 September 1872, BSBM, *Döllingeriana*, II; Huppertz, Transcription, vol. XII, p. 241. On 9 October 1872, Pusey compared his situation to that of the Old Catholics: 'We only ask, as you did before the Vatican Council, "leave us where we are; do nothing new; do not change our standing-ground". If that battle were lost, it would only be the first of a long series. The Establishment would lapse into Broad-Churchism. An active organization is being formed for the defence of the Ath[anasian] Creed. The future looks very dark, and so we should, for ourselves too; we should be thankful to see the Old Catholics take a clear doctrinal ground.' BSBM, *Döllingeriana*, II; Huppertz, Transcription, vol. XII, p. 242.

60 Mark D. Chapman, 'Liddon, Döllinger and the Bonn conferences of 1874 and 1875: A Case Study in Nationalism and Ecumenism', *IKZ*, 92 (2002), pp. 21–59. F. X. Bischof, *Theologie und Geschichte. Ignaz von Döllinger (1799–1890) in der zweiten Hälfte seines Lebens* (Stuttgart, 1997), pp. 404–37. On the role of Pusey, see Chadwick, 'Döllinger and Reunion', pp. 331–3.

61 Döllinger had suggested to Christopher Wordsworth, bishop of Lincoln, that he would chair the second Bonn Union conference: I. von Döllinger to Christopher Wordsworth, 29 July 1875, LPL, MS 2908, fols. 194–5.

62 The Anglo-Continental Society was established in 1853. Its aims were the promotion of the principles of the Church of England on the European continent through the publication of literature and to support the reformation of national Churches. In 1873 the society set up its own committee for corresponding with the Old Catholics and arranged for the dissemination of Old Catholic literature in England.

of the Old Catholic movement: that it is in fact declining if not moribund; that it is sinking financially, socially, personally; and that he cannot make the bishops understand how they are. Such an opinion, if it is indeed the opinion of a man like Dr. Döllinger, is of very great moment and claims … careful consideration. If on the other hand the opinion is not rightly ascribed to him, and the source to check the statement is finally traced [and] does not seem to be beyond doubt, it is important to be able to take his authority from it.[63]

John Mayor wrote to ask for an explanation from Döllinger, who in turn responded that 'as an 89-year-old he had more important things to do than continually write corrections'.[64] Bishop Joseph Hubert Reinkens (1811–96), since 1873 Catholic bishop for the Old Catholics in the German *Kaiserreich*, wrote to provide Mayor with a correct account of Döllinger's views.[65] He added that Döllinger, however, had remembered 'claiming something unfavourable about the church in Munich', which suggests that this 'rumour' had been triggered simply by one of Döllinger's offhand comments.

A month after Döllinger's death on 10 January 1890, Bishop Reinkens wrote to the Church of England clergyman Frederick Meyrick (1827–1906), secretary of the Anglo-Continental Society, to inform him of the death of 'our greatest confessor J. J. Ignatius von Döllinger'. He summarised Döllinger's significance as follows:

It is also certain that this lord among scholars who has now returned home did not only belong to us, but also provided an immortal service to the powerful Anglican Church with his treasures of thought. Hence on both sides we grieve justly because of our irreplaceable loss, but we are also thankful to God who gave us so much in this one who is now laid to rest, that neither death nor foe can take away from us. His call for the reunification of Christians will not lose its resonance, until the shepherd, Jesus Christ, who is known to his followers, has called to himself all those who know his voice.[66]

CONCLUSION

This chapter has offered only a brief account of the relationship between Anglicans and Ignaz von Döllinger, a relationship that deserves to be further examined and – as far as the period after 1870 is concerned – put in

63 B. F. Westcott to J. W. Mayor 25 January 1888, LPL, LC 27, fol. 90.

64 Bishop Joseph Hubert Reinkens to a resident of Merton House, Bonn, 29 February 1888, LPL.

65 Döllinger responded to Reinkens on 12 February 1888 by writing that 'It is with pleasure that I authorise you to provide the desired explanation, for I truly did not say this and, when something similar was suggested to me as a question, I contradicted it.' Quoted by Bishop Joseph Hubert Reinkens in his letter to a resident of Merton House, Bonn, 29 February 1888, LPL.

66 Joseph Hubert Reinkens to Frederick Meyrick, Bonn, 14 February 1890, Pusey House, Oxford, Meyrick Papers, no. 78.

the broader context of Old Catholic–Anglican relations, using the existing source material in Germany and England. Many Anglicans considered Döllinger to be a key figure of Old Catholicism from the beginning of the Old Catholic movement in 1870 up to the end of his life. Nobody attempting to understand the relationship between Anglicans and Old Catholics in the period between 1870 and 1890 can avoid analysing Döllinger's many connections.

Döllinger's important Anglican connections included William Ewart Gladstone, Christopher Wordsworth and, after 1870, Malcolm MacColl and Alfred Plummer among others. The relationships with Pusey and Wordsworth started in the late 1830s as theological exchanges between fellow scholars. Döllinger was interested in Pusey primarily as an important member of the Oxford Movement, about which Döllinger wrote in influential publications of his time. After the First Vatican Council, Döllinger's relationship with England was marked by the rapprochement between Old Catholicism and the Church of England. While Döllinger's view of the Church of England changed during the course of his life, he never wavered in his high esteem for the principal figures of the Oxford Movement. Thus, at eighty-three years of age, he wrote to Gladstone after Pusey's death:

> While I had to disagree with his position in some (few) instances, I have nevertheless always admired him as a rare and refreshing phenomenon. Pusey stands before me as a great scholar, a deeply devout Christian, a complete gentleman and an exceedingly gentle and gracious character unified in one person. In 1851, when I went from London to Oxford to see him, a noble convert told me, *I would you could deprive him of that key, with which he holds imprisoned the hearts and minds of so many people* (he was making reference to those whom Pusey kept from defecting to the Roman Church). That key was just that deep trust which he instilled through his knowledge and his wisdom.[67]

[67] J. Döllinger to W. E. Gladstone, Munich, 15 October 1882, BL, Gladstone Papers, Add. Ms 44,477. Huppertz, *Correspondence between Ignaz von Döllinger and William Ewart Gladstone*, p. 89. The original letter is in German; the quotation that was in English in the original is in italics.

CHAPTER 14

Anglicans, Old Catholics and Reformed Catholics in late nineteenth-century Europe

Nigel Yates

One of the more profound effects of the Oxford Movement was its transforming of Anglican ecumenical attitudes. Until the nineteenth century, with various modifications and nuances, Anglicans had been proud to call themselves Protestants, to rejoice in the Reformation and to consider themselves part of the family of Churches that had emerged from that process. However, by 1840 some Anglican high churchmen were breaking ranks with their Protestant colleagues within the Church of England. One of the things that most shocked English opinion about the publication of the first two volumes of Richard Hurrell Froude's *Remains* in 1838 had been his vehement criticism of the Reformation and his obvious regret that it had ever taken place.[1] The difficulty for high churchmen who took such a critical view of the Reformation was how they were to position themselves in future. Open approval of the Roman Catholic Church would bring the same sort of disapproval down on their heads that, twenty years earlier, Samuel Wix had received from Bishop Thomas Burgess when he had suggested that a rapprochement between Rome and Canterbury was both possible and desirable.[2]

Some of those Anglicans who grew critical of Protestantism looked for a closer relationship with the Eastern Orthodox Churches, just as the Anglican non-jurors had done a century earlier, although this was not an attractive option for many. In 1842, for example, F. W. Faber thought that 'the Greek Church in Greece is in very disadvantageous circumstances, and the firm impressions of a traveller are likely to be unfavourable. The

[1] For a discussion of all these issues, see especially Peter Nockles, *The Oxford Movement in Context: Anglican High Churchmanship 1760–1857* (Cambridge, 1994), pp. 104–45, and James Pereiro, *'Ethos' and the Oxford Movement: At the Heart of Tractarianism* (Oxford, 2008), pp. 186–232.

[2] See Samuel Wix, *Reflections Concerning the Expediency of a Council of the Church of England and the Church of Rome being holden with a View to Accommodate Religious Differences* (London, 1818); Thomas Burgess, *Popery Incapable of Union with a Protestant Church … A Letter in Reply to the Rev Samuel Wix* (Carmarthen, 1820); Samuel Wix, *A Letter to the Bishop of St David's* (London, 1819).

shabby dirty edifices and ill-clothed priests are not likely to impress a man favourably.' Even without those disadvantages, which Faber blamed largely on the centuries of Turkish oppression before Greek independence, he did not believe that the Greek Church could compare with the Roman in the quality of its liturgy.[3]

Dismissive of Eastern Orthodoxy, unwilling to maintain relations with foreign Protestant Churches and wary of challenging the deep-rooted anti-Catholicism of the contemporary British establishment, both political and ecclesiastical, many Tractarians found themselves increasingly isolated from other manifestations of Christianity apart from their own, even from their fellow Anglicans, and unsure as to how Anglicanism should relate to the wider Christian community. Some, like Keble, found comfort in the 'branch' theory of Catholic Christendom, but support for the branch theory was not a position that either the Eastern Orthodox or Roman Catholic Churches would reciprocate, and in terms of practical ecumenism it was completely meaningless. As T. A. Lacey was later to express it:

> [T]he Branch Theory, in short, does not regard the Catholic Church as consisting of a confederation of several communions; it merely recognises the fact that the Church is organised in provinces and groups of provinces geographically circumscribed.[4]

Nevertheless the theory helped shape the response of many Anglican high churchmen to ecumenical initiatives, and it was a major ingredient in many late nineteenth-century ecumenical developments, including the establishment of the Eastern Churches Association, the Association for the Promotion of the Unity of Christendom and even the ill-fated Order of Corporate Reunion. Anglicans who embraced the branch theory often made individual submissions to one of the larger 'branch' Churches, usually the Roman Catholic Church, but occasionally to either the Greek or Russian Churches.

During the second half of the nineteenth century, one option for Anglican high churchmen was to establish friendly relations with, and often to offer practical assistance to, secessionist Catholic Churches in Europe, Churches which came into being largely in opposition to the triumph of ultramontanist thinking within the Roman Catholic Church. One of the secessionist Churches, the Old Catholic Church of the

[3] F. W. Faber, *Sights and Thoughts in Foreign Churches and among Foreign Peoples* (London, 1842), pp. 583, 590.

[4] T. A. Lacey, *The Unity of the Church as Treated by English Theologians* (London 1898), pp. 25–6.

Netherlands, had, of course, been in existence since the early eighteenth century, and there were allegations (which it denied) that its leadership had been taken over by Jansenists. Rather surprisingly, before the 1840s nobody in the Church of England seems to have known anything about the Dutch Old Catholics. Archbishop William Wake of Canterbury, who had conducted extensive correspondence in the early eighteenth century with members of the Gallican Church of France, had 'left no trace of any knowledge of events in Holland'. While William Palmer had published a report on the Dutch Old Catholics in 1842, Anglicans had not shown much interest in the Old Catholic Church until J. M. Neale visited the Netherlands in 1851 and 1854.[5] It was Neale's publication of his *History of the So-Called Jansenist Church of Holland* in 1858 that first made most Anglicans aware of the fact that such a Church, Catholic but not Roman, existed. Since the more advanced Tractarians were trying to make Anglicanism Catholic but not Roman, the existence of another Church with a similar agenda seemed to offer an opportunity for collaboration. In truth, this opportunity was nothing like as great as some might have thought. The Dutch Old Catholics had, before the re-establishment of a separate Roman Catholic archbishopric at Utrecht (with a dependent hierarchy) in 1853, vigorously attempted to heal the schism with Rome, even if they had always been rebuffed. Even after 1853, the Dutch Old Catholics continued to hope for reunion with Rome, resisting any changes to their liturgy, such as replacing Latin with Dutch (except for the readings) in the Eucharist, and refusing to grant permission for their clergy to marry, until the early twentieth century. Neale himself had not seen any real opportunities for collaboration and had not been favourably impressed with what he had witnessed of Old Catholic services. In a letter to Benjamin Webb on 9 October 1854, written from Utrecht, Neale recorded that on

> Sunday I went to Mass at St Gertrude's. It is a very curious Office. One forgets that 150 years of separation must give a different air and manner to the same ritual ... I cannot give you a better idea of it than by saying that it struck me as the same thing that it would be if a set of Puseyites went through Mass – a great deal of stiffness or awkwardness, and slowness ... the Archbishop celebrated – it was a Mass that I could neither call High or Low; he had no deacon or sub-deacon, but there was music, etc., and everything else as in High Mass. There was only a crucifix and pix, beside candles on the Altar; very few images anywhere – and those of plaster. The Archbishop's *submissa voce* was so loud that I could have

[5] E. W. Kemp, 'The Church of England and the Old Catholic Churches', in E. G. W. Bill (ed.), *Anglican Initiatives in Christian Unity* (London, 1967), pp. 145–62, at p. 151.

heard every word of the Consecration. On the whole I was not pleased with that Office.[6]

As we shall see, the Dutch Old Catholics also had their doubts about Anglicans.

Another factor that was to prove significant in the eventual development of relations with Old or Reformed Catholic Churches in late nineteenth-century Europe was the expansion of Anglican activity on the Continent. Before the early nineteenth century the only places at which one could attend Anglican services on the European continent were a few chapels attached to British embassies or those that had been set up to meet the needs of British merchants trading there. As early as 1593, freedom of worship had been guaranteed to foreign merchants at Leghorn, Italy, leading to the establishment of an English chapel there.[7] In 1747 the king of Sweden gave permission for the holding of English services in a rented room in Gothenburg.[8] In 1793 the king of Denmark permitted a similar arrangement at Helsingør, but under very stringent conditions.

The chaplain appointed by the Congregation has to be confirmed in his position by the King. The Congregation, after having prayed for the Danish King and the Royal family may then pray for the British King and Royal family. The Community must keep Sundays and Holy Days as in the Danish Church, together with the Days of Prayer and Thanksgiving then in force, or to be ordered in future.[9]

This permission was renewed, in similar terms, in 1815 and the congregation was specifically allowed to 'hold public service in their mother tongue, according to the Liturgy of the English Church'.[10] Similar conditions prevailed in Roman Catholic countries. The papacy permitted the establishment of an English chapel in rented premises in Rome in 1816. The demand for this must have been considerable since at the initial service there were ninety-seven communicants and the offertory raised £220.[11] In 1826 the Grand Duke of Tuscany permitted the establishment of a chapel in Florence by the Swiss Reformed Church and from 1828 this

[6] *Letters of John Mason Neale, DD, Selected and Edited by His Daughter* (London 1910), pp. 228–9; for the most recent account of Neale's visits to the Netherlands see Michael Chandler, *The Life and Work of John Mason Neale* (Leominster, 1995), pp. 141–6.

[7] C. D. Tassarini, *The History of the English Church in Florence* (Florence, 1905), p. 2.

[8] J. R. Ashton, *A Short History of the English Church in Gothenburg 1747–1997* (Gothenburg, 1997), p. 5.

[9] A. C. Jarvis, *Some Account of the English Episcopal Church in Denmark* (Copenhagen, 1934), p. 27.

[10] *Ibid.*, pp. 34–5.

[11] M. T. Wilson, *The History of the English Church in Rome from 1816 to 1916* (Rome, 1916), pp. 11, 13.

chapel was used for an English service according to the Book of Common Prayer every Sunday at 12.30 p.m.[12] In 1843 application was made to the Tuscan government to build a separate English chapel and permission for this was granted provided '*que l'Edifice en question serait construit de manière que rien n'annonce à l'extérieur l'existence de la chapelle privée que l'on voudrait y établir*'.[13] No one who was not a subscriber was allowed to enter the church for morning service without a ticket purchased from the *custode* at the door, and subscribers were not allowed to introduce strangers into their pews, even in the absence of a member of their own family.[14] Even so, allegations were made by the Tuscan government in 1851 that the chapel congregation was seeking to proselytise among the local population by having 'services and sermons ... conducted in the Italian language with the express object of perverting native Catholics'.[15] These charges were vigorously denied by the Chapel Committee:

> No language can be used in the Church Ministration save the English ... No one is admitted into the body of the Church who does not pay for his seat, and ... there is not a single Tuscan Roman Catholic among the number of those who occupy seats in the body of the Church. A Gallery is set apart for servants and poor people who cannot pay for seats. It is but very rarely that an Italian has been seen to enter, so very seldom that the Church Officers merely regarded them as persons sent by authority to ascertain whether any objection could be taken to the services.

Indeed, they noted that only recently some Italians did ask admittance, but 'the parties were questioned, and upon declaring themselves to be Police Officers acting under authority, no objection was made to their entry'.[16]

Not all chapels established during the first half of the nineteenth century to cater for the spiritual needs of English residents and visitors were quite as scrupulous as the Florence Chapel Committee in seeking to maintain good relations with the governments in Roman Catholic countries. The first English chapel in Nice was opened with a strongly anti-Catholic sermon by the Evangelical preacher, Lewis Way. Some English residents on the French Riviera 'caused offence in Roman Catholic churches by "talking loud, laughing and stamping their feet while the service was going on"'. When in 1847 a wealthy English resident of Cannes, Thomas Robinson Woolfield, fitted out a chapel in the grounds of his house and invited a French Reformed minister to officiate in it without

[12] Tassarini, *English Church*, pp. 11–18.
[13] *Ibid.*, pp. 52–3. [14] *Ibid.*, p. 68. [15] *Ibid.*, p. 80. [16] *Ibid.*, pp. 82–3.

official permission, it was closed by the local police as an unlawful assembly. Woolfield successfully appealed against the decision with the result that French Reformed services could be held in the chapel on Sunday mornings and an English service in Woolfield's drawing-room in the afternoon. Eight years later Woolfield received permission to build an English church, Christ Church, in Cannes.[17] The Consular Act of 1825

> Made provision for the support ... of churches and chapels in foreign parts and places where a chaplain was appointed and maintained by subscription. The Crown was authorised to advance for such purpose a sum equal to the amount subscribed ... The grant could be made for erecting, hiring, or purchasing a church or chapel [provided it had government approval].[18]

At the same time, the archbishop of Canterbury sanctioned, at the suggestion of W. F. Hook, the consecration of Matthew Luscombe by the bishops of the Scottish Episcopal Church. Luscombe was to provide episcopal oversight of both British and American congregations in Europe. In fact few congregations accepted his authority and he combined his episcopal duties with responsibility for the British embassy chaplaincy in Paris, a post he held until his death in 1846.[19] In Paris, the congregation at the embassy chapel outgrew the confines of the building, which resulted in permission being given by the French government for the foundation of a new chapel in the Hôtel Marbeuf in 1824 – which was eventually to become St George's, Paris. The first chaplain was the Evangelical, Lewis Way, who had formerly ministered at Nice; he remained there until 1830. In 1833 Bishop Luscombe purchased a site in the rue d'Aguesseau for the building of a new embassy chapel, later known as St Michael's, Paris.[20]

Before 1842, when the diocese of Gibraltar was established, Anglican services in Europe had normally been conducted in rented buildings, including non-Anglican churches. Thus Anglicans worshipped in Reformed churches in Amsterdam, Geneva, Lausanne and Vevey; in Lutheran ones at Aachen, Bonn, Karlsruhe, Liège and Wiesbaden; in the Moravian church at Dresden; and even in Roman Catholic churches at Antwerp, Bruges, Interlaken, Mainz and Munich.[21] The new diocese of Gibraltar covered only southern Europe and the adjacent parts of North

[17] P. Howarth, *When the Riviera Was Ours* (London, 1977), pp. 16, 21, 23.

[18] H. J. C. Knight, *The Diocese of Gibraltar* (London 1917), p. 29.

[19] Jarvis, *English Episcopal Church*, pp. 160–66.

[20] M. Harrison, *An Anglican Adventure: The History of Saint George's Anglican Church* (Paris, 2005), pp. 9–22.

[21] J. E. Pinnington, 'Anglican Chaplaincies in Post-Napoleonic Europe: A Strange Variation on the Pax Britannica', *Church History*, 39 (1970), pp. 327–44.

Africa, with the rest of the continent remaining under the jurisdiction of the bishop of London. There were, in 1842, only four permanent churches in the new diocese, the cathedral-designate at Gibraltar and the churches at Athens, Trieste and Valetta. The chaplaincies at Genoa, Naples, Turin and Rome refused to acknowledge the authority of the first bishop.

At Rome, the Anglican chapel had seating for 400, two services every Sunday, services on holy days and some other weekdays and Holy Communion weekly between Advent and Easter and monthly between Easter and Advent. The congregation in Rome appealed to the British Foreign Office to support their rejection of Gibraltar's authority, and in March 1851 the Foreign Office wrote to the archbishop of Canterbury to request him 'to take effectual measures for preventing the improper interference of the Bishop of Gibraltar in the affairs of the British chapel'. The main reason for the congregation's refusal to acknowledge the bishop was its fear that this might offend the papacy and lead to the banning of Anglican services in Rome. Following the fall of the Papal States in 1870, the congregation accepted the bishop's jurisdiction.[22]

During the thirty years after the establishment of the diocese of Gibraltar, the number of Anglican chaplaincies and permanent churches in southern Europe increased rapidly. This growth was much aided by the decision in 1863 of the Society for the Propagation of the Gospel to resume its activity in Europe – activity that had been abandoned in 1710 in favour of work in the American colonies. By 1873 the new diocese was responsible for fifty congregations in southern Europe, from Portugal to Turkey, and four in North Africa, compared with the four permanent churches in the diocese in 1843. Three new permanent churches had been opened in Turkey, two new churches in France (Cannes 1855 and Nice 1862), three new churches in Italy (Pisa 1844, Florence 1846, Naples 1865), one new one in Malta (Sliema 1867) and one in Portugal.[23]

The increasing number of Anglican churches on the European continent, especially in Roman Catholic countries, had two results. In the first place it made Anglicanism better known to the Roman Catholic authorities; in the second, it made Anglicans aware of the opposition of many Roman Catholics, both clerical and lay, to the growing ultramontanism within their own Church. Some Anglican high churchmen,

[22] Knight, *Diocese of Gibraltar*, pp. 50–52; Wilson, *English Church*, pp. 38, 48–53, 88; see also J. E. Pinnington, 'The Consular Chaplaincies and the Foreign Office under Palmerston, Aberdeen and Malmesbury. Two Case Histories: Rome and Funchal', *JEH*, 27 (1976), pp. 277–84.

[23] Knight, *Diocese of Gibraltar*, pp. 68–9, 93–4, 258–61.

who retained their party's traditional dislike of Roman Catholicism, saw this as an opportunity to encourage the development of schismatic 'reformed' Catholic Churches. Other high churchmen, however, perceived such moves as a repudiation of the 'branch' theory of Catholic Christendom and were nervous about dealings with schismatic bodies in southern Europe and even with the Old Catholic Churches that emerged in Austria, Germany and Switzerland in response to the Vatican decree of papal infallibility in 1870. The first Anglican organisation deliberately to collaborate with both Old and Reformed Catholics was the Anglo-Continental Society established by Frederick Meyrick in 1853. The objects of this society were twofold: 'to make the principles of the English Church known in the different countries of Europe [and] to help forward the internal reformation of national churches'.[24] Spurred on by the publication of Neale's *History*, the society's officers paid regular visits to the Old Catholic archbishop of Utrecht from 1858.

> These visits made the Archbishop better acquainted with the Church of England than he would otherwise have been, and caused him the better to understand the position which we hold in Christendom.[25]

One of these visitors was Dr Joseph Oldknow, incumbent of Holy Trinity, Bordesley (a moderate ritualist church) and 'the well-known writer of pro-ritualist polemical tracts'.[26] Oldknow attended several services in Dutch Old Catholic churches and was no more impressed than Neale had been.

> Vespers were sung very slowly, the antiphons, &c, in Dutch, and when they were done, there was benediction, accompanied with long Dutch hymns, so that I was somewhat tired before the service was over.[27]

The society must also have been aware that the Dutch Old Catholics regarded the Church of England, whatever information they had been given to the contrary, as just one of the national Protestant Churches of northern Europe. They had no interest in developing ecumenical relations in that direction, however much they disliked Rome. They certainly had no interest in the society's other objective, the establishment of schismatic Reformed Catholic Churches in other parts of Europe. Before 1870 there were three parts of southern Europe in which such movements were beginning to get underway – Italy, Spain and Portugal.

[24] Frederick Meyrick, *The Old Catholics and the Anglo-Continental Society* (London 1875), p. 2.
[25] *Report of the Anglo-Continental Society* (London, 1873), pp. 33–4.
[26] Nigel Yates, *Anglican Ritualism in Victorian Britain 1830–1910* (Oxford, 1999), p. 259.
[27] *Report*, 1873, p. 35.

The Anglo-Continental Society had some powerful supporters, including E. H. Browne, bishop of Ely and later of Winchester, and William Gladstone (though the latter declined 'to join its executive committee').[28] However, some bishops and leading high churchmen were highly dubious about the society. They believed that the greater long-term goal, reunion of the Anglican Church with the Western Catholic and Eastern Orthodox Churches, could be compromised by offering support to schismatic members of mainstream Churches. Nevertheless, the society pressed ahead with its objectives. In 1860 it undertook an investigation into Catholic reform movements in Italy and was deeply disappointed when the reformers decided instead to seek an accommodation with the papacy.[29] A later attempt at establishing a Reformed Catholic Church in Italy was more successful, and it had six parishes in 1882. However, by that time the influence of the Anglo-Continental Society was on the wane and most English bishops refused to get involved, convinced that any support given to the new Italian Church would damage relations with the Roman Catholic Church. As a result the Italian Reformed Catholic Church had a very short existence.[30]

The situation in Portugal and Spain seemed more promising. In 1868 a Reformed Catholic Church was established and by 1878 it had nine congregations served by four former Roman Catholic priests. They asked Charles Sandford, bishop of Gibraltar, to act as their bishop but he declined. They then petitioned the Church of England to provide them with a bishop, but, after some agonising, the English bishops decided that they were not prepared to risk the ecumenical consequences. A similar appeal to the newly formed Old Catholic Churches in the aftermath of the First Vatican Council was also rejected, as the Old Catholics regarded the Reformed Catholics as Protestant. Eventually the Church of Ireland agreed to help, though its own bishops were divided on the matter. In 1894 the Evangelical Archbishop Plunket of Dublin, assisted by the bishops of Clogher and of Down, Connor and Dromore, consecrated a bishop for the Spanish Reformed Catholic Church. Bishop Sandford refused to have anything to do with this Spanish consecration, regarding it as 'an act of intrusion'. The Portuguese Reformed Catholic Church, meanwhile, had no bishop but it received much help from the

[28] G. W. Kitchin, *Edward Harold Browne, DD, Lord Bishop of Winchester* (London 1895), p. 407; H. C. G. Matthew, 'Gladstone, Vaticanism and the Question of the East', *Studies in Church History*, 15 (1978), pp. 417–42, at p. 424.

[29] Meyrick, *Old Catholics*, pp. 3, 5.

[30] C. B. Moss, *The Old Catholic Movement: Its Origins and History* (London 1948), pp. 284–5.

English chaplain at Lisbon, T. G. P. Pope, who assisted in the compilation of its prayer book.[31]

In contrast to the general Anglican desire to maintain a distance from the Reformed Catholic churches in Italy and the Iberian Peninsula, there was far more interest, in England certainly, in the work of Père Hyacinthe Loyson in France. Loyson (1827–1912) was a well-known Carmelite preacher who resigned from the order after a dispute with his superiors in 1869, and who in 1872 married an American woman in London. The following year he briefly took charge of an Old Catholic parish in Geneva, though the Dutch Old Catholics refused to have anything to do with him as he was married. In 1874 he returned to France and established a congregation in Paris in 1879. Between then and 1893, when he resigned because of his increasingly radical theological position, Loyson was placed under the pastoral oversight of four Anglican bishops: Robert Eden, bishop of Moray, Ross and Caithness, Henry Cotterill, bishop of Edinburgh, Henry Lascelles Jenner (of whom more later) and Cleveland Coxe, bishop of Western New York. After Loyson's resignation the Dutch Old Catholics agreed to accept responsibility for his Paris congregation, which moved to a new church, St-Denys, consecrated in 1895, in the boulevard Auguste Blanqui. The remnants of this congregation were worshipping in St Michael's Anglican church in Paris in the early 1960s.[32] Not surprisingly the Anglo-Continental Society was enthusiastic about Loyson. Commenting on his chaplaincy at Geneva the annual report noted that the services were no longer in Latin but in French, that confession was no longer compulsory and that Loyson himself had declared 'his adhesion to the decisions ... by the Synod of German Old Catholics at Bonn'.[33] In 1876 Loyson was entertained by William Gladstone, and in 1878 Bishop Browne of Winchester invited Loyson and one of his Old Catholic supporters, Bishop Herzog of Switzerland, to stay with him at Farnham Castle.[34]

Loyson turned out to be quite useful to the Church of England as he offered a way of providing episcopal employment for Henry Lacelles Jenner. Jenner (1820–98) was a rather sad character. As an undergraduate at Cambridge he was one of those who had combined with

[31] *Ibid.*, pp. 285–6; Knight, *Diocese of Gibraltar*, pp. 168–9, 171–5; the relevant Church of Ireland correspondence is in the papers of Bishop Graves of Limerick in the Representative Church Body Library, Dublin, D13.

[32] Moss, *Old Catholic Movement*, pp. 283–4; Peter Anson, *Bishops at Large* (London 1964), pp. 304–5.

[33] *Report of the Anglo-Continental Society* (London, 1874), p. 37.

[34] Matthew, 'Gladstone', p. 439; Moss, *Old Catholic Movement*, p. 331.

J. M. Neale, Benjamin Webb and others to found the Cambridge Camden Society, later renamed the Ecclesiological Society, in 1839. In 1853 he was appointed to the committee to supervise the publication of the second part of Thomas Helmore's *Hymnal Noted*. Deciding against a career in law, Jenner had been ordained deacon in 1843 and priest in 1844 to the curacy of Chevening in Kent, moving to curacies at St Columb Major (1846–9) and Antony (1849–51), both in Cornwall. At Antony both the incumbent and the squire were sympathetic to Tractarianism and Jenner was allowed to introduce daily services, coloured stoles, an altar cross and lighted candles, and to adopt the eastward position at Holy Communion. In 1851 Jenner moved briefly to Leigh in Essex and in the following year to serve as curate to Dr W. H. Mill, Regius Professor of Hebrew at Cambridge (and father-in-law of Benjamin Webb), at Brasted in Kent.[35] Mill was recovering from having had complaints of illegal ritual against him upheld by Archbishop Sumner of Canterbury and would no doubt have welcomed the services of a committed ritualist and highly musical curate.[36] Jenner, however, did not stay at Brasted long. In 1852 he was appointed to a minor canonry at Canterbury Cathedral – where he founded the Canterbury Amateur Musical Society – and in 1854 he was presented to the nearby chapter living of Preston-next-Wingham. Here he started daily services and weekly communion, and established a choir which sang plainsong settings of the psalms and canticles. In 1856 the churchwardens of Brasted – where Mill had been replaced by a successor who had 'no use for popish furniture' – presented Jenner with a set of choir surplices and a pair of candlesticks. In the same year Jenner replaced Thomas Helmore as music secretary of the Ecclesiological Society, a post he held until 1863. In 1862, he was instrumental in establishing the Canterbury Diocesan Choral Union, acting as its precentor for the next five years (1862–7).[37]

But for an extraordinary set of events (which would eventually bring him into contact with Père Hyacinthe Loyson), Jenner might have remained a country clergyman with a deep interest in church music. In 1865, G. A. Selwyn, bishop of New Zealand, wrote to C. T. Longley, archbishop of Canterbury, asking him to nominate and consecrate a bishop for a new diocese at Dunedin. Longley duly nominated and consecrated Jenner, who was in many ways a somewhat surprising choice, since he was known

[35] D. Adelmann, *The Contribution of the Cambridge Ecclesiologists to the Revival of Anglican Choral Worship 1839–62* (Aldershot, 1997), pp. 19, 64, 129–30.

[36] Yates, *Anglican Ritualism*, pp. 98–9.

[37] Adelmann, *Cambridge Ecclesiologists*, pp. 130–32, 177, 192–4, 196–7, 210–11.

to be a member of various ritualist societies, including the Confraternity of the Blessed Sacrament and the Society of the Holy Cross. Meanwhile, the Standing Committee of the Otago and Southland Rural Deanery Board had decided that it did not have the financial resources to establish the proposed bishopric at the present time. Remaining in England, Jenner decided to use his episcopal status to help out various friends in ritualist churches in London. On 10 April 1867, Arthur Stanton, curate at St Alban's, Holborn, reported to his sister that

> yesterday we had a Confirmation ... the Bishop of Dunedin by permission of the Bishop of London confirmed, and must have astonished our people by his enthusiastic praise for our teaching and ceremonial.[38]

In the same year, a member of the Otago and Southland Rural Deanery Board, while on a visit to England, chanced to attend a service at St Matthias, Stoke Newington, at which Jenner presided. In this service, the visitor claimed to have 'witnessed the most extravagant scenes and heard the grossest doctrines ... that ever disgraced a so-called Protestant church'. There were, to his horror, lighted candles on the altar and a procession with incense. When reports of this reached New Zealand, the Church's general synod tried to persuade Jenner to resign as bishop of Dunedin. Bishop Selwyn, who had returned to England and was shortly to be enthroned as bishop of Lichfield, supported Jenner. Archbishop Longley denied that he knew that Jenner was a ritualist. Bishop Harper of Christchurch, New Zealand, who was then acting as bishop of Dunedin, inhibited Jenner from carrying out any ministerial functions in the diocese. Although the clerical members of the diocesan synod voted four to three to accept Jenner, the lay members voted fifteen to ten against him on the grounds that they could not 'sanction the appointment of a bishop in whose religious opinions and practices they had not full confidence and assurance'. Jenner appealed against the inhibition to the new archbishop of Canterbury, A. C. Tait, who accepted that Jenner had a just claim to his diocese but advised him to abandon it. Jenner wrote to Harper reasserting his claim and enclosing Tait's letter. The New Zealand general synod met in February 1871 and refused to accept Jenner's nomination. In March 1871, the diocesan synod elected another English clergyman, S. J. Nevill, as bishop of Dunedin. But Jenner never acquiesced in Nevill's election, despite Nevill's subsequent consecration, and he refused to renounce his claim to the diocese. As late as 1875 he was still claiming

[38] G. W. E. Russell, *Arthur Stanton: A Memoir* (London, 1917), p. 94.

that he had been wrongly deprived of his bishopric.[39] Fortunately Jenner had not resigned his English benefice on his consecration and he was thus able to remain at Preston-next-Wingham until his death – although, with his sense of personal affront and betrayal, he remained a thorn in the flesh for Tait and his immediate successors as archbishop of Canterbury, E. W. Benson and Frederick Temple.

One of Jenner's principal concerns was to seek recognition of his episcopal status. In 1875 he wrote to Archbishop Tait to seek his guidance on the wearing of episcopal vestments. He pointed out that, as a result of the recently passed Public Worship Regulation Act, he was in an ambiguous position. As a bishop he could not be prosecuted, but as an incumbent in the diocese of Canterbury he could. As a bishop he was, in his opinion, obliged by the ornaments rubric in the Book of Common Prayer to wear a cope or vestment and either to carry a pastoral staff or else have it carried for him by a chaplain; in addition to this, he believed that the canons of 1604 required him to wear a cope if celebrating in cathedrals or collegiate churches. In response, Tait merely advised Jenner not to wear vestments that others might consider illegal. Jenner then told Tait that this was highly unsatisfactory and pointed out that at least two English diocesan bishops (probably Magee of Peterborough and Wordsworth of Lincoln[40]) were now wearing copes when celebrating in their respective cathedrals.[41] It is fairly clear that Jenner ignored Tait's advice. On 28 March 1887, the rural dean and vicar of St Mary's, Dover, John Puckle, informed Archbishop Benson that he had seen a photograph of Jenner taken after a service at the ritualist St Bartholomew's church, Dover, in which he was dressed in full pontifical vestments, including a mitre.[42]

In this difficult situation, the English bishops found it convenient to encourage Jenner to exercise his episcopal functions outside the Church of England, by offering them to Père Hyacinthe Loyson and his Paris congregation. Moreover, being beneficed in East Kent, with easy access to the rail and ferry connections to Paris, it was much easier for Jenner

[39] H. J. Purchas, *History of the English Church in New Zealand* (Christchurch, NZ, 1914), pp. 212–14; W. P. Morrell, *The Anglican Church in New Zealand* (Dunedin 1973), pp. 90–96; see also John Pearce, *Seeking a See: A Journal of the Right Reverend Henry Lascelles Jenner, DD, of His Visit to Dunedin, New Zealand in 1868–1869* (Dunedin, 1984).

[40] For the evidence on this see J. C. Macdonald, *Life and Correspondence of William Connor Magee*, 2 vols. (London, 1896), vol. II, p. 82 and J. H. Overton and E. Wordsworth, *Christopher Wordsworth* (London, 1888), p. 266.

[41] Tait Papers, LPL, vol. 239, fols. 53–60.

[42] Benson Papers, LPL, vol. 47, fols. 410–12.

to assist Loyson than for friendly Scottish or American bishops to do so. Jenner took a great risk, however, in accepting the office, as English ritualists were strongly divided over relations between Anglicans and either Old or Reformed Catholics. The Society of the Holy Cross, for example, took a very hostile stance. Not only did the society disapprove of any encouragement being given to schismatic Catholic bodies in Europe, but it also deprecated the establishment of English chaplaincies in Roman Catholic countries, believing that Anglicans resident in, or visiting them, should worship in Roman Catholic churches. When a member of the Society of the Holy Cross, the English chaplain at Pau in the French Pyrenees, appealed for a donation to support his work there, the society refused on the grounds that the establishment of a chaplaincy in Pau had been a schismatical action.[43] Although by then Jenner had ceased to be a member of the Society of the Holy Cross, his actions in giving episcopal support to Loyson were vigorously condemned. A motion stating that Jenner's actions constituted 'a grave violation of the discipline of the church' was defeated by thirteen votes to nine, but one describing them as a 'schismatical intrusion' was carried by fifteen votes to eleven.[44]

The divisions among Anglicans over their relations with Reformed Catholic churches in Europe were replicated in regard to those Old Catholic churches which came into being in Austria, Germany and Switzerland after the First Vatican Council. In these latter cases the situation was further complicated by the attitudes of the Dutch Old Catholics, both to the secessionists and to Anglicans. It had, indeed, become an exceedingly complicated ecclesiastical triangle. As might have been expected, the Anglo-Continental Society revealed a naive enthusiasm for the developments in Austria, Germany and Switzerland.

> The principle on which the Old Catholic Reformation is being carried out is the same as that on which the English Reformation was effected … for Old Catholics are prepared to give up whatever cannot be proved by Scripture, or is unaccordant with the practice of the Primitive Church.[45]

Some high church Anglicans agreed with the advice they were receiving from those who had seemed to have a sound knowledge of the situation on the ground.

[43] Pusey House, Oxford, Records of the Society of the Holy Cross, Ch 71/A5, pp. 314–16.

[44] *Ibid.*, pp. 270–5. These records have recently been transferred to Pusey House from the Centre for Kentish Studies in Maidstone and currently retain the same call numbers. See also J. Embry, *The Catholic Movement and the Society of the Holy Cross* (London, 1931), pp. 167–9.

[45] Meyrick, *Old Catholics*, p. 14.

Old Catholics are, then, a mere handful of the faithful protesting against the Pope and the whole Episcopate, preferring their own *private* judgement to that of the whole teaching body of the Catholic Church.[46]

They were encouraged in this view by the fact that the Old Catholic archbishop of Utrecht had advised the Austrian, German and Swiss dissidents, at the second Old Catholics' Congress in Cologne in 1872, against separating from the Roman Catholic Church – even though the Dutch bishops did later agree to consecrate a bishop for the German Old Catholics.[47] In England, calls for support of the Austrian, German and Swiss Old Catholics were led by old-fashioned high churchmen, such as Bishop E. H. Browne and Christopher Wordsworth, or by moderate Tractarians, such as William Gladstone. Support for the Old Catholics did include some ritualists; for example, Charles Lowder, the ritualist vicar of St Peter, London Docks, attended the Old Catholics' Congress at Constance in 1873. The Lambeth Conference of 1878 passed a resolution of sympathy for the Old Catholic Churches. In 1881 Bishop Browne invited bishops Reinkens of Germany and Herzog of Switzerland to visit England as his guests, and during this visit they also met bishops Christopher Wordsworth of Lincoln, William Maclagan of Lichfield, James Woodford of Ely and Archbishop Tait. In 1879, the Swiss Old Catholics allowed Anglicans to communicate at their altars and the German Old Catholics followed suit in 1883. In 1887, Bishop John Wordsworth of Salisbury (Christopher Wordsworth's son) visited the German and Swiss Old Catholic Churches, and in 1888 he and Bishop Ernest Wilberforce of Newcastle had a meeting with Archbishop Heykamp of Utrecht. In the same year the Lambeth Conference agreed to develop friendly relations with all the Old Catholic Churches, excluding the Reformed Catholic groups in southern Europe, and to admit Old Catholics to communion in Anglican churches.

None the less, although the First Bonn Union Conference in 1874 had agreed to accept the validity of Anglican orders, this agreement was not honoured by all the Old Catholic Churches. Those of Germany and Switzerland were quick to do so, but the Old Catholic Church of the Netherlands held out against this view. In 1908 a Society of St Willibrord was established, under the joint presidency of Bishop William Collins of

[46] Caesarius Tondini, *Anglicanism, Old Catholicism and the Union of the Christian Episcopal Churches* (London, 1875), p. 30.

[47] H. R. T. Brandreth, 'Approaches to the Churches towards Each Other in the Nineteenth Century', in Ruth Rouse and Stephen Neill (eds.), *A History of the Ecumenical Movement 1517–1948*, 2nd edn (London, 1967), pp. 263–306, at p. 292.

Gibraltar and Bishop Prins of Haarlem, to foster closer relations between Anglicans and Dutch Old Catholics. In 1913 Prins became the first Dutch Old Catholic bishop to visit England, where he attended a Solemn Eucharist at All Saints, Margaret Street, in London's West End. Even so, it was not until 1925 that the Dutch Old Catholics recognised Anglican orders, a decision that led to intercommunion between Anglicans and Old Catholics in 1931–2.[48]

In the context of the broader issues of Christian unity, the attention given by Anglicans to developing relations with the Old Catholic and the Reformed Catholic Churches in Europe in the late nineteenth century seems to have involved a great deal of effort for relatively modest, and long-delayed, results. The numbers of Old Catholics covered by the agreements of 1931–2 were comparatively small. There were certainly those in the more Protestant groupings within Anglicanism who felt that relations with the Old Catholic and Reformed Catholic Churches had been pushed at the expense of more fruitful schemes of union with either Protestant Churches in Europe or Protestant Free Churches at home. There were also Anglo-Catholics who felt the emphasis on relations with the Old and Reformed Catholics had not assisted attempts at reunion with Rome, though these attempts had been largely torpedoed by the opposition of the British Roman Catholic hierarchy, the papal bull *Apostolicae Curae* of 1896 and the collapse of the Malines Conversations of 1921–6. To some extent the complaints of Protestant Anglicans were answered with the agreement of intercommunion between Anglicans and the Lutheran Churches of Sweden and Finland, though here the essential ingredient for agreement was the fact that both churches had maintained the apostolic succession of their bishops. This was officially recognised at the Lambeth Conference of 1920 and intercommunion was thereafter established.[49] It was not until after the Second World War that further unions between Anglicans and other Protestants took place in some parts of the world.

On the positive side, the discussions between Anglicans and Old Catholics, and even to some extent between Anglicans and Reformed Catholics, did help to secure within Anglicanism the commitments to the historic episcopate, a broadly Catholic doctrine of the Eucharist and an appreciation of Catholic order which high churchmen had always held,

48 Moss, *Old Catholic Movement*, pp. 258, 332–5, 337–8; S. C. Neill, 'Plans of Union and Reunion 1910–1948', in Rouse and Neill (eds.), *History of the Ecumenical Movement*, pp. 445–95, at pp. 469–70.

49 Neill, 'Plans of Union and Reunion 1910–1948', pp. 471–3.

and which had been reasserted by the Oxford Movement, but which had in the nineteenth century, at least in their eyes, come under increasing threat from Evangelicals and liberals. These discussions also brought Anglicans into close association with other Christian bodies in Europe who had had a very different religious history from their own. In this way, the legacy of the Oxford Movement eventually helped to underpin and strengthen Anglican ecumenical engagement in Europe and the wider world.

Index

Milton Keynes UK
Ingram Content Group UK Ltd.
UKHW021050010924
447435UK00024B/204

9 781107 680272